W9-BZB-800

ENERGY
SUPPLIES, SUSTAINABILITY, AND COSTS

ENERGY
SUPPLIES, SUSTAINABILITY, AND COSTS

Kim Masters Evans

INFORMATION PLUS® REFERENCE SERIES
Formerly Published by Information Plus, Wylie, Texas

GALE
CENGAGE Learning·

Farmington Hills, Mich • San Francisco • New York • Waterville, Maine
Meriden, Conn • Mason, Ohio • Chicago

GALE
CENGAGE Learning

Energy: Supplies, Sustainability, and Costs

Kim Masters Evans

Kepos Media, Inc.: Steven Long and Janice Jorgensen, Series Editors

Project Editor: Laura Avery

Rights Acquisition and Management: Ashley M. Maynard, Carissa Poweleit

Composition: Evi Abou-El-Seoud, Mary Beth Trimper

Manufacturing: Rita Wimberley

Cover photograph: ©Lisa S./Shutterstock.com.

While every effort has been made to ensure the reliability of the information presented in this publication, Gale, a part of Cengage Learning, does not guarantee the accuracy of the data contained herein. Gale accepts no payment for listing; and inclusion in the publication of any organization, agency, institution, publication, service, or individual does not imply endorsement of the editors or publisher. Errors brought to the attention of the publisher and verified to the satisfaction of the publisher will be corrected in future editions.

Gale
27500 Drake Rd.
Farmington Hills, MI 48331-3535

ISBN-13: 978-0-7876-5103-9 (set)
ISBN-13: 978-1-4103-2545-7

ISSN 1534-1585

This title is also available as an e-book.
ISBN-13: 978-1-4103-3270-7 (set)
Contact your Gale sales representative for ordering information.

Printed in the United States of America
1 2 3 4 5   21 20 19 18 17

TABLE OF CONTENTS

PREFACE

Energy: Supplies, Sustainability, and Costs is part of the *Information Plus Reference Series*. The purpose of each volume of the series is to present the latest facts on a topic of pressing concern in modern American life. These topics include today's most controversial and studied social issues of the 21st century: abortion, capital punishment, care for the elderly, child abuse, crime, the environment, health care, high technology, immigration, national security, social welfare, youth, and many more. Although this series is written especially for high school and undergraduate students, it is an excellent resource for anyone in need of factual information on current affairs.

By presenting the facts, it is the intention of Gale, Cengage Learning, to provide its readers with everything they need to reach an informed opinion on current issues. To that end, there is a particular emphasis in this series on the presentation of scientific studies, surveys, and statistics. These data are generally presented in the form of tables, charts, and other graphics placed within the text of each book. Every graphic is directly referred to and carefully explained in the text. The source of each graphic is presented within the graphic itself. The data used in these graphics are drawn from the most reputable and reliable sources, such as from the various branches of the U.S. government and from private organizations and associations. Every effort was made to secure the most recent information available. Readers should bear in mind that many major studies take years to conduct, and that additional years often pass before the data from these studies are made available to the public. Therefore, in many cases the most recent information available in 2017 is dated from 2014 or 2015. Older statistics are sometimes presented as well, if they are landmark studies or of particular interest and no more-recent information exists.

Although statistics are a major focus of the *Information Plus Reference Series*, they are by no means its only content. Each book also presents the widely held positions and important ideas that shape how the book's subject is discussed in the United States. These positions are explained in detail and, where possible, in the words of their proponents. Some of the other material to be found in these books includes historical background, descriptions of major events related to the subject, relevant laws and court cases, and examples of how these issues play out in American life. Some books also feature primary documents or have pro and con debate sections that provide the words and opinions of prominent Americans on both sides of a controversial topic. All material is presented in an evenhanded and unbiased manner; readers will never be encouraged to accept one view of an issue over another.

HOW TO USE THIS BOOK

The United States is the world's largest consumer of energy in all its forms. Gasoline and other fossil fuels power its automobiles, trucks, trains, and aircraft. Electricity generated by burning oil, coal, and natural gas—or from nuclear or hydroelectric plants—runs Americans' lights, telephones, televisions, computers, and appliances. Without a steady, affordable, and massive amount of energy, modern America could not exist. This book presents the latest information on U.S. energy consumption and production and compares it with years past. Controversial issues such as U.S. dependence on foreign oil and government subsidies for the fossil fuel industries are explored.

Energy: Supplies, Sustainability, and Costs consists of nine chapters and three appendixes. Each of the major elements of the U.S. energy system—such as coal, nuclear energy, renewable energy sources, and electricity generation—has a chapter devoted to it. For a summary of the information that is covered in each chapter, please see the synopses that are provided in the Table of Contents. Chapters generally begin with an overview of the basic facts and background information on the chapter's topic, then proceed to examine subtopics of particular interest.

For example, Chapter 3: Natural Gas describes the various types of natural gas and their geological sources. Historically, the United States obtained much of its supply from conventional deposits trapped beneath nonporous rock formations. In the 21st century, however, natural gas is increasingly produced from dense shale and sandstone formations. The gas is typically liberated via hydraulic fracturing, a controversial technique that uses large amounts of water. The chapter delves into the extraction, processing, transporting, storage, and distribution of natural gas and provides import and export statistics. Domestic and international production and consumption are also examined. The chapter ends with a discussion of the factors that affect natural gas prices, and a brief overview of the environmental issues associated with the natural gas industry. Readers can find their way through a chapter by looking for the section and subsection headings, which are clearly set off from the text. They can also refer to the book's extensive Index, if they already know what they are looking for.

Statistical Information

The tables and figures featured throughout *Energy: Supplies, Sustainability, and Costs* will be of particular use to readers in learning about this topic. These tables and figures represent an extensive collection of the most recent and valuable statistics on energy production and consumption—for example, the amount of coal mined in the United States in a year, the rate at which energy consumption is increasing in the United States, and the percentage of U.S. energy that comes from renewable sources. Gale, Cengage Learning, believes that making this information available to readers is the most important way to fulfill the goal of this book: to help readers understand the topic of energy and reach their own conclusions about controversial issues related to energy use and conservation in the United States.

Each table or figure has a unique identifier appearing above it, for ease of identification and reference. Titles for the tables and figures explain their purpose. At the end of each table or figure, the original source of the data is provided.

To help readers understand these often complicated statistics, all tables and figures are explained in the text. References in the text direct readers to the relevant statistics. Furthermore, the contents of all tables and figures are fully indexed. Please see the opening section of the Index at the back of this volume for a description of how to find tables and figures within it.

Appendixes

Besides the main body text and images, *Energy: Supplies, Sustainability, and Costs* has three appendixes. The first is the Important Names and Addresses directory. Here, readers will find contact information for a number of organizations that study energy. The second appendix is the Resources section, which is provided to assist readers in conducting their own research. In this section, the author and editors of *Energy: Supplies, Sustainability, and Costs* describe some of the sources that were most useful during the compilation of this book. The final appendix is the Index. It has been greatly expanded from previous editions and should make it even easier to find specific topics in this book.

COMMENTS AND SUGGESTIONS

The editors of the *Information Plus Reference Series* welcome your feedback on *Energy: Supplies, Sustainability, and Costs*. Please direct all correspondence to:

Editors
Information Plus Reference Series
27500 Drake Rd.
Farmington Hills, MI 48331-3535

CHAPTER 1
AN ENERGY OVERVIEW

In scientific terms, energy is the capacity for doing work. Humans have learned to harness and use multiple energy sources to get work done. A perfect energy source would be widely available, safe, easy to procure and use, environmentally friendly, provide tremendous amounts of energy, and never run out. As yet, such an energy source has not been found. Instead, there are multiple energy sources with varying levels of suitability. This book will examine the various sources in terms of their availability (supplies), sustainability, and costs.

ENERGY CONVERSIONS

An important law of nature is that energy cannot be created or destroyed, it can only change forms. The most common form of energy conversion facilitated by humans is the conversion of chemical energy (e.g., the energy stored within fuels by virtue of their chemical structures) to thermal energy (heat). For example, the energy that is stored within wood and other combustible fuels is transferred to heat and light when the fuel is burned. Heat energy can be used directly, such as to heat buildings, or it can be converted to mechanical energy. Imagine a pot of boiling water. The steam rising above the pot is in motion. It is said to have kinetic energy. This energy, when concentrated, can be powerful enough to force movement in machines, such as to turn blades, move pistons, or open valves. In this context, steam is a working fluid. In fact, steam is a popular working fluid because once the desired work has been obtained, the steam can be condensed back to water and reused.

The chemical-to-heat-to-mechanical (C-H-M) energy conversion process powers vehicles, such as cars, trucks, ships, and bulldozers. The C-H-M process is also the main precursor for producing electricity at power plants. In a very simple power plant, coal or some other fuel is burned to produce steam that turns the blades of a turbine. The turbine rotates a magnet that is nestled within or around coiled wire, generating an electric current in the wire. Thus, mechanical energy is converted to electrical energy. This basic technology has been in use since the 19th century. Hydroelectric power also dates from that century. In this process water is the working fluid that helps convert mechanical energy to electrical energy. During the 20th century scientists developed yet another energy conversion process, one based on nuclear energy (the energy held within atomic nuclei). Splitting a uranium atom apart under controlled conditions produces heat that can be used to generate electricity. Wind and solar energy are also increasingly being converted to electrical energy using high-technology devices.

It is important to remember that at each energy conversion stage some of the capacity to do work is lost. For example, some of the heat that is generated by burning fuel escapes to the atmosphere rather than heating the desired target. Conversion losses are inevitable. Therefore, humans strive to find energy sources with large amounts of energy potential and to minimize energy losses at each conversion step.

ENERGY CONTENT

Energy content is the amount of energy that can be obtained from a given amount of energy source. Heat energy is the key factor by which various energy sources are compared. In the United States heat energy is measured using British thermal units (Btu). This term came into use during the 19th century as a benchmark measure: 1 Btu represented the amount of heat required to raise the temperature of 1 pound (0.5 kg) of water by 1 degree Fahrenheit (0.6 degrees Celsius). In modern times, the Btu is precisely defined by controlling the measurement variables, for example, the density of the water that is used in the measurement. In countries that rely on the metric system, the joule is the preferred unit for measuring heat, work, and energy; 1 Btu is equivalent to approximately 1,055 joules.

TABLE 1.1

Btu (British thermal units) content of common energy units

Btu content of common energy units
- 1 barrel (42 gallons) of crude oil = 5,800,000 Btu (for U.S. produced crude oil)
- 1 gallon of gasoline = 120,476 Btu
- 1 gallon of diesel fuel = 137,381 Btu (distillate fuel with less than 15 parts per million sulfur content)
- 1 gallon of heating oil = 138,500 Btu (distillate fuel with 15 to 500 parts per million sulfur content)
- 1 barrel of residual fuel oil = 6,287,000 Btu
- 1 cubic foot of natural gas = 1,028 Btu
- 1 gallon of propane = 91,333 Btu
- 1 short ton (2,000 pounds) of coal = 19,622,000 Btu
- 1 kilowatthour of electricity = 3,412 Btu

Note: The Btu content of each fuel reflects the average heat content for fuels consumed in the United States in 2014.

SOURCE: Adapted from "Btu Content of Common Energy Units," in *Energy Units Explained*, U.S. Energy Information Administration, July 29, 2015, http://www.eia.gov/energyexplained/print.cfm?page=about_energy_units (accessed August 7, 2016)

The Btu is a relatively small unit of measure. In "Energy Units and Calculators Explained: British Thermal Units (Btu)" (December 15, 2014, http://www.eia.gov/energyexplained/?page=about_btu), the U.S. Energy Information Administration (EIA) within the U.S. Department of Energy (DOE) explains that "one Btu is approximately equal to the energy released by burning a match."

Table 1.1 compares the Btu content of various fossil fuel energy sources and electricity. One ton (0.9 t) of coal provides 19.6 million Btu, compared with only 5.8 million Btu from a barrel (42 gallons [159 L]) of crude oil.

SUSTAINABILITY

In the United States most energy conversion processes begin with fossil fuels (fuels derived from the below-ground remains of prehistoric organisms that became energy enriched after millions of years of exposure to high temperatures and pressures). Examples include coal, petroleum, and natural gas. Chemically, they are known as hydrocarbons because they are compounds that contain hydrogen and carbon. These fuels and their derivatives have high energy contents because of their enormous carbon contents. Burning fossil fuels produces large amounts of heat, but also liberates large amounts of carbon into the atmosphere, which is an environmental problem.

Fossil fuels are considered to be nonrenewable energy sources. It takes nature millions of years to create them; as such, the amounts available to humans are finite. It is possible to exhaust these supplies because the replenishment time is so long. Uranium is also considered to be nonrenewable. It is found at low concentrations throughout the earth's soils and seawater. In theory, all of this uranium could be exhausted through massive use.

By contrast, other energy sources are said to be renewable because under the right circumstances they can be tapped again and again by humans without eliminating them. Examples include wind, sunlight, flowing water, and the heat stored beneath the earth's crust, which is called geothermal energy. Biomass (biologically based materials other than fossil fuels, such as trees and other vegetation) is also considered to be a renewable energy source because humans can regrow these materials in a relatively short amount of time. Likewise, combustible wastes produced by humans (e.g., garbage) are constantly being created and, thus, represent a renewable energy source.

ENERGY PRODUCTION AND CONSUMPTION

People have always found ways to harness energy, such as using animals for transportation and work or inventing machines such as windmills and waterwheels to tap the power of wind and water, respectively. Before the 1800s much of the thermal energy used in the United States for heating and cooking was obtained by burning wood. Lighting was provided by wax candles or by lanterns that burned whale oil or some other kind of animal fat.

The EIA indicates in "A Brief History of Coal Use" (February 12, 2013, http://www.fe.doe.gov/education/energylessons/coal/coal_history.html) that commercial coal mining in the United States began during the 1740s. Coal has a much higher heat content than wood, and this energy boost fueled the Industrial Revolution (1760–1848), a period of intense industrialization and modernization. One of the most important innovations of the Industrial Revolution was the steam engine (a machine that converted the thermal energy of burning fuel, such as coal, to mechanical energy). Steam engines powered locomotives, ships, and industrial equipment during the 1800s. There were even some steam-powered cars.

The petroleum age began in the United States in 1859, when the first successful modern oil well was drilled. Scientists developed methods to process and refine crude oil into gasoline and other products to power vehicles, ships, and industrial equipment. By the early 20th century petroleum derivatives were in high demand by consumers. Oil also became a vital commodity in regards to national security. The United States' large supply of domestic oil was a crucial component to its success in World War II (1939–1945).

Modern U.S. Energy Production

Table 1.2 shows energy production, by fuel, in the United States between 1950 and 2015. The units are quadrillion Btu, with 1 quadrillion Btu equal to 1,000,000,000,000,000 Btu. In 1950 the primary energy sources were coal (14.1 quadrillion Btu) and crude oil

TABLE 1.2

Primary energy production, by source, selected years 1950–2015

[Quadrillion Btu]

	Fossil fuels					Nuclear electric power	Renewable energy[a]							Total
	Coal[b]	Natural gas (dry)	Crude oil[c]	NGPL[d]	Total		Hydro-electric power[e]	Geothermal	Solar/PV	Wind	Biomass	Total	
1950 Total	14.060	6.233	11.447	0.823	32.563	0.000	1.415	NA	NA	NA	1.562	2.978	35.540
1955 Total	12.370	9.345	14.410	1.240	37.364	0.000	1.360	NA	NA	NA	1.424	2.784	40.148
1960 Total	10.817	12.656	14.935	1.461	39.869	0.006	1.608	NA	NA	NA	1.320	2.928	42.803
1965 Total	13.055	15.775	16.521	1.883	47.235	0.043	2.059	(s)	NA	NA	1.335	3.396	50.674
1970 Total	14.607	21.666	20.401	2.512	59.186	0.239	2.634	0.002	NA	NA	1.431	4.070	63.495
1975 Total	14.989	19.640	17.729	2.374	54.733	1.900	3.155	0.034	NA	NA	1.499	4.687	61.320
1980 Total	18.598	19.908	18.249	2.254	59.008	2.739	2.900	0.053	NA	NA	2.475	5.428	67.175
1985 Total	19.325	16.980	18.992	2.241	57.539	4.076	2.970	0.097	(s)	NA	3.016	6.084	67.698
1990 Total	22.488	18.326	15.571	2.175	58.560	6.104	3.046	0.171	0.059	0.029	2.735	6.041	70.705
1995 Total	22.130	19.082	13.887	2.442	57.540	7.075	3.205	0.152	0.069	0.033	3.099	6.558	71.174
2000 Total	22.735	19.662	12.358	2.611	57.366	7.862	2.811	0.164	0.066	0.057	3.006	6.104	71.332
2001 Total	23.547	20.166	12.282	2.547	58.541	8.029	2.242	0.164	0.064	0.070	2.624	5.164	71.735
2002 Total	22.732	19.382	12.160	2.559	56.834	8.145	2.689	0.171	0.063	0.105	2.705	5.734	70.713
2003 Total	22.094	19.633	11.960	2.346	56.033	7.960	2.793	0.173	0.062	0.113	2.805	5.946	69.938
2004 Total	22.852	19.074	11.550	2.466	55.942	8.223	2.688	0.178	0.063	0.142	2.996	6.067	70.232
2005 Total	23.185	18.556	10.974	2.334	55.049	8.161	2.703	0.181	0.063	0.178	3.101	6.226	69.436
2006 Total	23.790	19.022	10.768	2.356	55.935	8.215	2.869	0.181	0.068	0.264	3.212	6.594	70.744
2007 Total	23.493	19.786	10.749	2.409	56.436	8.459	2.446	0.186	0.076	0.341	3.472	6.520	71.415
2008 Total	23.851	20.703	10.616	2.419	57.590	8.426	2.511	0.192	0.089	0.546	3.868	7.206	73.223
2009 Total	21.624	21.139	11.335	2.574	56.672	8.355	2.669	0.200	0.098	0.721	3.953	7.641	72.667
2010 Total	22.038	21.806	11.592	2.781	58.217	8.434	2.539	0.208	0.126	0.923	4.316	8.112	74.764
2011 Total	22.221	23.406	11.934	2.970	60.531	8.269	3.103	0.212	0.171	1.168	4.501	9.155	77.955
2012 Total	20.677	24.610	13.747	3.246	62.279	8.062	2.629	0.212	0.227	1.340	4.406	8.813	79.155
2013 Total	20.001	24.859	15.781	3.532	64.173	8.244	2.562	0.214	0.305	1.601	4.647	9.330	81.747
2014 Total	20.286	26.552	18.434	4.096	69.368	8.338	2.467	0.214	0.420	1.728	4.849	9.678	87.383
2015 Total	17.927	27.926E	19.720E	4.474	70.047	8.338	2.389	0.224	0.550	1.816	4.715	9.694	88.078

[a]Most data are estimates.

[b]Beginning in 1989, includes waste coal supplied. Beginning in 2001, also includes a small amount of refuse recovery.

[c]Includes lease condensate.

[d]Natural gas plant liquids.

[e]Conventional hydroelectric power.

E = Estimate. NA = Not available. (s) = Less than 0.5 trillion Btu.

Notes: Totals may not equal sum of components due to independent rounding. Geographic coverage is the 50 states and the District of Columbia. Btu = British thermal units. PV = photovoltaic. NGPL = Natural gas plant liquids.

SOURCE: Adapted from "Table 1.2. Primary Energy Production by Source (Quadrillion Btu)," in *Monthly Energy Review: July 2016*, U.S. Energy Information Administration, July 2016, http://www.eia.gov/totalenergy/data/monthly/pdf/mer.pdf (accessed August 7, 2016)

(11.4 quadrillion Btu). Natural gas (6.2 quadrillion Btu) was a distant third. In "The History of Natural Gas" (February 12, 2013, http://www.fe.doe.gov/education/energylessons/gas/gas_history.html), the EIA explains that natural gas was mostly used during the 1800s as a fuel for street lights. It did not become widely available to individual homes and businesses until after World War II, when extensive pipelines were laid in U.S. cities.

By 1955 crude oil production surpassed that of coal; however, petroleum's reign at the top was short lived. (See Table 1.2.) In 1970 natural gas production surpassed that of crude oil. During the early 1980s these three fossil fuels were roughly equal in terms of domestic production. Over the following decades domestic production fell dramatically for crude oil, but grew stronger for coal and natural gas.

Figure 1.1 shows energy production by source between 1949 and 2015. Note that natural gas plant liquids (NGPL) are hydrocarbons separated from natural gas during processing. Figure 1.1 illustrates that, for decades, the production of fossil fuels (coal, natural gas, crude oil, and NGPL) vastly overshadowed the production of other energy sources. Among the latter, the top competitors were nuclear electric power and renewable energy, specifically biomass and hydroelectric power. (See Table 1.2.)

Figure 1.2 shows energy production, by source, in 2015. At 27.9 quadrillion Btu, natural gas accounted for more energy production in the United States in 2015 than any other energy source. Energy produced from crude oil was second (19.7 quadrillion Btu), followed by coal (17.9 quadrillion Btu) and nuclear electric power (8.3 quadrillion Btu). The total energy produced domestically (within the United States) more than doubled, from 35.5 quadrillion Btu in 1950 to 88.1 quadrillion Btu in 2015. (See Table 1.2.)

Modern U.S. Energy Consumption

Between 1950 and 2015 total domestic energy consumption (the amount of energy consumed in the United States) nearly tripled, from 34.6 quadrillion Btu in 1950 to 97.5 quadrillion Btu in 2015. (See Table 1.3.)

One of the reasons that energy consumption has increased in the United States is a growing population. According to the U.S. Census Bureau, in *Measuring America: The Decennial Censuses from 1790 to 2000* (September 2002, http://www.census.gov/prod/2002pubs/pol02marv.pdf), the U.S. population numbered 151.3 million in 1950. In "U.S. and World Population Clock" (September 16, 2014, http://www.census.gov/popclock), the Census Bureau estimates the U.S. population was

FIGURE 1.1

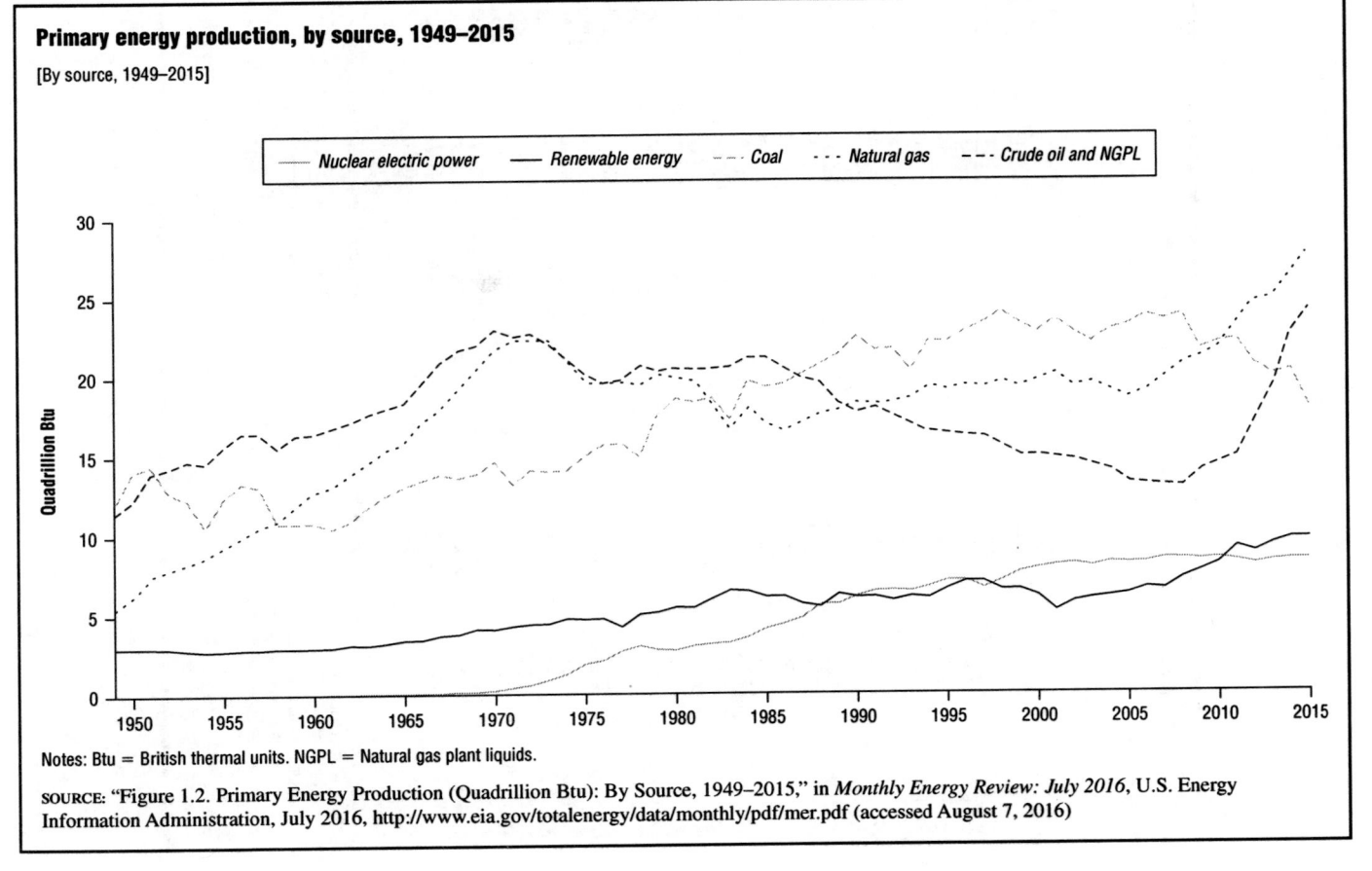

Primary energy production, by source, 1949–2015

[By source, 1949–2015]

Notes: Btu = British thermal units. NGPL = Natural gas plant liquids.

SOURCE: "Figure 1.2. Primary Energy Production (Quadrillion Btu): By Source, 1949–2015," in *Monthly Energy Review: July 2016*, U.S. Energy Information Administration, July 2016, http://www.eia.gov/totalenergy/data/monthly/pdf/mer.pdf (accessed August 7, 2016)

FIGURE 1.2

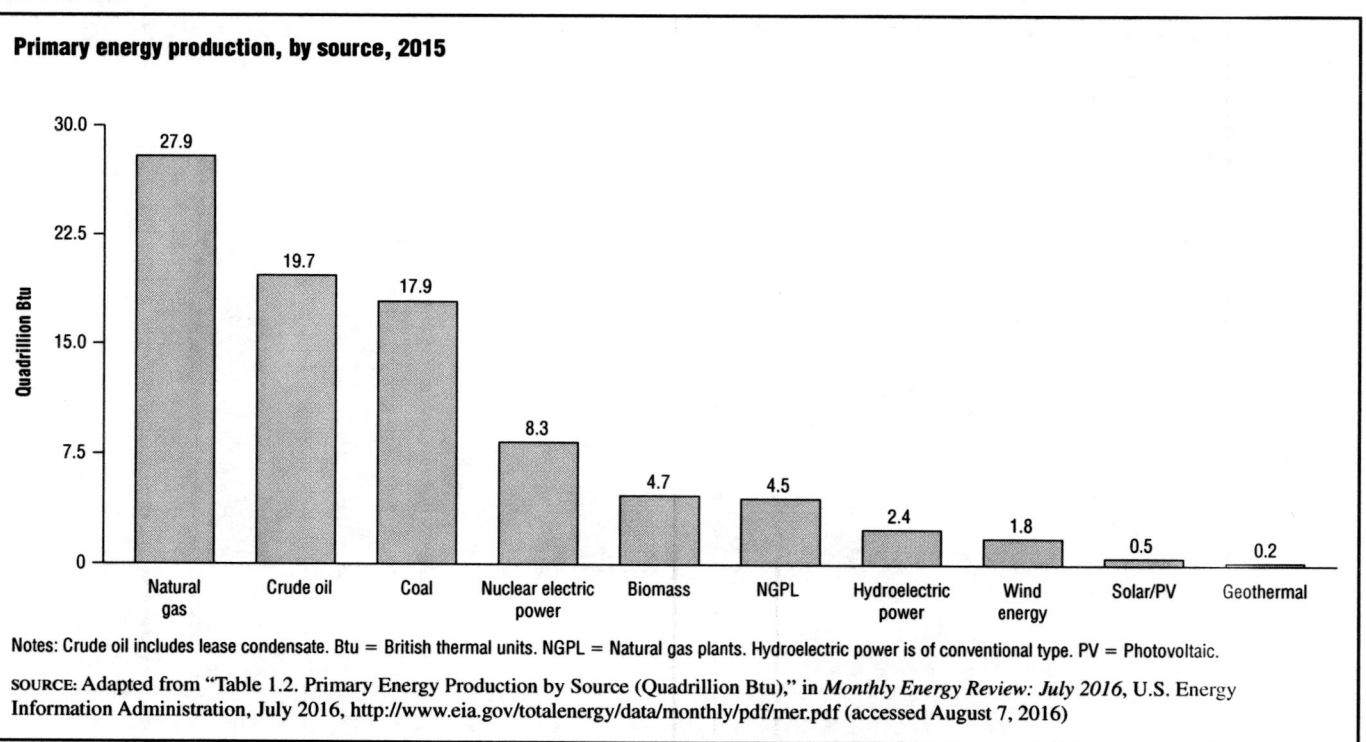

Primary energy production, by source, 2015

Notes: Crude oil includes lease condensate. Btu = British thermal units. NGPL = Natural gas plants. Hydroelectric power is of conventional type. PV = Photovoltaic.

SOURCE: Adapted from "Table 1.2. Primary Energy Production by Source (Quadrillion Btu)," in *Monthly Energy Review: July 2016*, U.S. Energy Information Administration, July 2016, http://www.eia.gov/totalenergy/data/monthly/pdf/mer.pdf (accessed August 7, 2016)

322.8 million at year-end 2015. Thus, the population more than doubled between 1950 and 2015. As noted earlier, energy consumption grew even faster, nearly tripling during the same period.

In *Monthly Energy Review: July 2016* (July 2016, http://www.eia.gov/totalenergy/data/monthly/archive/00351607.pdf), the EIA divides U.S. energy consumers into five broad sectors: electric power, residential, industrial, commercial, and transportation.

ELECTRIC POWER SECTOR. This sector consumes energy at facilities it operates to sell electricity to the public. Examples include electric utilities and combined heat-and-power plants that sell heat and electricity. It should be noted that this sector does not include power plants that are operated by factories and other industrial enterprises that produce electricity or electricity and heat for their own use. Figure 1.3 shows the primary fuels that were used by the electric power sector between 1949 and 2015. Coal has historically been the main fuel source for electric power generation.

The EIA considers the electric power sector an intermediary in the energy supply chain, not an end user of energy. As is explained in Chapter 8, electricity generation is inherently inefficient; energy content is lost as fuels are converted to electricity and as the electricity travels across transmission lines and distribution systems. Thus, the heat content of the energy sources that enter the electric power sector is far greater than the heat content of the electricity that is delivered to end users.

RESIDENTIAL SECTOR. This end-use sector consumes energy in residential living quarters. Common uses include space heating, water heating, air conditioning, lighting, refrigeration, cooking, and running other appliances. Figure 1.4 shows the major energy sources that were consumed by this sector between 1949 and 2015. Natural gas was historically the most-used source; its dominance, however, was matched by electricity during the first decade of the 21st century. Petroleum, renewable energy, and coal are minor energy sources to this sector.

INDUSTRIAL SECTOR. Energy consumption by this end-use sector powers equipment and facilities that are engaged in producing, processing, or assembling goods. Figure 1.5 shows the major energy sources that were consumed by the industrial sector between 1949 and 2015. During the 1950s petroleum and natural gas replaced coal as the preferred fuel. In 2015 petroleum and natural gas were the top fuels and were used roughly equally. Electricity, renewable energy, and coal played much smaller roles.

COMMERCIAL SECTOR. This end-use sector includes the equipment and facilities that are operated by businesses; federal, state, and local governments; and other private and public organizations, such as religious, social, or fraternal groups. The commercial sector includes institutional living quarters and sewage treatment facilities. Figure 1.6 shows that electricity and natural gas have been the preferred fuels in this sector for decades. In 2015 electricity was the main energy source, followed by natural gas, petroleum, renewable energy, and coal.

Energy

TABLE 1.3

Primary energy consumption, by source, selected years 1950–2015

[Quadrillion Btu]

	Fossil fuels				Nuclear electric power	Renewable energy[a]						Total[f]
	Coal	Natural gas[b]	Petroleum[c]	Total[d]		Hydro-electric power[e]	Geothermal	Solar/PV	Wind	Biomass	Total	
1950 Total	12.347	5.968	13.315	31.632	0.000	1.415	NA	NA	NA	1.562	2.978	34.616
1955 Total	11.167	8.998	17.255	37.410	0.000	1.360	NA	NA	NA	1.424	2.784	40.208
1960 Total	9.838	12.385	19.919	42.137	0.006	1.608	(s)	NA	NA	1.320	2.928	45.086
1965 Total	11.581	15.769	23.246	50.577	0.043	2.059	0.002	NA	NA	1.335	3.396	54.015
1970 Total	12.265	21.795	29.521	63.522	0.239	2.634	0.006	NA	NA	1.431	4.070	67.838
1975 Total	12.663	19.948	32.732	65.357	1.900	3.155	0.034	NA	NA	1.499	4.687	71.965
1980 Total	15.423	20.235	34.205	69.828	2.739	2.900	0.053	NA	NA	2.475	5.428	78.067
1985 Total	17.478	17.703	30.925	66.093	4.076	2.970	0.097	(s)	(s)	3.016	6.084	76.392
1990 Total	19.173	19.603	33.552	72.332	6.104	3.046	0.171	0.059	0.029	2.735	6.041	84.485
1995 Total	20.089	22.671	34.441	77.262	7.075	3.205	0.152	0.069	0.033	3.101	6.560	91.032
2000 Total	22.580	23.824	38.266	84.735	7.862	2.811	0.164	0.066	0.057	3.008	6.106	98.819
2001 Total	21.914	22.773	38.190	82.906	8.029	2.242	0.164	0.064	0.070	2.622	5.163	96.172
2002 Total	21.904	23.510	38.226	83.700	8.145	2.689	0.171	0.063	0.105	2.701	5.729	97.647
2003 Total	22.321	22.831	38.790	83.992	7.960	2.793	0.173	0.062	0.113	2.806	5.948	97.921
2004 Total	22.466	22.923	40.227	85.754	8.223	2.688	0.178	0.063	0.142	3.008	6.079	100.094
2005 Total	22.797	22.565	40.303	85.709	8.161	2.703	0.181	0.063	0.178	3.114	6.239	100.193
2006 Total	22.447	22.239	39.824	84.570	8.215	2.869	0.181	0.068	0.264	3.262	6.645	99.492
2007 Total	22.749	23.663	39.491	85.928	8.459	2.446	0.186	0.068	0.341	3.485	6.533	101.027
2008 Total	22.387	23.843	36.907	83.178	8.426	2.511	0.192	0.076	0.546	3.851	7.189	98.906
2009 Total	19.691	23.416	34.959	78.042	8.355	2.669	0.200	0.098	0.721	3.936	7.624	94.138
2010 Total	20.834	24.575	35.489	80.891	8.434	2.539	0.208	0.126	0.923	4.270	8.066	97.480
2011 Total	19.658	24.955	34.824	79.447	8.269	3.103	0.212	0.171	1.168	4.405	9.059	96.902
2012 Total	17.378	26.089	34.016	77.487	8.062	2.629	0.212	0.227	1.340	4.369	8.777	94.487
2013 Total	18.039	26.805	34.613	79.440	8.244	2.562	0.214	0.305	1.601	4.673	9.356	97.238
2014 Total	17.998	27.488	34.881	80.345	8.338	2.467	0.214	0.420	1.728	4.812	9.641	98.505R
2015 Total	15.614	28.320R	35.373	79.289R	8.338	2.389	0.224	0.550	1.816	4.696	9.675	97.528R

[a]Most data are estimates.

[b]Natural gas only; excludes supplemental gaseous fuels.

[c]Petroleum products supplied, including natural gas plant liquids and crude oil burned as fuel. Does not include biofuels that have been blended with petroleum—biofuels are included in "Biomass."

[d]Includes coal coke net imports.

[e]Conventional hydroelectric power.

[f]Includes coal coke net imports and electricity net imports, which are not separately displayed.

R = Revised. NA = Not available. (s) = Less than 0.5 trillion Btu. Btu = British thermal units.

Notes: Totals may not equal sum of components due to independent rounding. Geographic coverage is the 50 states and the District of Columbia.

SOURCE: Adapted from "Table 1.3. Primary Energy Consumption by Source (Quadrillion Btu)," in *Monthly Energy Review: July 2016*, U.S. Energy Information Administration, July 2016, http://www.eia.gov/totalenergy/data/monthly/pdf/mer.pdf (accessed August 7, 2016)

FIGURE 1.3

Electric power sector energy consumption, by major source, 1949–2015

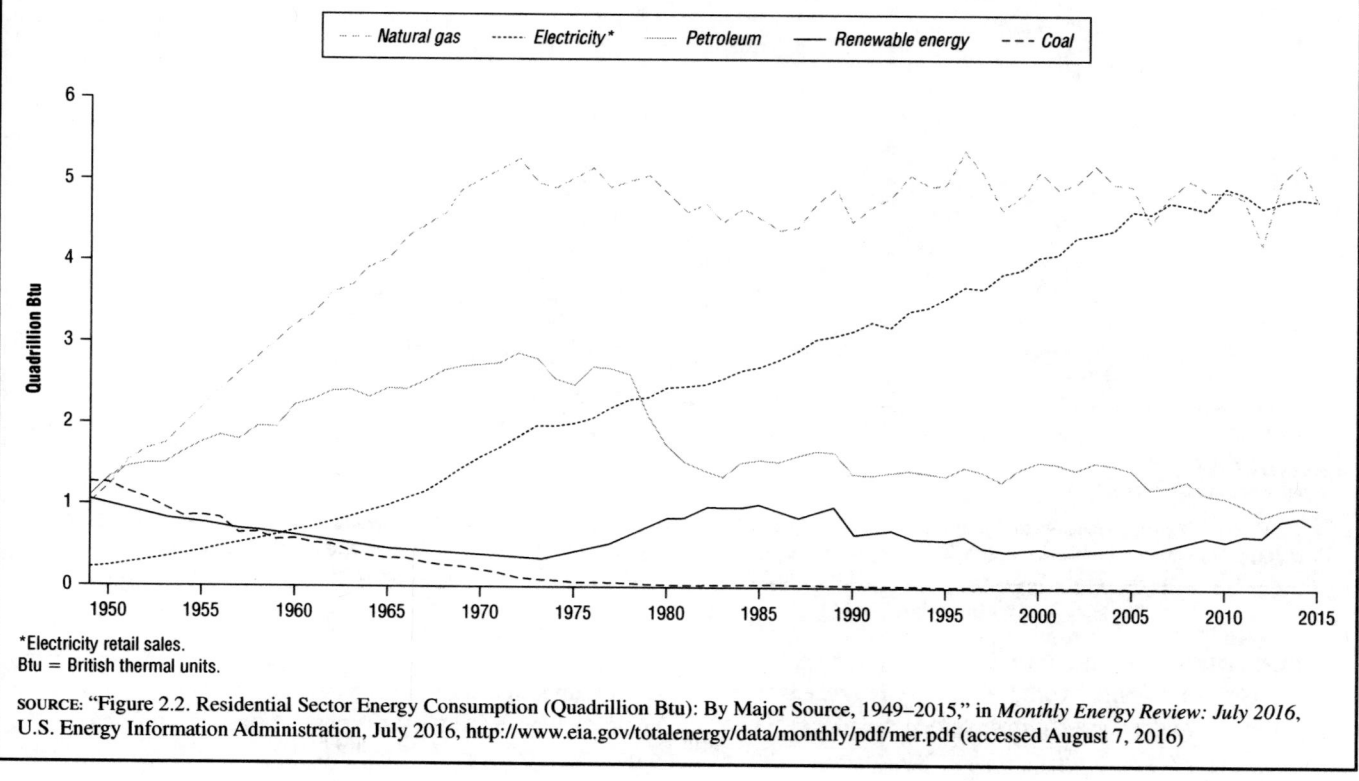

Note: Btu = British thermal units.

SOURCE: "Figure 2.6. Electric Power Sector Energy Consumption (Quadrillion Btu): By Major Source, 1949–2015," in *Monthly Energy Review: July 2016*, U.S. Energy Information Administration, July 2016, http://www.eia.gov/totalenergy/data/monthly/pdf/mer.pdf (accessed August 7, 2016)

FIGURE 1.4

Residential sector energy consumption, by major source, 1949–2015

*Electricity retail sales.
Btu = British thermal units.

SOURCE: "Figure 2.2. Residential Sector Energy Consumption (Quadrillion Btu): By Major Source, 1949–2015," in *Monthly Energy Review: July 2016*, U.S. Energy Information Administration, July 2016, http://www.eia.gov/totalenergy/data/monthly/pdf/mer.pdf (accessed August 7, 2016)

FIGURE 1.5

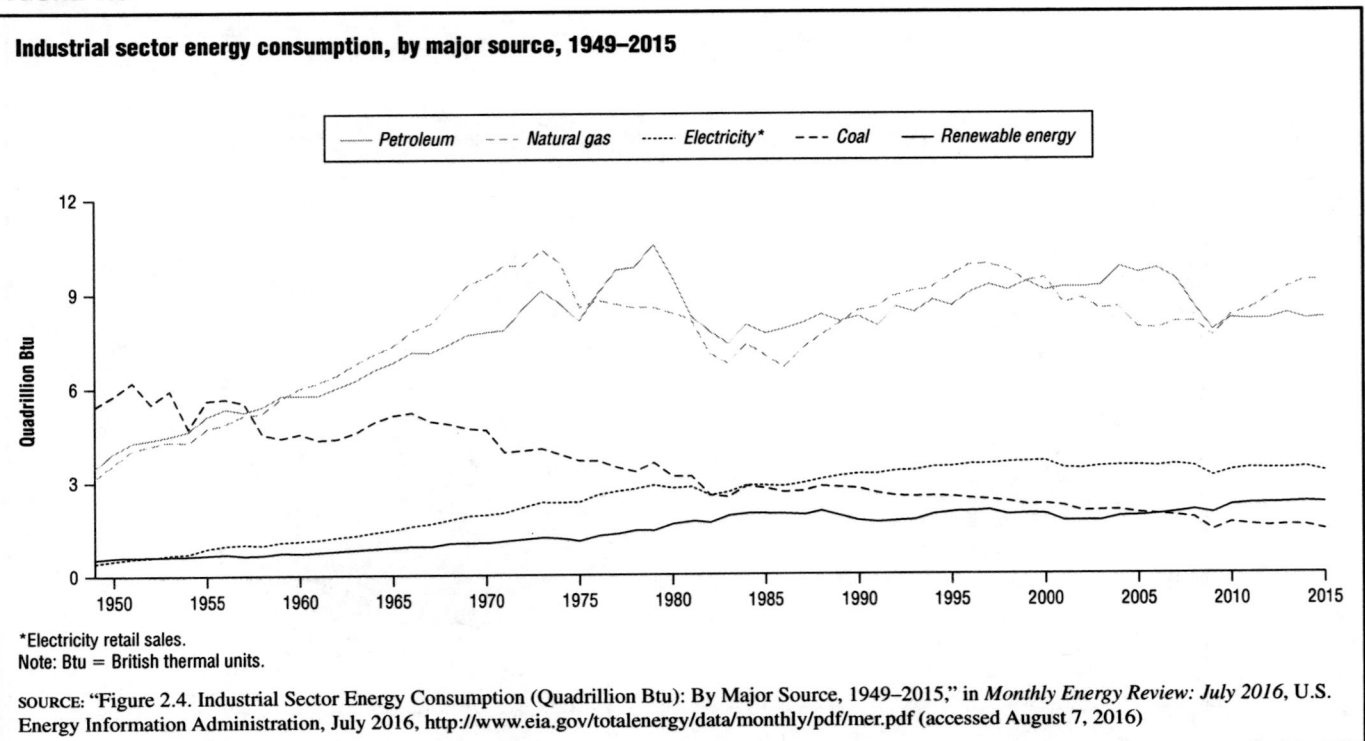

Industrial sector energy consumption, by major source, 1949–2015

— Petroleum   - - - Natural gas   ······· Electricity*   - - - Coal   —— Renewable energy

*Electricity retail sales.
Note: Btu = British thermal units.

SOURCE: "Figure 2.4. Industrial Sector Energy Consumption (Quadrillion Btu): By Major Source, 1949–2015," in *Monthly Energy Review: July 2016*, U.S. Energy Information Administration, July 2016, http://www.eia.gov/totalenergy/data/monthly/pdf/mer.pdf (accessed August 7, 2016)

FIGURE 1.6

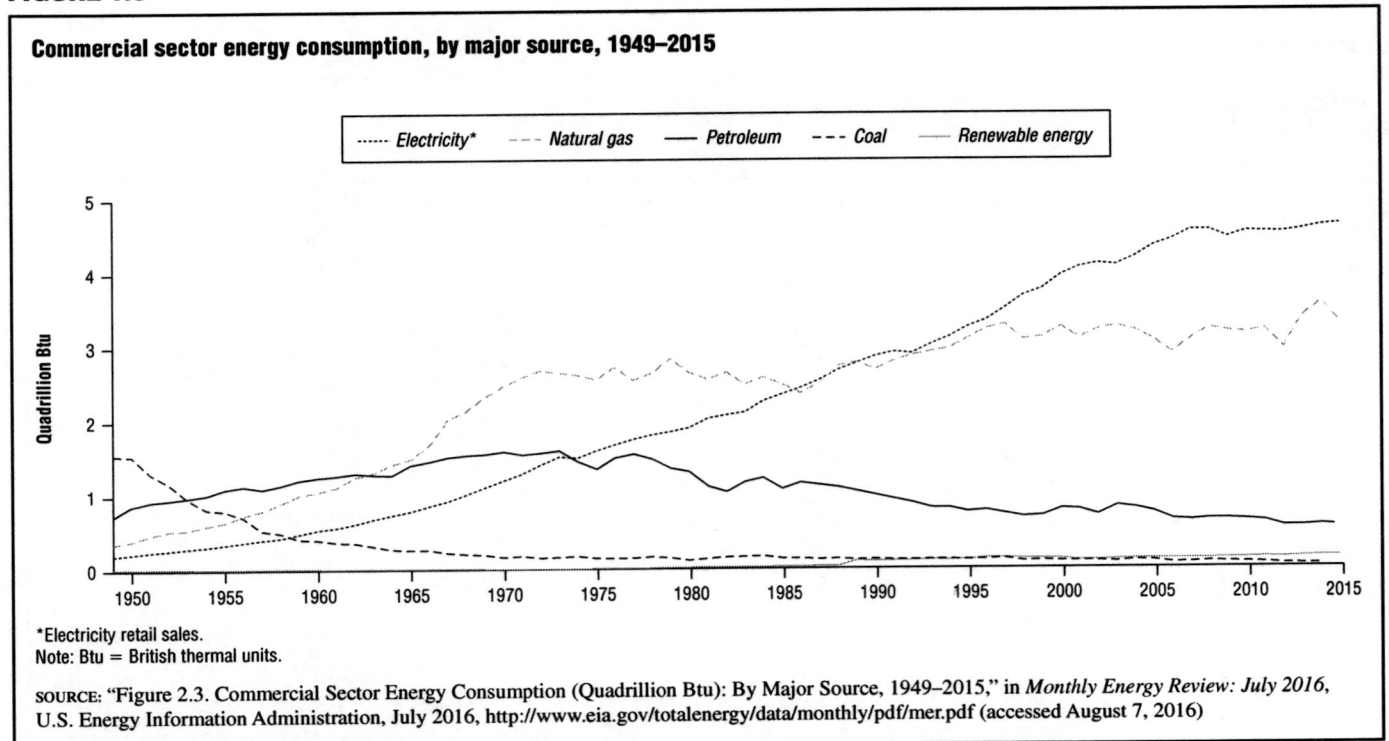

Commercial sector energy consumption, by major source, 1949–2015

······· Electricity*   - - - Natural gas   —— Petroleum   - - - Coal   —— Renewable energy

*Electricity retail sales.
Note: Btu = British thermal units.

SOURCE: "Figure 2.3. Commercial Sector Energy Consumption (Quadrillion Btu): By Major Source, 1949–2015," in *Monthly Energy Review: July 2016*, U.S. Energy Information Administration, July 2016, http://www.eia.gov/totalenergy/data/monthly/pdf/mer.pdf (accessed August 7, 2016)

TRANSPORTATION SECTOR. Energy consumed by this end-use sector is for vehicles whose primary purpose is transporting people and/or goods from place to place. These vehicles include automobiles; trucks; buses; motorcycles; trains, subways, and other rail vehicles; aircraft; and ships, barges, and other waterborne vehicles. It should be noted that vehicles whose primary purpose is not transportation (e.g., bulldozers, tractors, and forklifts) are classified in the sector of their primary use. Petroleum dominates, by far, the energy consumption in the transportation sector. (See Figure 1.7.) Other energy sources are minor players.

SECTORS OVERALL. Historically, industry has been the largest energy consumer of the end-use sectors. (See Figure 1.8.) In 2015 industry used 31 quadrillion Btu,

FIGURE 1.7

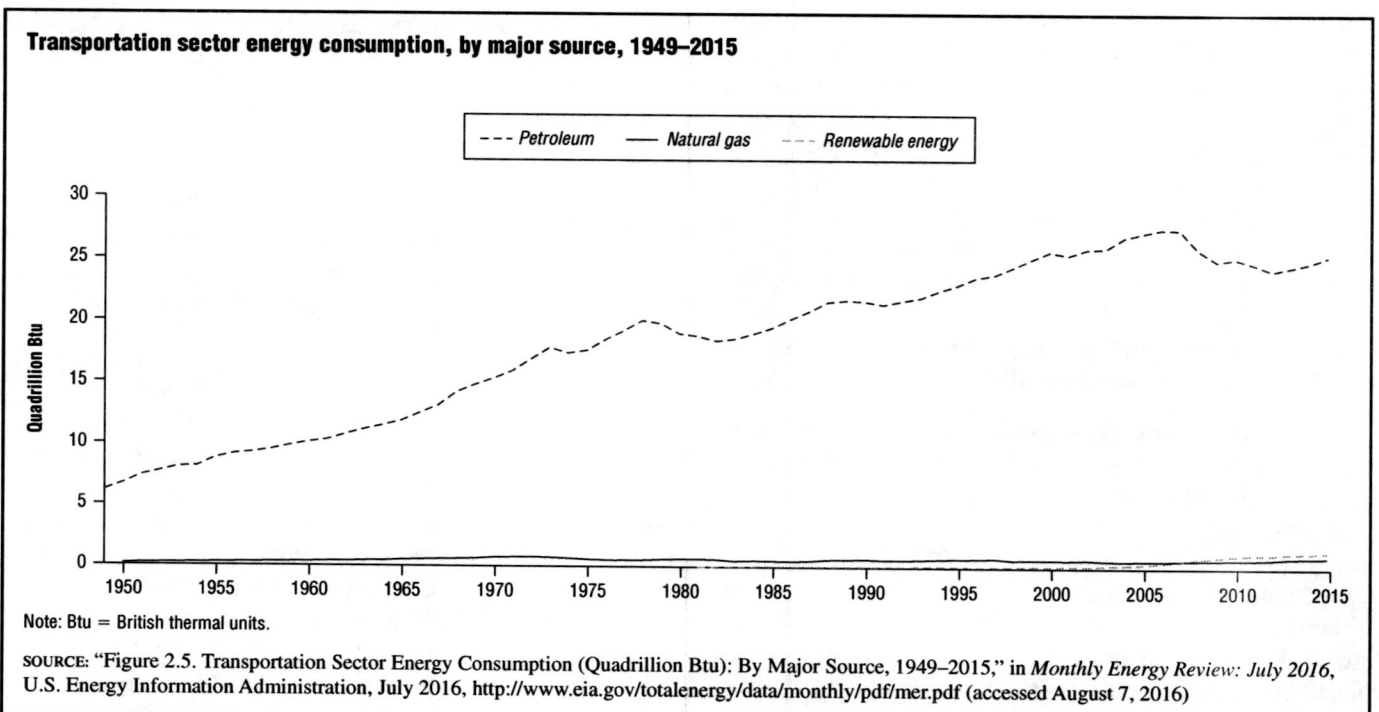

Transportation sector energy consumption, by major source, 1949–2015

Note: Btu = British thermal units.

SOURCE: "Figure 2.5. Transportation Sector Energy Consumption (Quadrillion Btu): By Major Source, 1949–2015," in *Monthly Energy Review: July 2016*, U.S. Energy Information Administration, July 2016, http://www.eia.gov/totalenergy/data/monthly/pdf/mer.pdf (accessed August 7, 2016)

FIGURE 1.8

Total energy consumption, by end-use sector, 1949–2015

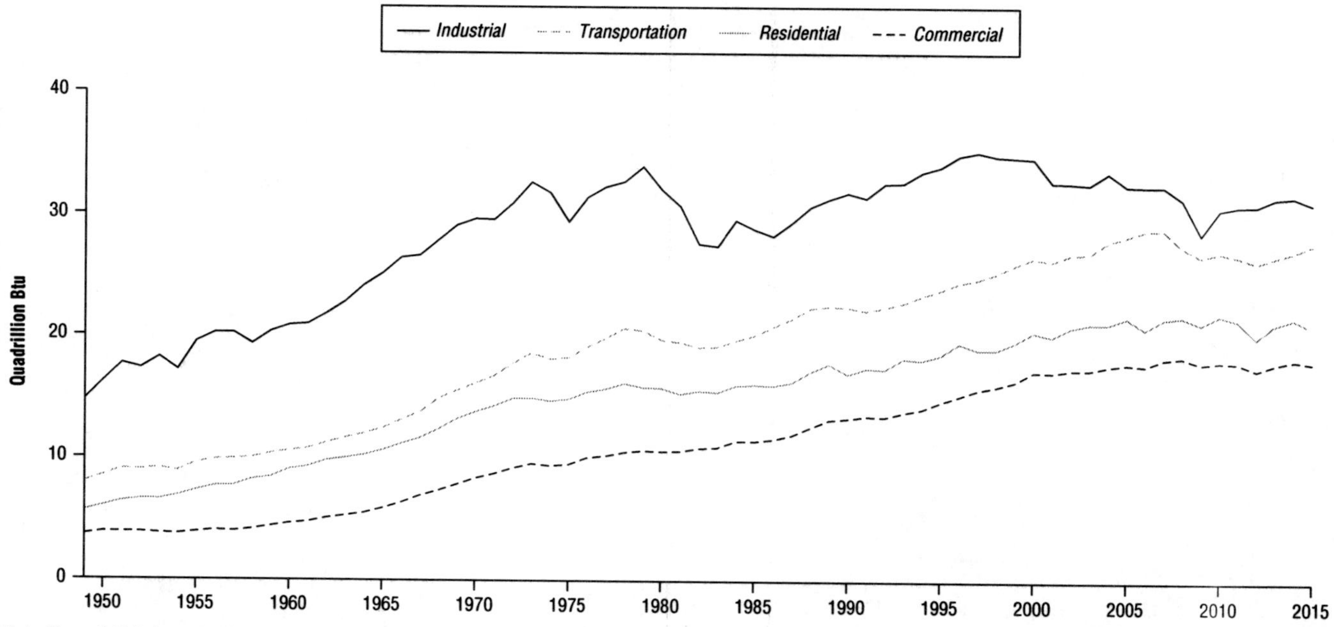

Note: Btu = British thermal units.

SOURCE: "Figure 2.1. Energy Consumption by Sector (Quadrillion Btu): Total Consumption by End-Use Sector, 1949–2015," in *Monthly Energy Review: July 2016*, U.S. Energy Information Administration, July 2016, http://www.eia.gov/totalenergy/data/monthly/pdf/mer.pdf (accessed August 7, 2016)

compared with 27.7 quadrillion Btu for the transportation sector, 20.8 quadrillion Btu for the residential sector, and 18 quadrillion Btu for the commercial sector.

ENERGY SELF-SUFFICIENCY

Before the 20th century, the United States was largely energy self-sufficient, in that it produced enough energy domestically to satisfy domestic demand. Through the 1950s domestic energy production and consumption were nearly equal. (See Figure 1.9.) During the 1960s consumption slightly outpaced production. During the 1970s the gap widened considerably; it narrowed somewhat during the early 1980s, and then began to widen again. By around 2005 the gap between domestic energy production and consumption was quite significant, but it then narrowed significantly through 2015.

Since the 1970s energy imports (particularly of petroleum) have been used to close the gap between domestic energy production and consumption. Petroleum imports have historically accounted for the vast majority of total energy imports. (See Figure 1.10.) The United States' dependence on other countries for oil first became a cause for concern during the 1970s. By this time the nation was hugely dependent on foreign oil, particularly from countries in the Middle East. A political disagreement led some of those countries to temporarily limit the amount of oil they sold to the United States. Lower supply in the face of growing demand sent prices soaring for gasoline and other oil products. The energy embargo had severe repercussions on the overall economy. Energy self-sufficiency became a new national goal, but, as shown in Figure 1.9, this goal has been difficult to achieve.

The United States does export some energy commodities. (See Figure 1.11.) Through the 1990s coal was the predominant export. Since that time petroleum exports have surged dramatically, totaling 9.1 quadrillion Btu in 2015. According to the EIA, in *Monthly Energy Review: July 2016*, U.S. petroleum exports are almost all petroleum products. The United States exports very little crude oil due to regulatory restrictions that are described in Chapter 2.

Figure 1.12 shows domestic energy production, import, export, and consumption flows in 2015. Overall, domestic production was 88.6 quadrillion Btu. Imports added another 23.6 quadrillion Btu, mostly from crude oil and petroleum products. Thus, the total U.S. energy supply was 110.8 quadrillion Btu, of which 80% was domestically produced and 20% was imported. Approximately 13.1 quadrillion Btu (12%) of the U.S. supply was exported. This included 9.3 quadrillion Btu of petroleum products and 3.8 quadrillion Btu of other commodities, such as natural gas, coal, coal coke, biofuels, and electricity. Total U.S. energy consumption in 2015 was 97.7 quadrillion Btu. The majority

FIGURE 1.9

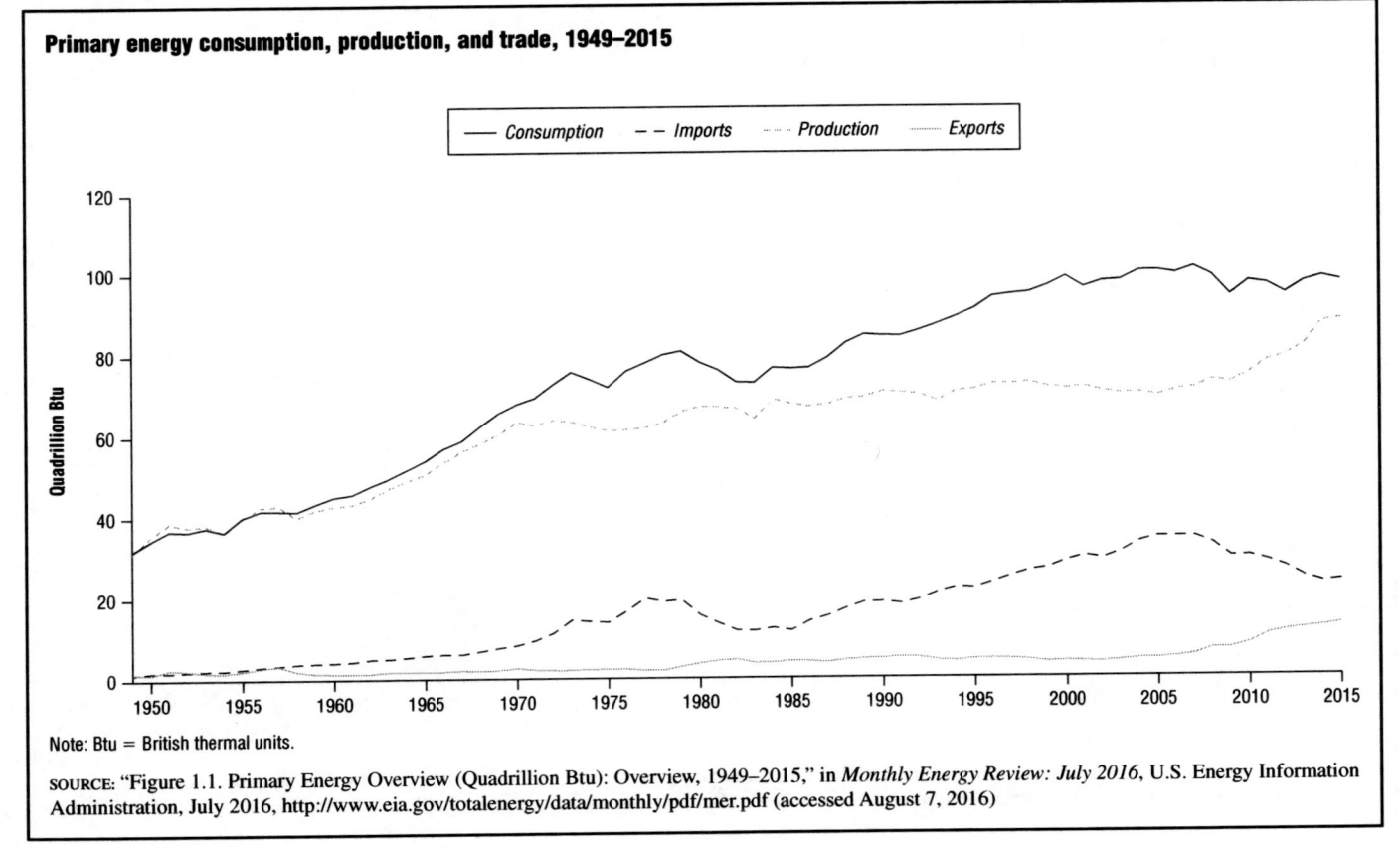

Primary energy consumption, production, and trade, 1949–2015

Note: Btu = British thermal units.

SOURCE: "Figure 1.1. Primary Energy Overview (Quadrillion Btu): Overview, 1949–2015," in *Monthly Energy Review: July 2016*, U.S. Energy Information Administration, July 2016, http://www.eia.gov/totalenergy/data/monthly/pdf/mer.pdf (accessed August 7, 2016)

FIGURE 1.10

Primary energy imports, by source, 1949–2015

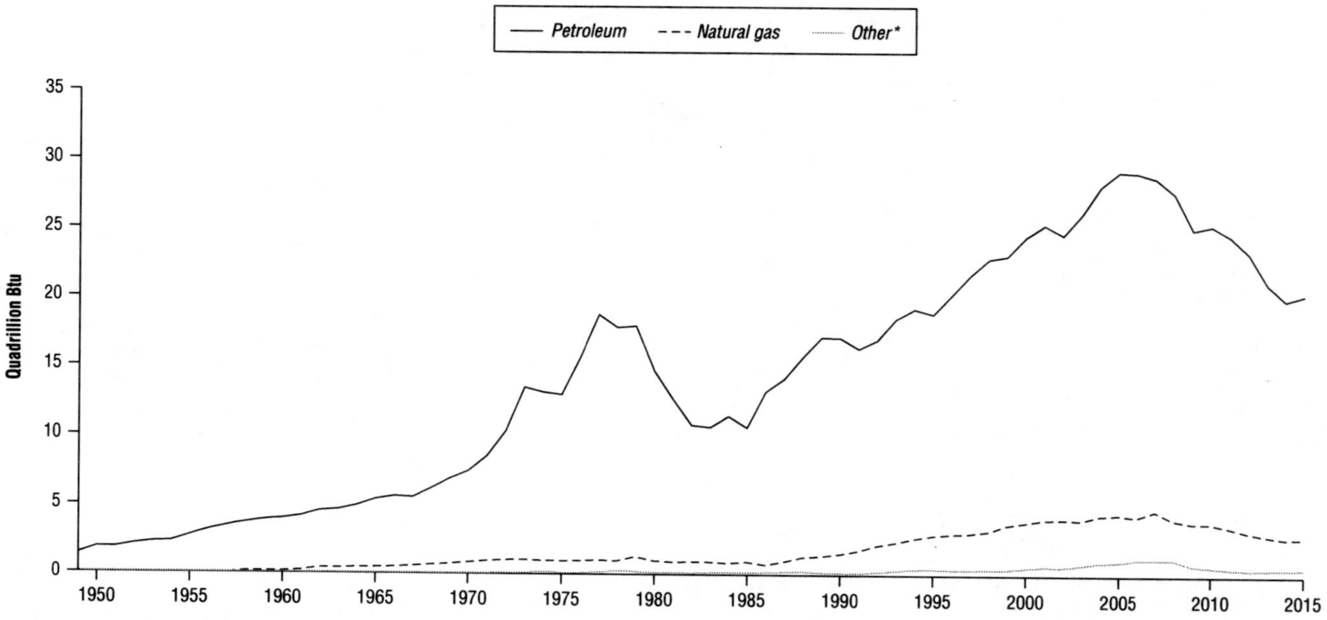

*Coal, coal coke, biofuels, and electricity.
Note: Btu = British thermal units.

SOURCE: Adapted from "Figure 1.4a. Primary Energy Imports and Exports (Quadrillion Btu): Imports by Source, 1949–2015," in *Monthly Energy Review: July 2016*, U.S. Energy Information Administration, July 2016, http://www.eia.gov/totalenergy/data/monthly/pdf/mer.pdf (accessed August 7, 2016)

FIGURE 1.11

Primary energy exports, by source, 1949–2015

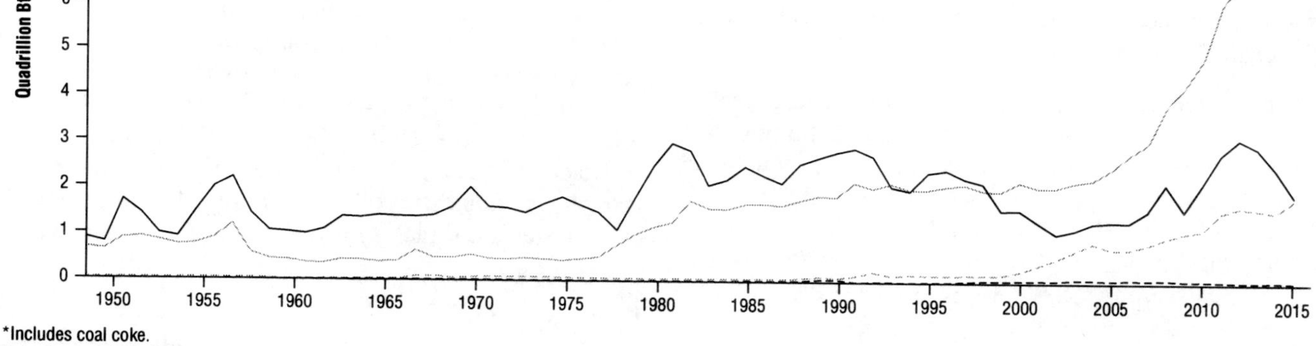

*Includes coal coke.
Note: Btu = British thermal units.

SOURCE: Adapted from "Figure 1.4a. Primary Energy Imports and Exports (Quadrillion Btu): Imports by Source, 1949–2015," in *Monthly Energy Review: July 2016*, U.S. Energy Information Administration, July 2016, http://www.eia.gov/totalenergy/data/monthly/pdf/mer.pdf (accessed August 7, 2016)

FIGURE 1.12

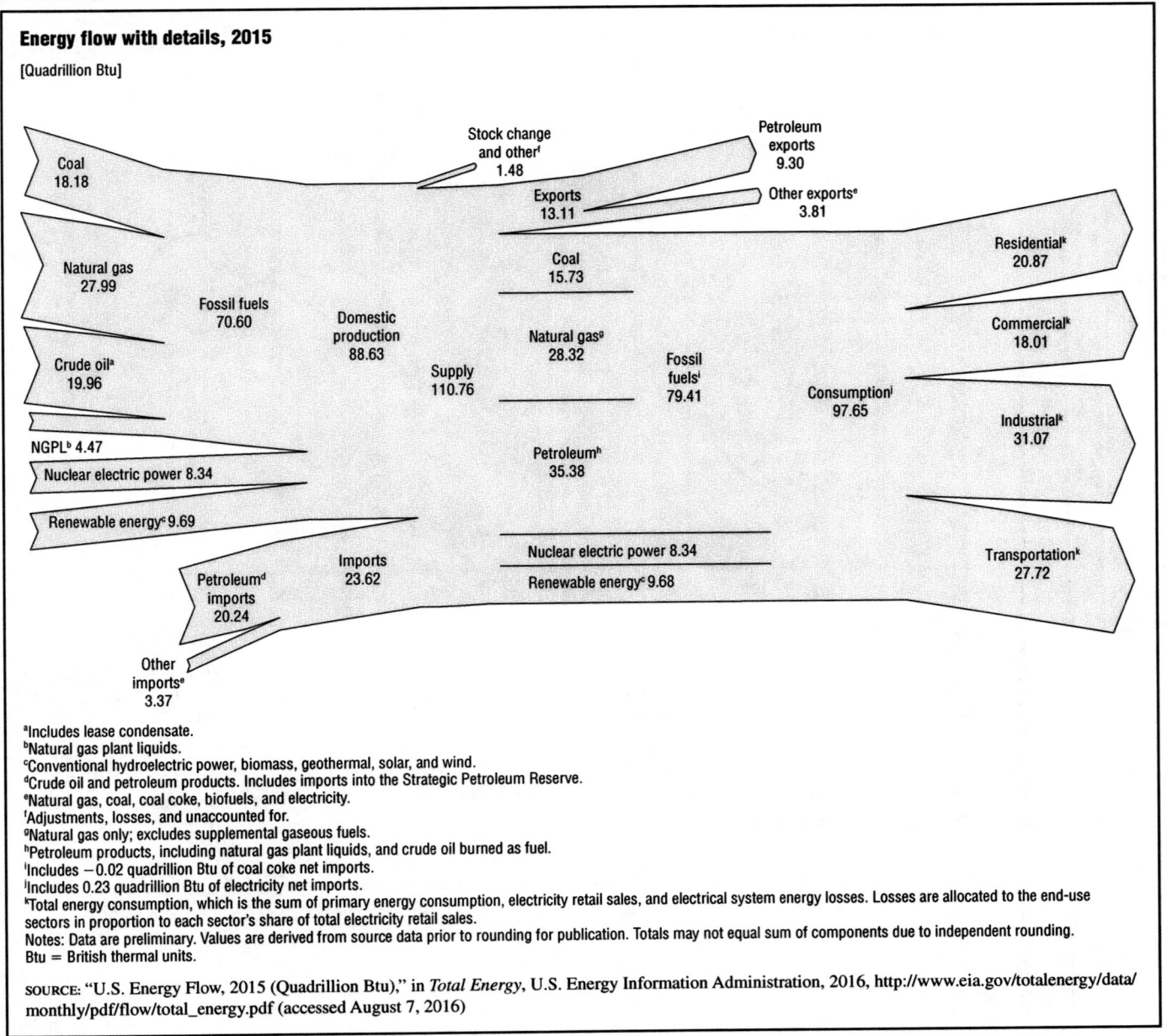

Energy flow with details, 2015

[Quadrillion Btu]

^aIncludes lease condensate.
^bNatural gas plant liquids.
^cConventional hydroelectric power, biomass, geothermal, solar, and wind.
^dCrude oil and petroleum products. Includes imports into the Strategic Petroleum Reserve.
^eNatural gas, coal, coal coke, biofuels, and electricity.
^fAdjustments, losses, and unaccounted for.
^gNatural gas only; excludes supplemental gaseous fuels.
^hPetroleum products, including natural gas plant liquids, and crude oil burned as fuel.
ⁱIncludes −0.02 quadrillion Btu of coal coke net imports.
^jIncludes 0.23 quadrillion Btu of electricity net imports.
^kTotal energy consumption, which is the sum of primary energy consumption, electricity retail sales, and electrical system energy losses. Losses are allocated to the end-use sectors in proportion to each sector's share of total electricity retail sales.
Notes: Data are preliminary. Values are derived from source data prior to rounding for publication. Totals may not equal sum of components due to independent rounding.
Btu = British thermal units.

SOURCE: "U.S. Energy Flow, 2015 (Quadrillion Btu)," in *Total Energy*, U.S. Energy Information Administration, 2016, http://www.eia.gov/totalenergy/data/monthly/pdf/flow/total_energy.pdf (accessed August 7, 2016)

(74 quadrillion Btu, or 76%) of total consumption came from domestic energy products, while 23.6 quadrillion Btu (24%) came from imports.

The United States cannot obtain total energy self-sufficiency without replacing energy imports (almost all of which are petroleum based) with domestic production. Figure 1.13 shows various scenarios for future U.S. oil use as projected by the EIA in *Annual Energy Outlook 2016 with Projections to 2040* (August 2016, https://www.eia.gov/forecasts/aeo/pdf/0383(2016).pdf). The EIA calculates that net imports (imports minus exports) of oil accounted for around a quarter of total U.S. liquid fuels consumption in 2015. Under a scenario in which oil prices are high (thus encouraging production) and domestic oil production increases robustly, the United States could

reduce its net oil imports to zero by 2025. The oil company BP (formerly British Petroleum) presents its prediction in *BP Energy Outlook: Outlook to 2035* (March 2016, http://www.bp.com/content/dam/bp/pdf/energy-economics/energy-outlook-2016/bp-energy-outlook-2016.pdf). BP forecasts that the United States will become oil self-sufficient by 2030. Chapter 2 describes the tremendous growth in domestic oil production that has put the United States on track to achieve energy self-sufficiency.

ENERGY COSTS

Energy costs, like the costs for all commodities, depend on supply and demand factors. These factors are quite complex, and some of the major drivers are discussed in this chapter. In addition, source-specific

FIGURE 1.13

Net imports (imports minus exports) as a share of liquid fuels consumption, 1990–2015 and projected through 2040

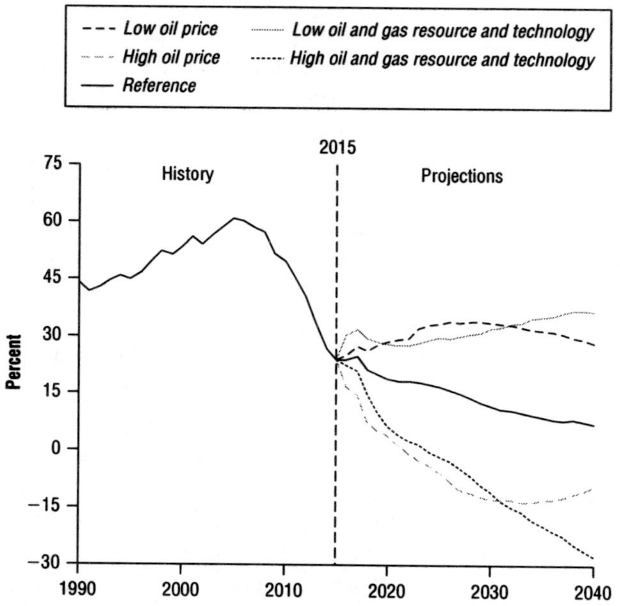

SOURCE: "Figure MT-56. Net Import Share of U.S. Petroleum and Other Liquid Fuels Consumption in Five Cases, 1990–2040 (Percent)," in *Annual Energy Outlook 2016 with Projections to 2040*, U.S. Energy Information Administration, August 2016, https://www.eia.gov/forecasts/aeo/pdf/0383(2016).pdf (accessed September 16, 2016)

TABLE 1.4

Energy price estimates, by type, 2014

[Dollars per million BTU]

Primary energy	
Coal	2.51
Natural gas[a]	7.20
Petroleum	
Distillate fuel oil	26.17
Jet fuel[b]	20.52
LPG[c]	19.03
Motor gasoline[d]	27.48
Residual fuel oil	15.06
Other[e]	25.02
Total	25.38
Nuclear fuel	0.75
Biomass: wood and waste[f]	4.12
Total[g, h, i]	12.67
Electric power sector[g, h]	2.80
Retail electricity	30.74
Total energy[a, i]	21.33

[a]Natural gas as it is consumed; includes supplemental gaseous fuels that are commingled with natural gas.
[b]Includes kerosene-type jet fuel only; naphtha-type jet fuel is included in "Other petroleum."
[c]Liquefied petroleum gases, includes ethane and olefins.
[d]Motor gasoline as it is consumed; includes fuel ethanol blended into motor gasoline.
[e]Includes asphalt and road oil, aviation gasoline, kerosene, lubricants, and the other petroleum products.
[f]Wood, wood-derived fuels, and biomass waste.
[g]There are no direct fuel costs for hydroelectric, geothermal, wind, photovoltaic, or solar thermal energy.
[h]Electricity imports are included in these prices but not shown separately.
[i]The U.S. average includes coal coke net imports, which are not allocated to the states.
— = No consumption, including cases where adjustments were made.

SOURCE: Adapted from "Table E1. Primary Energy, Electricity, and Total Energy Price Estimates, 2014 (Dollars per Million Btu)," in *State Energy Data System (SEDS): 1960–2014 (Complete)*, U.S. Energy Information Administration, June 29, 2016, http://www.eia.gov/state/seds/sep_sum/html/pdf/sum_pr_tot.pdf (accessed August 12, 2016)

supply and demand factors are discussed in detail in Chapter 2 for oil, in Chapter 3 for natural gas, in Chapter 4 for coal, in Chapter 5 for nuclear energy, in Chapter 6 for renewable energy, and in Chapter 8 for electricity.

Energy costs can be divided into two broad categories: market costs and external costs.

Market Costs

Market costs are the prices paid in the marketplace for energy products. The EIA tracks various kinds of market costs, including energy production costs, import and export energy costs, and consumer costs for energy. Source-specific costs are discussed in detail in the relevant chapters. Some general information about costing trends, however, is presented here.

In *Annual Energy Review 2011* (September 2012, http://www.eia.gov/totalenergy/data/annual/pdf/aer.pdf), the EIA notes that the nation's overall price tag for total energy purchased by consumers increased from less than $2 per million Btu in 1970 to more than $20 per million Btu in the early 21st century. It should be noted that these are nominal prices, meaning that they do not reflect the effects of inflation over time. As shown in Table 1.4, average U.S. energy prices in 2014 varied considerably

from $30.74 per million Btu for retail electricity to $0.75 per million Btu for nuclear fuel. The overall average for all energy types was $21.33 per million Btu.

Overall, consumers spent nearly $1.4 trillion on energy in 2014. (See Table 1.5.) Petroleum had the highest expenditures, at $863.9 billion. Motor gasoline accounted for more than half of the petroleum total. In addition, consumers spent $390 billion on retail electricity.

External Costs

External costs are costs other than market costs. In economics, externalities are benefits (positive consequences) and harms (negative consequences) that are not included in marketplace prices. There are positive externalities that are associated with the energy industry. For example, the research and development of energy technologies has produced scientific knowledge that has benefited other industries, and hence the overall economy. Energy externalities, however, are most often discussed in terms of negative consequences, meaning the external costs that are associated with energy.

TABLE 1.5

U.S. energy expenditure estimates, by type, 2014

Primary energy		
Coal		
	Coking coal	2,796
	Steam coal	42,323
	Total	**45,119**
Coal coke		
	Exports	233
	Imports	9
Natural gas[a]		174,019
Petroleum		
	Distillate fuel oil	222,606
	Jet fuel[b]	62,421
	LPG[c]	58,652
	Motor gasoline[d]	452,805
	Residual fuel oil	8,861
	Other[e]	58,563
	Total	**863,909**
Nuclear fuel		6,252
Biomass: wood and waste[f, g]		8,845
	Total[g, h, i, j]	**1,100,940**
Electric power sector[h, i]		−95,837
Retail electricity		389,872
	Total energy[g, h, i]	**1,394,974**

[a]Natural gas as it is consumed; includes supplemental gaseous fuels that are commingled with natural gas.
[b]Through 2004, includes kerosene-type and naphtha-type jet fuel. Beginning in 2005, includes kerosene-type jet fuel only; naphtha-type jet fuel is included in "Other petroleum."
[c]Liquefied petroleum gases, includes ethane and olefins.
[d]Beginning in 1993, includes fuel ethanol blended into motor gasoline.
[e]Includes asphalt and road oil, aviation gasoline, kerosene, lubricants, and other petroleum products.
[f]Wood, wood-derived fuels, and biomass waste. Prior to 2001, includes non-biomass waste.
[g]There is a discontinuity in this time series between 1988 and 1989 due to the expanded coverage of the use of wood and biomass waste beginning in 1989.
[h]There are no direct fuel costs for hydroelectric, geothermal, wind, photovoltaic, or solar thermal energy.
[i]For 1981 through 1992, includes fuel ethanol blended into motor gasoline that is not included in the motor gasoline column.
[j]Electricity imports are included in total primary energy and electric power sector but are not shown separately.
Note: Expenditure totals may not equal sum of components due to independent rounding.

SOURCE: Adapted from "Table ET1. Primary Energy, Electricity, and Total Energy Price and Expenditure Estimates, Selected Years, 1970–2014, United States," in *State Energy Data System (SEDS): 1960–2014 (Complete)*, U.S. Energy Information Administration, June 29, 2016, http://www.eia.gov/state/seds/sep_prices/total/pdf/pr_US.pdf (accessed August 12, 2016)

Although these costs are believed to be substantial, they are difficult to quantify.

The most obvious external cost associated with energy is environmental degradation. Extracting, processing, and burning fossil fuels has environmental consequences, chiefly emissions of contaminants that degrade the air, water, and land and harm ecosystems and ultimately human health. Likewise, the production of nuclear energy and energy from renewable sources has negative environmental impacts to varying degrees.

The energy industry (like all industries) is bound by government regulations to limit its emissions and other environmental impacts through control measures. These measures are inherently imperfect, and the imposition of stricter controls is fraught with political controversy in the United States. Energy—especially domestically produced low-cost energy—is considered to be a vital commodity for the nation's economic well-being and national security. As a result, the U.S. government supports the energy industry via many measures, which is explained in detail later in this chapter.

Critics complain that the external environmental costs of fossil fuel use have for decades been borne by society at large, rather than by the producers and consumers of the fuels. The criticism grew especially loud during the first decade of the 21st century as energy prices soared and oil and natural gas companies made record profits. At the same time, there was growing concern about global warming and resulting climate change. Scientists believe that large-scale burning of fossil fuels for more than a century has pumped enormous amounts of carbon into the atmosphere. (The carbon-containing gases are often called greenhouse gases, because they act like the panes of a greenhouse to hold in heat.) The resulting atmospheric changes have been gradually warming the planet and changing historical climate patterns. These effects are expected to continue well into the future. Although there are other contributing factors to global warming, including deforestation, the combustion of coal, natural gas, and oil and its derivatives (such as gasoline) is believed to be the main culprit. Thus, the negative impacts of global warming, including melting ice caps, coastal flooding, and disruptive climate changes, are considered to be external costs of fossil fuel usage.

Some people believe the federal government should force external environmental costs into the market costs for fossil fuels, such as by taxing carbon emissions from fossil fuel combustion. Advocates of this approach argue that it would show consumers the "true" costs of fossil fuels. Of course, prices would be much higher for coal, natural gas, oil, gasoline, and electricity, which is largely fossil fuel based in the United States. Price shocks do lower demand for expensive commodities. Many consumers would likely switch to alternatives, in this case, to energy that is produced from renewable sources such as wind and solar power. A carbon tax or similar provision would certainly push the nation away from fossil fuels and toward renewables, which is a highly desirable outcome in some opinions. However, severe price shocks, especially for a widely used and vital commodity such as energy, would stress the nation's economy, perhaps on a large and calamitous scale. As a result, as of September 2016 the U.S. government had not implemented taxes that were specifically designed to capture the external environmental costs of fossil fuel use.

GOVERNMENT INTERVENTION

Government intervention has long been a factor in energy supply and demand in the United States. Over the decades presidents have set energy policies and proposed federal budgets that reflected their energy priorities. Congress has passed laws and spending bills that sometimes supported presidential priorities and sometimes reflected alternative priorities. Politics has always been a major consideration in the nation's energy decisions. At the heart of the debate is how large a role the government should play in a private market. In general, it is agreed that energy is so precious a commodity that the government should play some role, chiefly by promoting domestic production and conservation, which are both elements of the overall goal of energy self-sufficiency. This puts the government in the odd position of both encouraging domestic suppliers to bring more energy to market and encouraging buyers to use less energy. Also, because most U.S. energy is fossil fuel based, government support of domestic fossil fuel production engenders environmental problems, including global warming. These seemingly contradictory outcomes are just some of the difficulties involved in government manipulation of the energy market.

National Energy Policy

The energy policy of President Barack Obama (1961–) has been laid out in several key documents:

- *Blueprint for a Secure Energy Future* (March 30, 2011, http://www.whitehouse.gov/sites/default/files/blueprint _secure_energy_future.pdf)

- *The President's Climate Action Plan* (June 2013, http://www.whitehouse.gov/sites/default/files/image/ president27sclimateactionplan.pdf)

- *The All-of-the-Above Energy Strategy as a Path to Sustainable Economic Growth* (May 2014, http://www .whitehouse.gov/sites/default/files/docs/aota_energy _strategy_as_a_path_to_sustainable_economic_growth .pdf)

- *Quadrennial Energy Review: Energy Transmission, Storage, and Distribution Infrastructure* (April 2015, http://energy.gov/sites/prod/files/2015/07/f24/QER%20 Full%20Report_TS%26D%20April%202015_0.pdf)

In *The All-of-the-Above Energy Strategy as a Path to Sustainable Economic Growth*, President Obama establishes an energy agenda that supports energy sources, such as wind, solar, and nuclear power, with low or zero carbon emissions; reduces energy demand by promoting energy efficiency; and endorses the use of carbon capture, utilization, and storage for coal and natural gas power plants and industrial facilities. The president notes the unexpected energy boom that the United States began experiencing during the first decade of the 21st century. As is described in Chapters 2 and 3, domestic production of oil and natural gas has skyrocketed thanks to new technologies that allow extraction of previously unrealized sources of these fossil fuels. This ongoing

development provides key economic benefits, including job creation, and empowers the United States to become more energy independent in the future; however, continued reliance on fossil fuels has environmental consequences. The Obama administration is particularly worried about carbon emissions from fossil fuel combustion. Subsequent chapters will summarize federal programs and regulations aimed at limiting the energy sector's carbon emissions. These efforts are politically controversial because they are seen in some circles as an unnecessary financial burden on energy companies and hence the nation's economy overall.

In January 2014 President Obama (http://www.white house.gov/the-press-office/2014/01/09/presidential-memo randum-establishing-quadrennial-energy-review) created an interagency task force charged with gathering "ideas and advice" from government agencies, academia, businesses, consumers, and other stakeholders across the country for the quadrennial energy review (QER). (The term *quadrennial* means recurring every four years.) The first part of the QER was published in April 2015. In *Quadrennial Energy Review: Energy Transmission, Storage, and Distribution Infrastructure*, the QER task force provides a comprehensive overview of the nation's energy infrastructure (pipelines, electric wires, storage systems, waterways, railroads, and other facilities). The lengthy report includes numerous recommendations that are summarized in "Fact Sheet: Administration Announces New Agenda to Modernize Energy Infrastructure" (April 21, 2015, http://energy.gov/sites/prod/files/2015/ 04/f22/QER%20SUMMARY%20FACT%20SHEET%20 final.pdf) and would require at least $11 billion in federal spending through 2025. This ambitious spending proposal proved politically unattractive in 2015 and 2016 as Congress was racked by infighting over federal spending. The U.S. House of Representatives' Committee on Energy and Commerce, Subcommittee on Energy and Power notes in *Hearing on "The Fiscal Year 2017 Department of Energy Budget"* (February 29, 2016, http://docs .house.gov/meetings/IF/IF03/20160302/104593/HHRG-114- IF03-20160302-SD002.pdf) that the DOE was given only $31.3 million during fiscal year (FY) 2016 and asked for $31 million for FY 2017 to "carry out QER-related activities." (The federal government's fiscal year begins in October and ends in September.) As of September 2016, the DOE appropriations bill for FY 2017 had not been finalized.

Tax Provisions

The government collects taxes as a matter of course on economic activity. Energy products, like other commodities in commerce, are subject to these taxes. In addition, the government uses taxes in some areas of the energy industry to offset some of the external costs that are associated with energy development and consumption.

Taxes are sometimes imposed specifically to discourage certain activities, whereas tax breaks are granted to encourage other activities. For example, in *Fuel Economy Guide: Model Year 2016* (September 1, 2016, https://www.fueleconomy.gov/feg/pdfs/guides/FEG2016.pdf), the DOE and the U.S. Environmental Protection Agency describe a tax provision that was active in 2016. A "gas guzzler" tax was imposed on auto manufacturers that sold cars with "exceptionally low fuel economy." By contrast, a federal income tax credit was offered to consumers who bought certain electric or partially electric vehicles (cars using little to no gasoline). Both tax provisions directly support national goals for energy self-sufficiency.

TARGETED TAXES. Government entities at the federal, state, and local levels often use taxes that target particular energy sectors, such as coal mining. One purpose of these targeted taxes is to offset some of the external costs that are associated with energy production and consumption, such as health, social, and environmental consequences. The collected monies may be put into trust funds that are administered by government agencies. The trust funds provide monies to cover external costs that are ongoing or may occur in the future. One example is the Oil Spill Liability Trust Fund, which was created by Congress in 1986. Its purpose is to cover certain damages that are associated with oil spills.

Government entities also commonly impose excise taxes (taxes that target specific goods) on gasoline. These taxes are often used for building and maintaining transportation infrastructure, such as roads and bridges. A severance tax (a tax that targets the removal of nonrenewable resources) is another type of tax. Many states levy severance taxes on companies that extract subsurface resources, such as oil, natural gas, and coal, within their boundaries. Cassarah Brown of the National Council of State Legislators provides in *State Revenues and the Natural Gas Boom: An Assessment of State Oil and Gas Production Taxes* (June 2013, http://www.ncsl.org/documents/energy/pdf_version_final.pdf) a table that details how states typically spend the severance taxes they collect from oil and gas extraction. Some states allocate the money to their general funds, whereas others earmark it for specific programs or funds.

Whatever their purpose, taxes on energy products elevate the prices that consumers ultimately pay for those products.

Federal Financial Support

The federal government's financial support to the energy industry amounts to billions of dollars annually. In *Federal Support for the Development, Production, and Use of Fuels and Energy Technologies* (November 2015, https://www.cbo.gov/sites/default/files/114th-congress-2015-2016/reports/50980-EnergySupport-3.pdf), the Congressional Budget Office describes how the federal government financially supports the energy industry using two tools: tax preferences (special tax law provisions that reduce tax liabilities) and spending programs that are administered by the DOE.

FEDERAL TAX PREFERENCES. The United States has a long history of using tax preferences to encourage domestic energy development. Molly F. Sherlock of the Congressional Research Service notes in *Energy Tax Policy: Historical Perspectives on and Current Status of Energy Tax Expenditures* (May 2, 2011, http://www.leahy.senate.gov/imo/media/doc/R41227EnergyLegReport.pdf) that the first federal energy tax breaks were implemented in 1916. Sherlock indicates that from 1916 through 1970 tax policy "focused almost exclusively" on increasing domestic reserves and production of oil and natural gas. During the 1970s the United States suffered an energy crisis due to high reliance on foreign oil. At the same time, awareness was arising about the environmental consequences of fossil fuels.

Figure 1.14 shows the estimated costs for energy-related federal tax preferences between FYs 1985 and 2015. Preferences for the fossil fuel industry accounted for the majority of the yearly costs through 2007. Preferences for the renewable energy industry increased dramatically after that time.

It should be noted that government intervention does not always achieve the desired results. For example, tax preferences that were favorable to renewable energy sources had little effect during the late 1990s because oil prices were historically low. Consumers responded to the low oil prices by buying large sport-utility vehicles and other vehicles that had relatively poor fuel economy.

Energy economics changed as energy prices began rising. Congress responded with new laws, such as the Energy Policy Act of 2005. In *Energy Tax Policy: Issues in the 114th Congress* (June 15, 2016, http://fas.org/sgp/crs/misc/R43206.pdf), Molly F. Sherlock and Jeffrey M. Stupak note the law "included an estimated $9 billion, over five years, in tax incentives distributed among renewable energy, conservation, and traditional energy sources." The United States suffered from a severe economic downturn dubbed the Great Recession from late 2007 to mid-2009. In 2008 Congress passed the Emergency Economic Stabilization Act, which extended many previous energy tax breaks, mostly to the renewable energy industries. It also raised taxes on the oil and natural gas industries to help offset the lost revenues to the government from the tax breaks that were extended to the renewable energy industries. Provisions in the American Recovery and Reinvestment Act of 2009 (ARRA) also greatly affected the energy industry. Sherlock and Stupak state, "Collectively, ARRA's energy tax provisions lowered the cost of selected renewable energy [sources] relative to energy from other sources, such as

FIGURE 1.14

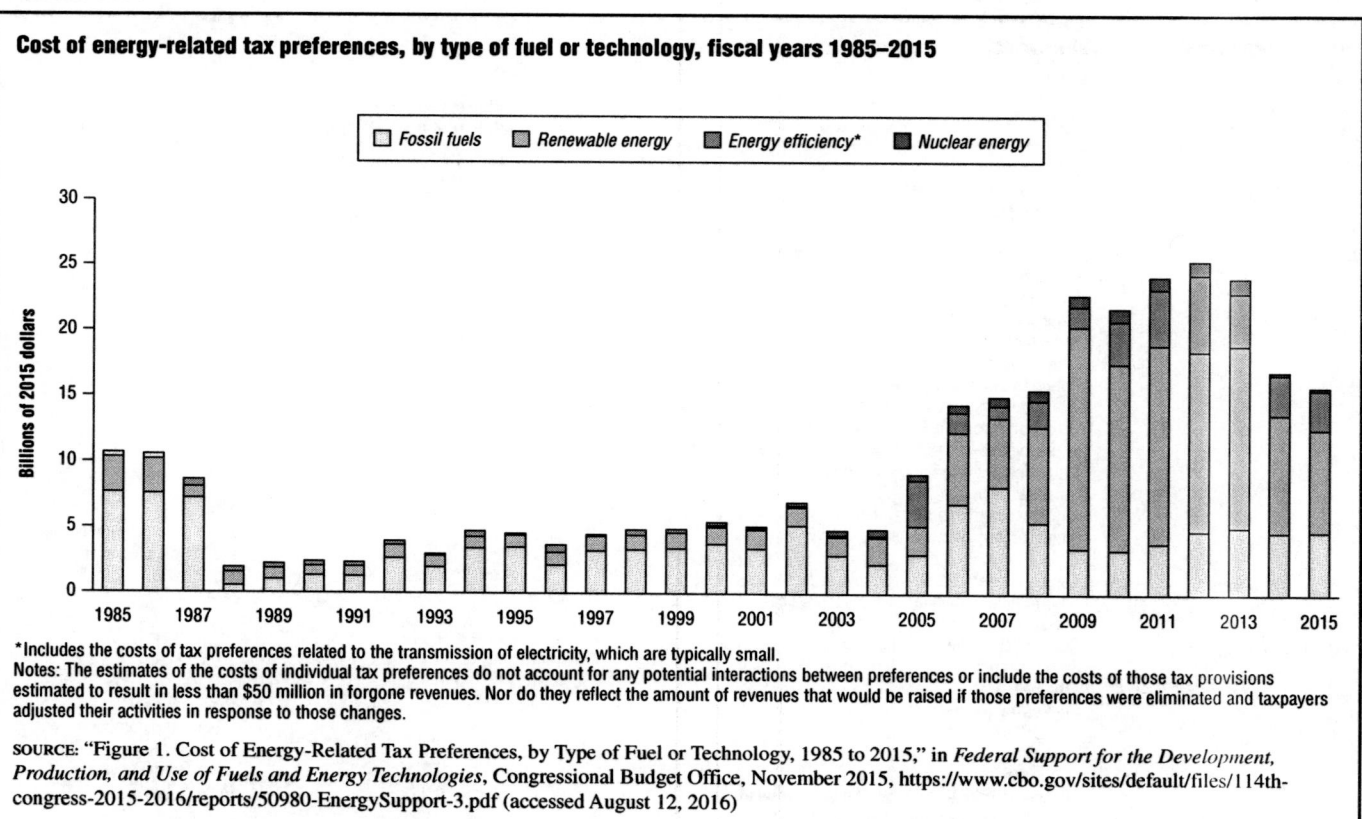

Cost of energy-related tax preferences, by type of fuel or technology, fiscal years 1985–2015

*Includes the costs of tax preferences related to the transmission of electricity, which are typically small.

Notes: The estimates of the costs of individual tax preferences do not account for any potential interactions between preferences or include the costs of those tax provisions estimated to result in less than $50 million in forgone revenues. Nor do they reflect the amount of revenues that would be raised if those preferences were eliminated and taxpayers adjusted their activities in response to those changes.

SOURCE: "Figure 1. Cost of Energy-Related Tax Preferences, by Type of Fuel or Technology, 1985 to 2015," in *Federal Support for the Development, Production, and Use of Fuels and Energy Technologies*, Congressional Budget Office, November 2015, https://www.cbo.gov/sites/default/files/114th-congress-2015-2016/reports/50980-EnergySupport-3.pdf (accessed August 12, 2016)

oil and gas." During the early years of the 21st century several more bills were passed that expanded and extended energy tax breaks devoted to renewable energy sources, energy efficiency, and alternative fuel vehicles.

Table 1.6 provides a breakdown of the $15.8 billion in total energy-related tax preferences that were in effect in FY 2015. As shown in Figure 1.15, renewable energy had the largest share (49%), followed by fossil fuels (30%), energy efficiency (17%), electricity (2%), and nuclear energy (1%). Nevertheless, most of the provisions for energy efficiency and renewable energy were temporary, whereas those for fossil fuels and nuclear energy were mostly permanent. (See Table 1.6.) This difference is emblematic of a long political struggle over what types of energy sources the government should and should not promote. During his eight years in office, President Obama repeatedly tried but failed to persuade Congress to end many of the financial incentives given to the fossil fuel industry.

DOE SPENDING PROGRAMS. Although federal tax laws are written and passed by Congress, the administrative branch (the president and the offices under his control) directly impacts the energy industry through spending programs administered by the DOE. According to the Congressional Budget Office, in *Federal Support for the Development, Production, and Use of Fuels and*

Energy Technologies, the DOE's support for energy technologies and energy efficiency takes two forms: direct investments (primarily for research and development purposes) and loans or loan guarantees. Figure 1.16 shows the total amounts of financial support by the DOE between FYs 1985 and 2015. Table 1.7 provides a breakdown of the $5.4 billion that was spent in FY 2015.

Resource Leases

Another way in which the government influences energy markets is through resource leases. U.S. law provides that underground resources, such as minerals or natural gas, belong to the property owner. Thus, individuals and companies that own land can sell their underground resources to others. The federal and state governments own huge swaths of land across the United States, both onshore and offshore (i.e., off the coastlines beneath ocean waters). Government entities can sell the resources beneath the land within their jurisdictions so long as those sales do not violate existing law. As is explained in later chapters, some government lands have been deemed off limits for resource exploration and extraction.

Resource sales by the government are carried out through legal contracts called leases. Leases cover particular tracts of land and are typically sold through auctions to the highest bidder. In addition, the leases require developers to pay the government royalties (a specific

TABLE 1.6

Cost of energy-related tax preferences, by type of fuel or technology, fiscal year 2015

Type of fuel or technology supported	Tax preference	Estimated total cost (billions of dollars)	Expiration date
	Tax preferences affecting income taxes		
Renewable energy	Credit for the production of electricity from renewable resources	2.9[a]	12/31/2014[b]
	Credit for investments in solar and geothermal equipment, fuel cells, and microturbines	0.6	12/31/2016
	Credit for investment in advanced energy property, including property used in producing energy from wind, the sun, or geothermal sources	0.3	Fixed $2.3 billion in credit; available until used
	Five-year depreciation for certain renewable energy equipment	0.3	None
Fossil fuels	Option to expense depletion costs on the basis of gross income rather than actual costs	1.7	None
	Exceptions for publicly traded partnerships with qualifying income derived from certain energy-related activities[c]	1.1	None
	Expensing of exploration and development costs for oil and natural gas	1.1	None
	Amortization of costs of air pollution control facilities	0.4	None
	Credit for investment in clean coal facilities	0.2	Fixed dollar amount of credit; available until used
	15-year depreciation for natural gas distribution lines	0.2	12/31/2010[d]
	Amortization of geological and geophysical expenditures associated with oil and gas exploration	0.1	None
Energy efficiency	Residential efficiency property credit	1.2	12/31/2016
	Credit for energy-effciency improvements to existing homes	0.8[a]	12/31/2014
	Credit for plug-in electric vehicles	0.2	Expires for each manufacturer when the number of vehicles it sells reaches the limit set by the federal government
	10-year depreciation for smart meters or other devices for monitoring and managing energy use	0.2	None
	Credit for new energy-efficient homes	0.2[a]	12/31/2014
	Deduction for energy-efficient commercial buildings	0.1[a]	12/31/2014
Electricity	Dispositions of property related to electricity transmission[e]	0.3	12/31/2014
	15-year depreciation of certain property related to electricity transmission	0.2	None
	Special rule to implement restructuring of the electricity transmission infrastructure	−0.2	12/31/2014[d]
Nuclear energy	Special tax rate for reserve funds for nuclear decommissioning	0.2	None
	Subtotal, tax preferences affecting income taxes	12.1	n.a.
	Tax preferences affecting energy-related excise taxes[f]		
Renewable energy	Biodiesel and renewable diesel credits[g]	1.3[a]	12/31/2014
	Tax incentives for alternative fuels	0.4[a]	12/31/2014
	Subtotal, tax preferences affecting excise taxes	1.7	n.a.
	Grants in lieu of tax credits affecting energy-related excise taxes		
Renewable energy	Section 1603 grants	2.0	12/31/2011[h]
	All energy-related tax preferences		
Total		**15.8**	**n.a.**

percentage of the value of any resources that are extracted). The government's control of resource leases on public lands is fraught with controversy. Policy makers, the energy industry, environmentalists, and other parties can have strong disagreements about where the leases should be offered and how much they should cost.

The Office of Natural Resources Revenue (ONRR) within the U.S. Department of the Interior manages the revenues that are raised through the private use of public natural resources (e.g., fossil fuels, minerals, and other commodities) on the outer continental shelf and onshore federal and Native American lands. According to the ONRR (2016, http://statistics.onrr.gov/ReportTool.aspx),

it collected $9.6 billion in FY 2015 from royalties, rents, and other revenues. More than half ($5.6 billion) of the total was from oil royalties alone.

Liability Limits

U.S. law includes provisions that limit the financial liability of certain energy sectors in the event of disasters within the industry. Energy accidents, such as oil spills and radiation leaks, can have enormous costs. The liability limits were set to grant the industries a level of financial protection in their exploration and production endeavors. Most of the limits were originally set decades ago. For example, the Atomic Energy Act of 1954

TABLE 1.6

Cost of energy-related tax preferences, by type of fuel or technology, fiscal year 2015 [CONTINUED]

n.a. = not applicable.

[a]This tax preference was extended through calendar year 2014 by the Tax Increase Prevention Act of 2014, which was enacted in December 2014. In this table, pending updated estimates by the staff of the Joint Committee on Taxation (JCT) of the cost of the tax preference, the Congressional Budget Office (CBO) used JCT's estimate of the revenue loss due to the one-year extension.

[b]The production tax credit is generally available for 10 years beginning on the date that the facility is put into service. The Tax Increase Prevention Act of 2014 defined eligible facilities as those whose construction began by December 31, 2014.

[c]This tax preference may be claimed for a variety of activities associated with the production of energy and natural resources; however, on the basis of industry estimates of the size of the industries in which the firms that would qualify for the tax preference operate, CBO expects that most of the $1.1 billion accrues to firms in the fossil fuel industry.

[d]Effects of the tax preference extend beyond the expiration date.

[e]After 2015, the changes in revenues become positive.

[f]Neither JCT nor the Administration generally estimates revenues forgone in the excise tax system. They do, however, provide information on revenue reductions from excise tax credits for alcohol and biodiesel.

[g]Estimate includes effects on both income and excise taxes.

[h]Companies that began constructing a facility and applied for the benefit by December 31, 2011, are eligible. Grants are not paid until facilities are placed into service; they are therefore still being disbursed.

Notes: The estimates of the costs of individual tax preferences do not account for any potential interactions between preferences or include the costs of those tax provisions estimated to result in less than $50 million in forgone revenues. Nor do they reflect the amount of revenues that would be raised if those preferences were eliminated and taxpayers adjusted their activities in response to those changes.

SOURCE: "Table 1. Energy-Related Tax Preferences, 2015," in *Federal Support for the Development, Production, and Use of Fuels and Energy Technologies*, Congressional Budget Office, November 2015, https://www.cbo.gov/sites/default/files/114th-congress-2015-2016/reports/50980-EnergySupport-3.pdf (accessed August 12, 2016)

FIGURE 1.15

Breakdown of the cost of energy-related tax preferences, by type of fuel or technology, fiscal year 2015

Electricity (2%)
Nuclear energy (1%)
Energy efficiency (17%)
Renewable energy (49%)
Fossil fuels (30%)

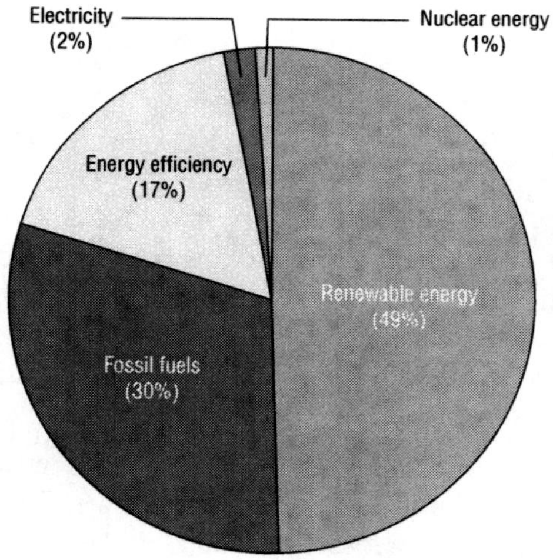

Total: $15.8 billion

SOURCE: "Figure 2. Estimated Allocation of Energy-Related Tax Preferences, by Type of Fuel or Technology, 2015," in *Federal Support for the Development, Production, and Use of Fuels and Energy Technologies*, Congressional Budget Office, November 2015, https://www.cbo.gov/sites/default/files/114th-congress-2015-2016/reports/50980-EnergySupport-3.pdf (accessed August 12, 2016)

established liability limits on accidents that were associated with the U.S. nuclear power industry. Lawmakers feared that without the limits, the fledgling industry would not grow because companies would not be able to afford the premiums for insurance policies protecting them against damages. In addition, the limits have served to keep energy prices lower because they represent a cost savings to energy producers. In the 21st century, however, the limits have become quite controversial because they are seen as relatively low in comparison to the massive costs that can arise from an energy-related disaster. Liability limits specific to various energy sectors are described in subsequent chapters.

Regulations and Mandates

The government uses regulations and mandates to exert control over energy production and consumption factors. For example, the energy industry is subject to extensive environmental regulations that limit the types and amounts of emissions that energy producers can release to the air, land, and water. These regulations are designed to minimize the external costs that are associated with energy production, but their imposition does increase the market costs of energy sources.

Mandates are usually directed at supporting a particular type of energy source. Chapter 6 describes federal and state government mandates for use of specified levels of biomass and other renewable energy sources.

THE DOMESTIC OUTLOOK

In *Annual Energy Outlook 2016 with Projections to 2040*, the EIA forecasts energy supply, demand, and prices through 2040 for various scenarios based on expected supply and demand factors. Table 1.8 summarizes key data for 2015 and projected for 2020 through 2040 for a reference case that assumes future energy markets and policies will be similar to those currently in place.

FIGURE 1.16

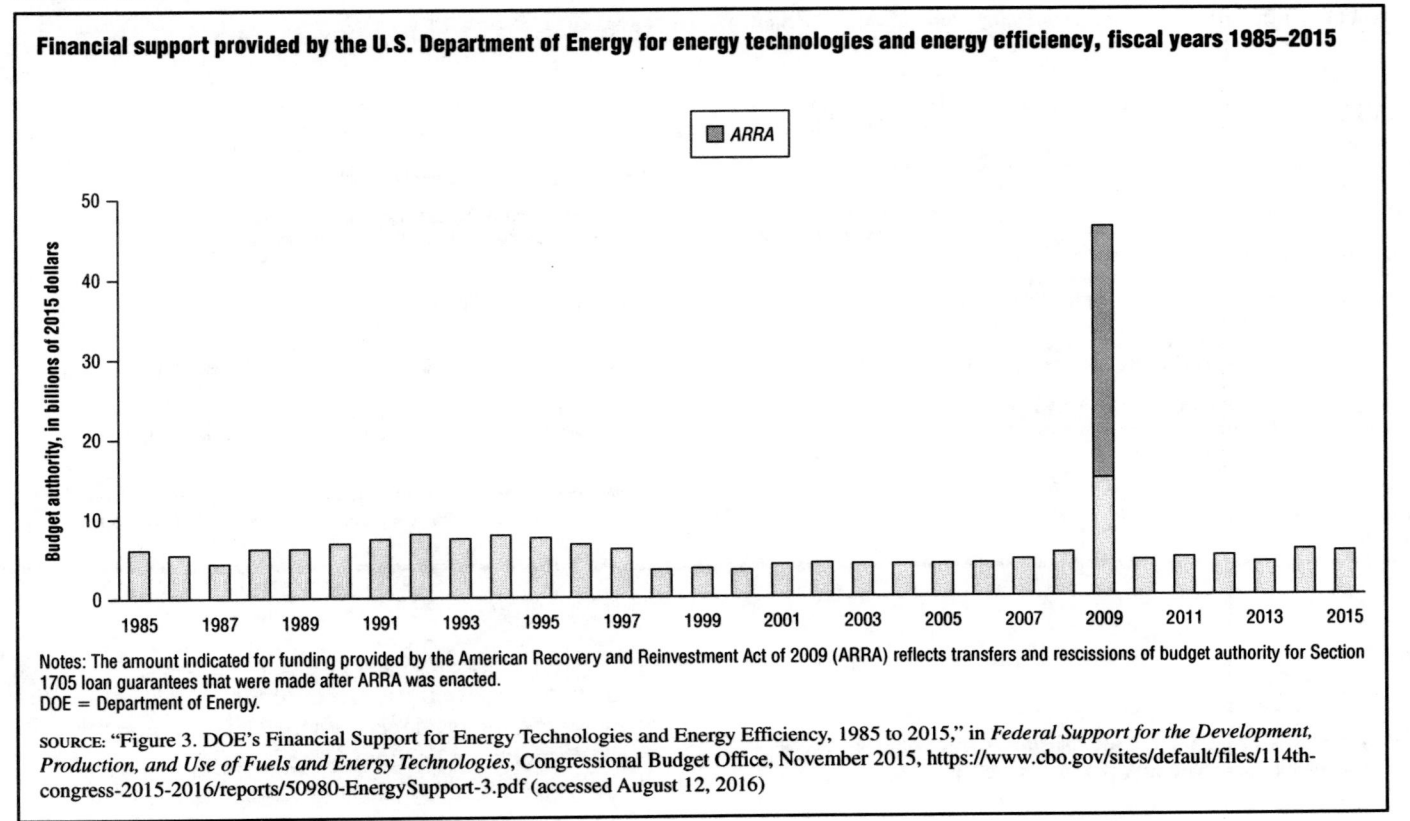

Financial support provided by the U.S. Department of Energy for energy technologies and energy efficiency, fiscal years 1985–2015

Notes: The amount indicated for funding provided by the American Recovery and Reinvestment Act of 2009 (ARRA) reflects transfers and rescissions of budget authority for Section 1705 loan guarantees that were made after ARRA was enacted.
DOE = Department of Energy.

SOURCE: "Figure 3. DOE's Financial Support for Energy Technologies and Energy Efficiency, 1985 to 2015," in *Federal Support for the Development, Production, and Use of Fuels and Energy Technologies*, Congressional Budget Office, November 2015, https://www.cbo.gov/sites/default/files/114th-congress-2015-2016/reports/50980-EnergySupport-3.pdf (accessed August 12, 2016)

TABLE 1.7

Financial support provided by the U.S. Department of Energy for energy technologies and energy efficiency, fiscal year 2015

	Budget authority (billions of dollars)
Direct investment programs	
Applied energy	
Renewable energy and energy efficiency	1.9
Nuclear energy	0.7
Fossil energy research and development	0.6
Electricity delivery and energy reliability	0.1
Advanced Research Projects Agency–energy	0.3
Subtotal	**3.6**
Science	
Basic energy sciences program	1.7
Subtotal, direct investments	**5.4**
Energy credit programs	
Title 17 Innovative Technology Loan Guarantee Program	*
Advanced Technology Vehicles Manufacturing Loan Program	*
Total	**5.4**

* = Between zero and $50 million.
Note: DOE = Department of Energy.

SOURCE: "Table 2. DOE's Financial Support for Energy Technologies and Energy Efficiency, 2015," in *Federal Support for the Development, Production, and Use of Fuels and Energy Technologies*, Congressional Budget Office, November 2015, https://www.cbo.gov/sites/default/files/114th-congress-2015-2016/reports/50980-EnergySupport-3.pdf (accessed August 12, 2016)

As shown in Table 1.8, total domestic energy production is projected to increase from 87.3 quadrillion Btu in 2015 to 112.2 quadrillion Btu in 2040, or 1% growth annually. Total energy imports are forecast to decrease 0.3% annually, whereas energy exports are forecast to increase 3% annually. Overall, domestic consumption is expected to increase from 96.7 quadrillion Btu in 2015 to 107.2 quadrillion Btu in 2040, or 0.4% annually.

Energy prices are shown in Table 1.8 for two price types: nominal and real. Nominal prices are not adjusted for inflation; they represent the actual dollar amounts that consumers pay at specific times. Real prices are adjusted for inflation—that is, they assume the dollar has the same value over time, in this case the value it had in 2015. Comparison of real prices between 2015 and 2040 shows effects due solely to market factors. Real prices for all energy commodities are expected to rise by 2040. Oil shows the largest annual price increase (3.9 to 4%), whereas electricity shows the lowest increase (0.1%).

WORLD ENERGY PRODUCTION AND CONSUMPTION

Table 1.9 shows world energy production in 2012 for the world, by region, and for the top-20 producers. Total world production in 2012 was 537.3 quadrillion Btu. The

TABLE 1.8

Total energy supply, disposition, and price summary, 2015 and forecast selected years 2020–40

[Quadrillion Btu, unless otherwise noted]

Supply, disposition, and prices	2015	2020	2025	2030	2035	2040	2015–2040
Production							
Crude oil and lease condensate	19.67	19.59	19.70	20.99	22.27	23.53	0.7%
Natural gas plant liquids	4.45	6.09	6.35	6.53	6.62	6.67	1.6%
Dry natural gas	28.03	31.45	35.89	38.93	41.16	43.42	1.8%
Coal[a]	17.25	17.55	15.35	13.26	13.44	13.11	−1.1%
Nuclear/uranium[b]	8.34	8.12	8.25	8.25	8.25	8.25	0.0%
Conventional hydroelectric power	2.34	2.79	2.80	2.81	2.81	2.83	0.8%
Biomass[c]	4.13	4.25	4.33	4.43	4.44	4.62	0.4%
Other renewable energy[d]	2.61	4.65	6.13	6.60	7.81	8.83	5.0%
Other[e]	0.48	0.90	1.03	0.90	0.93	0.97	2.8%
Total	**87.30**	**95.39**	**99.84**	**102.69**	**107.74**	**112.23**	**1.0%**
Imports							
Crude oil	16.10	16.81	16.77	16.02	15.76	15.88	−0.1%
Petroleum and other liquids[f]	3.86	4.52	4.46	4.27	4.21	4.30	0.4%
Natural gas[g]	2.79	2.10	1.80	1.55	1.40	1.43	−2.6%
Other[h]	0.43	0.18	0.20	0.17	0.16	0.16	−3.9%
Total	**23.19**	**23.61**	**23.23**	**22.02**	**21.53**	**21.77**	**−0.3%**
Exports							
Petroleum and other liquids[i]	9.02	11.62	12.48	13.54	14.39	15.24	2.1%
Natural gas[j]	1.78	4.98	7.14	7.61	8.62	9.02	6.7%
Coal	1.96	1.85	1.80	1.89	2.19	2.32	0.7%
Total	**12.76**	**18.45**	**21.43**	**23.04**	**25.21**	**26.59**	**3.0%**
Discrepancy[k]	**0.99**	**0.00**	**0.08**	**0.14**	**0.21**	**0.27**	**—**
Consumption							
Petroleum and other liquids[l]	36.49	37.85	37.31	36.62	36.81	37.52	0.1%
Natural gas	28.31	28.30	30.22	32.51	33.52	35.39	0.9%
Coal[m]	15.48	15.62	13.49	11.32	11.21	10.75	−1.4%
Nuclear/uranium[b]	8.34	8.12	8.25	8.25	8.25	8.25	0.0%
Conventional hydroelectric power	2.34	2.79	2.80	2.81	2.81	2.83	0.8%
Biomass[n]	2.75	2.78	2.91	3.00	3.00	3.14	0.5%
Other renewable energy[d]	2.61	4.65	6.13	6.60	7.81	8.83	5.0%
Other[o]	0.42	0.43	0.45	0.44	0.44	0.43	0.1%
Total	**96.74**	**100.55**	**101.56**	**101.54**	**103.85**	**107.15**	**0.4%**
Prices (2015 dollars per unit)							
Brent spot price (dollars per barrel)	52.32	76.57	91.59	104.00	119.64	136.21	3.9%
West Texas Intermediate spot price (dollars per unit)	48.67	71.12	85.41	97.06	112.45	129.11	4.0%
Natural gas at Henry Hub (dollars per mmBtu)	2.62	4.43	5.12	5.06	4.91	4.86	2.5%
Coal, minemouth (dollars per ton)[p]	33.80	33.60	33.99	33.84	37.58	38.68	0.5%
Coal, Minemouth (dollars per million Btu)[p]	1.69	1.68	1.71	1.71	1.86	1.91	0.5%
Coal, delivered (dollars per million Btu)[q]	2.37	2.43	2.49	2.55	2.61	2.68	0.5%
Electricity (cents per kilowatthour)	10.3	10.5	10.7	10.9	10.6	10.5	0.1%
Prices (nominal dollars per unit)							
Brent spot price (dollars per barrel)	52.32	84.59	112.10	140.69	180.68	229.22	6.1%
West Texas Intermediate spot price (dollars per unit)	48.67	78.57	104.54	131.30	169.81	217.26	6.2%
Natural gas at Henry Hub (dollars per mmBtu)	2.62	4.90	6.27	6.84	7.42	8.17	4.7%
Coal, minemouth (dollars per ton)[p]	33.80	37.12	41.60	45.77	56.76	65.09	2.7%
Coal, Minemouth (dollars per million Btu)[p]	1.69	1.86	2.09	2.31	2.81	3.21	2.6%
Coal, delivered (dollars per million Btu)[q]	2.37	2.69	3.05	3.45	3.94	4.50	2.6%
Electricity (cents per kilowatthour)	10.3	11.6	13.1	14.7	16.1	17.6	2.2%

two largest producing regions were Asia and Oceania (167 quadrillion Btu) and North America (107.1 quadrillion Btu). Top producers in 2012 were China, the United States, Russia, Saudi Arabia, and Canada. The U.S. production of 79.2 quadrillion Btu in 2012 accounted for 15% of the total world production.

The total world energy consumption in 2012 was 524.1 quadrillion Btu. (See Table 1.10.) Asia and Oceania (202.1 quadrillion Btu) and North America (116.2 quadrillion Btu) were the leading regions in terms of consumption. On a national basis China, the United

States, Russia, India, and Japan were the top-five consumers. The U.S. consumption of 95.1 quadrillion Btu in 2012 accounted for 18% of the total world consumption.

Analysts believe that energy consumption will grow as more people gain access to electricity. The World Bank is an international financial institution affiliated with the United Nations (UN) that specializes in giving financial advice and loans to developing nations. In "Energy Overview" (http://www.worldbank.org/en/topic/energy/overview), the World Bank estimates that as of April 2016 approximately 1.1 billion people around

ªIncludes waste coal.

ᵇThese values represent the energy obtained from uranium when it is used in light water reactors. The total energy content of uranium is much larger, but alternative processes are required to take advantage of it.

ᶜIncludes grid-connected electricity from wood and wood waste; biomass, such as corn, used for liquid fuels production; and non-electric energy demand from wood.

ᵈIncludes grid-connected electricity from landfill gas; biogenic municipal waste; wind; photovoltaic and solar thermal sources; and non-electric energy from renewable sources, such as active and passive solar systems. Excludes electricity imports using renewable sources and nonmarketed renewable energy.

ᵉIncludes non-biogenic municipal waste, liquid hydrogen, methanol, and some domestic inputs to refineries.

ᶠIncludes imports of finished petroleum products, unfinished oils, alcohols, ethers, blending components, and renewable fuels such as ethanol.

ᵍIncludes imports of liquefied natural gas that are later re-exported.

ʰIncludes coal, coal coke (net), and electricity (net). Excludes imports of fuel used in nuclear power plants.

ⁱIncludes crude oil, petroleum products, ethanol, and biodiesel.

ʲIncludes re-exported liquefied natural gas.

ᵏBalancing item. Includes unaccounted for supply, losses, gains, and net storage withdrawals.

ˡEstimated consumption. Includes petroleum-derived fuels and non-petroleum-derived fuels, such as ethanol and biodiesel, and coal-based synthetic liquids. Petroleum coke, which is a solid, is included. Also included are hydrocarbon gas liquids and crude oil consumed as a fuel.

ᵐExcludes coal converted to coal-based synthetic liquids and natural gas.

ⁿIncludes grid-connected electricity from wood and wood waste, non-electric energy from wood, and biofuels heat and coproducts used in the production of liquid fuels, but excludes the energy content of the liquid fuels.

ᵒIncludes non-biogenic municipal waste, liquid hydrogen, and net electricity imports.

ᵖIncludes reported prices for both open market and captive mines. Prices weighted by production, which differs from average minemouth prices published in EIA data reports where it is weighted by reported sales.

ᑫPrices weighted by consumption; weighted average excludes export free-alongside-ship (f.a.s.) prices.

Btu = British thermal units.

MmBtu = Million Btu.

— = Not applicable.

Note: Totals may not equal sum of components due to independent rounding. Data for 2014 are model results and may differ from official EIA data reports.

SOURCE: Adapted from "Table 1. Total Energy Supply, Disposition, and Price Summary," in *Annual Energy Outlook 2016 Early Release*, U.S. Energy Information Administration, June 2016, https://www.eia.gov/forecasts/aeo/excel/aeotab_1.xlsx (accessed August 12, 2016)

---

the world lacked access to electricity. An estimated 2.9 million people around the world were forced to cook their meals using solid fuels, such as wood, which had devastating consequences on the air quality in and around their homes. The organization's Sustainable Energy for All initiative seeks to achieve "universal access to electricity and clean cooking fuels" by 2030. Two related goals are to double the amount of the world's energy supplied by renewable sources and to double the improvement rate in energy efficiency.

THE WORLD OUTLOOK

The EIA provides in *International Energy Outlook 2016* (May 2016, http://www.eia.gov/forecasts/ieo/) its estimates of world energy consumption by country and by country grouping through 2040. The Organisation for Economic Co-operation and Development (OECD) is a collection of dozens of mostly Western nations that are devoted to global economic development. As shown in Figure 1.17, energy consumption by OECD nations was larger than that of non-OECD nations in 1990 and 2000. However, by 2012 non-OECD consumption had increased dramatically. The EIA projects that this trend will continue and that by 2040 non-OECD nations will consume nearly three times as much energy as OECD nations. Overall, the EIA expects world energy consumption to increase from 549 quadrillion Btu in 2012 to 815 quadrillion Btu in 2040, an increase of 48%. (See Table 1.11.)

Table 1.11 shows detailed EIA projections of future energy consumption for the world and its major regions and by country grouping. Some of the values reflect the expected influence of the U.S. Clean Power Plan (CPP). As is explained in Chapter 8, the CPP is a rule finalized by the U.S. Environmental Protection Agency in October 2015 that would impose limits beginning in 2022 on carbon emissions from existing power plants. The CPP is highly controversial and widely opposed by the energy industry and conservative Republican legislators. As of September 2016, the rule had been suspended pending a court review. Thus, its future status was unclear. As shown in Table 1.11, the EIA predicts that the CPP (if implemented) would have a very small dampening effect on future world energy consumption.

TABLE 1.9

World primary energy production, by region and selected country, 2012

[Quadrillion Btu]

	2012
World	**537.3**
Regions	
Asia & Oceania	167.0
North America	107.1
Middle East	77.7
Eurasia	73.7
Europe	44.0
Africa	36.0
Central & South America	31.8
Countries	
China	101.8
United States	79.2
Russia	55.3
Saudi Arabia	27.7
Canada	19.1
Indonesia	16.3
India	15.9
Iran	13.6
Australia	12.9
Qatar	9.9
Brazil	9.8
Norway	9.6
Mexico	8.7
United Arab Emirates	8.5
Venezuela	7.3
Algeria	7.2
Nigeria	6.7
Kuwait	6.5
Iraq	6.4
South Africa	6.3

Btu = British thermal units.

SOURCE: Adapted from "Table. Total Primary Energy Production (Quadrillion Btu)," in *International Energy Statistics: Total Energy*, U.S. Energy Information Administration, 2016, http://www.eia.gov/cfapps/ipdbproject/iedindex3.cfm?tid=44&pid=44&aid=1&cid=regions&syid=2012&eyid=2012&unit=QBTU (accessed August 12, 2016)

TABLE 1.10

World primary energy consumption, by region and selected country, 2012

[Quadrillion Btu]

	2012
World	**524.1**
Regions	
Asia & Oceania	202.1
North America	116.2
Europe	81.4
Eurasia	46.1
Middle East	32.2
Central & South America	28.7
Africa	17.3
Countries	
China	105.9
United States	95.1
Russia	31.5
India	23.9
Japan	20.3
Germany	13.5
Canada	13.4
Brazil	12.1
Korea, South	11.5
France	10.7
Iran	9.6
Saudi Arabia	9.3
United Kingdom	8.6
Mexico	7.8
Italy	7.2
Indonesia	6.4
Spain	6.0
Australia	6.0
South Africa	5.7
Thailand	5.2

SOURCE: Adapted from "Table. Total Primary Energy Consumption (Quadrillion Btu)," in *International Energy Statistics: Total Energy*, U.S. Energy Information Administration, 2016, http://www.eia.gov/cfapps/ipdbproject/iedindex3.cfm?tid=44&pid=44&aid=2&cid=regions&syid=2012&eyid=2012&unit=QBTU (accessed August 12, 2016)

FIGURE 1.17

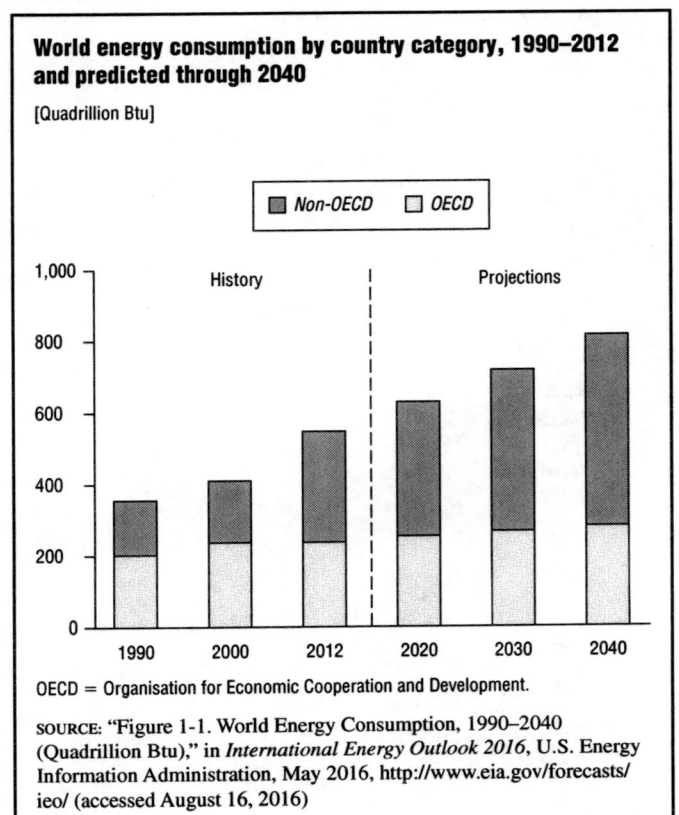

World energy consumption by country category, 1990–2012 and predicted through 2040

[Quadrillion Btu]

OECD = Organisation for Economic Cooperation and Development.

SOURCE: "Figure 1-1. World Energy Consumption, 1990–2040 (Quadrillion Btu)," in *International Energy Outlook 2016*, U.S. Energy Information Administration, May 2016, http://www.eia.gov/forecasts/ieo/ (accessed August 16, 2016)

TABLE 1.11

World energy consumption by country and country category, selected years, 2012–40

[Quadrillion Btu]

Region	2012	2020	2025	2030	2035	2040	Average annual percent change, 2012–40
OECD	**238**	**254**	**261**	**267**	**274**	**282**	**0.6**
Americas	118	126	128	131	134	138	0.6
Europe	81	85	87	90	93	96	0.6
Asia	39	43	45	46	47	48	0.8
OECD with U.S. CPP	**238**	**252**	**258**	**265**	**272**	**280**	**0.6**
OECD Americas with U.S. CPP	118	124	125	128	132	136	0.5
Non-OECD	**311**	**375**	**413**	**451**	**491**	**533**	**1.9**
Europe/Eurasia	51	52	55	56	58	58	0.5
Asia	176	223	246	270	295	322	2.2
Middle East	32	41	45	51	57	62	2.4
Africa	22	26	30	34	38	44	2.6
Americas	31	33	37	40	43	47	1.5
Total world	**549**	**629**	**674**	**718**	**766**	**815**	**1.4**
Total world with U.S. CPP	**549**	**627**	**671**	**715**	**763**	**813**	**1.4**

OECD = Organisation for Economic Cooperation and Development. CPP = U.S. Clean Power Play.

SOURCE: "Table 1-1. World Energy Consumption by Country Grouping, 2012–40 (Quadrillion Btu)," in *International Energy Outlook 2016*, U.S. Energy Information Administration, May 2016, http://www.eia.gov/forecasts/ieo/ (accessed August 16, 2016)

CHAPTER 2
OIL

On August 27, 1859, Edwin Drake (1819–1880) struck oil 69 feet (21 m) below the surface of the earth near Titusville, Pennsylvania. This was the first successful modern oil well and ushered in a new wave of modernization. Not only did oil help meet the growing demand for new and better fuels for heating and lighting but also it proved to be an excellent source of gasoline for the internal combustion engine, which was developed during the late 1800s. Oil has become one of the most valuable commodities on the earth. Its supply is finite, and the United States consumes more oil every year than any other country, primarily because of Americans' love of the automobile. This addiction has its price; the United States has been forced for decades to import oil from countries that are sometimes less than friendly, sometimes downright hostile. Thus, oil self-sufficiency is a major goal for the United States.

UNDERSTANDING OIL

Oil is a generic term for liquid fossil fuels. As is explained in Chapter 1, fossil fuels are the below-ground remains of prehistoric organisms that became energy enriched after millions of years of exposure to high temperatures and pressures. Oil and natural gas are often found together because they both originate from microscopic plants and animals that died in ancient water bodies (mostly swamps) and were gradually buried under many layers of sediment. Over several millennia the layers were compressed and baked into rock beds. The original microorganisms were chemically transformed into hydrocarbon chemicals, specifically oil and natural gas.

Oil and natural gas are less dense than their source rock, so once formed, they begin moving through the pores and fractures of surrounding rock formations. They migrate upward toward areas of lower pressure until a completely solid rock layer stops them or they seep from the ground into the open air. Underground oil and natural gas accumulations are called reservoirs, fields, or pools. They are typically found in sandstone or limestone formations that are overlaid with a shield layer of impermeable rock or shale. The oil and natural gas are trapped beneath the shield within the numerous pores and fractures of the reservoir rock. Because gas is lighter than liquid, the natural gas accumulates at the top of the traps above the oil pools. Anticlines (archlike folds in a bed of rock), faults, and salt domes are common trapping formations. (See Figure 2.1.) Oil fields can be found at varying depths below the ground surface.

Oil Properties

Some key properties of oil include density, viscosity (thickness, or resistance to flow), heat content, and the amounts of water, minerals, combustible gases, and sulfur (which is considered an impurity). Oil's viscosity can vary considerably. Oil that flows easily (like water) is said to be "light," while thick dense oil is said to be "heavy." In addition, oil is called "sweet" if it contains only a small amount of sulfur and "sour" if it contains a lot of sulfur. Lighter oils are the easiest to extract from the ground because they flow readily into wells. Refiners prefer sweet light oil because it is easy to pump and does not require extensive treatment for sulfur removal.

Conventional and Unconventional Oils

Raw (unprocessed) oil is known as crude oil and can be sourced from hydrocarbons in liquid, semisolid, and solid forms. Liquid crude oil is called a conventional oil because historically it has been the preferred type due to its ease of extraction. Evolving technologies, however, have allowed the collection of unconventional oils that are much more difficult to extract from the ground.

Unconventional oils can be derived from oily solids or semisolids, such as kerogen and bitumen. Kerogen is a waxy material found in formations of sedimentary rock

FIGURE 2.1

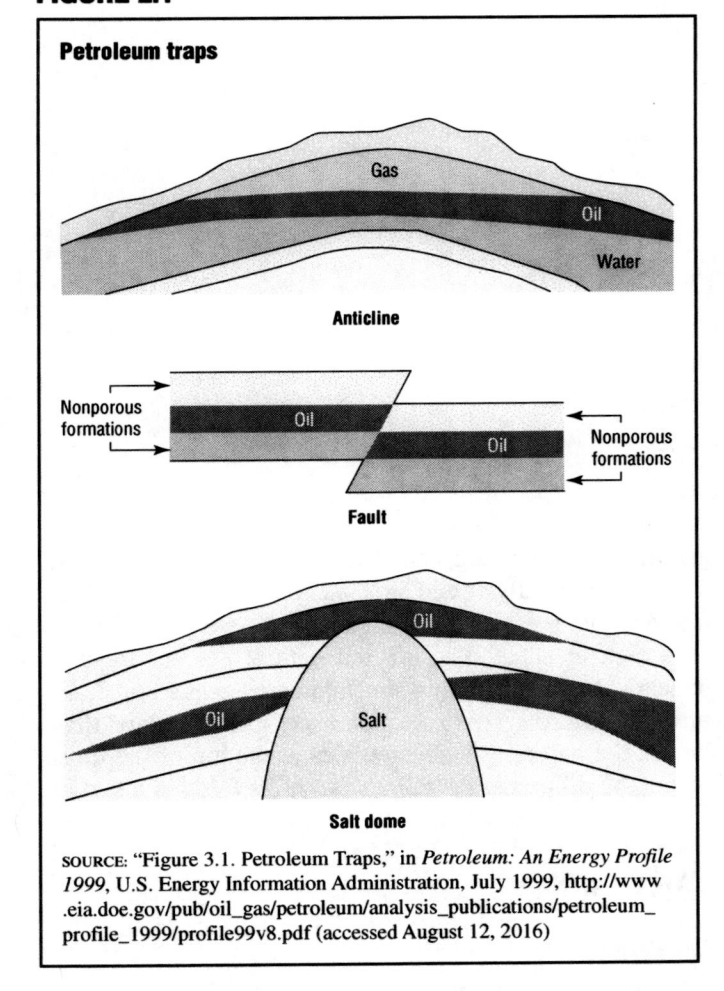

Petroleum traps

Gas

Oil

Water

Anticline

Nonporous formations

Oil

Oil

Nonporous formations

Fault

Oil

Oil

Salt

Salt dome

SOURCE: "Figure 3.1. Petroleum Traps," in *Petroleum: An Energy Profile 1999*, U.S. Energy Information Administration, July 1999, http://www.eia.doe.gov/pub/oil_gas/petroleum/analysis_publications/petroleum_profile_1999/profile99v8.pdf (accessed August 12, 2016)

Petroleum

The generic term *petroleum* is often used as a synonym for oil. The word *petroleum* is derived from the Latin words *petra* (meaning "rock") and *oleum* (meaning "oil"). In *Monthly Energy Review: July 2016* (July 2016, http://www.eia.gov/totalenergy/data/monthly/archive/00351607.pdf), the U.S. Energy Information Administration (EIA) notes that petroleum is "a broadly defined class of liquid hydrocarbon mixtures" that includes crude oil and its derivatives and other liquids, particularly liquids associated with natural gas extraction. The latter include lease condensate and natural gas plant liquids (NGPL). Lease condensate is a liquid recovered from natural gas at the well (the extraction point). It consists primarily of chemical compounds called pentanes and heavier hydrocarbons and is generally blended with crude oil for refining. NGPL, such as butane and propane, are recovered during the refinement of natural gas in processing plants. The EIA also includes in its definition of petroleum the refined products that are obtained from the processing of raw oils.

Oil Deposit Locations

The locations of oil deposits around the world are driven solely by geology. Regions and countries that are known to have large oil fields include the Middle East, Russia, China, northern South America, Mexico, Canada, and the United States.

Many of the earth's oil fields are offshore (i.e., they lie beneath the oceans). The EIA explains in "Oil: Crude and Petroleum Products Explained: What Is Offshore?" (January 7, 2016, http://www.eia.gov/energyexplained/index.cfm?page=oil_offshore) that the United States lays claim to an Exclusive Economic Zone (EEZ) that extends outward 200 miles (322 km) from its coastline. This applies to the U.S. mainland, Alaska, Hawaii, and all U.S. territories. (See Figure 2.2.) Figure 2.3 shows the extent of the EEZ and a conceptual side view of a continental shelf. The latter is the "shelf" of underwater land that extends outward from the coastline of each continent. The outward extent of the North American continental shelf ranges from around 12 miles (20 km) to 250 miles (400 km). According to the EIA, the water depth above this continental shelf is typically less than 492 feet (150 m) to 656 feet (200 m) at its deepest point. The continental shelf ends with a sharp drop off to the continental slope, which underlies deep ocean. (See Figure 2.3.) The United States claims exclusive rights to the resources (such as oil) underlying the continental shelf off its coastlines.

In general, the continental shelf is relatively narrow along the Pacific coast, wide along much of the Atlantic coast and the Gulf of Alaska, and widest in the Gulf of Mexico. Most coastal states have resource rights

known as oil shale. The U.S. Department of the Interior's Bureau of Land Management notes in "Frequently Asked Questions" (2016, http://ostseis.anl.gov/faq/index.cfm) that petroleum-like liquids are released when the rock is heated. Bitumen is a black tarry substance found in underground formations called tar sands, oil sands, or tight sands. It can be diluted with liquid chemicals to flow through pipelines.

Unconventional oils also include liquid deposits that are trapped in very dense rocks, such as shale, sandstone, or carbonate. These formations have very low permeability, meaning that liquids (and gases) do not move easily through them. In the United States the term *tight oil* is used to refer to the oil extracted from such formations. Tight oil obtained from shale formations is known as "shale oil." In the rest of the world the terms *tight oil* and *shale oil* are often used interchangeably.

As will be explained later, the extraction of unconventional oils is far more difficult than that of crude oil. However, technological advances and rising oil prices have made it more economically worthwhile to extract unconventional oils. They can then be processed and refined along with conventional crude oil.

FIGURE 2.2

Map of U.S. Exclusive Economic Zone

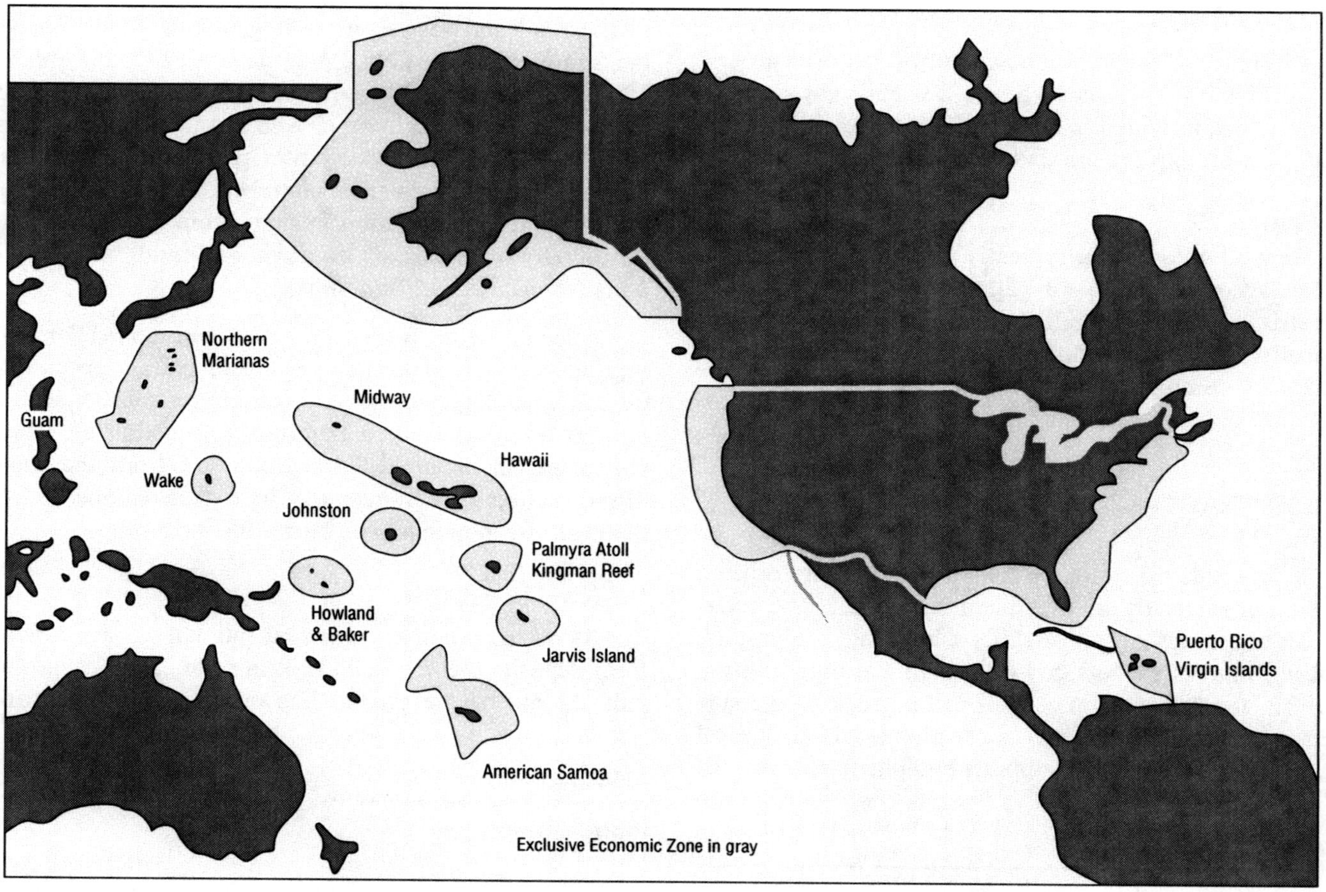

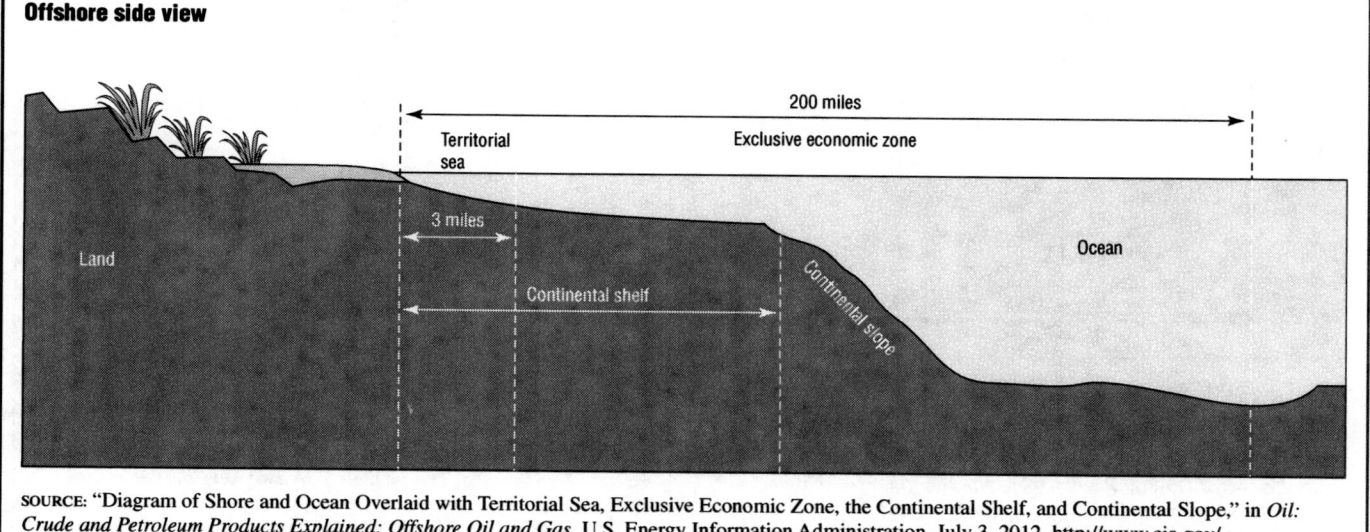

SOURCE: "Map Showing Exclusive Economic Zone around the United States and Territories," in *Oil: Crude and Petroleum Products Explained: Offshore Oil and Gas*, U.S. Energy Information Administration, July 3, 2012, http://www.eia.gov/energyexplained/images/charts/EEZmap.png (accessed August 12, 2016)

FIGURE 2.3

Offshore side view

SOURCE: "Diagram of Shore and Ocean Overlaid with Territorial Sea, Exclusive Economic Zone, the Continental Shelf, and Continental Slope," in *Oil: Crude and Petroleum Products Explained: Offshore Oil and Gas*, U.S. Energy Information Administration, July 3, 2012, http://www.eia.gov/energyexplained/images/continentalshelf.gif (accessed August 12, 2016)

extending outward 3 miles (5 km) from their coastlines. Resources beyond that limit fall under federal government control in an area called the outer continental shelf. Water above the outer continental shelf can be up to 600 feet (183 m) deep.

Estimates of the total amounts of oil deposits around the world and in the United States that have not yet been extracted are provided in Chapter 7, along with information about oil exploration and development activities.

Measuring Oil

Raw oil volumes are typically measured in barrels. A barrel is equivalent to 42 gallons (159 L). Because a barrel is a relatively small unit of measure, oil data are typically expressed in units of thousand barrels or million barrels. A commonly used unit for production and consumption data is million barrels per day (mbpd).

OIL EXTRACTION
Crude Oil

Most crude oil wells are drilled with a rotary drilling system, or rotary rig, as illustrated in Figure 2.4. A rotating bit at the end of a pipe drills a hole into the ground. Drilling mud is pushed down through the pipe and the drill bit, forcing small pieces of drilled rock to the surface. As the well gets deeper, more pipe is added. The oil derrick above the ground supports equipment that can lift

the pipe and drill bit from the well when drill bits need to be changed or replaced.

Drilling takes place both onshore and offshore. Figure 2.5 shows a typical offshore rig. The development of offshore oil and gas resources began with the drilling of the Summerland oil field along the coast of California in 1896, where about 400 wells were drilled. Since then, the industry has continually improved drilling technology. In the early 21st century deepwater petroleum and natural gas exploration occurs from platforms and drill ships, and shallow-water exploration occurs from gravel islands (artificially made islands of gravel and sand) and mobile units (ship-based drilling units).

After crude oil reservoirs have been tapped for several years or decades, their supply of readily accessible oil becomes depleted. Several techniques can be used to recover additional oil, including the injection of water, chemicals, or steam to force more oil from the rock. These recovery techniques can be expensive and add to the cost of producing each barrel of crude oil.

Unconventional Oils

As noted earlier, some unconventional oils are derived from deposits that are solid or semisolid. They cannot be pumped out of the ground like crude oil. Kerogen and

FIGURE 2.4

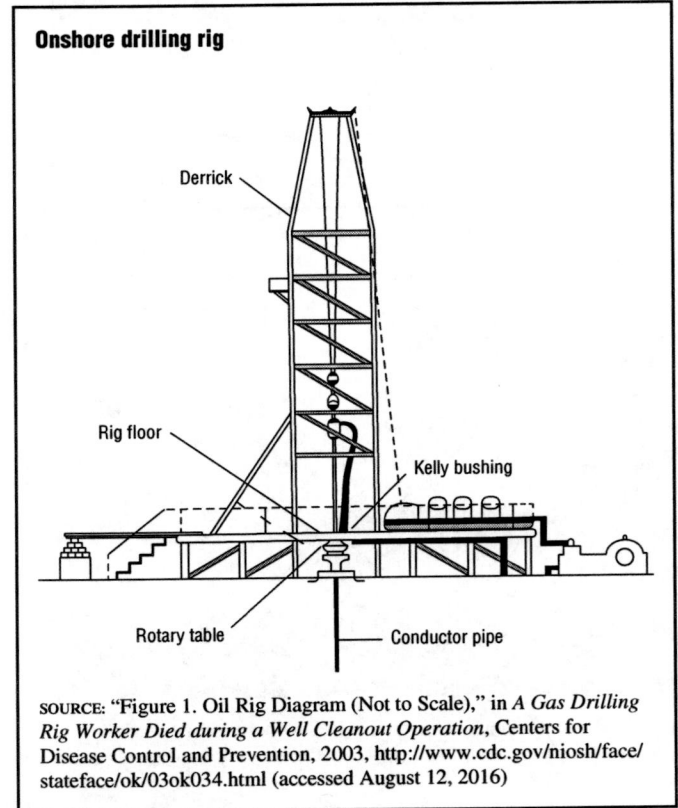

Onshore drilling rig

SOURCE: "Figure 1. Oil Rig Diagram (Not to Scale)," in *A Gas Drilling Rig Worker Died during a Well Cleanout Operation*, Centers for Disease Control and Prevention, 2003, http://www.cdc.gov/niosh/face/stateface/ok/03ok034.html (accessed August 12, 2016)

FIGURE 2.5

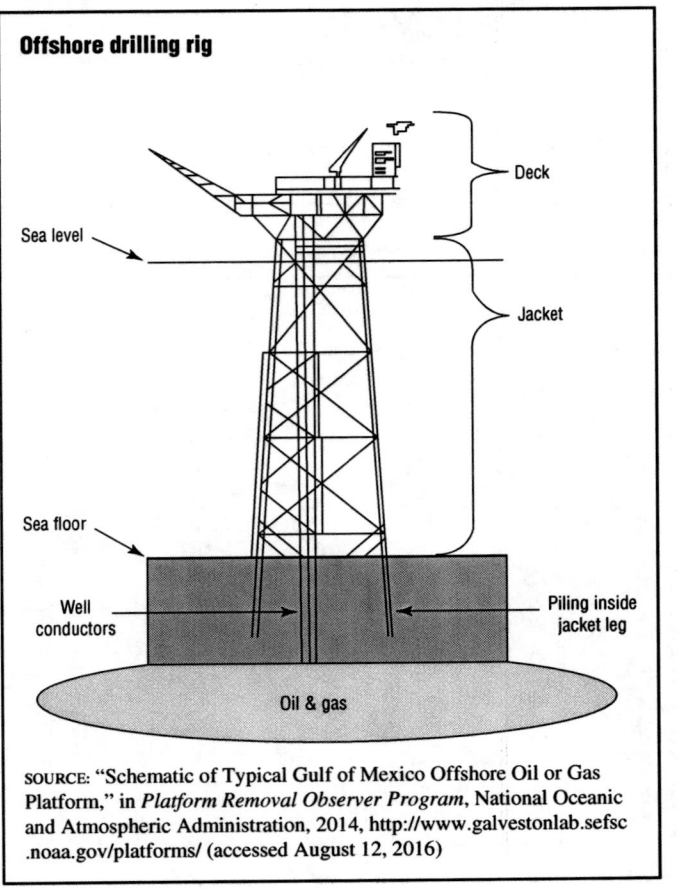

Offshore drilling rig

SOURCE: "Schematic of Typical Gulf of Mexico Offshore Oil or Gas Platform," in *Platform Removal Observer Program*, National Oceanic and Atmospheric Administration, 2014, http://www.galvestonlab.sefsc.noaa.gov/platforms/ (accessed August 12, 2016)

bitumen lying near the surface are typically dug out using mining techniques, which can have large land impacts. This makes their extraction extremely controversial from an environmental standpoint. Once mined, the materials are heated (or retorted) to liquefy the oil. Deposits that are deep within the earth can be heated in situ (in place) by injecting steam through drilled wells. The liquefied oil is then pumped to the surface. Other methods are used as well, but all efforts amount to expensive and specialized processes.

Tight oil is typically liberated from dense rock formations using horizontal drilling or hydraulic fracturing. A horizontal well extends vertically down to the formation of interest and then extends horizontally across it. (See well A in Figure 2.6.) This arrangement exposes a greater surface area of the producing formation to extraction than does a completely vertical well. Hydraulic fracturing (fracking) is a specialized well-based technique for extracting oil and natural gas from unconventional geological sources, such as shale.

Figure 2.7 shows a typical fracking operation. A vertical well is drilled down and into the desired geological formation. Then, a horizontal leg extends through the formation. Perforated pipes are inserted into the horizontal leg, and water is forced through the perforations under very high pressure, which causes numerous small fractures in the rock. The water contains sand, tiny ceramic beads, or other solids that serve as propping agents (they prop open the fractures so they do not close

FIGURE 2.6

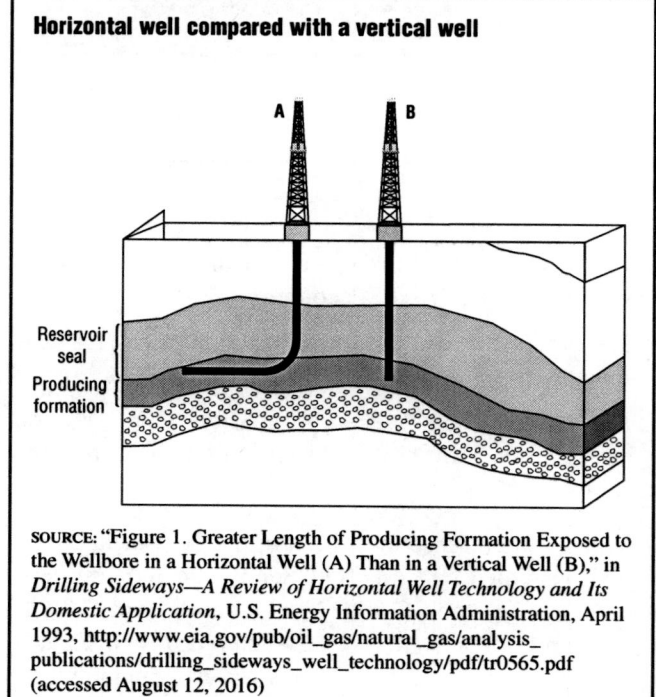

Horizontal well compared with a vertical well

SOURCE: "Figure 1. Greater Length of Producing Formation Exposed to the Wellbore in a Horizontal Well (A) Than in a Vertical Well (B)," in *Drilling Sideways—A Review of Horizontal Well Technology and Its Domestic Application*, U.S. Energy Information Administration, April 1993, http://www.eia.gov/pub/oil_gas/natural_gas/analysis_publications/drilling_sideways_well_technology/pdf/tr0565.pdf (accessed August 12, 2016)

when the pressure is released and the water is removed). Oil and natural gas then escape from the rock fractures into the well and flow to the surface.

Fracking is a relatively new extraction process, in that it has only been used for a few decades. It is controversial because large amounts of water are required and there is a danger that oil and natural gas could be accidentally introduced into aquifers (underground freshwater pools).

Because unconventional oil is typically blended into crude oil, many analysts refer to all "raw" oil as crude oil. This naming convention will be followed in this book when referring to oil past the extraction stage.

CRUDE OIL TRANSPORT

According to the EIA, in "Petroleum and Other Liquids: Imports by Area of Entry" (August 31, 2016, http://www.eia.gov/dnav/pet/pet_move_imp_dc_NUS-Z00_mbbl_a.htm), 2.7 billion barrels of crude oil and 52.6 million barrels of NGPL and liquefied refinery gases were imported into the United States in 2015. Much of this oil traveled by sea in enormous oil tankers. In addition, there are more than a dozen oil pipelines connecting the United States and Canada. Two of the largest Canadian companies involved in piping crude oil to the United States are Enbridge Inc. (2016, http://www.enbridge.com/map#map:infrastructure) and TransCanada Corporation (2016, http://www.transcanada.com/oil-pipelines.html).

The United States features a massive, mostly interconnected network of pipelines for moving crude oil around the country. (For a map of the pipelines, see the American Petroleum Institute's "U.S. Refineries, Crude Oil, and Refined Products Pipelines" [2016, http://www.api.org/oil-and-natural-gas/wells-to-consumer/transporting-oil-natural-gas/pipeline].)

The Keystone XL Project

In 2010 TransCanada sought permission from the U.S. government to construct a new crude oil pipeline from Canada into the United States. The project was named Keystone XL (http://keystone-xl.com) and was proposed to run from Alberta, Canada, across the U.S. border into Montana and down to Steele City, Nebraska. There, it would connect with an existing TransCanada pipeline called the Keystone pipeline. The latter ends in Cushing, Oklahoma, which is a key hub for U.S. oil resources.

The Keystone XL project encountered stiff resistance from environmentalists and the administration of President Barack Obama (1961–). Presidential permission is required for a pipeline to cross the U.S. border. In 2011 TransCanada submitted a comprehensive report, called an Environmental Impact Statement (EIS), for the

FIGURE 2.7

Hydraulic fracturing (fracking)

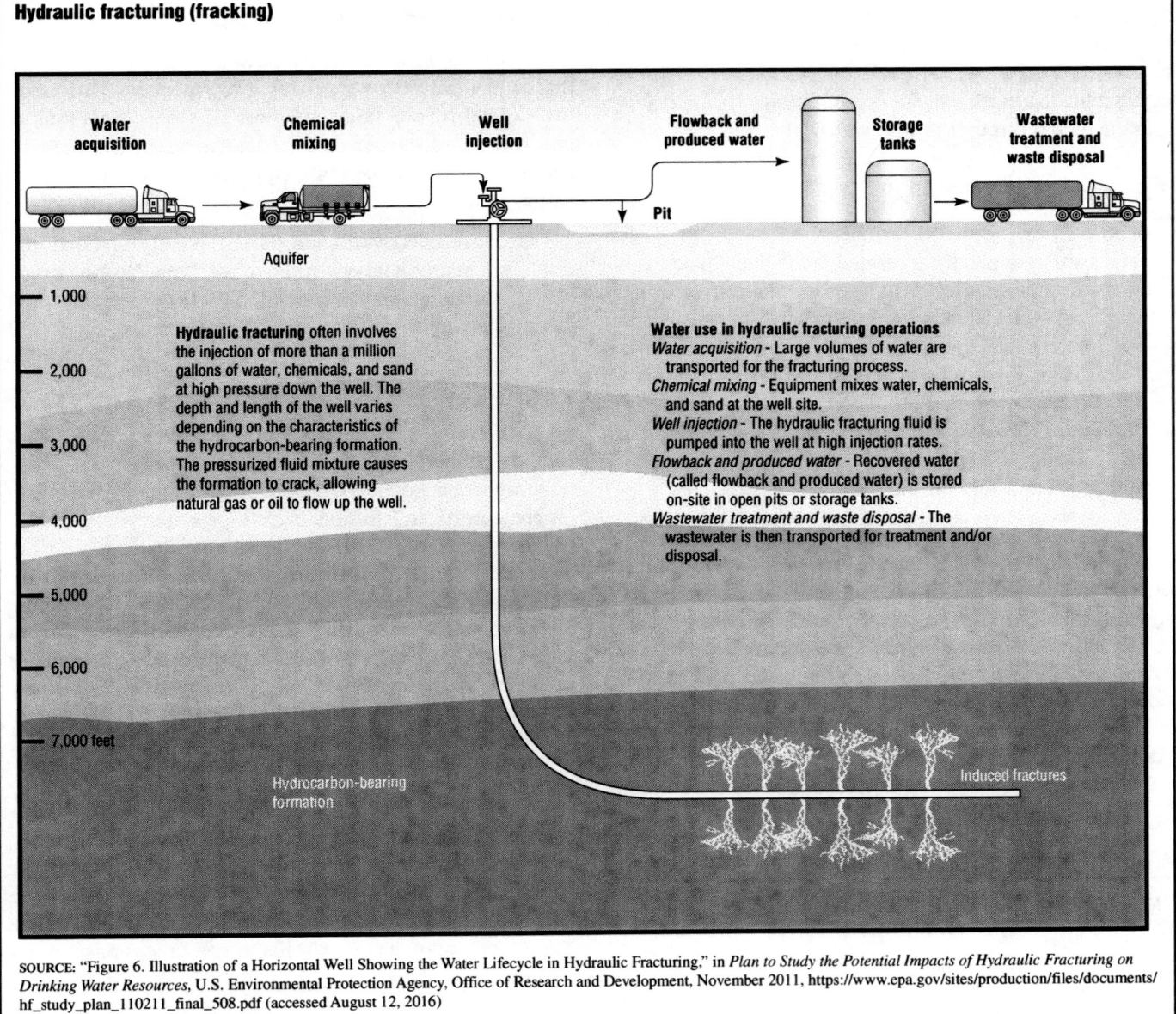

Water use in hydraulic fracturing operations
Water acquisition - Large volumes of water are transported for the fracturing process.
Chemical mixing - Equipment mixes water, chemicals, and sand at the well site.
Well injection - The hydraulic fracturing fluid is pumped into the well at high injection rates.
Flowback and produced water - Recovered water (called flowback and produced water) is stored on-site in open pits or storage tanks.
Wastewater treatment and waste disposal - The wastewater is then transported for treatment and/or disposal.

SOURCE: "Figure 6. Illustration of a Horizontal Well Showing the Water Lifecycle in Hydraulic Fracturing," in *Plan to Study the Potential Impacts of Hydraulic Fracturing on Drinking Water Resources*, U.S. Environmental Protection Agency, Office of Research and Development, November 2011, https://www.epa.gov/sites/production/files/documents/hf_study_plan_110211_final_508.pdf (accessed August 12, 2016)

project. At that time the pipeline was designed to traverse the Sand Hills region of Nebraska, an environmentally sensitive area. Obama declined to approve the permit. The president's critics were dismayed by his decision because they believed the pipeline would benefit the U.S. economy and reduce reliance on oil imported from overseas. TransCanada developed an alternative route that avoided the Sand Hills region and submitted a revised EIS. The final version of the document (http://keystonepipeline-xl.state.gov/finalseis/index.htm) was published in January 2014. In November 2015 Obama again denied a permit for the project. He explained in a statement (https://www.whitehouse.gov/the-press-office/2015/11/06/statement-president-keystone-xl-pipeline) that the project was rejected for three primary reasons:

- The pipeline would not make a meaningful long-term contribution to the U.S. economy

- The pipeline would not lower gasoline prices for U.S. consumers

- The United States' energy security would not be increased by shipping "dirtier crude oil" into the country

Obama's reference to "dirtier crude oil" is explained by Jeremy Van Loon, in "Oil Sands and the Environment: Why Keystone Counts" (Bloomberg.com, July 1, 2016). Van Loon notes that "fuels derived from Canada's tar sands do produce more greenhouse gas than conventional forms of gasoline and heating oil." As is explained in Chapter 1, emissions of greenhouse gases are blamed in large part for warming the earth's atmosphere and causing climate change. During his two terms in office President Obama devoted much attention to the negative effects of climate change. However, this issue does not resonate with many Republicans who dismiss global warming concerns as hysteria.

According to Ethan Lou, in "TransCanada Formally Seeks NAFTA Damages in Keystone XL Rejection" (Reuters.com, June 25, 2016), TransCanada sued the United States in federal court following Obama's decision. In addition, the company raised a claim under the North American Free Trade Agreement (a treaty that governs trade among Canada, Mexico, and the United States). Lou indicates that the company was seeking $15 billion in damages in the latter suit. As of September 2016, decisions had not been reached in either case.

Dakota Access Pipeline

Dakota Access is a subsidiary of Energy Transfer Partners, LP, a Texas-based corporation. During the summer of 2016 the company began construction on the Dakota Access Pipeline (DAPL; http://www.daplpipelinefacts.com/) to transport crude oil from the Bakken/Three Forks region in North Dakota to Illinois. (The location of the Bakken region is depicted in Figure 2.8.) The $3.7 billion project was scheduled to be completed by the end of 2016. It was fiercely opposed, however, by Native American tribes and environmentalists who sought to stop the DAPL in court. Lawyers for the Standing Rock Sioux Tribe of North Dakota argued that the pipeline had been improperly permitted and would destroy or desecrate areas considered to be sacred by the tribe. They also feared that oil leaks could pollute the tribe's drinking water supply. The pipeline was intended to cross beneath the Missouri River just upstream of the tribe's reservation. In August and early September 2016 protests along the pipeline route turned violent and attracted widespread media attention. In mid-September a federal appeals court ordered a halt to construction near the water crossing to give the court more time to consider the tribe's request for an emergency injunction. It remained to be seen how the legal battle would play out.

OIL REFINING

Crude oil has little practical use in its raw state. It is a mixture of different liquid hydrocarbons that are separable

FIGURE 2.8

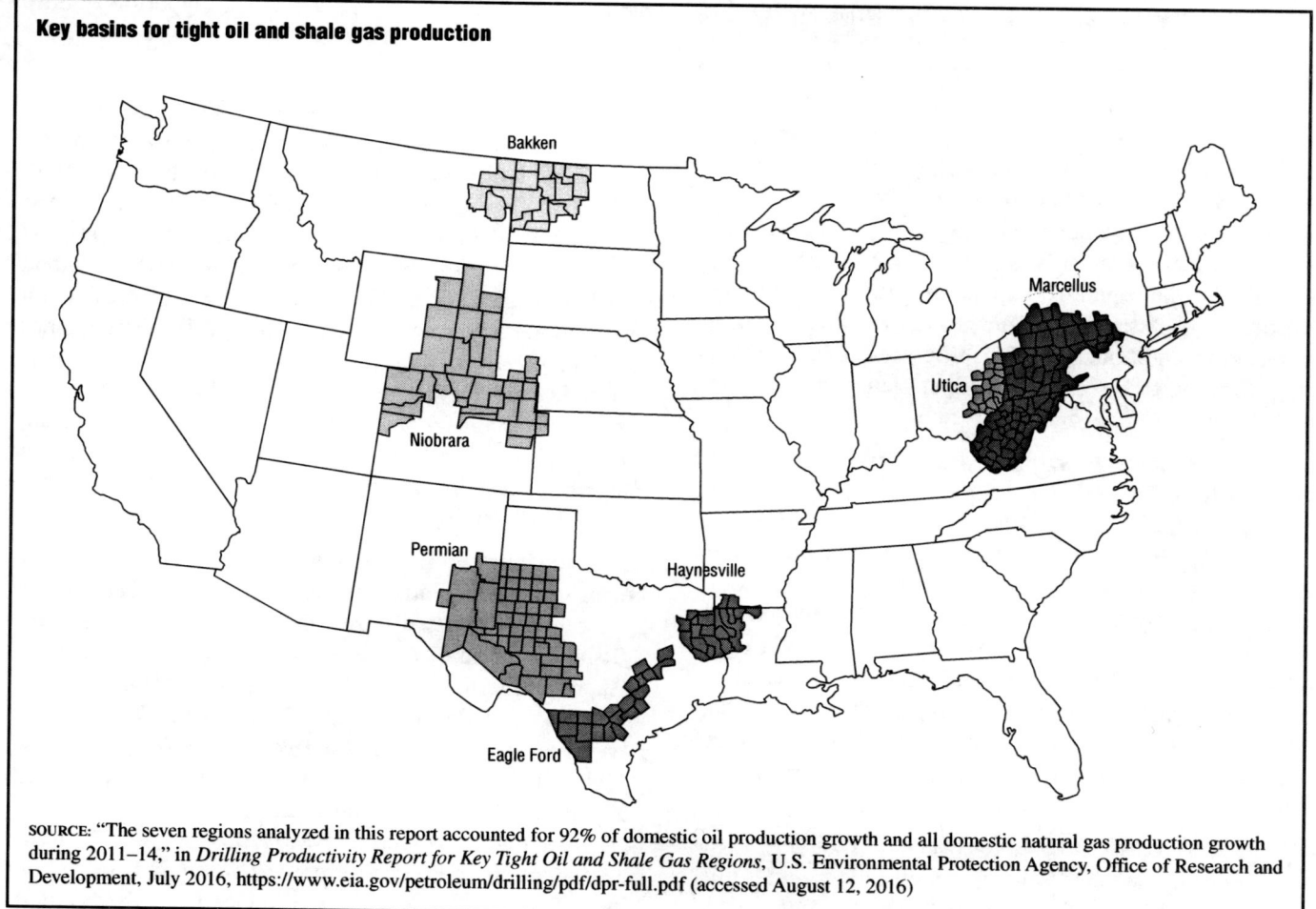

Key basins for tight oil and shale gas production

SOURCE: "The seven regions analyzed in this report accounted for 92% of domestic oil production growth and all domestic natural gas production growth during 2011–14," in *Drilling Productivity Report for Key Tight Oil and Shale Gas Regions*, U.S. Environmental Protection Agency, Office of Research and Development, July 2016, https://www.eia.gov/petroleum/drilling/pdf/dpr-full.pdf (accessed August 12, 2016)

FIGURE 2.9

Crude oil distillation fractions

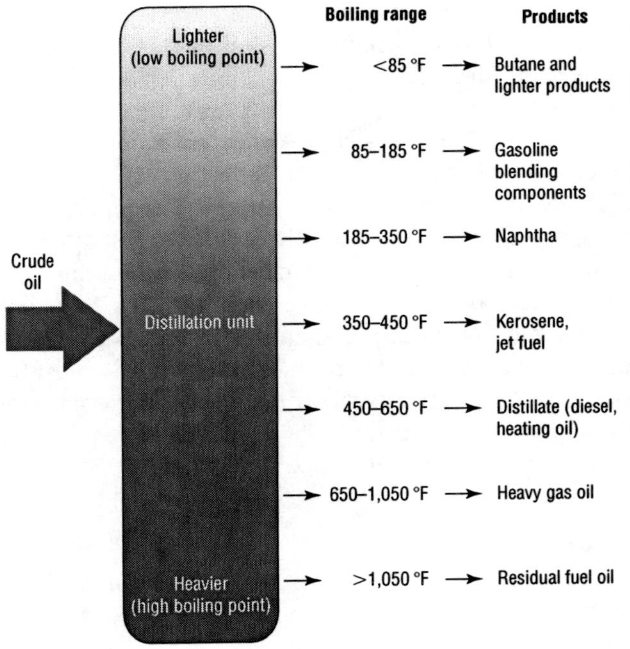

SOURCE: "Crude Oil Distillation Unit and Products," in *Today in Energy: Crude Oil Distillation and the Definition of Refinery Capacity*, U.S. Energy Information Administration, July 5, 2012, http://www.eia.gov/todayinenergy/detail.cfm?id=6970# (accessed August 12, 2016)

by distillation. (See Figure 2.9.) The liquid components (or fractions) vaporize at different boiling points. Light fractions, such as butane, boil off at relatively low temperatures. Heavy components with high boiling points, such as residual fuel oil, must be heated to high temperatures to boil off. All the separated vapors are then cooled to condense them back to liquids. The heavier fractions are often subjected to additional refining processes called cracking and reforming to break up heavy petroleum products into lighter ones.

Refining produces numerous petroleum products, all of which have different physical and chemical properties. These products include gasoline, diesel fuel, jet fuel, and lubricants for transportation; heating oil, residual oil, and kerosene for heat; butane, ethane, and propane; and heavy residuals for paving and roofing. Petroleum by-products are also vital to the chemical industry, ending up in many different foams, plastics, synthetic fabrics, paints, dyes, inks, and even pharmaceutical drugs. Because of their dependence on petroleum, many chemical plants are directly connected by pipelines to nearby refineries.

REFINERY NUMBERS AND CAPACITY

According to the EIA, in "Petroleum and Other Liquids: Number and Capacity of Petroleum Refineries"

(June 22, 2016, http://www.eia.gov/dnav/pet/pet_pnp_cap1_dcu_nus_a.htm), as of January 1, 2016, there were 139 operable refineries in the United States, down from 150 in 2009. Refinery capacity in 2016 was about 18.3 mbpd. The number of refineries has dropped for a variety of reasons, including retirement of older inefficient plants and consolidation within the oil industry. In addition, some countries that export oil to the United States have begun refining their own oil and selling the petroleum products directly.

In "When Was the Last Refinery Built in the United States?" (June 22, 2016, http://www.eia.gov/tools/faqs/faq.cfm?id=29&t=6), the EIA notes that as of 2016, the last large U.S. refinery to begin operating was built during the late 1970s in Louisiana. In 2016 it had an operating capacity of 539,000 barrels per calendar day. Four small refineries in Texas and North Dakota began operating in 2015 with capacities of between 19,500 and 84,000 barrels per calendar day.

In 2010 Hyperion Energy, a Texas-based company, obtained an air permit for a proposed $10 billion refinery in South Dakota. Environmental groups, including the Sierra Club, challenged the project in court. In early 2013 the South Dakota Supreme Court ruled in favor of Hyperion; however, the company's air permit expired later that year. As of September 2016, Hyperion Energy had not reapplied for a permit for the proposed refinery.

DOMESTIC CRUDE OIL PRODUCTION

Figure 2.10 shows domestic production of crude oil (including lease condensate) and NGPL between 1949 and 2015. Production peaked at 9.6 mbpd in 1970 and then slowly declined into the first decade of the 21st century. Production then rose sharply, topping 9.4 mbpd in 2015. Table 2.1 provides a breakdown of production by oil type and jurisdiction. Chiefly, it distinguishes Alaskan oil from that produced in the 48 contiguous states. During the 1990s Alaskan production accounted for more than 22% of total domestic production; however, its share has since fallen. As is explained in Chapter 7, certain pristine areas of northern Alaska are off limits to drilling.

The sharp uptick in domestic oil production that began during the latter half of the first decade of the 21st century is due almost entirely to tight oil. Figure 2.8 shows a map of the seven regions that accounted for 92% of domestic oil production growth between 2011 and 2014. The Permian, Eagle Ford, and Bakken basins have been particularly productive. The EIA indicates in "Tight Oil Production Pushes U.S. Crude Supply to over 10% of World Total" (March 26, 2014, http://www.eia.gov/todayinenergy/detail.cfm?id=15571) that U.S. tight oil production in 2005 was around 0.3 mbpd. In "How Much Shale (Tight) Oil Is Produced in the United

FIGURE 2.10

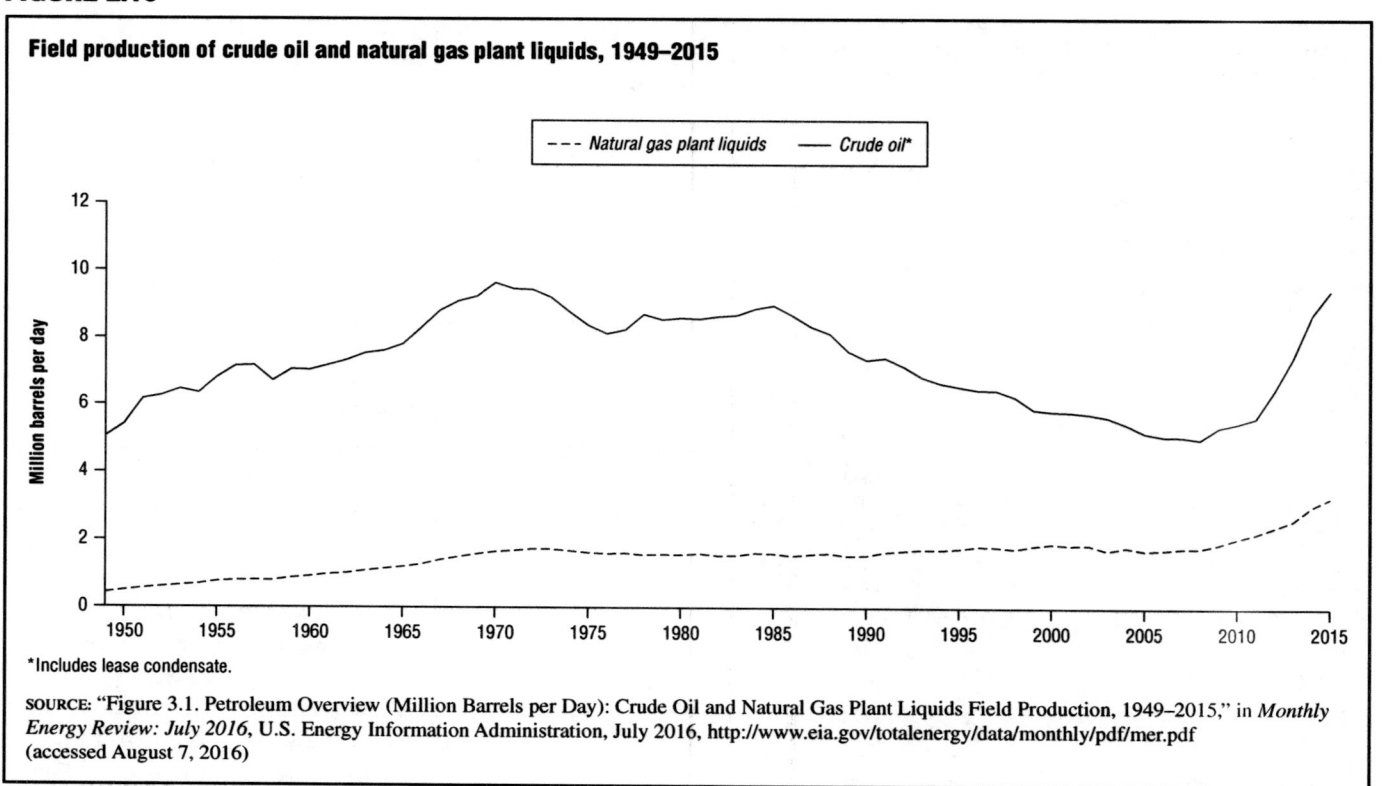

Field production of crude oil and natural gas plant liquids, 1949–2015

- - - Natural gas plant liquids   —— Crude oil*

*Includes lease condensate.

SOURCE: "Figure 3.1. Petroleum Overview (Million Barrels per Day): Crude Oil and Natural Gas Plant Liquids Field Production, 1949–2015," in *Monthly Energy Review: July 2016*, U.S. Energy Information Administration, July 2016, http://www.eia.gov/totalenergy/data/monthly/pdf/mer.pdf (accessed August 7, 2016)

States?" (June 14, 2016, https://www.eia.gov/tools/faqs/faq.cfm?id=847&t=6), the EIA notes that production soared to 4.9 mbpd in 2015.

U.S. oil production is affected by crude oil availability and legislative, legal, and cost issues related to drilling and extraction. For example, U.S. producers spend more money than do Middle Eastern producers to drill and extract crude oil because oil is available in enormous, easily accessible reservoirs in the Middle East. U.S. oil is not as easily recovered. When the cost of oil recovery severely reduces the profit margin on a barrel of oil, U.S. producers may shut down their most expensive wells, especially in times when oil prices are low. When oil prices are high, even the most expensive extraction methods can become cost effective.

The Domestic Production Outlook

The EIA publishes annual projections of future U.S. and world production of crude oil and petroleum products. In *Annual Energy Outlook 2016 with Projections to 2040* (August 2016, https://www.eia.gov/forecasts/aeo/pdf/0383(2016).pdf), the EIA indicates that it considers six future scenarios: a reference case, low and high economic growth cases, low and high oil price cases, and a high oil and gas resource case. All of the projections are based on the assumption that existing energy-related laws and regulations will remain in effect. Table 2.2 shows EIA projections for U.S. crude oil production through

2040 for the reference case by extraction location. Alaskan production is predicted to decline 4.7% between 2015 and 2040. By contrast, production in the lower 48 states is expected to rise 0.9% during the same period. According to the EIA, this growth is largely due to further development of the tight oil resources in the Bakken, Eagle Ford, and Permian basin formations.

DOMESTIC CRUDE OIL TRADE

The United States has been importing crude oil since World War II (1939–1945). Initially, the imported amounts were very small. Figure 2.11 shows historical imports of crude oil and petroleum products between 1949 and 2015. At first, imported oil was cheap and readily available, suiting the demands of a growing American population and economy. Furthermore, relatively low world crude oil prices often dampened domestic oil production: when the world price was lower than the cost of producing oil from some U.S. wells, domestic oil became unprofitable and was not produced. Consequently, more oil was imported.

Concern about Foreign Oil Dependency

The Organization of the Petroleum Exporting Countries (OPEC) is a cartel (a group of countries that agree to control production and marketing to avoid competing with one another). It was formed in 1960 by five major oil-producing countries: Iran, Iraq, Kuwait, Saudi Arabia,

TABLE 2.1

Field production of crude oil and natural gas plant liquids, by location, selected years 1950–2015

[Thousand barrels per day]

| | Field production[a] | | | | |
| | Crude oil[b, c] | | | | |
	48 States[d]	Alaska	Total	NGPL[e]	Total[c]
1950 Average	5,407	0	5,407	499	5,906
1955 Average	6,807	0	6,807	771	7,578
1960 Average	7,034	2	7,035	929	7,965
1965 Average	7,774	30	7,804	1,210	9,014
1970 Average	9,408	229	9,637	1,660	11,297
1975 Average	8,183	191	8,375	1,633	10,007
1980 Average	6,980	1,617	8,597	1,573	10,170
1985 Average	7,146	1,825	8,971	1,609	10,581
1990 Average	5,582	1,773	7,355	1,559	8,914
1995 Average	5,076	1,484	6,560	1,762	8,322
2000 Average	4,851	970	5,822	1,911	7,733
2001 Average	4,839	963	5,801	1,868	7,670
2002 Average	4,759	985	5,744	1,880	7,624
2003 Average	4,675	974	5,649	1,719	7,369
2004 Average	4,533	908	5,441	1,809	7,250
2005 Average	4,320	864	5,184	1,717	6,901
2006 Average	4,346	741	5,087	1,739	6,825
2007 Average	4,355	722	5,077	1,783	6,860
2008 Average	4,318	683	5,001	1,784	6,785
2009 Average	4,709	645	5,354	1,910	7,264
2010 Average	4,876	600	5,476	2,074	7,550
2011 Average	5,076	561	5,637	2,216	7,853
2012 Average	5,950	526	6,476	2,408	8,884
2013 Average	6,939	515	7,454	2,606	10,060
2014 Average	8,211	496	8,708	3,015	11,722
2015 Average	8,948[E]	483[E]	9,431[E]	3,273	12,704[E]

[a]Crude oil production on leases, and natural gas liquids (liquefied petroleum gases, pentanes plus, and a small amount of finished petroleum products) production at natural gas processing plants. Excludes what was previously classified as "Field Production" of finished motor gasoline, motor gasoline blending components, and other hydrocarbons and oxygenates; these are now included in Adjustments."
[b]Includes lease condensate.
[c]Once a month, data for crude oil production, total field production, and adjustments are revised going back as far as the data year of the U.S. Energy Information Administration's (EIA) last published *Petroleum Supply Annual (PSA)*—these revisions are released at the same time as EIA's *Petroleum Supply Monthly*. Once a year, data for these series are revised going back as far as 10 years—these revisions are released at the same time as the PSA.
[d]United States excluding Alaska and Hawaii.
[e]Natural gas plant liquids.
E = Estimate and greater than –500 barrels per day.
Notes: Totals may not equal sum of components due to independent rounding.
Geographic coverage is the 50 states and the District of Columbia.

SOURCE: Adapted from "Table 3.1. Petroleum Overview (Thousand Barrels per Day)," in *Monthly Energy Review: July 2016*, U.S. Energy Information Administration, July 2016, http://www.eia.gov/totalenergy/data/monthly/pdf/mer.pdf (accessed August 7, 2016)

and Venezuela. Since 1973 OPEC has tried to influence the worldwide oil supply to achieve higher prices. Over the decades various countries have joined and quit the cartel. As of September 2016, OPEC (http://www.opec.org/opec_web/en/about_us/25.htm) had 14 member countries:

- Algeria
- Angola
- Ecuador
- Gabon
- Indonesia
- Iran
- Iraq
- Kuwait
- Libya
- Nigeria
- Qatar
- Saudi Arabia
- United Arab Emirates
- Venezuela

The United States was hugely dependent on OPEC oil during the 1970s and early 1980s. (See Figure 2.12.) In 1973 some Arab countries, including those in OPEC, cut their oil exports to the United States in retaliation for U.S. aid to Israel during the Yom Kippur War, which was fought between Israel and neighboring Arab countries. The embargo lasted only six months, but the price of oil rose dramatically during that period. Americans experienced sudden price hikes for products that were produced from oil, such as gasoline and home heating oil, and faced temporary shortages. The energy problem quickly became an energy crisis, which led to occasional blackouts in cities and industries, temporary shutdowns of factories and schools, and frequent lines at gasoline service stations. The sudden increase in energy prices during the early 1970s is widely considered to have been a major cause of the economic recession of 1974 and 1975. Nevertheless, the United States obtained nearly three-fourths of its imported oil from OPEC by 1977. (See Figure 2.12.)

U.S. leaders became concerned that so much of the country's economic structure, based heavily on imported oil, was dependent on decisions in OPEC countries. Oil resources became an issue of national security, and OPEC countries, especially the Arab members, were often portrayed as potentially strangling the U.S. economy. Efforts were made to reduce imports by raising public awareness and by encouraging industry to create more energy-efficient products, such as automobiles with better gas mileage. These measures are described in detail in Chapter 9. Nonetheless, total petroleum imports rose through the end of the 1970s. (See Figure 2.11 and Figure 2.12.) Imports declined and then rebounded over the following decades as conservation efforts waned in the face of low oil prices. In fact, fuel efficiency gains in automobiles during the 1990s were offset by the public's growing preference for large vehicles, such as sport-utility vehicles. As a result, total oil imports grew steadily. However, as shown in Figure 2.12, by this time the United States was obtaining more than half of its imported oil from non-OPEC countries, such as Canada and Mexico.

TABLE 2.2

Crude oil supply, imports, and exports, 2015 and forecast through 2040

[Million barrels per day, unless otherwise noted]

Supply and disposition	2015	2020	2025	2030	2035	2040	2015–2040
Crude oil							
Domestic crude production[a]	9.42	9.38	9.43	10.06	10.66	11.26	0.7%
Alaska	0.48	0.41	0.32	0.24	0.19	0.15	−4.7%
Lower 48 states	8.94	8.96	9.12	9.82	10.48	11.11	0.9%
Net imports	6.88	6.97	6.95	6.57	6.24	6.10	−0.5%
Gross imports	7.28	7.60	7.58	7.20	7.07	7.12	−0.1%
Exports	0.40	0.63	0.63	0.63	0.83	1.02	3.8%
Other crude supply[b]	−0.11	0.01	0.07	0.00	0.00	0.00	—
Total crude supply	**16.19**	**16.36**	**16.46**	**16.63**	**16.91**	**17.36**	**0.3%**

[a]Includes lease condensate.
[b]Strategic petroleum reserve stock additions plus unaccounted for crude oil and crude oil stock withdrawals.
— = Not applicable.
Note: Totals may not equal sum of components due to independent rounding.

SOURCE: Adapted from "Table 11. Petroleum and Other Liquids Supply and Disposition," in *Annual Energy Outlook 2016 Early Release*, U.S. Energy Information Administration, May 2016, https://www.eia.gov/forecasts/aeo/excel/aeotab_11.xlsx (accessed August 12, 2016)

FIGURE 2.11

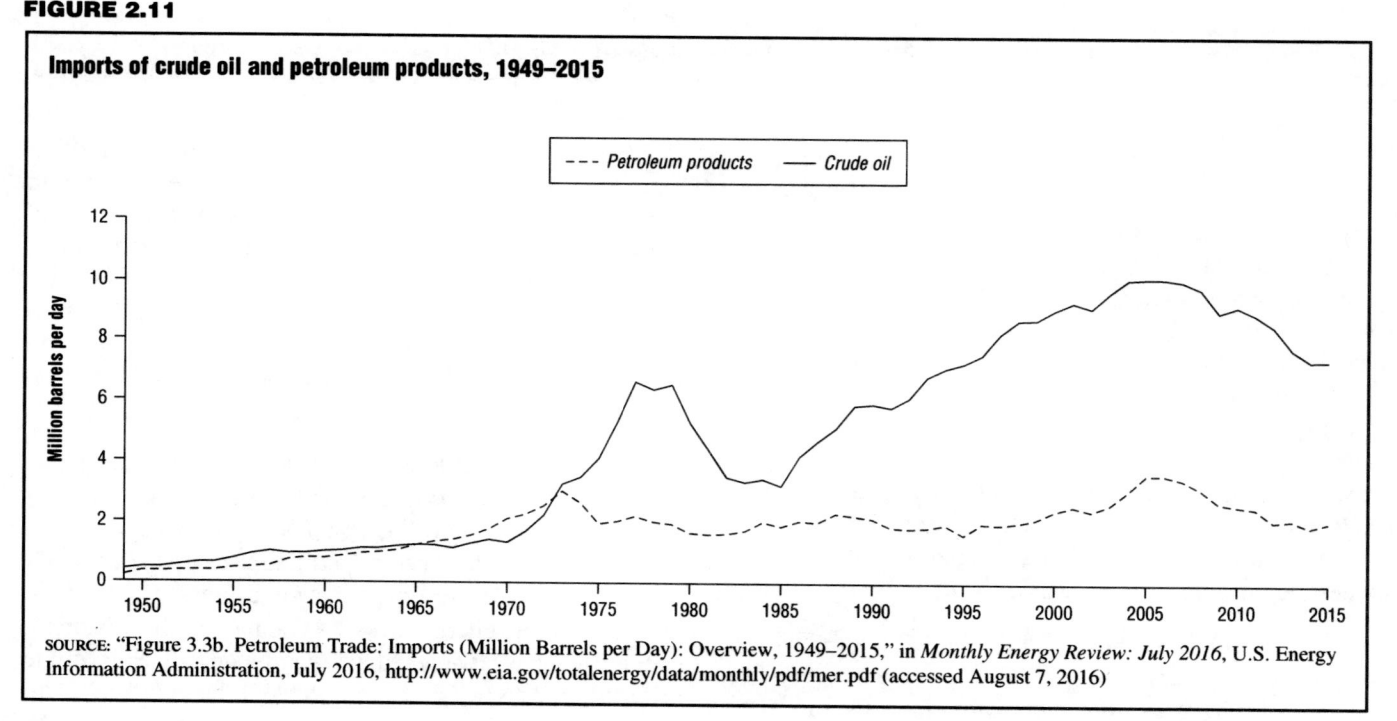

Imports of crude oil and petroleum products, 1949–2015

SOURCE: "Figure 3.3b. Petroleum Trade: Imports (Million Barrels per Day): Overview, 1949–2015," in *Monthly Energy Review: July 2016*, U.S. Energy Information Administration, July 2016, http://www.eia.gov/totalenergy/data/monthly/pdf/mer.pdf (accessed August 7, 2016)

Concern about continued U.S. reliance on OPEC oil grew after the terrorist attacks of September 11, 2001. The concern was heightened by the war with Iraq and the subsequent unrest in Middle Eastern nations. Nevertheless, demand for the product persisted, and total oil imports peaked in 2005. (See Figure 2.11.) Later that decade the United States experienced a dramatic rise in domestic tight oil production that lowered U.S. need for imported oil.

As shown in Figure 2.13, in 2015 imports accounted for 7.4 mbpd (44%) of the total U.S. crude oil supply of 16.8 mbpd. A breakdown of the imports by supplying entity is provided in Table 2.3. In 2015 the United States obtained 4.7 mbpd (64%) of its imported crude oil from non-OPEC countries. The major suppliers were Canada, Mexico, and Colombia. The remaining 2.7 mbpd (36%) of imported crude oil came from OPEC countries, primarily Saudi Arabia, Venezuela, and Iraq. Overall, Canada provided 3.2 mbpd (43% of U.S. imports), while Saudi Arabia provided 1.1 mbpd (14%). These two countries were the leading importers of crude oil to the United States in 2015.

FIGURE 2.12

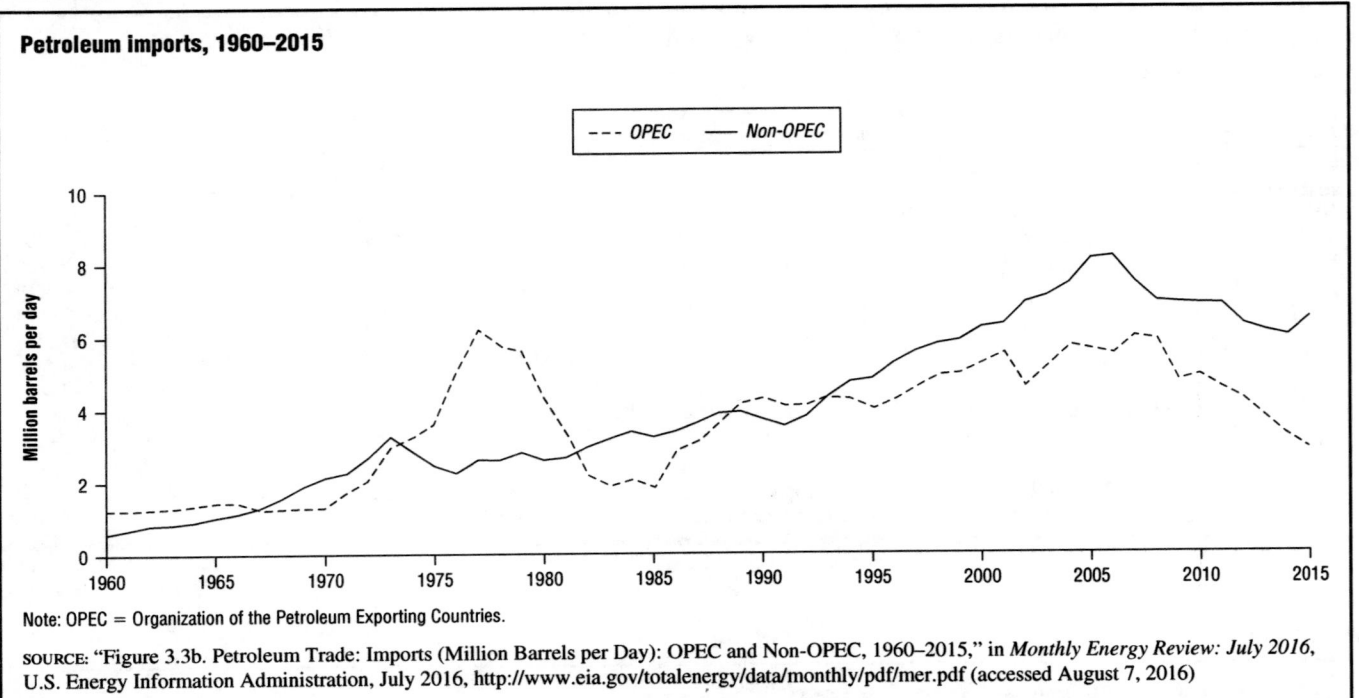

Petroleum imports, 1960–2015

Note: OPEC = Organization of the Petroleum Exporting Countries.

SOURCE: "Figure 3.3b. Petroleum Trade: Imports (Million Barrels per Day): OPEC and Non-OPEC, 1960–2015," in *Monthly Energy Review: July 2016*, U.S. Energy Information Administration, July 2016, http://www.eia.gov/totalenergy/data/monthly/pdf/mer.pdf (accessed August 7, 2016)

The Canadian Connection

According to the EIA, in *Monthly Energy Review: July 2016*, Canada, unlike the United States, almost balanced its domestic oil supply and petroleum consumption during the latter decades of the 20th century. Portions of Canada, particularly the province of Alberta, have vast deposits of bitumen. As described earlier, crude oil can be obtained from this black tarry substance, which is typically found in rock formations called tar sands, oil sands, or tight sands. Canada's bitumen industry has grown dramatically, allowing the nation to produce more crude oil than it needs. The EIA indicates that in 2015 Canada's crude oil production averaged 3.7 mbpd, while its petroleum consumption was only 2.3 mbpd.

Canada's close proximity to the United States and the existing pipelines and transportation systems between the two countries have facilitated cross-border trade of Canadian crude oil. As shown in Figure 2.14, U.S. imports of the oil soared from around 0.2 mbpd in 1980 to more than 3 mbpd in 2015.

U.S. Strategic Petroleum Reserve

In 1975, in response to growing concern over U.S. dependence on imported oil, Congress created the Strategic Petroleum Reserve (SPR). Crude oil is stored in deep salt caverns in Louisiana and Texas. (The caverns are used because oil does not dissolve salt the way water does.) If the United States suddenly finds its crude oil imports cut, the reserves can be accessed via existing pipelines.

At the end of 2015 the SPR contained 695 million barrels of crude oil. (See Figure 2.15.) As shown in Figure 2.13, crude oil imports in 2015 averaged 7.4 mbpd. At that usage rate the SPR would last the United States a maximum of 94 days (i.e., assuming no crude oil imports at all). The non-SPR crude oil stocks shown in Figure 2.15 are amounts in the hands of the U.S. oil industry, including Alaskan crude oil in transit to the 48 contiguous states.

Although the SPR was created to compensate against drastic import disruptions, it has been tapped under other circumstances. In "SPR Quick Facts and FAQs" (2016, http://energy.gov/fe/services/petroleum-reserves/strategic-petroleum-reserve/spr-quick-facts-and-faqs#Q1), the U.S. Department of Energy describes some of the historical events that have triggered sales or loans of SPR crude oil. SPR loans to oil companies have to be paid back with interest—that is, including an extra amount above the borrowed amount. In 2012 the Marathon Oil Company borrowed 1 million barrels after Hurricane Isaac disrupted oil production in the U.S. Gulf Coast. Major sales of SPR oil took place in 1990 due to the Persian Gulf War and in 2011 following a revolution in Libya. The latter sale occurred at the direction of the International Energy Agency (IEA), which is an independent organization devoted to energy issues. As of 2016, the United States and 28 other developed countries were IEA members.

Management of the SPR is a highly politicized topic in the United States. During times of high oil and gasoline prices some politicians clamor for a release of SPR

FIGURE 2.13

Petroleum flow, 2015

[Million barrels per day]

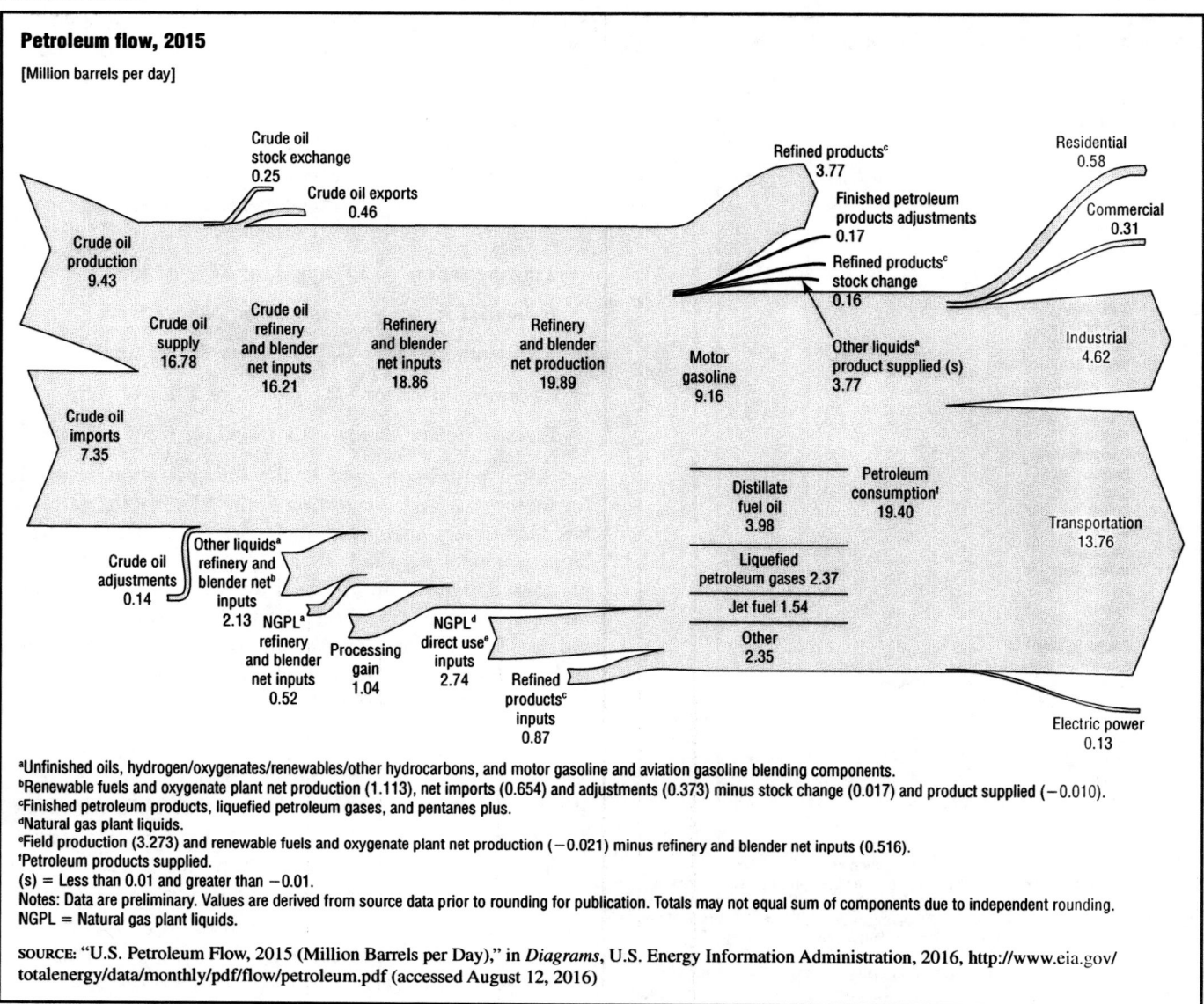

aUnfinished oils, hydrogen/oxygenates/renewables/other hydrocarbons, and motor gasoline and aviation gasoline blending components.
bRenewable fuels and oxygenate plant net production (1.113), net imports (0.654) and adjustments (0.373) minus stock change (0.017) and product supplied (−0.010).
cFinished petroleum products, liquefied petroleum gases, and pentanes plus.
dNatural gas plant liquids.
eField production (3.273) and renewable fuels and oxygenate plant net production (−0.021) minus refinery and blender net inputs (0.516).
fPetroleum products supplied.
(s) = Less than 0.01 and greater than −0.01.
Notes: Data are preliminary. Values are derived from source data prior to rounding for publication. Totals may not equal sum of components due to independent rounding.
NGPL = Natural gas plant liquids.

SOURCE: "U.S. Petroleum Flow, 2015 (Million Barrels per Day)," in *Diagrams*, U.S. Energy Information Administration, 2016, http://www.eia.gov/totalenergy/data/monthly/pdf/flow/petroleum.pdf (accessed August 12, 2016)

oil to dampen prices and ease the financial burden on consumers. The U.S. government, however, has historically maintained that releases should take place only because of special events that lower (or threaten to lower) crude oil supply availability to the United States. The United States is also bound by IAE requirements regarding crude oil reserves. According to the Department of Energy, the IAE requires each member nation to maintain at least a 90-day reserve including both private and government supplies.

Domestic Crude Oil Exports

As shown in Table 2.4, the United States historically exported very little crude oil. Annual exports ranged from a low of 3,000 barrels per day (bpd) in 1965 to a high of 458,000 bpd in 2015. The latter value was up dramatically from earlier years in the 21st century. During the 1970s the U.S. government imposed strict export

requirements on crude oil to keep as much of it as possible in the domestic supply and hold prices down. Christian Berthelsen and Lynn Cook explain in "U.S. Ruling Loosens Four-Decade Ban on Oil Exports" (WSJ.com, June 24, 2014) that U.S. companies have long been free to export refined oil (petroleum products), such as gasoline.

The U.S. tight oil boom encouraged domestic producers to seek permission to export some minimally processed crude oil. According to Berthelsen and Cook, the U.S. Department of Commerce decided in 2014 to allow two U.S. companies to sell condensate (a type of ultralight oil) that had been stabilized and distilled. In December 2015 Congress passed a massive spending bill that lifted the decades-old limitations on exporting crude oil. However, this change in policy did not immediately boost exports. According to the EIA, in *Monthly Energy*

TABLE 2.3

Crude oil imports, by supplying nation or group, 2015

All countries	**7,351**
Persian Gulf	**1,488**
OPEC*	**2,679**
Saudi Arabia	1,051
Venezuela	779
Iraq	229
Ecuador	225
Kuwait	206
Angola	124
Nigeria	57
Indonesia	34
Algeria	3
Libya	3
United Arab Emirates	2
Non OPEC*	**4,672**
Canada	3,169
Mexico	688
Colombia	370
Brazil	189
Chad	72
Russia	28
Argentina	16
Azerbaijan	13
United Kingdom	11
Australia	10
Norway	9
Vietnam	9
Congo (Brazzaville)	8
Guatemala	8
Gabon	7
Trinidad and Tobago	7
Peru	6
Albania	5
Equatorial Guinea	5
India	2
Belize	1
Egypt	1
Italy	1

OPEC = Organization of the Petroleum Exporting Countries.
Notes: *Countries listed under OPEC and non-OPEC are based on current affiliations. Crude oil includes imports for storage in the Stategic Petroleum Reserve. The Persian Gulf includes Bahrain, Iran, Iraq, Kuwait, Qatar, Saudi Arabia, and United Arab Emirates. Totals may not equal sum of components due to independent rounding.

SOURCE: Adapted from "U.S. Imports by Country of Origin," in *Petroleum and Other Liquids: Data*, U.S. Energy Information Administration, July 29, 2016, http://www.eia.gov/dnav/pet/pet_move_impcus_a2_nus_epc0_im0_mbblpd_a.htm (accessed August 12, 2016)

Review: July 2016, crude oil exports between January and June 2016 averaged 467,000 bpd, only slightly above the 2015 average of 458,000 bpd.

PETROLEUM PRODUCT CONSUMPTION

Crude oil is a raw material that is refined and processed into multiple petroleum products. In "Oil: Crude and Petroleum Products Explained" (June 16, 2016, http://www.eia.gov/energyexplained/?page=oil_home), the EIA states that in 2015 a barrel (42 gallons [159 L]) of crude oil provided approximately 45 gallons' (170 L) worth of petroleum products. The agency notes that "this increase in volume is similar to what happens to popcorn when it is popped."

The United States makes petroleum products from domestically produced and imported crude oil. In addition, petroleum products are imported directly from foreign nations. As shown in Figure 2.13, average domestic consumption of petroleum products in 2015 was 19.4 mbpd.

Figure 2.16 shows petroleum product consumption by energy-using sector between 1949 and 2015. (It should be noted that the sectors are defined in detail in Chapter 1.) The transportation sector has historically been the largest consumer of petroleum. Average consumption by sector in 2015 was:

- Transportation—13.8 mbpd, or 71% of total
- Industrial sector—4.6 mbpd, or 24% of total
- Residential sector—0.6 mbpd, or 3% of total
- Commercial sector—0.3 mbpd, or 1.5% of total
- Electric power sector—0.1 mbpd, or 0.5% of total

Most petroleum used in the transportation sector is for motor gasoline. According to the EIA, motor gasoline has historically accounted for nearly half of total petroleum products supplied. (See Figure 2.17.) Other major products are shown in Figure 2.18. They include distillate fuel oils (such as diesel oil), jet fuel, propane, and residual fuel oil. In *Monthly Energy Review: July 2016*, the EIA explains that residual fuel oil is a heavy oil used to power U.S. Navy ships and in industrial and commercial heating and electric power generation.

WORLD OIL PRODUCTION AND CONSUMPTION

Table 2.5 shows total oil production for 2014 for the world, by region, and for the top-20 producers. The values include crude oil, lease condensate, NGPL, other liquids, and refinery processing gains, which are due to chemicals added during refining. A majority of the leading oil-producing nations in 2014 were OPEC members, including the second most prolific supplier, Saudi Arabia.

Total world oil production was 93.2 mbpd in 2014. (See Table 2.5.) The Middle East was the largest producing region, accounting for 27.8 mbpd (30% of the world total). North America was second with 21.2 mbpd (23%). The United States led all countries with 14 mbpd (15% of the world total). Saudi Arabia was second with 11.6 mbpd (12%), followed by Russia, China, and Canada.

As of September 2016, complete consumption data were not available from the EIA for 2014 for all countries. As shown in Table 2.6, total world petroleum consumption in 2013 was 91.3 mbpd. The United States was the leading petroleum consumer, at 19 mbpd (21% of the world total). Other top consumers in 2013 included China, Japan, India, and Russia.

World Outlook

As noted earlier, the EIA prepares forecasts in which it considers scenarios including a reference case and high

FIGURE 2.14

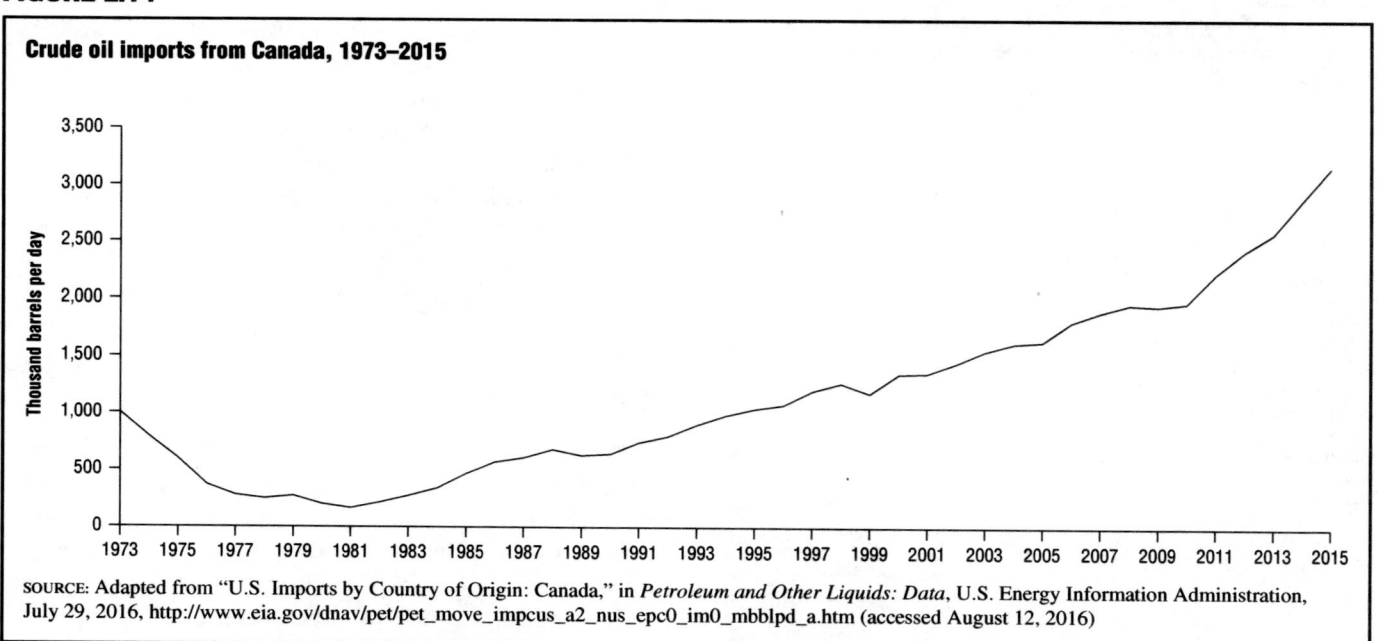

Crude oil imports from Canada, 1973–2015

SOURCE: Adapted from "U.S. Imports by Country of Origin: Canada," in *Petroleum and Other Liquids: Data*, U.S. Energy Information Administration, July 29, 2016, http://www.eia.gov/dnav/pet/pet_move_impcus_a2_nus_epc0_im0_mbblpd_a.htm (accessed August 12, 2016)

FIGURE 2.15

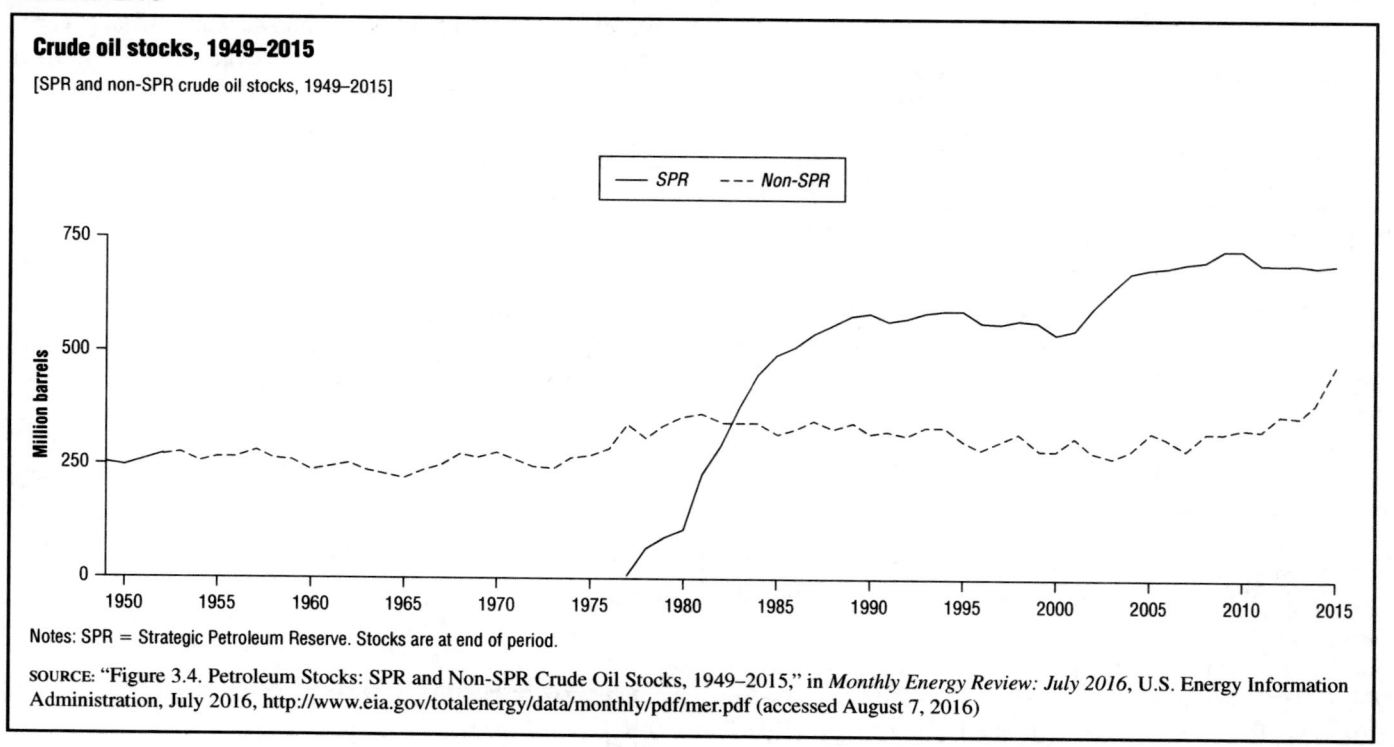

Crude oil stocks, 1949–2015

[SPR and non-SPR crude oil stocks, 1949–2015]

Notes: SPR = Strategic Petroleum Reserve. Stocks are at end of period.

SOURCE: "Figure 3.4. Petroleum Stocks: SPR and Non-SPR Crude Oil Stocks, 1949–2015," in *Monthly Energy Review: July 2016*, U.S. Energy Information Administration, July 2016, http://www.eia.gov/totalenergy/data/monthly/pdf/mer.pdf (accessed August 7, 2016)

and low oil price cases. As shown in Table 2.7, the agency predicts world petroleum consumption will rise 1.1% between 2015 and 2040. The EIA categorizes nations by whether they are members of the Organisation for Economic Co-operation and Development (OECD). The OECD is a collection of dozens of mostly Western nations (including the United States) that are devoted to global economic development. Developed nations concentrate on energy conservation measures and alternative fuel sources to reduce their reliance on oil. The EIA expects OECD petroleum consumption to grow only 0.1% between 2015 and 2040. By contrast, consumption among non-OECD members (such as China, India, and Russia) is projected to increase by 1.8%.

TABLE 2.4

Crude oil and petroleum product exports, selected years 1950–2015

[Thousand barrels per day]

	Crude oil*	Exports Petroleum products	Total
1950 Average	95	210	305
1955 Average	32	336	368
1960 Average	8	193	202
1965 Average	3	184	187
1970 Average	14	245	259
1975 Average	6	204	209
1980 Average	287	258	544
1985 Average	204	577	781
1990 Average	109	748	857
1995 Average	95	855	949
2000 Average	50	990	1,040
2001 Average	20	951	971
2002 Average	9	975	984
2003 Average	12	1,014	1,027
2004 Average	27	1,021	1,048
2005 Average	32	1,133	1,165
2006 Average	25	1,292	1,317
2007 Average	27	1,405	1,433
2008 Average	29	1,773	1,802
2009 Average	44	1,980	2,024
2010 Average	42	2,311	2,353
2011 Average	47	2,939	2,986
2012 Average	67	3,137	3,205
2013 Average	134	3,487	3,621
2014 Average	351	3,824	4,176
2015 Average	458	4,292	4,750

Notes: Totals may not equal sum of components due to independent rounding. Geographic coverage is the 50 states and the District of Columbia.

SOURCE: Adapted from "Table 3.3b. Petroleum Trade: Imports and Exports by Type (Thousand Barrels per Day)," in *Monthly Energy Review: July 2016*, U.S. Energy Information Administration, July 2016, http://www.eia.gov/totalenergy/data/monthly/pdf/mer.pdf (accessed August 7, 2016)

Many non-OECD members are considered developing nations that are undergoing rapid industrialization and heavy use of resources, much as the United States and western Europe did during the mid-20th century. At that time the world oil industry was dominated by Western companies, most of which were based in the United States. The article "Supermajordämmerung" (Economist.com, August 3, 2013) notes that during the 1950s the industry leaders were the so-called seven sisters: BP (formerly British Petroleum), Esso, Gulf Oil, Mobil, Royal Dutch Shell, Southern Oil Company of California, and Texaco. All were based in the United States except BP, which was based in the United Kingdom, and Royal Dutch Shell, which was based in the United Kingdom and the Netherlands. These companies held enormous economic power and wielded great control over the world's oil resources. Over time, they and their successors were dubbed "Big Oil." (It is important to note that most large oil companies also trade in natural gas because the two fuels are often found together.)

The oil industry performs a range of tasks, such as finding and extracting oil, refining it into multiple petroleum products, and distributing the products. The Big Oil companies grew to domination by practicing vertical integration, meaning that they performed (or purchased smaller companies that performed) all of these tasks. This gave them broad economic power, for example, from the oil well to the gas pump. Over the decades the big companies have undergone ownership transitions, such as mergers and acquisitions, and have changed names in some cases. However, the industry has sustained only a handful of Big Oil companies. As of 2016, they were generally considered to include BP, Chevron (U.S. based), ExxonMobil (U.S. based), Royal Dutch Shell, and Total (France based).

As developing nations began to mature during the 20th century, many of them created national oil companies (NOCs) that eventually grew to rival the commercial firms. The United States and other countries that embrace capitalism and free enterprise allow private companies to develop and sell natural resources, such as oil. This is not the case in nations where oil is viewed as a commodity best managed by the national government. NOCs are companies that are wholly or majority-owned by the national government. The article "Supermajordämmerung" explains that many of the NOCs were initially very dependent on the Big Oil firms to develop and process their oil resources. Over time, however, the NOCs grew into powerful industry forces that operate much more independently. As of 2016, some of the most notable NOCs were:

- Abu Dhabi National Oil Corporation (United Arab Emirates)
- China National Offshore Oil Corporation, China National Petroleum Corporation, China Petroleum and Chemical Corporation, and PetroChina Company (China)
- Gazprom (Russia)
- Iraqi Oil Ministry (Iraq)
- Kuwait Petroleum Corporation (Kuwait)
- National Iranian Oil Company (Iran)
- Nigerian National Petroleum (Nigeria)
- Petróleo Brasileiro S.A. (Brazil)
- Petróleos de Venezuela S.A (Venezuela)
- Petróleos Mexicanos (Mexico)
- Petroliam Nasional Berhad (Malaysia)
- Qatar Petroleum (Qatar)
- Rosneft (Russia)
- Saudi Aramco (Saudi Arabia)
- Statoil ASA (Norway)

FIGURE 2.16

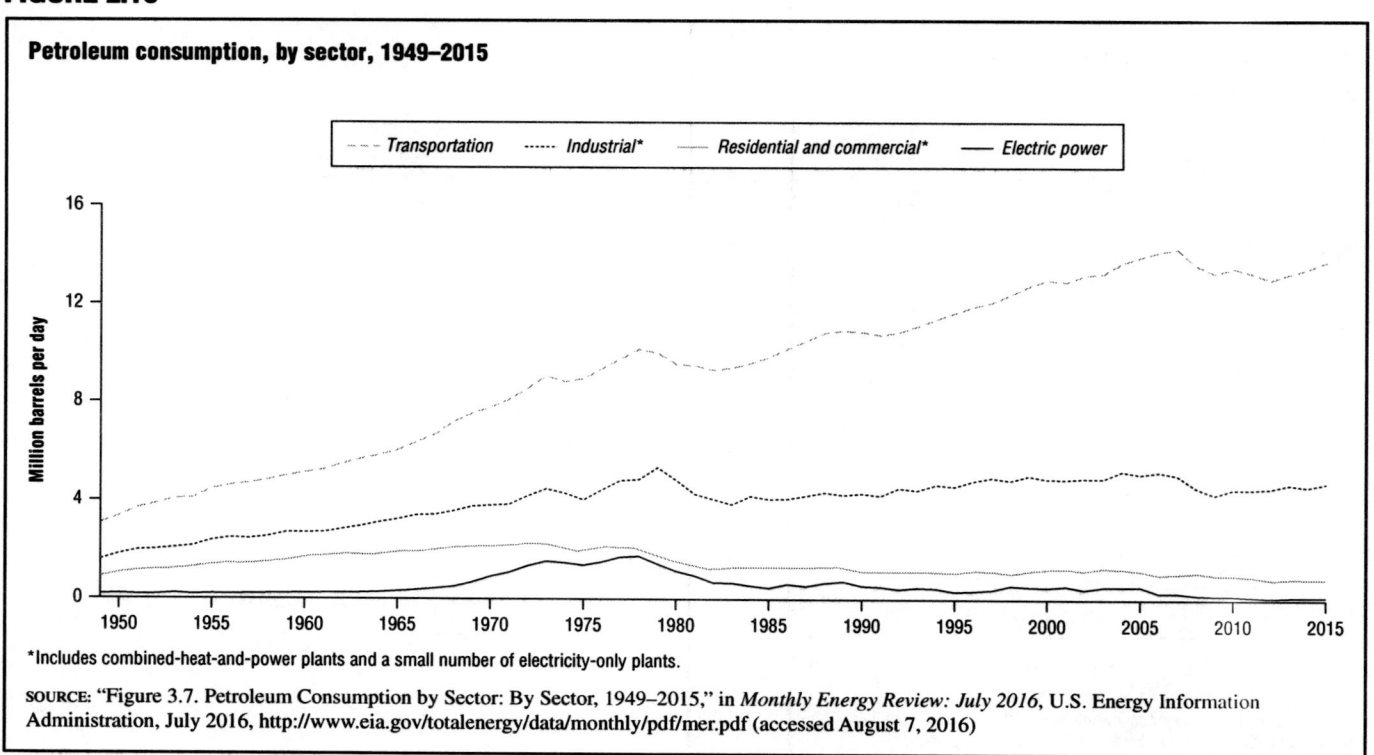

Petroleum consumption, by sector, 1949–2015

*Includes combined-heat-and-power plants and a small number of electricity-only plants.

SOURCE: "Figure 3.7. Petroleum Consumption by Sector: By Sector, 1949–2015," in *Monthly Energy Review: July 2016*, U.S. Energy Information Administration, July 2016, http://www.eia.gov/totalenergy/data/monthly/pdf/mer.pdf (accessed August 7, 2016)

FIGURE 2.17

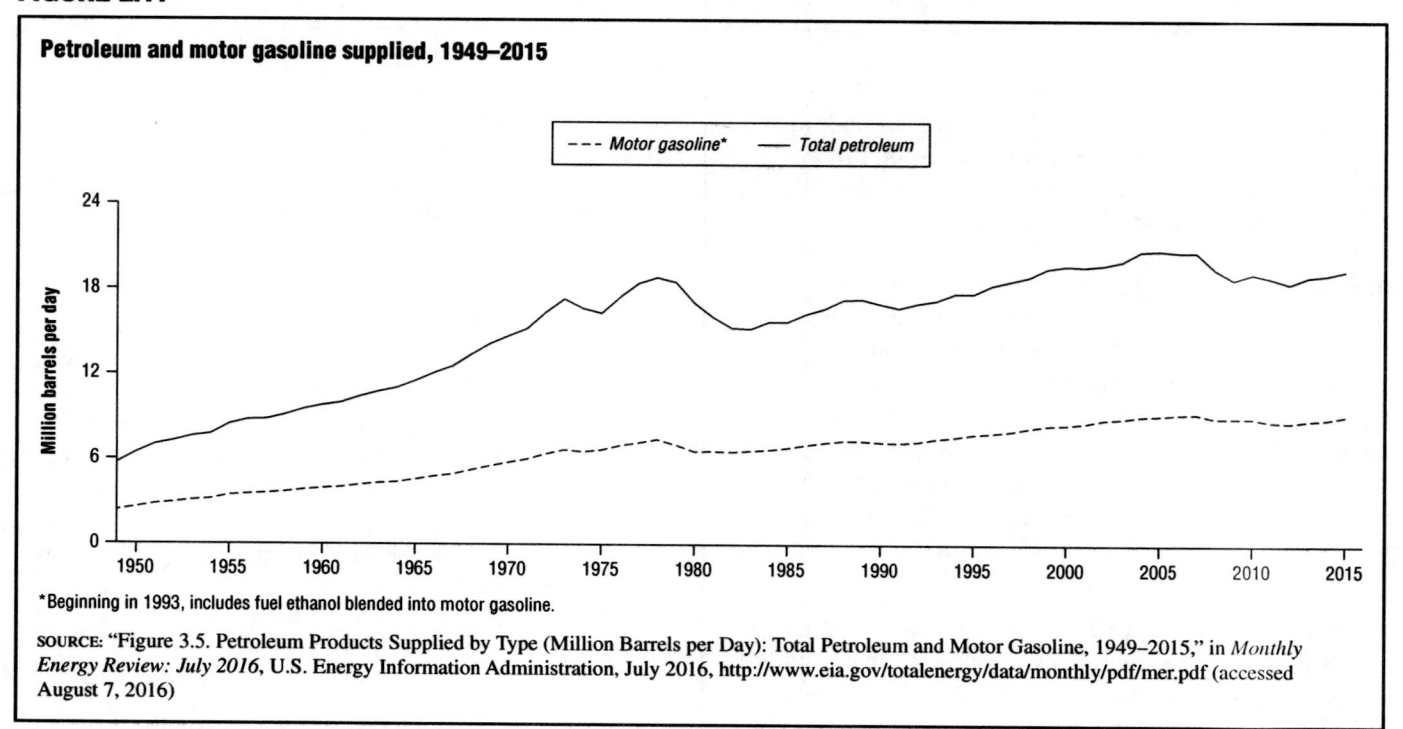

Petroleum and motor gasoline supplied, 1949–2015

*Beginning in 1993, includes fuel ethanol blended into motor gasoline.

SOURCE: "Figure 3.5. Petroleum Products Supplied by Type (Million Barrels per Day): Total Petroleum and Motor Gasoline, 1949–2015," in *Monthly Energy Review: July 2016*, U.S. Energy Information Administration, July 2016, http://www.eia.gov/totalenergy/data/monthly/pdf/mer.pdf (accessed August 7, 2016)

In addition, as of 2016, the Italian government owned nearly one-third of the shares in Eni S.p.A., a company based in Italy. This ownership does not technically constitute majority control of the company; however, the government's shares are "golden shares," meaning it has special powers over how the company is managed.

OIL PRICES

When discussing oil prices, it is important to understand that there is no single price for a barrel of oil in the marketplace. Instead, analysts and investors monitor several benchmark prices. Table 2.8 shows various prices for crude oil and for liquid fuels produced from crude oil

FIGURE 2.18

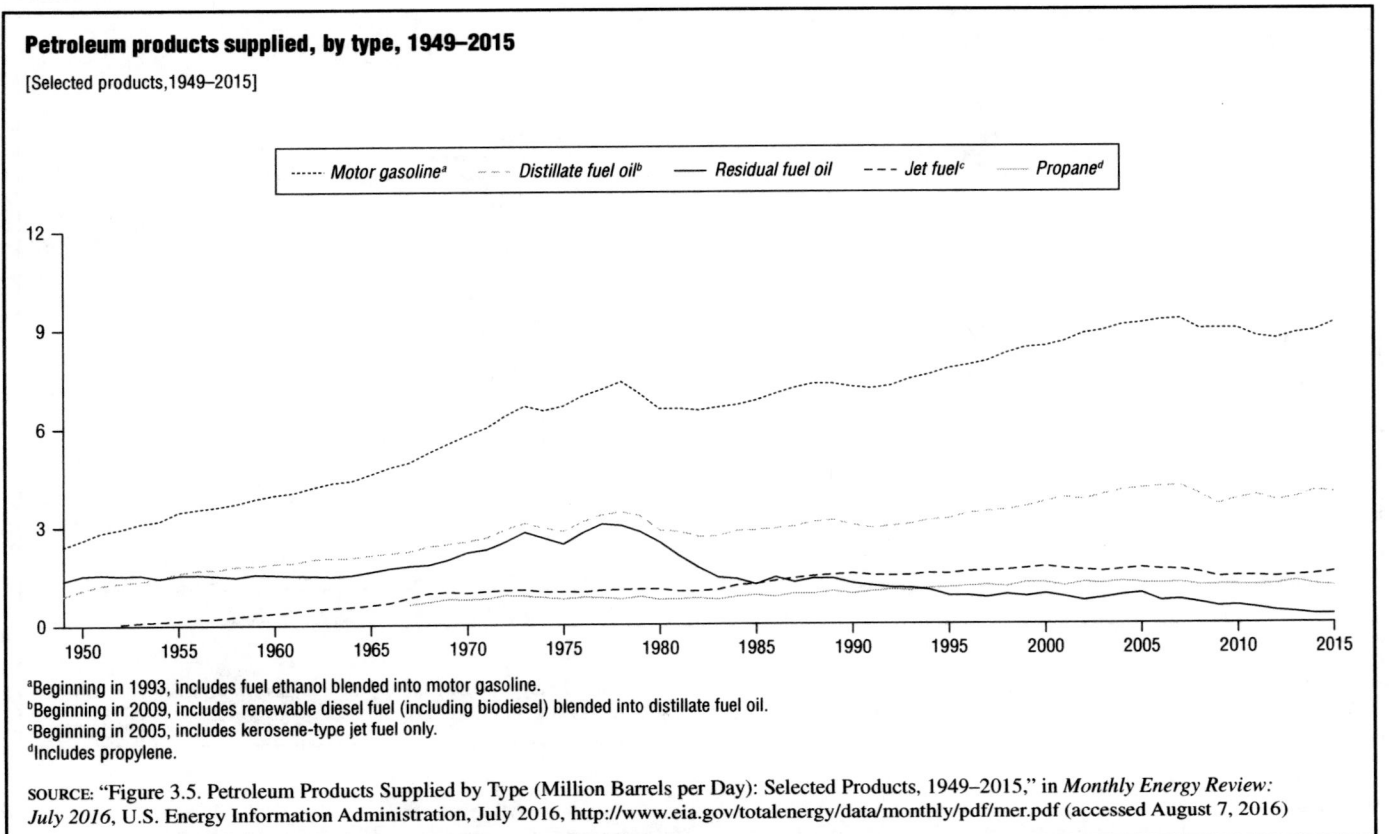

Petroleum products supplied, by type, 1949–2015

[Selected products,1949–2015]

Legend: ------ Motor gasoline[a] - - - Distillate fuel oil[b] —— Residual fuel oil - - - Jet fuel[c] ········ Propane[d]

[a]Beginning in 1993, includes fuel ethanol blended into motor gasoline.
[b]Beginning in 2009, includes renewable diesel fuel (including biodiesel) blended into distillate fuel oil.
[c]Beginning in 2005, includes kerosene-type jet fuel only.
[d]Includes propylene.

SOURCE: "Figure 3.5. Petroleum Products Supplied by Type (Million Barrels per Day): Selected Products, 1949–2015," in *Monthly Energy Review: July 2016*, U.S. Energy Information Administration, July 2016, http://www.eia.gov/totalenergy/data/monthly/pdf/mer.pdf (accessed August 7, 2016)

between the first quarter of 2015 and the second quarter of 2016. The West Texas intermediate spot average for crude oil was around $45 per barrel as of the second quarter of 2016. West Texas intermediate oil is a light sweet grade, and its price serves as a reference point for other U.S. oil prices. Another benchmark price of note is the Brent spot average. It represents a light sweet crude oil sourced from the North Sea in northern Europe. As of the second quarter of 2016, the Brent spot price for crude oil was nearly $46 per barrel. The two other crude oil prices shown in Table 2.8 are the imported average (the average price of a barrel of crude oil imported to the United States) and the refiner average acquisition cost (the average price paid by U.S. refiners for a barrel of crude oil).

Table 2.9 shows crude oil refiner acquisition costs between 1965 and 2015. According to the EIA, in *Monthly Energy Review: July 2016*, the costs include the price of the oil purchased plus transportation costs and fees. The costs are expressed in nominal dollars (current to that year), which do not take into account the effects of inflation over time. Refiner acquisition costs grew steadily through 2008. As is noted in Chapter 1, the United States suffered a severe economic downturn called the Great Recession, which lasted from December 2007 to June 2009. Consumer demand dropped severely during that period. Correspondingly, refiner acquisition

costs plummeted to less than $60 per barrel in 2009, but then rebounded to around $100 per barrel over subsequent years. In 2014 and 2015 the costs declined again, dropping to below $50 per barrel in 2015.

Gasoline Prices

As noted earlier, motor gasoline has historically accounted for nearly half of total petroleum products supplied each year. Thus, the price of gasoline is very dependent on crude oil prices. In "Petroleum and Other Liquids: Gasoline and Diesel Fuel Update" (September 19, 2016, http://www.eia.gov/petroleum/gasdiesel), the EIA provides the following average breakdown of costs for each gallon of regular gasoline that was sold to consumers in July 2016:

- Crude oil—46% of total
- Taxes—20% of total
- Distribution and marketing—19% of total
- Refining—16% of total

A similar breakdown is provided by the EIA for diesel fuel in July 2016:

- Crude oil—43% of total
- Distribution and marketing—22% of total

TABLE 2.5

World production of crude oil, including lease condensate and other petroleum liquids, by region and selected country, 2014

[Million barrels per day]

	2014
World	**93.2**
Regions	
Middle East	27.8
North America	21.2
Eurasia	13.9
Asia & Oceania	9.3
Africa	8.7
Central & South America	8.4
Europe	3.9
Countries	
United States	14.0
Saudi Arabia	11.6
Russia	10.8
China	4.6
Canada	4.4
United Arab Emirates	3.5
Iran	3.4
Iraq	3.4
Brazil	3.0
Mexico	2.8
Kuwait	2.8
Venezuela	2.7
Nigeria	2.4
Qatar	2.1
Norway	1.9
Angola	1.8
Algeria	1.7
Kazakhstan	1.7
Colombia	1.0
India	1.0

SOURCE: Adapted from "Table: Total Oil Supply (Thousand Barrels per Day)," in *International Energy Statistics: Petroleum Production*, U.S. Energy Information Administration, 2016, http://www.eia.gov/cfapps/ipdbproject/iedindex3.cfm?tid=5&pid=53&aid=1&cid=regions&syid=2014&eyid=2014&unit=TBPD (accessed August 13, 2016)

TABLE 2.6

World petroleum consumption, by region and selected country, 2013

[Million barrels per day]

	2013
World	**91.3**
Regions	
Asia & Oceania	30.1
North America	23.4
Europe	14.2
Middle East	8.1
Central & South America	7.1
Eurasia	4.7
Africa	3.6
Countries	
United States	19.0
China	10.5
Japan	4.6
India	3.7
Russia	3.5
Brazil	3.0
Saudi Arabia	3.0
Germany	2.4
Canada	2.4
Korea, South	2.3
Mexico	2.1
Iran	1.9
Indonesia	1.7
France	1.7
United Kingdom	1.5
Italy	1.3
Singapore	1.2
Spain	1.2
Thailand	1.2
Australia	1.1

SOURCE: Adapted from "Table: Total Oil Supply (Thousand Barrels per Day)," in *International Energy Statistics: Petroleum Production*, U.S. Energy Information Administration, 2016, http://www.eia.gov/cfapps/ipdbproject/iedindex3.cfm?tid=5&pid=53&aid=1&cid=regions&syid=2014&eyid=2014&unit=TBPD (accessed August 13, 2016)

- Taxes—22% of total

- Refining—14% of total

It should be noted that the individual amounts sum to more than 100% due to rounding.

Table 2.10 shows average annual gasoline and diesel prices for selected years between 1950 and 2015 and monthly prices from January to June 2016. Different gasoline grades and formulations are represented. The prices are in nominal dollars, meaning they are not adjusted for inflation. In general, they peaked in 2012 or 2013 then declined through 2016.

Oil Pricing Factors

As is true for all commodities, oil pricing is dependent on supply and demand factors. In general, when demand outpaces supply, prices go up. Likewise, when supply outpaces demand, prices go down. Higher prices encourage oil producers to produce more. They may start new wells that are more expensive to operate due to higher developmental and operational expenses, for example, wells in off-shore and remote areas. Higher prices, however, tend to spur consumers to cut back on their petroleum consumption. This demand drop can then push prices lower. Energy markets are quite complex, and this is particularly true for oil because so much of it is imported into the United States. In addition, the U.S. government takes actions that affect the oil markets and hence oil pricing.

WEATHER CONDITIONS. The demand for petroleum products varies. Heating oil demand rises during the winter. A cold spell, which leads to a sharp rise in demand, may result in a corresponding price increase. A warm winter may be reflected in lower prices as suppliers try to clear out their inventory. Gasoline demand rises during the summer—people drive more for recreation—so gas prices rise as a consequence.

Weather disasters, such as Hurricane Katrina along the Gulf Coast during the summer of 2005, can disrupt production and refining capabilities and temporarily raise oil and petroleum product prices.

TABLE 2.7

World petroleum and related liquids consumption, by region and country, 2015 and predicted for 2040

[Million barrels per day, unless otherwise noted]

Supply, disposition, and prices	2015	2020	2025	2030	2035	2040	2015–2040
Petroleum and other liquids consumption[a]							
OECD							
United States (50 states)	19.42	20.11	19.90	19.54	19.69	20.14	0.1%
United States territories	0.30	0.31	0.32	0.34	0.36	0.38	1.0%
Canada	2.39	2.39	2.38	2.39	2.44	2.51	0.2%
Mexico and Chile	2.30	2.38	2.36	2.50	2.67	2.87	0.9%
OECD Europe[b]	13.83	13.70	13.57	13.65	13.79	13.98	0.0%
Japan	4.14	3.91	3.75	3.66	3.56	3.40	−0.8%
South Korea	2.38	2.41	2.42	2.44	2.48	2.55	0.3%
Australia and New Zealand	1.28	1.35	1.39	1.41	1.45	1.53	0.7%
Total OECD consumption	**46.03**	**46.56**	**46.08**	**45.93**	**46.44**	**47.35**	**0.1%**
Non-OECD							
Russia	3.35	3.65	3.79	3.75	3.73	3.59	0.3%
Other Europe and Eurasia[c]	2.07	2.18	2.34	2.43	2.48	2.53	0.8%
China	11.18	12.71	13.81	14.81	15.65	16.36	1.5%
India	3.97	4.54	5.19	5.94	6.97	8.26	3.0%
Other Asia[d]	8.15	9.40	10.35	11.42	12.73	14.29	2.3%
Middle East	8.29	9.96	10.42	11.28	12.31	13.23	1.9%
Africa	3.86	4.54	5.06	5.50	6.08	6.93	2.4%
Brazil	3.15	3.41	3.74	4.06	4.39	4.71	1.6%
Other Central and South America	3.85	4.11	4.28	4.41	4.60	4.89	1.0%
Total Non-OECD consumption	**47.87**	**54.49**	**58.99**	**63.60**	**68.93**	**74.79**	**1.8%**
Total liquids consumption	**93.90**	**101.05**	**105.06**	**109.52**	**115.37**	**122.14**	**1.1%**

[a]Estimated consumption. Includes both OPEC and non-OPEC consumers in the regional breakdown.
[b]OECD Europe = Austria, Belgium, Czech Republic, Denmark, Estonia, Finland, France, Germany, Greece, Hungary, Iceland, Ireland, Israel, Italy, Luxembourg, the Netherlands, Norway, Poland, Portugal, Slovakia, Slovenia, Spain, Sweden, Switzerland, Turkey, and the United Kingdom.
[c]Other Europe and Eurasia = Albania, Armenia, Azerbaijan, Belarus, Bosnia and Herzegovina, Bulgaria, Croatia, Georgia, Kazakhstan, Kosovo, Kyrgyzstan, Latvia, Lithuania, Macedonia, Malta, Moldova, Montenegro, Romania, Serbia, Tajikistan, Turkmenistan, Ukraine, and Uzbekistan.
[d]Other Asia = Afghanistan, Bangladesh, Bhutan, Brunei, Cambodia (Kampuchea), Fiji, French Polynesia, Guam, Hong Kong, India (for production), Indonesia, Kiribati, Laos, Malaysia, Macau, Maldives, Mongolia, Myanmar (Burma), Nauru, Nepal, New Caledonia Niue, North Korea, Pakistan, Papua New Guinea, Philippines, Samoa, Singapore, Solomon Islands, Sri Lanka, Taiwan, Thailand, Tonga, Vanuatu, and Vietnam.
OECD = Organization for Economic Cooperation and Development.
Note: Totals may not equal sum of components due to independent rounding.

SOURCE: Adapted from "Table 21. International Petroleum and Other Liquids Supply, Disposition, and Prices," in *Annual Energy Outlook 2016 Early Release*, U.S. Energy Information Administration, May 2016, https://www.eia.gov/forecasts/aeo/excel/aeotab_21.xlsx (accessed August 12, 2016)

FOREIGN UNREST. Wars and other types of political unrest in oil-producing nations add volatility to petroleum prices, which fluctuate—sometimes dramatically—depending on the situation at the time. In *Energy Supply Security: Emergency Response of IEA Countries* (2014, https://www.iea.org/publications/freepublications/publication/ENERGYSUPPLYSECURITY2014.pdf), the IEA describes events that have occurred since the last half of the 20th century that have caused major disruptions in the world's oil supply. Most of the events were wars or other violent upheavals in the Middle East, including the war in Iraq in 2003 and a revolution in Libya in 2011.

FOREIGN PRICE MANIPULATION. Some top oil-producing countries have used their market power to manipulate oil prices upward for their own economic and political benefit. They do this by limiting the amount of oil they produce and/or export. Diminished supply (unless accompanied by diminished demand) increases the prices that buyers must pay. As described earlier, OPEC members and other oil-producing countries used their collective clout during the oil embargo of the 1970s.

At other times, OPEC has used production quotas to put upward pressure on prices. This approach, however, sometimes backfires. For example, high oil prices during the late 1970s to the mid-1980s encouraged conservation, which reduced demand for oil and led to a sharp decline in oil prices. As a result of the decreased demand for oil and lower prices, OPEC lost some of its ability to control its members and, consequently, prices. In addition, OPEC has faced increased competition since the 1970s from nonmember nations, such as Canada, Mexico, and Russia, that have expanded their oil production activities. Nevertheless, OPEC actions can still influence the worldwide petroleum market and the U.S. market. According to the EIA, in *Monthly Energy Review: July 2016*, the United States obtained 30.8% of its imported oil from OPEC in 2015.

GOVERNMENT INTERVENTION. U.S. government actions also affect oil pricing. Taxes push oil prices upward. For example, as noted earlier, taxes accounted on average for 20% of the cost of each gallon of gasoline sold in July 2016. Other government actions push oil

TABLE 2.8

Prices for crude oil and petroleum products, 1st quarter 2015–2nd quarter 2016

	2015				2016	
	1st	2nd	3rd	4th	1st	2nd
Crude oil (dollars per barrel)						
West Texas intermediate spot average	48.48	57.85	46.55	41.94	33.35	45.46
Brent spot average	53.91	61.65	50.43	43.55	33.89	45.57
U.S. imported average	46.38	56.07	45.59	37.88	28.83	41.21
U.S. refiner average acquisition cost	47.94	57.46	47.68	40.48	30.84	43.10
U.S. liquid fuels (cents per gallon)						
Refiner prices for resale						
Gasoline	159	201	184	145	119	158
Diesel fuel	176	189	161	141	109	140
Heating oil	178	180	151	129	99	124
Refiner prices to end users						
Jet fuel	172	186	156	138	107	133
No. 6 residual fuel oil[a]	137	154	123	101	69	89
Retail prices including taxes						
Gasoline regular grade[b]	227	267	260	216	190	225
Gasoline all grades[b]	236	275	269	226	200	235
On-highway diesel fuel	292	285	263	243	208	230
Heating oil	288	276	247	224	195	206

[a]Average for all sulfur contents.
[b]Average self-service cash price.
[c]Includes fuel oils No. 4, No. 5, No. 6, and topped crude.
Notes: Prices exclude taxes unless otherwise noted. Prices are not adjusted for inflation.

SOURCE: Adapted from "Table 2. Energy Prices," in *Short-Term Energy Outlook (STEO)*, U.S. Energy Information Administration, August 2016, http://www.eia.gov/forecasts/steo/pdf/steo_full.pdf (accessed August 13, 2016)

prices downward, mainly financial incentives, such as tax breaks and subsidies, which encourage domestic oil (and natural gas) production. As is shown in Figure 1.14 in Chapter 1, the fossil fuel industry as a whole has long enjoyed these kinds of incentives, which totaled around $4.8 billion in 2015. (See Table 1.6 in Chapter 1.)

The oil industry also benefits from liability limits on oil spills. Quinn Bowman explains in "Oil Spill Liability a Complicated Legal Web" (PBS.org, June 7, 2010) that the Oil Pollution Act, as amended in 1990, limited to $75 million the damages that a responsible party had to pay to "make up for lost economic activity, lost tax revenue and damage to natural resources as a result of an oil spill" from an offshore facility. (It should be noted that the costs of "cleaning up and containing" spilled oil are separate costs and have no limit.) In December 2014 the Bureau of Ocean Energy Management (http://www.boem.gov/press12112014/) raised the damages limit to $134 million. Bowman indicates that the damages limit does not apply if the responsible party is found to have committed "gross negligence, willful misconduct or a failure to comply with operating or safety regulations."

In addition, federal law limits liability amounts for tankers that spill oil in U.S. waters. In "Limits of Liability" (September 12, 2016, http://www.uscg.mil/npfc/Response/RPs/limits_of_liability.asp), the U.S. Coast Guard notes that the limits vary based on the type and tonnage of the vessels involved.

Critics suggest that all the oil spill liability limits are too low given the enormous economic and ecological consequences that a large oil spill can cause. Other provisions, however, are in place to help pay for damages from an oil spill. One is the Oil Spill Liability Trust Fund, which was created by Congress in 1986. According to the Coast Guard, in "The Oil Spill Liability Trust Fund (OSLTF)" (September 12, 2016, http://www.uscg.mil/npfc/About_NPFC/osltf.asp), the fund contained more than $1 billion in 2016. Over the decades oil industry companies have sometimes been required to pay (depending on changing federal laws) into the fund via taxes on oil products. As of 2016, the tax was $0.08 per barrel of oil produced domestically or imported into the United States. The rate is scheduled to increase to $0.09 per barrel in 2017.

ENVIRONMENTAL ISSUES

Environmental concerns related to the oil industry primarily involve the extraction, transport, refining, and combustion stages. Extraction impacts the environment via invasive drilling and mining to find and remove oil deposits. As noted earlier, fracking is worrisome because oil and natural gas could be accidentally introduced into freshwater aquifers. Water impacts and other environmental concerns associated with fracking are addressed by the U.S. Environmental Protection Agency (EPA) in *Assessment of the Potential Impacts of Hydraulic*

Crude oil refiner acquisition costs, selected years 1965–2015

[Dollars per barrel]

	Refiner acquisition cost		
	Domestic	**Imported**	**Composite**
1965 Average	NA	NA	NA
1970 Average	3.46[E]	2.96[E]	3.40[E]
1975 Average	8.39	13.93	10.38
1980 Average	24.23	33.89	28.07
1985 Average	26.66	26.99	26.75
1990 Average	22.59	21.76	22.22
1995 Average	17.33	17.14	17.23
2000 Average	29.11	27.70	28.26
2001 Average	24.33	22.00	22.95
2002 Average	24.65	23.71	24.10
2003 Average	29.82	27.71	28.53
2004 Average	38.97	35.90	36.98
2005 Average	52.94	48.86	50.24
2006 Average	62.62	59.02	60.24
2007 Average	69.65	67.04	67.94
2008 Average	98.47	92.77	94.74
2009 Average	59.49	59.17	59.29
2010 Average	78.01	75.86	76.69
2011 Average	100.71	102.63	101.87
2012 Average	100.72	101.09	100.93
2013 Average	102.91	98.11	100.49
2014 Average	94.05	89.56	92.02
2015 Average	49.94	46.38	48.39

E = Estimate.
Note: Prices are in nominal dollars; they are not adjusted for inflation. Annual averages are the averages of the monthly prices, weighted by volume. Geographic coverage is the 50 states, the District of Columbia, Puerto Rico, the Virgin Islands, and all U.S. Territories and Possessions.

SOURCE: Adapted from "Table 9.1. Crude Oil Price Summary (Dollars per Barrel)," in *Monthly Energy Review: July 2016*, U.S. Energy Information Administration, July 2016, http://www.eia.gov/totalenergy/data/monthly/pdf/mer.pdf (accessed August 7, 2016)

Fracturing for Oil and Gas on Drinking Water Resources (June 2015, http://ofmpub.epa.gov/eims/eimscomm .getfile?p_download_id=523540). For example, the EPA indicates that "very small amounts of seismic energy [are] generated during subsurface fracturing." Greater seismic events are believed to be triggered by the use of deep injection wells for the disposal of the massive amounts of wastewater that are produced during oil and natural gas extraction. On September 3, 2016, Oklahoma was shaken by a magnitude 5.8 earthquake, the strongest tremor in state history. In "New Fault Line Discovered after 5.8 Oklahoma Earthquake" (Kansas.com, September 13, 2016), Sean Murphy notes that state and federal regulators ordered dozens of disposal wells in Oklahoma to cease operating after the quake. According to the U.S. Geological Survey, in "Myths and Misconceptions" (April 6, 2016, http://earthquake.usgs.gov/research/induced/ myths.php), most oil and natural gas industry wastewater results from conventional extraction methods.

Crude oil is transported daily across the world's oceans and through a near-global network of pipelines. Although large spills during drilling and transport are relatively rare, when they do occur they have devastating environmental and economic effects. Oil refining and the combustion of petroleum products have air quality impacts due to the release of contaminants such as carbon monoxide, nitrogen dioxide, sulfur dioxide, volatile organic compounds, and particulate matter. In addition, the combustion of oil, a carbon-rich fossil fuel, contributes to global warming and related climate change.

Oil Spills

In recent decades, the modern oil industry has experienced some environmental failures with serious consequences. Two of the most well-known events are the *Exxon Valdez* spill of 1989 and the BP spill in the Gulf of Mexico in 2010.

On March 24, 1989, the oil tanker *Exxon Valdez* hit a reef in Alaska and spilled 11 million gallons (41.6 million L) of crude oil into the waters of Prince William Sound. The spill was an environmental disaster for a formerly pristine area. Exxon was originally levied a $5 billion fine for damages, but that amount was later reduced by the U.S. Supreme Court to about $500 million.

The BP spill happened after an offshore oil platform located 40 miles (64 km) from the Louisiana coast exploded on April 20, 2010, and killed 11 workers. Engineers were unable to quickly cap the well on the ocean floor, which was about 1 mile (1.6 km) under the water's surface. Over a period of nearly three months millions of barrels of crude oil gushed into the Gulf, damaging the aquatic ecosystem and harming the area's fisheries and tourism industries. In November 2012 the U.S. government imposed a $4 billion fine on BP for damages. In addition, two BP oil rig supervisors were charged with manslaughter. The company and its business partners in the oil rig venture still faced private court cases and potentially billions of dollars more in damages. As of September 2016, the spill was considered to be the worst oil spill in U.S. history.

TABLE 2.10

Retail motor gasoline and highway diesel fuel prices, selected years 1950–2015 and January–June 2016

[Dollars[a] per gallon, including taxes]

| | Platt's / Bureau of Labor Statistics data | | | | U.S. Energy Information Administration data | | | |
| | Motor gasoline by grade | | | | Regular motor gasoline by area type | | | |
	Leaded regular	Unleaded regular	Unleaded premium[b]	All grades[c]	Conventional gasoline areas[d]	Reformulated gasoline areas[e]	All areas	On-highway diesel fuel
1950 Average	0.268	NA	NA	NA	—	—	—	—
1955 Average	0.291	NA	NA	NA	—	—	—	—
1960 Average	0.311	NA	NA	NA	—	—	—	—
1965 Average	0.312	NA	NA	NA	—	—	—	—
1970 Average	0.357	NA	NA	NA	—	—	—	—
1975 Average	0.567	NA	NA	NA	—	—	—	—
1980 Average	1.191	1.245	NA	1.221	—	—	—	—
1985 Average	1.115	1.202	1.340	1.196	—	—	—	—
1990 Average	1.149	1.164	1.349	1.217	NA	NA	NA	NA
1995 Average	—	1.147	1.336	1.205	1.103	1.163	1.111	1.109
2000 Average	—	1.510	1.693	1.563	1.462	1.543	1.484	1.491
2001 Average	—	1.461	1.657	1.531	1.384	1.498	1.420	1.401
2002 Average	—	1.358	1.556	1.441	1.313	1.408	1.345	1.319
2003 Average	—	1.591	1.777	1.638	1.516	1.655	1.561	1.509
2004 Average	—	1.880	2.068	1.923	1.812	1.937	1.852	1.810
2005 Average	—	2.295	2.491	2.338	2.240	2.335	2.270	2.402
2006 Average	—	2.589	2.805	2.635	2.533	2.654	2.572	2.705
2007 Average	—	2.801	3.033	2.849	2.767	2.857	2.796	2.885
2008 Average	—	3.266	3.519	3.317	3.213	3.314	3.246	3.803
2009 Average	—	2.350	2.607	2.401	2.315	2.433	2.353	2.467
2010 Average	—	2.788	3.047	2.836	2.742	2.864	2.782	2.992
2011 Average	—	3.527	3.792	3.577	3.476	3.616	3.521	3.840
2012 Average	—	3.644	3.922	3.695	3.552	3.757	3.618	3.968
2013 Average	—	3.526	3.843	3.584	3.443	3.635	3.505	3.922
2014 Average	—	3.367	3.713	3.425	3.299	3.481	3.358	3.825
2015 Average	—	2.448	2.866	2.510	2.334	2.629	2.429	2.707
2016 January	—	1.967	2.455	2.034	1.843	2.170	1.949	2.143
February	—	1.767	2.248	1.833	1.681	1.936	1.764	1.998
March	—	1.958	2.411	2.021	1.895	2.124	1.969	2.090
April	—	2.134	2.585	2.196	2.027	2.293	2.113	2.152
May	—	2.264	2.710	2.324	2.199	2.413	2.268	2.315
June	—	2.363	2.807	2.422	2.303	2.497	2.366	2.423
July	—	2.225	2.702	2.287	2.157	2.411	2.239	2.405
August	—	2.155	2.629	2.218	2.119	2.300	2.178	2.351

[a]Prices are not adjusted for inflation.
[b]The 1981 average (available in Web file) is based on September through December data only.
[c]Also includes grades of motor gasoline not shown separately.
[d]Any area that does not require the sale of reformulated gasoline.
[e]"Reformulated Gasoline Areas" are ozone nonattainment areas designated by the U.S. Environmental Protection Agency that require the use of reformulated gasoline (RFG). Areas are reclassified each time a shift in or out of an RFG program occurs due to federal or state regulations.
NA = Not available. — = Not applicable.
Notes: Geographic coverage: for columns 1–4, current coverage is 85 urban areas; for columns 5–7, coverage is the 50 states and the District of Columbia; for column 8, coverage is the 48 contiguous states and the District of Columbia.

SOURCE: Adapted from "Table 9.4 Retail Motor Gasoline and On-Highway Diesel Fuel Prices (Dollars per Gallon, Including Taxes)," in *Monthly Energy Review: July 2016*, U.S. Energy Information Administration, July 2016, http://www.eia.gov/totalenergy/data/monthly/pdf/mer.pdf (accessed August 7, 2016)

CHAPTER 3
NATURAL GAS

In 1821 William A. Hart, a gunsmith, drilled a well down 27 feet (8 m) and found a reservoir of natural gas in Fredonia, New York. This was the first successful modern natural gas well and resulted in the formation of the first U.S. natural gas company. Natural gas soon became popular as a fuel source for city street lighting, but by the start of the 20th century it had been largely supplanted in this capacity by electricity. Following World War II (1939–1945), the United States constructed a massive pipeline network to carry natural gas to individual homes and businesses. The fuel is available in large amounts domestically at low prices and is widely used in industrial applications and for producing electricity.

UNDERSTANDING NATURAL GAS

The term *natural gas* refers to a gaseous mixture of hydrocarbon compounds, mainly methane. This mixture is found naturally in certain geological formations and can be manufactured in relatively small quantities.

Naturally derived natural gas falls into two categories, depending on its means of formation. Thermogenic natural gas results from the actions of pressure and heat over millions of years on prehistoric aquatic microorganisms. Thus, it is a fossil fuel. Biogenic natural gas results from the decomposition of organic (carbon-containing) matter by bacteria. This process can happen relatively quickly and is not limited to underground spaces; in fact, biogenic natural gas forms in landfills that contain organic garbage. When it is found underground, biogenic natural gas is typically at much shallower depths than thermogenic natural gas.

Thermogenic Natural Gas

Thermogenic natural gas can be further categorized based on its geological source as conventional gas, coal-bed methane, shale gas, or tight sand gas. (See Figure 3.1.)

CONVENTIONAL NATURAL GAS. Conventional natural gas, like crude oil, formed from prehistoric microscopic organisms that were converted to hydrocarbons deep underground after millions of years of being exposed to intense pressures and high temperatures. The gas was baked and squeezed more intensely than the crude oil. Thus, the hydrocarbons in natural gas are smaller and lighter than those found in crude oil and are in a gaseous state. Methane, ethane, and propane are the primary constituents of natural gas, with methane making up the vast majority of the total. Once formed, crude oil and natural gas migrated away from their source rocks and toward the surface until they were either trapped beneath a nonporous rock formation (the seal shown in Figure 3.1) or seeped out into the open air. Conventional natural gas trapped above oil pools is called associated gas, while conventional natural gas found by itself is called non-associated gas.

COAL-BED METHANE. Coal-bed methane is methane gas that naturally occurs as coal is formed. Coal is a dense solid fossil fuel that contains heavy hydrocarbons. In "Natural Gas: Definitions, Sources and Explanatory Notes" (2016, http://www.eia.gov/dnav/ng/TblDefs/ng_prod_coal bed_tbldef2.asp), the U.S. Energy Information Administration (EIA) within the U.S. Department of Energy notes that coal-bed methane is trapped within the coal microstructure but can be liberated and brought to the surface.

SHALE GAS. Shale is a dark dense type of sedimentary rock that is made up of fine tightly packed grains. Shale that contains high concentrations of organic matter is sometimes called black shale. Some shale formations contain significant accumulations of natural gas. The natural gas originally formed within the shale and became trapped in its pores. The gas is typically liberated by a process called hydraulic fracturing (fracking). As shown in Figure 3.2, a vertical well is drilled down into a shale formation and then continues horizontally across the formation. The horizontal portion contains numerous

FIGURE 3.1

Schematic geology of natural gas resources

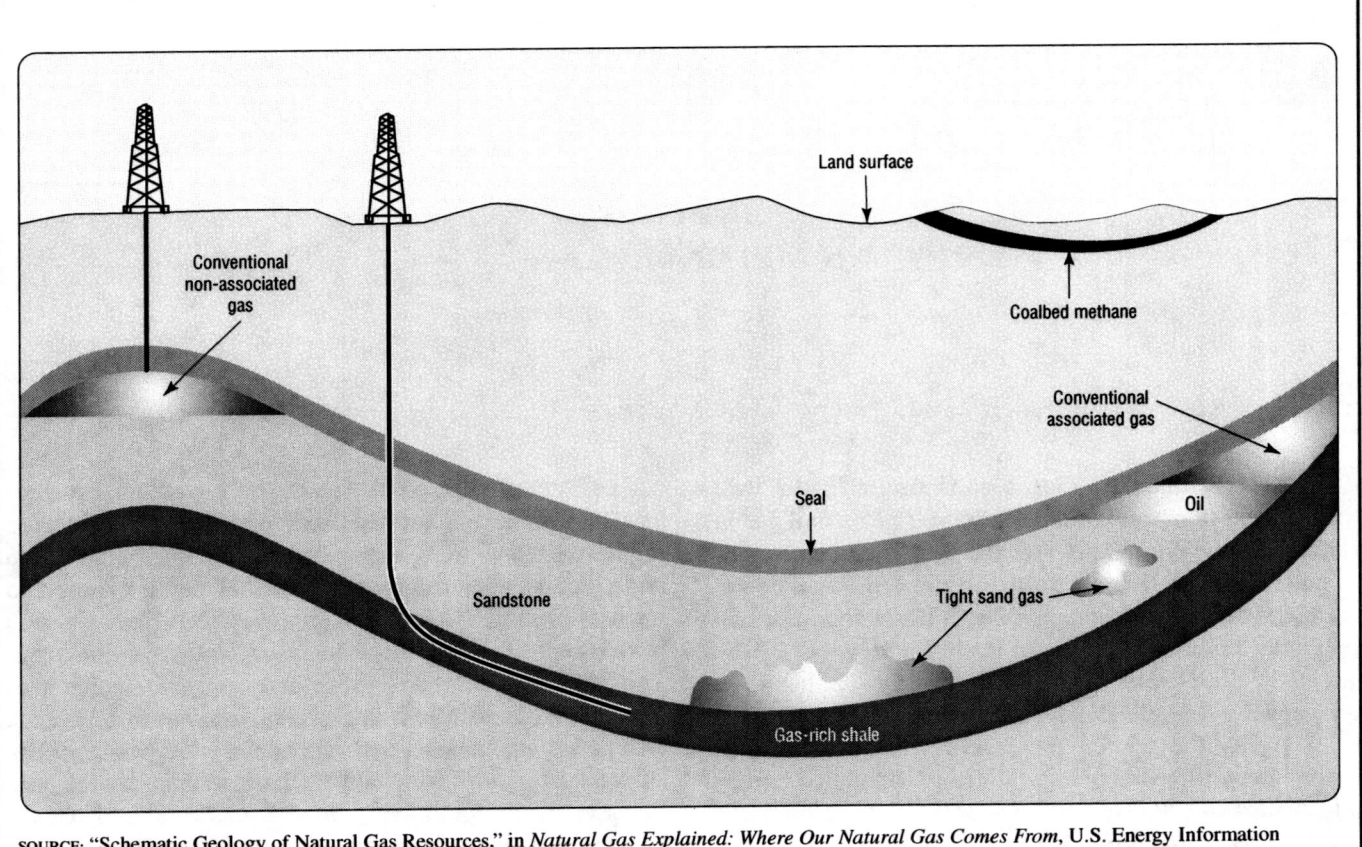

Land surface

Coalbed methane

Conventional
non-associated
gas

Conventional
associated gas

Seal

Oil

Sandstone

Tight sand gas

Gas-rich shale

SOURCE: "Schematic Geology of Natural Gas Resources," in *Natural Gas Explained: Where Our Natural Gas Comes From*, U.S. Energy Information Administration, June 26, 2012, http://www.eia.gov/energyexplained/images/charts/NatGasSchematic-large.jpg (accessed August 14, 2016)

small perforations. Water containing chemicals and tiny ceramic beads or other solids is pumped into the well under high pressure. As it blasts out of the perforations it creates fractures in the shale. The fractures are held open by the beads or other solids and allow trapped natural gas to seep into the well and flow to the surface.

TIGHT SAND GAS. The EIA defines in *Annual Energy Review 2011* (September 2012, http://www.eia.gov/total energy/data/annual/pdf/aer.pdf) tight sand gas as "natural gas produced from a non-shale formation with extremely low permeability." Tight sand gas is found in sandstone, a type of sedimentary rock that is made up of sand-sized particles. (See Figure 3.1.) Sandstone is more porous than shale, but still typically requires fracking to release the natural gas that is trapped within it. Tight sand gas, or tight gas, is believed to have originated from the same thermogenic processes that produced conventional gas.

Natural Gas Deposits

Like crude oil deposits, natural gas deposits are found only in certain geological formations. Regions and countries that are known to have large natural gas deposits include North America, Russia, the Middle East,

and northwestern Europe. Many of the earth's deposits are offshore (i.e., they lie beneath the oceans). Figure 2.2 and Figure 2.3 in Chapter 2 show the extent of offshore underground lands to which the United States claims exclusive rights to extract resources, such as crude oil and natural gas. Many U.S. natural gas deposits lie in the nation's outer continental shelf, the outermost reaches of the continental shelf that are under federal control.

Estimates of the amounts of natural gas deposits that have not yet been extracted are provided in Chapter 7, along with information about natural gas exploration and development activities.

Measuring Natural Gas

In the United States natural gas volumes are measured in cubic feet. Because a cubic foot is a relatively small unit of measure, natural gas data are often presented in units of billion cubic feet (bcf) or trillion cubic feet (tcf). In countries that rely on the metric system, the cubic meter is the preferred unit for measuring natural gas volumes. Thus, natural gas data are typically expressed in units of billion cubic meters (bcm) or trillion cubic meters (tcm).

FIGURE 3.2

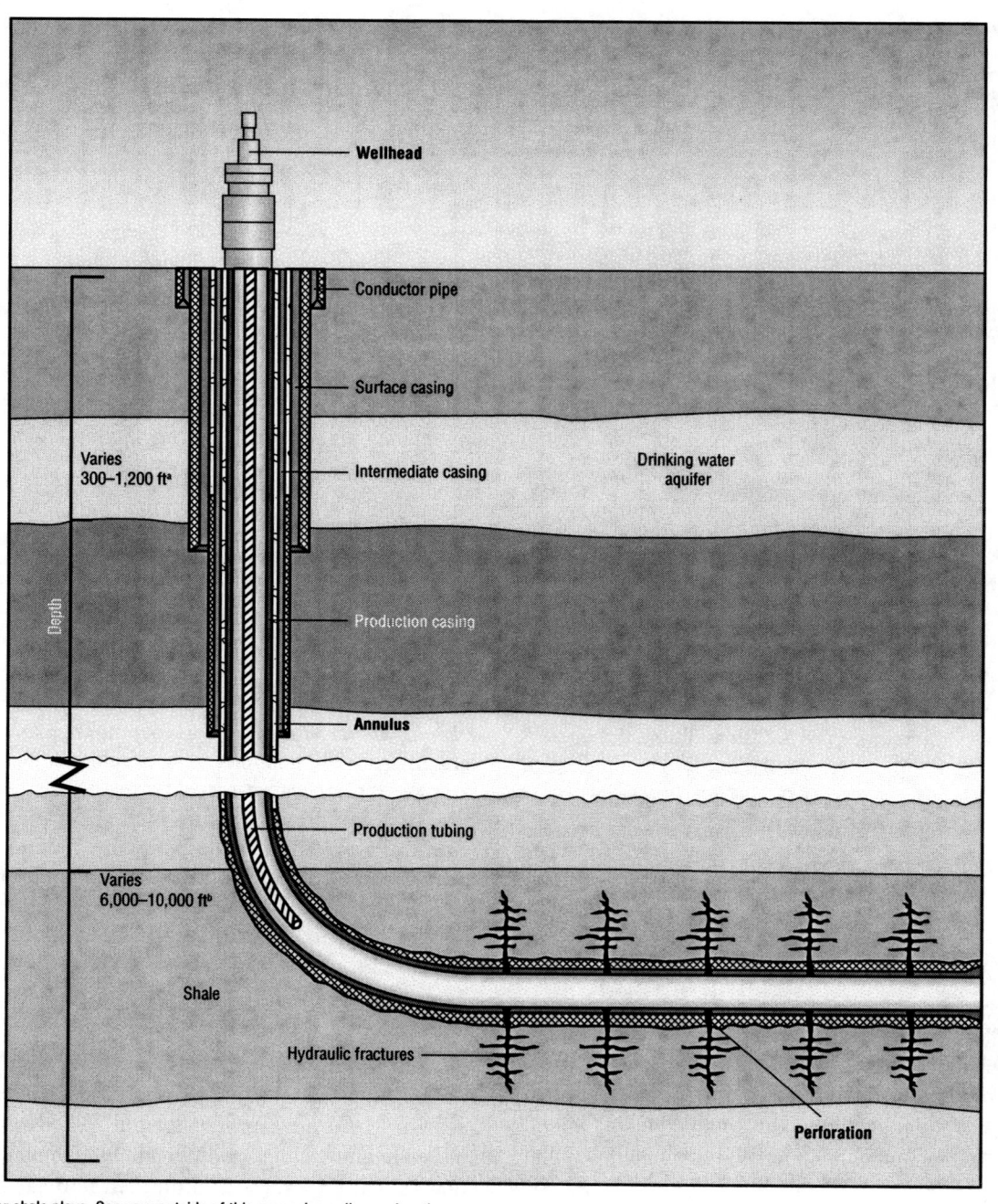

Typical configuration for a horizontally drilled, hydraulically fractured shale gas well

⊠ Cement   ⊡ Drilling mud

Wellhead

Conductor pipe

Surface casing

Varies
300–1,200 ft[a]

Intermediate casing

Drinking water
aquifer

Depth

Production casing

Annulus

Production tubing

Varies
6,000–10,000 ft[b]

Shale

Hydraulic fractures

Perforation

[a]For several major shale plays. Can vary outside of this range depending on location.
[b]Typically for the Marcellus shale play. Depths will vary based on local geology.
Notes: Illustration not to scale. ft = feet.

SOURCE: C. Clark et al., "Figure 1. Typical Configuration for a Horizontally Drilled, Hydraulically Fractured Shale Gas Well," in *Hydraulic Fracturing and Shale Gas Production: Technology, Impacts, and Regulations*, U.S. Department of Energy, Argonne National Laboratory, April 2013, http://www.afdc.energy.gov/uploads/publication/anl_hydraulic_fracturing.pdf (accessed August 12, 2016)

NATURAL GAS EXTRACTION

In many cases natural gas is extracted like crude oil, that is, via deeply drilled wells. The EIA notes in *Monthly Energy Review: July 2016* (July 2016, http://www.eia.gov/totalenergy/data/monthly/archive/00351607.pdf) that an average of 226 rotary wells were in operation in 2015

FIGURE 3.3

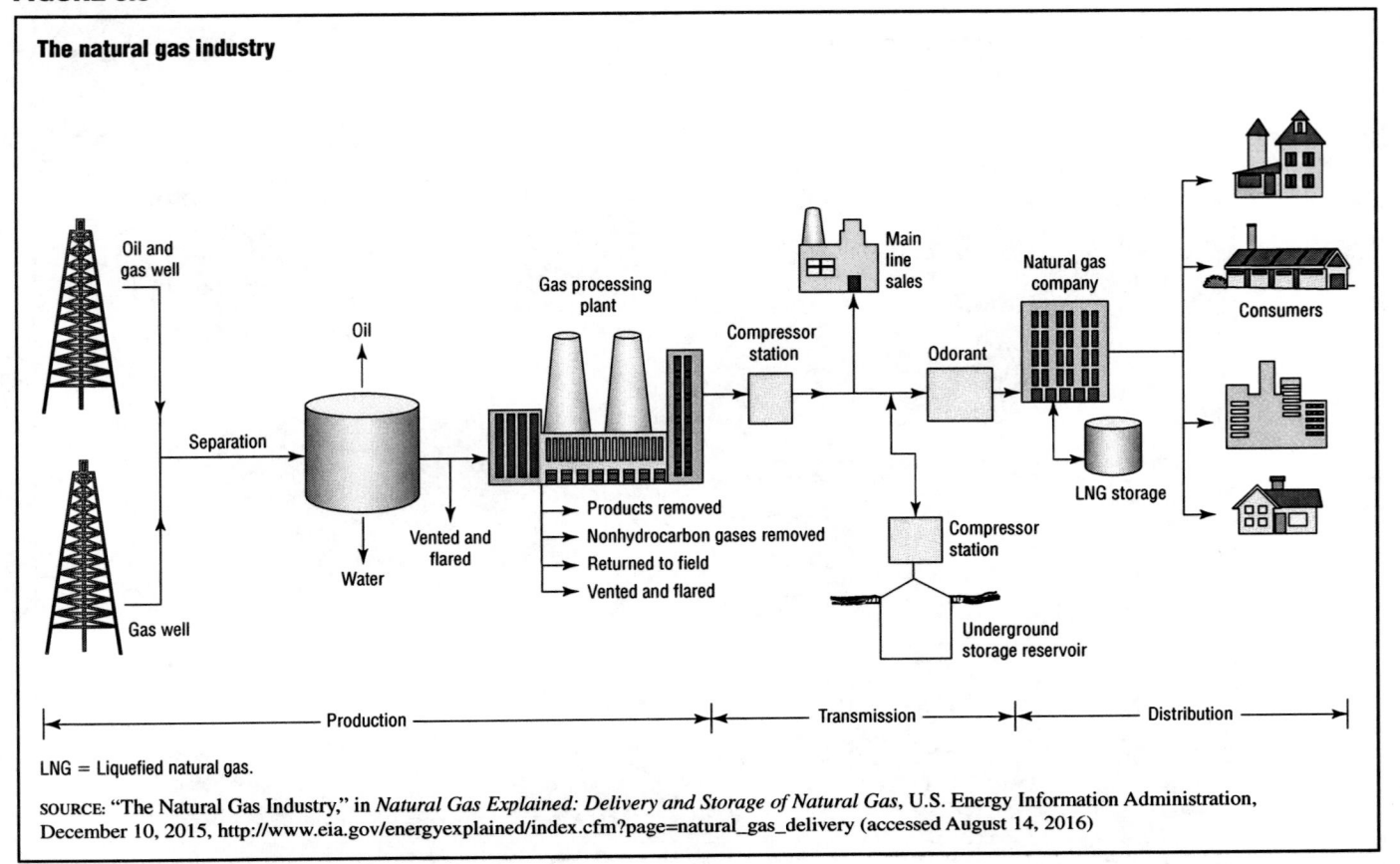

The natural gas industry

LNG = Liquefied natural gas.

SOURCE: "The Natural Gas Industry," in *Natural Gas Explained: Delivery and Storage of Natural Gas*, U.S. Energy Information Administration, December 10, 2015, http://www.eia.gov/energyexplained/index.cfm?page=natural_gas_delivery (accessed August 14, 2016)

solely for natural gas production. Natural gas is also extracted via fracking, as shown in Figure 3.2. In addition, the agency indicates that some oil wells "productively encounter both crude oil and natural gas." (See Figure 3.3.) The number of total wells in operation fluctuates from year to year because new wells are opened and old wells are closed. Weather and economic conditions also affect well operations.

PROCESSING AND TRANSPORTING NATURAL GAS

Most natural gas that is extracted from deep underground is considered "wet" because it contains water vapor and hydrocarbons that easily liquefy at the cooler temperatures found above ground. The hydrocarbon liquids include lease condensate and natural gas plant liquids (NGPL). Lease condensate is a liquid mix of heavy hydrocarbons that are recovered during natural gas processing at a lease, or field separation, facility. NGPL are a mixture of compounds such as propane and butane that are recovered as liquids at facilities later in the processing stage.

Consumer-grade natural gas is "dry," which means that it has been processed to remove water vapor, nonhydrocarbon gases (such as helium and nitrogen), and lease condensate and NGPL. (See Figure 3.3.) The dry gas flows into a compressor station. In *Natural Gas*

Compressor Stations on the Interstate Pipeline Network: Developments since 1996 (November 2007, http://www.eia.gov/pub/oil_gas/natural_gas/analysis_publications/ngcompressor/ngcompressor.pdf), the EIA states "the purpose of a compressor station is to boost the pressure in a natural gas pipeline and move the natural gas further downstream." There are more than a thousand compressor stations located along the nation's massive natural gas pipeline network. In addition, the network includes multiple underground storage reservoirs.

Underground Storage

Because of seasonal, daily, and even hourly changes in demand, substantial natural gas storage facilities have been created. Many are depleted natural gas reservoirs that are located near transmission lines and high-consumption areas, such as major cities. Gas is injected into storage when the produced supply exceeds demand, and withdrawn from storage when it is needed. Table 3.1 shows the amount of natural gas that was in underground storage between 1955 and 2015. It consisted of base gas (permanently stored gas needed to maintain the proper pressure in the storage area) and working gas (gas that can be released from storage and used). At year-end 2015, 8 tcf (227.7 bcm) was in storage, including 4.4 tcf (123.5 bcm) of base gas and 3.7 tcf (104.1 bcm) of working gas.

TABLE 3.1

Natural gas in underground storage, selected years 1955–2015

[Volumes in billion cubic feet]

	Natural gas in underground storage, end of period		
	Base gas	Working gas	Total[a]
1955 Total	863	505	1,368
1960 Total	NA	NA	2,184
1965 Total	1,848	1,242	3,090
1970 Total	2,326	1,678	4,004
1975 Total	3,162	2,212	5,374
1980 Total	3,642	2,655	6,297
1985 Total	3,842	2,607	6,448
1990 Total	3,868	3,068	6,936
1995 Total	4,349	2,153	6,503
2000 Total	4,352	1,719	6,071
2001 Total	4,301	2,904	7,204
2002 Total	4,340	2,375	6,715
2003 Total	4,303	2,563	6,866
2004 Total	4,201	2,696	6,897
2005 Total	4,200	2,635	6,835
2006 Total	4,211	3,070	7,281
2007 Total	4,234	2,879	7,113
2008 Total	4,232	2,840	7,073
2009 Total	4,277	3,130	7,407
2010 Total	4,301	3,111	7,412
2011 Total	4,302	3,462	7,764
2012 Total	4,372	3,413	7,785
2013 Total	4,365	2,890	7,255
2014 Total	4,365	3,141	7,506
2015 Total	4,363	3,677	8,040

NA = Not applicable.

SOURCE: Adapted from "Table 4.4. Natural Gas in Underground Storage (Volumes in Billion Cubic Feet)," in *Monthly Energy Review: July 2016*, U.S. Energy Information Administration, July 2016, http://www.eia.gov/totalenergy/data/monthly/pdf/mer.pdf (accessed August 7, 2016)

According to the EIA, in "Underground Natural Gas Storage Capacity" (August 31, 2016, http://www.eia.gov/dnav/ng/ng_stor_cap_dcu_NUS_m.htm), there were 415 storage fields in the U.S. natural gas pipeline network as of June 2016, with a total capacity of 9.2 tcf (261.4 bcm).

Facilitating Natural Gas Transport and Usage

The physical state of natural gas is sometimes changed to facilitate its transport and usage. For example, a volume of natural gas can be compressed under high pressure so that it takes up less space. The EIA (2016, http://www.eia.gov/tools/glossary/index.cfm?id=C) indicates that natural gas can be compressed to a pressure at or above 2,900 to 3,600 pounds per square inch (203.9 to 253.1 kg per square cm) and stored in "high-pressure containers." Compressed natural gas (CNG) is used as a fuel for vehicles that burn natural gas.

Natural gas can also be liquefied by cooling it to a very cold temperature. In "Natural Gas Explained: Liquefied Natural Gas" (May 10, 2016, http://www.eia.gov/energyexplained/index.cfm?page=natural_gas_lng), the EIA explains that a liquefied volume of natural gas takes up far less space than the same volume of natural gas in a gaseous state. Liquefied natural gas (LNG) can be moved long distances, such as across the oceans, for importation and exportation. Liquefaction is an energy-intensive process in that a lot of energy is required to cool the natural gas to the liquefaction temperature, which is around −260 degrees Fahrenheit (−162 degrees Celsius). LNG can be transported or stored in tanks and returned to a gaseous state, as needed, by heating it above the liquefaction temperature.

Another storage alternative for natural gas involves the use of porous carbon materials. The gas can be tightly packed into the numerous tiny pores because the gas molecules adsorb (adhere in thin compressed layers) to the pore walls. As of 2016, adsorbed natural gas containers were being developed for commercial use by several companies, including Energtek (http://energtek.com/adsorbed-natural-gas) and United Technologies Research Center in partnership with Adsorbed Natural Gas Products, Inc. (http://www.utrc.utc.com/20160204_angp.html).

Transmission and Distribution

A vast network of natural gas pipelines crisscrosses the mainland United States. The EIA provides in "About U.S. Natural Gas Pipelines" (2016, http://www.eia.gov/pub/oil_gas/natural_gas/analysis_publications/ngpipeline/index.html) a map of this network. The agency also notes that the natural gas in this 305,000-mile (491,000-km) system generally flows northeastward, primarily from Texas and Louisiana, the two major gas-producing states, and from Oklahoma and New Mexico. It also flows west to California.

In its original state, natural gas is odorless. An odorant is added to it before it is sold to consumers. (See Figure 3.3.) The odorant, which smells like rotten eggs, helps people notice when natural gas is leaking around their homes or businesses so they can take action quickly by cutting off the gas flow. This safety precaution is necessary because natural gas is highly flammable and can cause tremendous explosions when ignited.

DOMESTIC WITHDRAWALS AND PRODUCTION

Table 3.2 shows natural gas gross withdrawals and production data between 1950 and 2015. The withdrawals include gas from natural gas, crude oil, coal bed, and shale gas wells. They totaled 32.9 tcf (931.5 bcm) in 2015 and provided 27 tcf (765.4 bcm) of dry gas for consumers. In addition, 1.7 tcf (48.7 bcm) of NGPL was produced during natural gas processing.

Overall, dry gas production climbed dramatically from 1949 through the early 1970s and then fell through the mid-1980s. (See Figure 3.4.) It then rose at a moderate rate through the beginning of the 21st century before sharply increasing. The uptick is due almost entirely to shale gas, which is being extracted from the same basins that provide the tight oil, as is described in Chapter 2. Figure 2.8 in Chapter 2 shows a map of the seven basins

TABLE 3.2

Natural gas withdrawals, production, trade, and consumption, selected years 1950–2015

[Billion cubic feet]

	Gross withdrawals[a]	Marketed production (wet)[b]	NGPL production[c]	Dry gas production[d]	Supplemental gaseous fuels	Trade			Net storage withdrawals[e]	Balancing item[f]	Consumption
						Imports	Exports	Net imports			
1950 Total	8,480	6,282[g]	260	6,022[g]	NA	0	26	−26	−54	−175	5,767
1955 Total	11,720	9,405[g]	377	9,029[g]	NA	11	31	−20	−68	−247	8,694
1960 Total	15,088	12,771[g]	543	12,228[g]	NA	156	11	144	−132	−274	11,967
1965 Total	17,963	16,040[g]	753	15,286[g]	NA	456	26	430	−118	−319	15,280
1970 Total	23,786	21,921[g]	906	21,014[g]	NA	821	70	751	−398	−228	21,139
1975 Total	21,104	20,109[g]	872	19,236[g]	NA	953	73	880	−344	−235	19,538
1980 Total	21,870	20,180	777	19,403	155	985	49	936	23	−640	19,877
1985 Total	19,607	17,270	816	16,454	126	950	55	894	235	−428	17,281
1990 Total	21,523	18,594	784	17,810	123	1,532	86	1,447	−513	307	19,174
1995 Total	23,744	19,506	908	18,599	110	2,841	154	2,687	415	396	22,207
2000 Total	24,174	20,198	1,016	19,182	90	3,782	244	3,538	829	−306	23,333
2001 Total	24,501	20,570	954	19,616	86	3,977	373	3,604	−1,166	99	22,239
2002 Total	23,941	19,885	957	18,928	68	4,015	516	3,499	467	65	23,027
2003 Total	24,119	19,974	876	19,099	68	3,944	680	3,264	−197	44	22,277
2004 Total	23,970	19,517	927	18,591	60	4,259	854	3,404	−114	461	22,403
2005 Total	23,457	18,927	876	18,051	64	4,341	729	3,612	52	236	22,014
2006 Total	23,535	19,410	906	18,504	66	4,186	724	3,462	−436	103	21,699
2007 Total	24,664	20,196	930	19,266	63	4,608	822	3,785	192	−203	23,104
2008 Total	25,636	21,112	953	20,159	61	3,984	963	3,021	34	2	23,277
2009 Total	26,057	21,648	1,024	20,624	65	3,751	1,072	2,679	−355	−103	22,910
2010 Total	26,816	22,382	1,066	21,316	65	3,741	1,137	2,604	−13	115	24,087
2011 Total	28,479	24,036	1,134	22,902	60	3,469	1,506	1,963	−354	−94	24,477
2012 Total	29,542	25,283	1,250	24,033	61	3,138	1,619	1,519	−9	−66	25,538
2013 Total	29,523	25,562	1,357	24,206	55	2,883	1,572	1,311	546	38	26,155
2014 Total	31,346	27,337	1,608	25,728	60	2,695	1,514	1,181	−253	−21	26,695
2015 Total	32,895[E]	28,752[E]	1,718	27,034[E]	60	2,718	1,784	935	−539	−14[R]	27,475[R]

[a]Gases withdrawn from natural gas, crude oil, coalbed, and shale gas wells. Includes natural gas, natural gas plant liquids, and nonhydrocarbon gases; but excludes lease condensate.
[b]Gross withdrawals minus repressuring, nonhydrocarbon gases removed, and vented and flared.
[c]Natural gas plant liquids (NGPL) production, gaseous equivalent. This data series was previously called "Extraction Loss."
[d]Marketed production (wet) minus NGPL production.
[e]Net withdrawals from underground storage. For 1980–2014, also includes net withdrawals of liquefied natural gas in above-ground tanks.
[f]Beginning in 1980, excludes transit shipments that cross the U.S.-Canada border (i.e., natural gas delivered to its destination via the other country).
[g]Through 1979, may include unknown quantities of nonhydrocarbon gases.
R = Revised. E = Estimate. NA = Not available.
Notes: Through 1964, all volumes are shown on a pressure base of 14.65 psia (pounds per square inch absolute) at 60° Fahrenheit; beginning in 1965, the pressure base is 14.73 psia at 60° Fahrenheit. Totals may not equal sum of components due to independent rounding. Geographic coverage is the 50 states and the District of Columbia (except Alaska, for which underground storage is excluded from "Net Storage Withdrawals" through 2012).

SOURCE: Adapted from "Table 4.1. Natural Gas Overview (Billion Cubic Feet)," in *Monthly Energy Review: July 2016*, U.S. Energy Information Administration, July 2016, http://www.eia.gov/totalenergy/data/monthly/pdf/mer.pdf (accessed August 7, 2016)

that accounted for 100% of domestic natural gas production growth between 2011 and 2014. The Marcellus, Permian, Haynesville, and Eagle Ford basins have been particularly productive. As shown in Figure 3.5, natural gas production from the Marcellus basin soared from less than 1 bcf/day (0.03 bcm/day) in 2007 to around 18 bcf/day (0.5 bcm/day) in 2016.

Figure 3.6 provides a breakdown of domestic production by source from 1990 to 2015 and a forecast through 2040. Half of the 27 tcf (765.4 bcm) produced in 2015 was from shale gas and tight oil plays. (Oil plays are groups of oil fields in similar geological environments.) Tight gas (also known as tight sand gas) made up 18% of the total, while gas from other onshore sources in the lower 48 states accounted for 24% of the total. Very small amounts of natural gas were obtained from Alaskan wells, coal beds, and offshore wells.

IMPORTS AND EXPORTS

As shown in Table 3.2, domestic dry gas production met or nearly met U.S. consumption through the mid-1980s; thus, little natural gas was imported. Thereafter, consumption began to outpace production, and the volume of imported natural gas increased as well. Natural gas imports peaked at 4.6 tcf (130.5 bcm) in 2007 before falling as the U.S. shale gas boom unfolded. In 2015 the United States imported 2.7 tcf (77 bcm) of natural gas and exported almost 1.8 tcf (50.5 bcm). Figure 3.4 shows dry production, consumption, and net imports (imports minus exports) between 1949 and 2015. During the first decade of the 21st century the United States dramatically narrowed the gap between its production and consumption of natural gas.

According to the EIA, in *Monthly Energy Review: July 2016*, Canada supplied 2.6 tcf (74.4 bcm), or 97% of the natural gas imported to the United States in

FIGURE 3.4

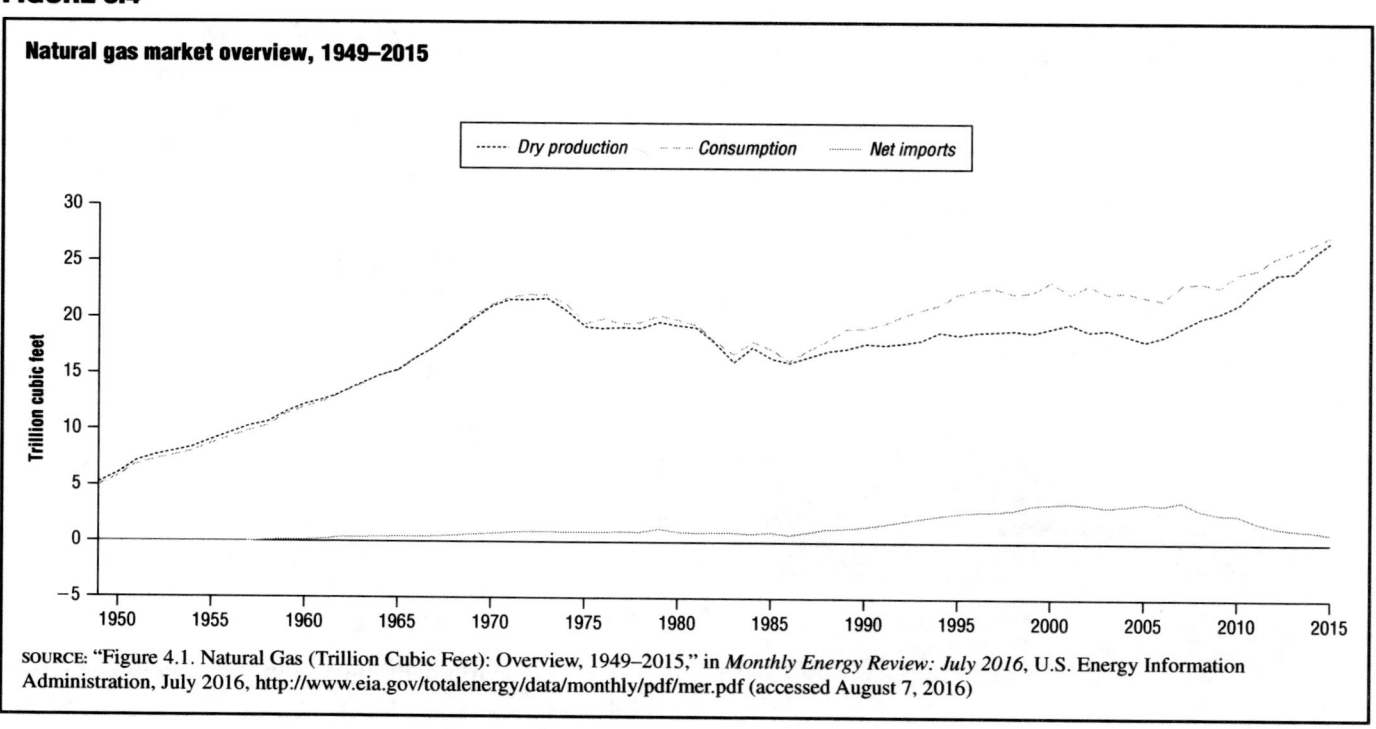

Natural gas market overview, 1949–2015

SOURCE: "Figure 4.1. Natural Gas (Trillion Cubic Feet): Overview, 1949–2015," in *Monthly Energy Review: July 2016*, U.S. Energy Information Administration, July 2016, http://www.eia.gov/totalenergy/data/monthly/pdf/mer.pdf (accessed August 7, 2016)

FIGURE 3.5

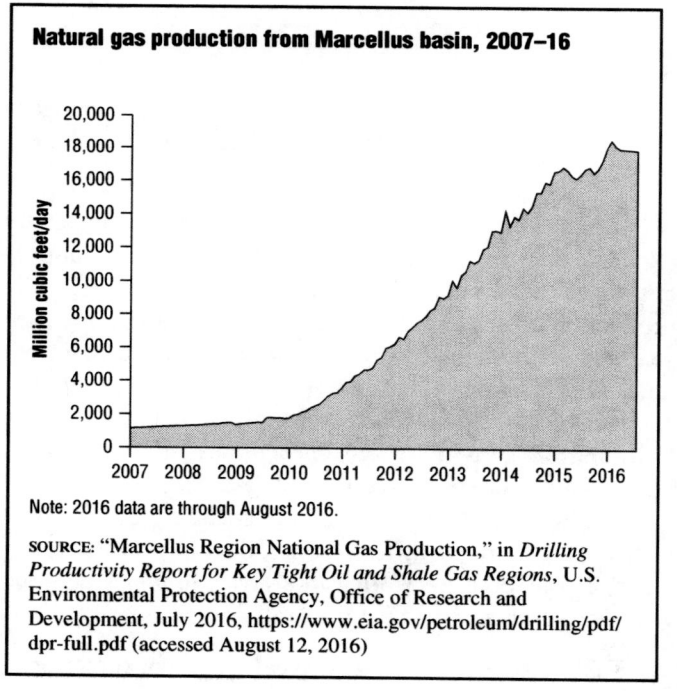

Natural gas production from Marcellus basin, 2007–16

Note: 2016 data are through August 2016.

SOURCE: "Marcellus Region National Gas Production," in *Drilling Productivity Report for Key Tight Oil and Shale Gas Regions*, U.S. Environmental Protection Agency, Office of Research and Development, July 2016, https://www.eia.gov/petroleum/drilling/pdf/dpr-full.pdf (accessed August 12, 2016)

2015. Mexico was the largest market for U.S. exports in 2015, receiving nearly 1.1 tcf (29.9 bcm), or 59% of the total. Most of the remaining exports—701 bcf (19.9 bcm), or 40% of the total—went to Canada. The EIA notes that most natural gas travels to and from the United States by pipelines; very small amounts travel as LNG or CNG.

DOMESTIC CONSUMPTION

Natural gas fulfills an important part of the country's energy needs. It is an attractive fuel not only because its price is relatively low but also because it burns relatively cleanly and efficiently, which helps the country meet its environmental goals.

Natural gas consumption rose between 1949 and 1972 and then generally declined through 1986. (See Table 3.2 and Figure 3.4.) Since 1986 natural gas consumption has been rising. As shown in Table 3.2, it hit an all-time high of 27.5 tcf (778.1 bcm) in 2015.

Table 3.3 shows natural gas consumption by energy-using sector between 1950 and 2015. The industrial sector was historically the largest consumer. In 2012 and 2015, however, this sector was surpassed by the electric power sector. (See Figure 3.7.)

The EIA notes in "Natural Gas Explained: Use of Natural Gas" (July 29, 2015, http://www.eia.gov/energy explained/index.cfm?page=natural_gas_use) that the industrial sector uses natural gas to produce products that require large amounts of heat for manufacture. Examples include steel, glass, and paper. Natural gas hydrocarbons are used as raw materials to make products such as paints, plastics, and medicines. The industrial sector also uses natural gas in its own power plants to generate electricity and in combined heat and power plants that generate heat and electricity. In addition, natural gas is used by the oil and gas industry in its extraction and processing activities. These are designated in Table 3.3 as "lease and plant fuel." According to the EIA, in "Natural Gas: Definitions,

FIGURE 3.6

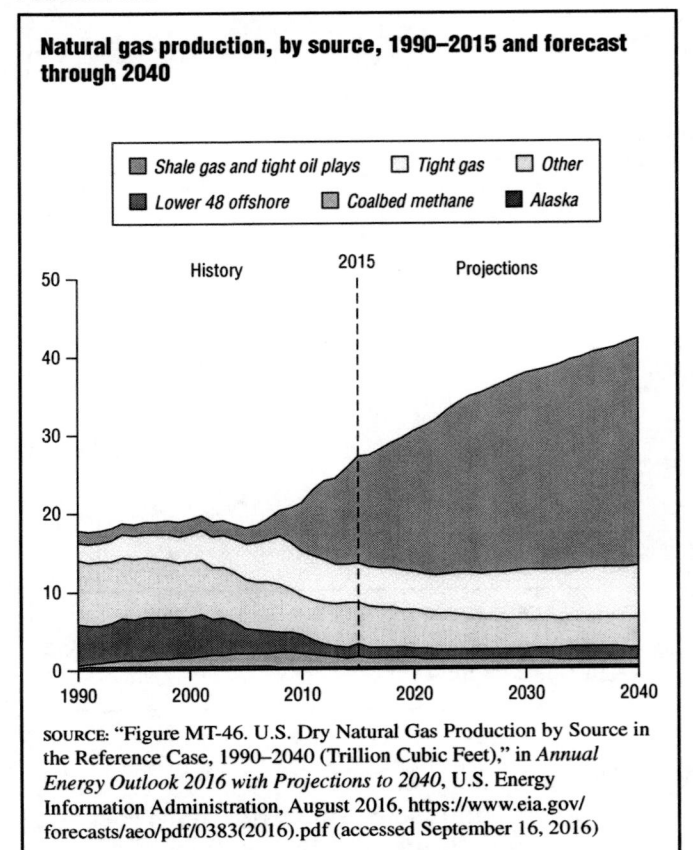

Natural gas production, by source, 1990–2015 and forecast through 2040

Legend:
- Shale gas and tight oil plays
- Tight gas
- Other
- Lower 48 offshore
- Coalbed methane
- Alaska

SOURCE: "Figure MT-46. U.S. Dry Natural Gas Production by Source in the Reference Case, 1990–2040 (Trillion Cubic Feet)," in *Annual Energy Outlook 2016 with Projections to 2040*, U.S. Energy Information Administration, August 2016, https://www.eia.gov/forecasts/aeo/pdf/0383(2016).pdf (accessed September 16, 2016)

Sources and Explanatory Notes" (2016, http://www.eia.gov/dnav/ng/tbldefs/ng_cons_sum_tbldef2.asp), lease fuel is natural gas used in well, field, and lease operations, such as drilling. Plant fuel is natural gas used as fuel in plants that process natural gas.

Consumption in the electric power sector was nearly 9.7 tcf (273.9 bcm) in 2015. (See Table 3.3 and Figure 3.7.) The industrial sector was the second-largest consumer of natural gas, with 9.1 tcf (257.2 bcm). As is explained in Chapter 8, the share of fossil fuel–fired electric power generation held by natural gas grew tremendously between the 1980s and 2015 for a variety of reasons.

The residential and commercial sectors ranked third and fourth, respectively, in natural gas consumption in 2015. (See Table 3.3 and Figure 3.7.) The residential sector used 4.6 tcf (130.7 bcm) and the commercial sector used 3.2 tcf (90.9 bcm). Usage by both sectors has been relatively flat since the 1970s. In "Use of Natural Gas," the EIA notes that about half of U.S. homes used natural gas as their primary heating fuel in 2014. Other residential uses include cooking, water heating, and clothes drying. Natural gas consumption for heating homes and commercial buildings depends heavily on weather conditions, in that colder winters result in increased demand. Residential consumption is also affected by conservation

practices and the efficiency of gas appliances such as water heaters, stoves, and clothes dryers.

The transportation sector consumed only 895 bcf (25.3 bcm) of natural gas in 2015. (See Table 3.3 and Figure 3.7.) The gas is used within the natural gas industry (e.g., during piping and distribution) and as a vehicle fuel.

WORLD NATURAL GAS PRODUCTION AND CONSUMPTION

Table 3.4 shows total natural gas production for 2013 for the world, by region, and for the top-20 producers. Total production was 121.3 tcf (3.4 tcm). North America was the largest producing region, accounting for 31.1 tcf (880.7 bcm), or 26% of world production. Eurasia was second with 29.4 tcf (831.4 bcm), or 24% of the total. The United States led all countries with 24.3 tcf (688.9 bcm), or 20% of world production. Russia was second with 22.1 tcf (626.9 bcm), or 18% of the total, followed by Iran, Qatar, and Canada.

The total world natural gas consumption in 2013 was 121.4 tcf (3.4 tcm). (See Table 3.5.) The United States was the leading consumer at 26.2 tcf (741 bcm), accounting for 22% of the world total. Other top consumers in 2013 included Russia, China, Iran, and Japan.

NATURAL GAS PRICES

Analysts typically track three types of natural gas prices: wellhead prices, citygate prices, and consumer prices.

In *Monthly Energy Review: July 2016*, the EIA explains that the wellhead is the point at which natural gas exits the ground. The wellhead price includes all production costs, such as gathering and compressing the gas, and state charges. The citygate price is "a point or measuring station at which a distribution gas utility receives gas from a natural gas pipeline company or transmission system." Consumer prices are the prices paid by consumers to their local gas utilities. Natural gas prices vary across the nation because federal and state rate structures differ. Location also plays a role. For example, consumer prices are lower in major natural gas–producing areas where transmission costs are lower.

Table 3.6 lists wellhead, citygate, and consumer prices, by sector, between 1950 and 2015 on an average annual basis. These are nominal prices, meaning that they reflect the prices at the time of purchase and have not been adjusted for inflation. Overall, residential customers paid the highest price ($10.38 per thousand cubic feet) for natural gas in 2015, followed by commercial customers ($7.89 per thousand cubic feet), industrial customers ($3.84 per thousand cubic feet), and electric power customers ($3.37 per thousand cubic feet).

TABLE 3.3

Natural gas consumption, by sector, selected years 1950–2015

[Billion cubic feet]

				End-use sectors				Transportation				
				Industrial				Pipelines^d and distribution^e	Vehicle fuel	Total	Electric power sector^f,g	Total
	Residential	Commercial^a	Lease and plant fuel	Other industrial			Total					
				CHP^b	Non-CHP^c	Total						
1950 Total	1,198	388	928	h	2,498	2,498	3,426	126	NA	126	629	5,767
1955 Total	2,124	629	1,131	h	3,411	3,411	4,542	245	NA	245	1,153	8,694
1960 Total	3,103	1,020	1,237	h	4,535	4,535	5,771	347	NA	347	1,725	11,967
1965 Total	3,903	1,444	1,156	h	5,955	5,955	7,112	501	NA	501	2,321	15,280
1970 Total	4,837	2,399	1,399	h	7,851	7,851	9,249	722	NA	722	3,932	21,139
1975 Total	4,924	2,508	1,396	h	6,968	6,968	8,365	583	NA	583	3,158	19,538
1980 Total	4,752	2,611	1,026	h	7,172	7,172	8,198	635	NA	635	3,682	19,877
1985 Total	4,433	2,432	966	h	5,901	5,901	6,867	504	NA	504	3,044	17,281
1990 Total	4,391	2,623	1,236	1,055	5,963^i	7,018^i	8,255	660	(s)	660	3,245^i	19,174^i
1995 Total	4,850	3,031	1,220	1,258	6,906	8,164	9,384	700	5	705	4,237	22,207
2000 Total	4,996	3,182	1,151	1,386	6,757	8,142	9,293	642	13	655	5,206	23,333
2001 Total	4,771	3,023	1,119	1,310	6,035	7,344	8,463	625	15	640	5,342	22,239
2002 Total	4,889	3,144	1,113	1,240	6,287	7,527	8,640	667	15	682	5,672	23,027
2003 Total	5,079	3,179	1,122	1,144	6,007	7,150	8,273	591	18	610	5,135	22,277
2004 Total	4,869	3,129	1,098	1,191	6,066	7,256	8,354	566	21	587	5,464	22,403
2005 Total	4,827	2,999	1,112	1,084	5,518	6,601	7,713	584	23	607	5,869	22,014
2006 Total	4,368	2,832	1,142	1,115	5,412	6,527	7,669	584	24	608	6,222	21,699
2007 Total	4,722	3,013	1,226	1,050	5,604	6,655	7,881	621	25	646	6,841	23,104
2008 Total	4,892	3,153	1,220	955	5,715	6,670	7,890	648	26	674	6,668	23,277
2009 Total	4,779	3,119	1,275	990	5,178	6,167	7,443	670	27	697	6,873	22,910
2010 Total	4,782	3,103	1,286	1,029	5,797	6,826	8,112	674	29	703	7,387	24,087
2011 Total	4,714	3,155	1,323	1,063	5,931	6,994	8,317	688	30	718	7,574	24,477
2012 Total	4,150	2,895	1,396	1,149	6,077	7,226	8,622	731	30	761	9,111	25,538
2013 Total	4,897	3,295	1,483	1,170	6,255	7,425	8,909	833	30	863	8,191	26,155
2014 Total	5,087	3,467	1,500	1,145	6,479	7,624	9,124	836	35	871	8,146	26,695
2015 Total	4,616^R	3,209^R	1,578^E	1,170	6,336^R	7,506^R	9,084^R	860^E	34^E	895^R,E	9,671	27,475^R

^a All commercial sector fuel use, including that at commercial combined-heat-and-power (CHP) and commercial electricity-only plants.
^b Industrial combined-heat-and-power (CHP) and a small number of industrial electricity-only plants.
^c All industrial sector fuel use other than that in "Lease and Plant Fuel" and "CHP."
^d Natural gas consumed in the operation of pipelines, primarily in compressors. Beginning in 2009, includes line loss, which is known volumes of natural gas that are the result of leaks, damage, accidents, migration, and/or blow down.
^e Natural gas used as fuel in the delivery of natural gas to consumers. Beginning in 2009, includes line loss, which is known volumes of natural gas that are the result of leaks, damage, accidents, migration, and/or blow down.
^f The electric power sector comprises electricity-only and combined-heat-and-power (CHP) plants within the NAICS 22 category whose primary business is to sell electricity, or electricity and heat, to the public.
^g Through 1988, data are for electric utilities only. Beginning in 1989, data are for electric utilities and independent power producers.
^h Included in "Non-CHP."
^i For 1989–1992, a small amount of consumption at independent power producers may be counted in both "Other Industrial" and "Electric Power Sector."
R = Revised. E = Estimate. NA = Not available. (s) = Less than 500 million cubic feet.
Notes: Data are for natural gas, plus a small amount of supplemental gaseous fuels. Through 1964, all volumes are shown on a pressure base of 14.65 psia (pounds per square inch absolute) at 60° Fahrenheit; beginning in 1965, the pressure base is 14.73 psia at 60° Fahrenheit. Totals may not equal sum of components due to independent rounding. Geographic coverage is the 50 states.

SOURCE: Adapted from "Table 4.3. Natural Gas Consumption by Sector (Billion Cubic Feet)," in *Monthly Energy Review: July 2016*, U.S. Energy Information Administration, July 2016, http://www.eia.gov/totalenergy/data/monthly/pdf/mer.pdf (accessed August 7, 2016)

Natural Gas Pricing Factors

Some of the factors described in Chapter 2 as affecting oil pricing, such as supply and demand and weather, also affect natural gas pricing. However, because the United States produces all or nearly all of the natural gas it consumes and obtains almost all of its imports from Canada, natural gas pricing in the United States is far less dependent on foreign events and manipulation than oil pricing. Chapter 2 also explains various government interventions that are designed to benefit the oil and natural gas industry.

The biggest impact on natural gas pricing within the United States in the 20th century was the deregulation of the natural gas industry, which began during the 1970s. Deregulation meant an end to government-protected monopolies and opened the industry to competition. These events and the subsequent restructuring of companies within the industry brought about a period of sharply rising prices. However, once the industry adjusted to deregulation, prices dropped.

Natural gas prices began to climb at the turn of the century and by 2008 the citygate price reached a record high of $9.18 per thousand cubic feet. (See Table 3.6.) This period coincides with the skyrocketing demand for natural gas from the electric power sector. (See Figure 3.7.) Because supply could not keep up with demand, natural gas prices rose. The industry responded with greater production, and prices began to come down. By 2015 the citygate price was down to $4.26 per thousand cubic feet.

FIGURE 3.7

Natural gas consumption, by sector, 1949–2015

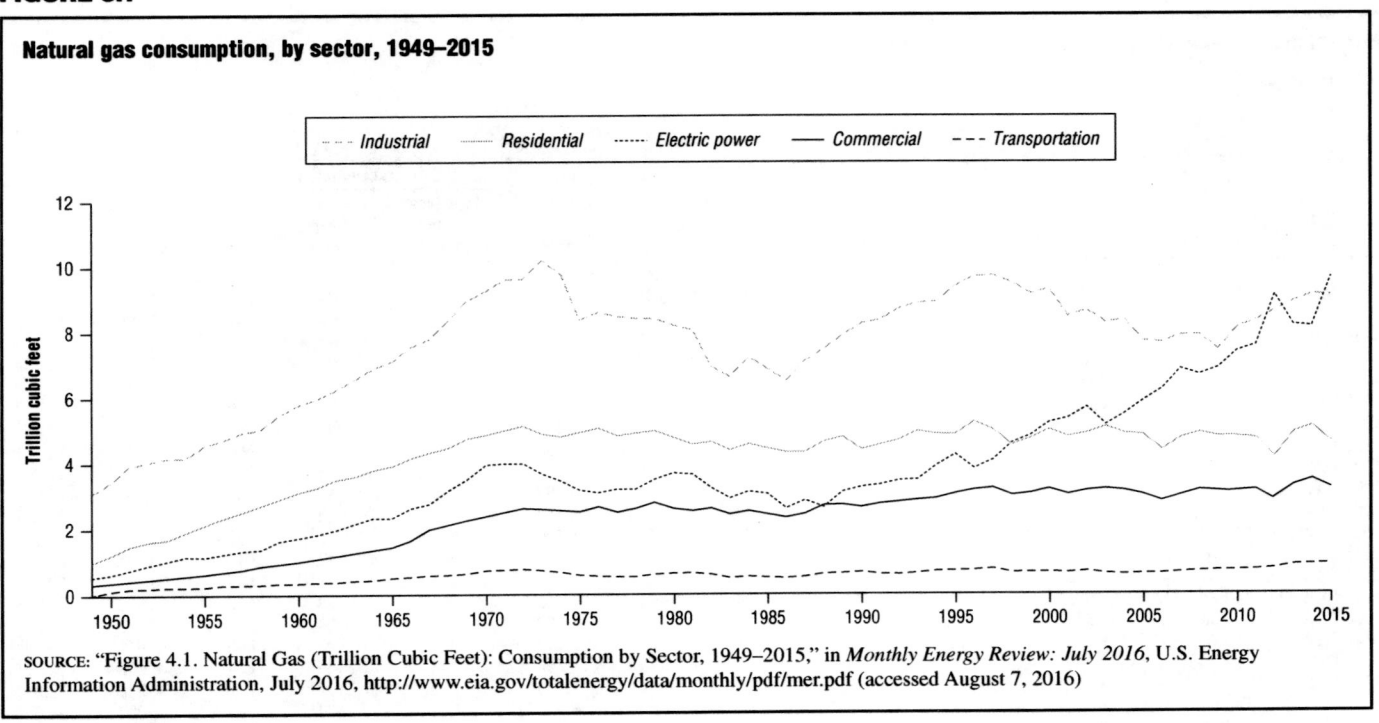

SOURCE: "Figure 4.1. Natural Gas (Trillion Cubic Feet): Consumption by Sector, 1949–2015," in *Monthly Energy Review: July 2016*, U.S. Energy Information Administration, July 2016, http://www.eia.gov/totalenergy/data/monthly/pdf/mer.pdf (accessed August 7, 2016)

FUTURE TRENDS IN THE NATURAL GAS INDUSTRY

The EIA predicts in *Annual Energy Outlook 2016 with Projections to 2040* (August 2016, https://www.eia.gov/forecasts/aeo/pdf/0383(2016).pdf) that domestic natural gas production will greatly increase in the coming decades to keep pace with rising demand. (See Figure 3.6.) The agency expects that much of the new production will be gas obtained from unconventional geological sources—that is, shale gas and tight oil and tight gas (also known as tight sand gas). In fact, by 2040 natural gas from shale and tight oil plays is projected to supply 69% of the nation's natural gas supply. Another 16% is expected to be tight gas, while 11% is projected to come from other onshore sources in the lower 48 states. Overall, domestic production is forecast to increase by 55%, from 27 tcf (764.6 bcm) in 2015 to 41.9 tcf (1.2 tcm) in 2040.

ENVIRONMENTAL ISSUES

The natural gas industry is associated with fewer environmental concerns than the oil and coal industries for two main reasons. First, leaks of natural gas (which do occur) do not contaminate ecosystems in the same way that oil spills do. Second, natural gas burns much cleaner than oil and coal. Nevertheless, leaks and the combustion of natural gas release large amounts of carbon into the atmosphere, which, as is explained in Chapter 1, contributes to global warming and climate change. For example, in October 2015 a leak developed in a natural gas storage facility in California. According to Joby Warrick, in "California Gas Leak Was the Worst Man-Made Greenhouse-Gas Disaster in U.S. History, Study Says" (WashingtonPost.com, February 25, 2016), the leak lasted for four months and spewed about 5 bcf (0.1 bcm) of methane into the atmosphere. Warrick notes that the heat-trapping effect of the release was equivalent to the annual exhaust emissions of nearly 600,000 cars. As of September 2016, it held the record for the largest climate impact from a single incident in the United States.

Chapter 2 examines environmental issues associated with the extraction of both natural gas and oil. For example, large amounts of wastewater are produced by the industry. Disposal of this wastewater via underground injection into deep wells has been implicated in causing earthquakes. Likewise, the fracking of natural gas is highly controversial because it requires large amounts of water and could allow natural gas to seep into and contaminate freshwater aquifers (underground freshwater pools).

TABLE 3.4

World production of dry natural gas, by region and selected country, 2013

[Billion cubic feet]

	2013
World	**121,283.2**
Regions	
North America	31,102.6
Eurasia	29,357.2
Middle East	19,831.0
Asia & Oceania	17,738.4
Europe	9,982.1
Africa	7,328.3
Central & South America	5,943.6
Countries	
United States	24,334.0
Russia	22,139.3
Iran	5,696.1
Qatar	5,597.5
Canada	5,128.8
China	3,986.0
Norway	3,840.0
Saudi Arabia	3,526.2
Netherlands	3,052.0
Turkmenistan	2,994.7
Algeria	2,812.8
Indonesia	2,486.2
Malaysia	2,260.2
Australia	2,178.9
Uzbekistan	2,105.8
Egypt	2,034.1
United Arab Emirates	1,928.2
Mexico	1,639.8
Trinidad and Tobago	1,511.5
Thailand	1,476.2

SOURCE: Adapted from "Dry Natural Gas Production (Billion Cubic Feet)," in *International Energy Statistics: Natural Gas Production*, U.S. Energy Information Administration, 2016, http://www.eia.gov/cfapps/ipdbproject/iedindex3.cfm?tid=3&pid=26&aid=1&cid=regions&syid=2013&eyid=2013&unit=BCF (accessed August 14, 2016)

TABLE 3.5

World consumption of dry natural gas, by region and selected country, 2013

[Billion cubic feet]

	2013
World	**121,357.1**
Regions	
North America	32,103.4
Asia & Oceania	23,626.8
Eurasia	21,944.6
Europe	18,511.9
Middle East	15,078.2
Central & South America	5,518.8
Africa	4,573.4
Countries	
United States	26,168.0
Russia	15,599.0
China	5,760.1
Iran	5,555.6
Japan	4,492.4
Canada	3,654.8
Saudi Arabia	3,532.6
Germany	3,123.4
United Kingdom	2,734.9
Italy	2,474.5
United Arab Emirates	2,355.2
Mexico	2,280.6
Korea, South	1,877.2
Egypt	1,861.8
Thailand	1,846.0
India	1,822.3
Argentina	1,694.8
Ukraine	1,659.8
Netherlands	1,637.2
Uzbekistan	1,629.1

SOURCE: Adapted from "Dry Natural Gas Consumption (Billion Cubic Feet)," in *International Energy Statistics: Natural Gas Consumption*, U.S. Energy Information Administration, 2016, http://www.eia.gov/cfapps/ipdbproject/iedindex3.cfm?tid=3&pid=26&aid=2&cid=regions&syid=2013&eyid=2013&unit=BCF (accessed August 14, 2016)

TABLE 3.6

Natural gas prices, by pricing location and consuming sector, selected years 1950–2015

[Dollars^a per thousand cubic feet]

	Wellhead price	Citygate price	Consuming sectors							
			Residential		Commercial^b		Industrial^c		Transportation	Electric power^d	
			Price^e	Percentage of sector	Price^e	Percentage of sector	Price^e	Percentage of sector	Vehicle fuel^f price^e	Price^e	Percentage of sector^g
1950 Average	0.07	NA	NA	NA	NA	NA	NA	NA	NA	NA	NA
1955 Average	0.10	NA	NA	NA	NA	NA	NA	NA	NA	NA	NA
1960 Average	0.14	NA	NA	NA	NA	NA	NA	NA	NA	NA	NA
1965 Average	0.16	NA	NA	NA	NA	NA	NA	NA	NA	NA	NA
1970 Average	0.17	NA	1.09	NA	0.77	NA	0.37	NA	NA	0.29	NA
1975 Average	0.44	NA	1.71	NA	1.35	NA	0.96	NA	NA	0.77	96.1
1980 Average	1.59	NA	3.68	NA	3.39	NA	2.56	NA	NA	2.27	96.9
1985 Average	2.51	3.75	6.12	NA	5.50	NA	3.95	68.8	NA	3.55	94.0
1990 Average	1.71	3.03	5.80	99.2	4.83	86.6	2.93	35.2	3.39	2.38	76.8
1995 Average	1.55	2.78	6.06	99.0	5.05	76.7	2.71	24.5	3.98	2.02	71.4
2000 Average	3.68	4.62	7.76	92.6	6.59	63.9	4.45	19.8	5.54	4.38	50.5
2001 Average	4.00	5.72	9.63	92.4	8.43	66.0	5.24	20.8	6.60	3.68^e	40.2
2002 Average	2.95	4.12	7.89	97.9	6.63	77.4	4.02	22.7	5.10	5.57	83.9
2003 Average	4.88	5.85	9.63	97.5	8.40	78.2	5.89	22.1	6.19	5.57	91.2
2004 Average	5.46	6.65	10.75	97.7	9.43	78.0	6.53	23.6	7.16	6.11	89.8
2005 Average	7.33	8.67	12.70	98.1	11.34	82.1	8.56	24.0	9.14	8.47	91.3
2006 Average	6.39	8.61	13.73	98.1	12.00	80.8	7.87	23.4	8.72	7.11	93.4
2007 Average	6.25	8.16	13.08	98.0	11.34	80.4	7.68	22.2	8.50	7.31	92.2
2008 Average	7.97	9.18	13.89	97.5	12.23	79.7	9.65	20.4	11.75	9.26	101.1
2009 Average	3.67	6.48	12.14	97.4	10.06	77.8	5.33	18.8	8.13	4.93	101.1
2010 Average	4.48	6.18	11.39	97.4	9.47	77.5	5.49	18.0	6.25	5.27	100.8
2011 Average	3.95	5.63	11.03	96.3	8.91	67.3	5.13	16.3	7.48	4.89	101.2
2012 Average	2.66^E	4.73	10.65	95.8	8.10	65.2	3.88	16.2	8.04	3.54	95.5
2013 Average	NA	4.88	10.32	95.7	8.08	65.8	4.64	16.6	9.76	4.49	94.9
2014 Average	NA	5.71	10.97	95.5	8.90	65.8	5.55	15.9	NA	5.19	94.6
2015 Average	NA	4.26^R	10.38	95.7	7.89	65.9	3.84	15.9	NA	3.37	94.4

^aPrices are not adjusted for inflation.
^bCommercial sector, including commercial combined-heat-and-power (CHP) and commercial electricity-only plants.
^cIndustrial sector, including industrial combined-heat-and-power (CHP) and industrial electricity-only plants.
^dThe electric power sector comprises electricity-only and combined-heat-and-power (CHP) plants within the NAICS 22 category whose primary business is to sell electricity, or electricity and heat, to the public. Through 2001, data are for electric utilities only; beginning in 2002, data also include independent power producers.
^eIncludes taxes.
^fMuch of the natural gas delivered for vehicle fuel represents deliveries to fueling stations that are used primarily or exclusively by fleet vehicles. Thus, the prices are often those associated with the cost of gas in the operation of fleet vehicles.
^gPercentages exceed 100% when reported natural gas receipts are greater than reported natural gas consumption—this can occur when combined-heat-and-power plants report fuel receipts related to non-electric generating activities.
R = Revised. NA = Not available. E = Estimate.
Notes: Prices are for natural gas, plus a small amount of supplemental gaseous fuels. Prices are intended to include all taxes. Wellhead annual and year-to-date prices are simple averages of the monthly prices; all other annual and year-to-date prices are volume-weighted averages of the monthly prices. Geographic coverage is the 50 states and the District of Columbia.

SOURCE: Adapted from "Table 9.10. Natural Gas Prices (Dollars per Thousand Cubic Feet)," in *Monthly Energy Review: July 2016*, U.S. Energy Information Administration, July 2016, http://www.eia.gov/totalenergy/data/monthly/pdf/mer.pdf (accessed August 7, 2016)

CHAPTER 4
COAL

Although it had been a source of energy for many centuries, coal was first used on a large scale during the Industrial Revolution (1760–1848). Its use expanded over the following decades with the building of railroads across the country. Coal eventually replaced wood as the fuel for steam engines, which became the new workhorses of the modern age. However, coal's widespread use in industry waned during the latter 20th century as petroleum became more popular. Coal found a new niche in electricity generation, a field it now dominates. Coal's strong appeal is driven by its high abundance and easy accessibility in the United States. Nevertheless, coal has its problems, chiefly environmental ones.

UNDERSTANDING COAL

Coal is a dark, combustible, mineral solid. Coal beds, or seams, are found in the earth between beds of sandstone, shale, and limestone. Like oil and thermogenic natural gas, coal developed underground over millions of years as organic (carbon-containing) material was subjected to intense temperatures and pressures. Oil and thermogenic natural gas originated from microscopic organisms, whereas coal is believed to have developed from vegetation, particularly plant fibers. These materials were first transformed into peat (a fibrous sodlike mass of partially disintegrated organic material). Peat is typically found near the ground surface and is very moist; however, once dried it can be burned as fuel. Peat created several millennia ago was baked and squeezed by the earth and eventually turned into coal.

Measuring Coal

In the United States coal amounts are measured in tons, which are also known as short tons. One ton is equivalent to 2,000 pounds (907.2 kg). In countries that rely on the metric system, the metric tonne (t) is the preferred unit for measuring coal amounts. One ton is equivalent to 0.9 t.

Coal Ranks

There are different coal ranks (classifications), which are based on coal maturity. Stanley P. Schweinfurth of the U.S. Geological Survey explains in *An Introduction to Coal Quality* (July 2009, http://pubs.usgs.gov/pp/1625f/downloads/ChapterC.pdf) that coal rank depends on heat, moisture, carbon, and volatile matter contents. Heat content is the amount of heat that can be produced from a given unit of fuel. In general, more mature coal has a higher heat content and less moisture than younger coal. Moisture content is very important because drier coals are easier to handle and burn hotter than wetter coals.

In *Monthly Energy Review: July 2016* (July 2016, http://www.eia.gov/totalenergy/data/monthly/archive/00351607.pdf), the U.S. Energy Information Administration (EIA) within the U.S. Department of Energy explains that the United States uses four coal ranks:

- Lignite (brown coal) is the lowest-ranked coal and the first true coal produced by the earth from peat. As such, it is relatively soft and moist compared with other coals. Lignite is brownish-black in color and has a high moisture content (as much as 45%). Lignite's heat content is about 9 million to 17 million British thermal units (Btu) per ton.

- Subbituminous coal ranks above lignite. Subbituminous coal ranges from dark brown to jet black in color and typically contains 20% to 30% moisture. Its heat content is approximately 17 million to 24 million Btu per ton.

- Bituminous coal is more mature than subbituminous coal and is the most abundant type of coal in the United States. Bituminous coal is dense and usually black, with a moisture content of less than 20%. It has a heat content of approximately 21 million to 30 million Btu per ton.

- Anthracite is the highest-ranked coal and the most mature. It is hard, brittle, and lustrous and typically jet-black in color, with a moisture content of less than 15%. Its heat content is approximately 22 million to 28 million Btu per ton. Anthracite is highly valued for its low moisture content and high heat content, but is very rare.

Coal Grades

Coal is also divided into grades based on its quality and intended end use. Two of the most common grades are metallurgical (or coking) coal and thermal (or steam) coal. The EIA (2016, http://www.eia.gov/tools/glossary/index .cfm?id=C) notes that coking coal has low sulfur and ash contents and is typically drawn from the bituminous rank. It is used to make coke, a high-value solid substance that is used in certain industrial processes, such as steel-making. According to the EIA, all coal not classified as coking coal is steam coal, which is mostly used to generate steam to produce electricity or for heating purposes.

COAL DEPOSITS

The locations of coal deposits around the world are driven solely by geology. Regions and countries known to have large coal deposits include the United States, Eurasia (particularly China, Russia, and India), Australia, South Africa, and northern South America.

Geologists divide U.S. coalfields into the Appalachian, interior, and western regions. (See Figure 4.1.) The Appalachian region encompasses the Appalachian Mountains in the eastern United States and stretches from Pennsylvania south to Alabama. The interior region covers parts of the Midwest and Deep South, including Texas. The western region includes Alaska and a huge swath of territory from Montana and North Dakota in the north to the upper portions of Arizona and New Mexico in the south.

Like oil and natural gas, coal is located both onshore and offshore (i.e., beneath the earth's oceans). Offshore

FIGURE 4.1

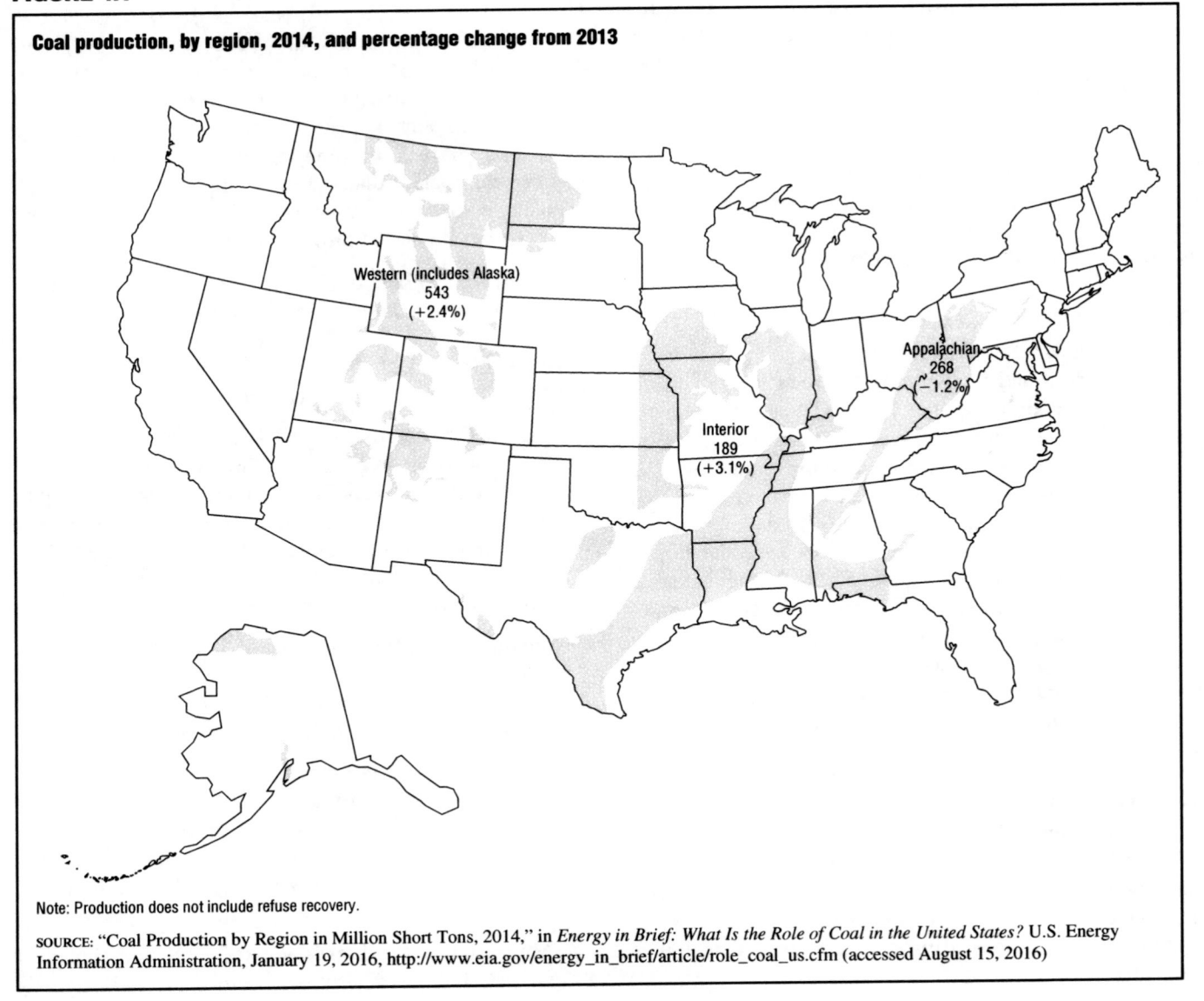

Coal production, by region, 2014, and percentage change from 2013

Western (includes Alaska)
543
(+2.4%)

Appalachian
268
(−1.2%)

Interior
189
(+3.1%)

Note: Production does not include refuse recovery.

SOURCE: "Coal Production by Region in Million Short Tons, 2014," in *Energy in Brief: What Is the Role of Coal in the United States?* U.S. Energy Information Administration, January 19, 2016, http://www.eia.gov/energy_in_brief/article/role_coal_us.cfm (accessed August 15, 2016)

coal deposits were first mined during the 1800s, and some offshore mining is still conducted. Nevertheless, huge offshore coal deposits remain almost entirely untouched because of the difficulties and costs involved in extracting them.

Estimates of the amounts of coal deposits around the world and in the United States that have not yet been extracted are provided in Chapter 7, along with information about coal exploration and development activities.

COAL EXTRACTION

Coal exists in the earth in solid form. As such, it is typically mined out of the ground. The method used to mine coal depends on the terrain and depth of the coal.

Surface mining is used for deposits that lie relatively near the ground surface—that is, less than about 200 feet (61 m) deep. Surface mines can be developed in flat or hilly terrain. On large plots of relatively flat ground, workers use a technique known as area surface mining. Rock and soil that lie above the coal—called overburden or spoil—are loosened by drilling and blasting and then dug away.

Underground mining is required when the coal lies more than about 200 feet (61 m) below ground. The depth of most underground mines is less than 1,000 feet (305 m), but a few are 2,000 feet (610 m) deep. In underground mines, some coal must be left untouched to form pillars that prevent the mines from caving in. It should be noted that underground cave mining is inherently dangerous. The U.S. Department of Labor notes in the fact sheet "Injury Trends in Mining" (2016, http://www.msha.gov/MSHA INFO/FactSheets/MSHAFCT2.HTM#.U71L455dWra) that more than 3,200 coal miners died on the job in 1907, the deadliest year for the industry. Since then stricter regulations and improved safety measures have dramatically lowered the casualty rates. According to the Department of Labor, in "Mine Safety and Health at a Glance" (July 20, 2015, http:// arlweb.msha.gov/MSHAINFO/FactSheets/MSHAFCT10 .asp), 45 coal miners lost their lives in U.S. mines in 2014. Coal mining death tolls are much higher in other parts of the world. For example, more than 300 miners died in a mine explosion in Turkey in May 2014.

Table 4.1 shows regional and U.S. totals for the number of mining operations, number of employees, and productivity (tons extracted per hour worked) in 2014. There were 1,354 coal mining operations around the country that employed 74,931 people. Average productivity in 2014 was nearly 6 tons (5.4 t) per employee hour. Most (1,231) of the mining operations were located east of the Mississippi River. Only 90 operated west of the river; however, their average productivity of nearly 16 tons (14.5 t) per employee hour was much higher than that for the eastern mines, which was 3.1 tons (2.8 t) per employee hour.

TABLE 4.1

Coal mining operations, employees, and productivity, 2014

Coal-producing state, region and mine type	Number of mining operations[a] 2014	Number of employees[b] 2014	Average production per employee hour (short tons)[c] 2014
Alabama	46	3,694	1.88
Underground	13	2,852	1.84
Surface	33	842	2.02
Alaska	1	120	5.43
Surface	1	120	5.43
Arizona	1	387	8.06
Surface	1	387	8.06
Arkansas	2	84	0.53
Underground	1	82	0.49
Surface	1	2	6.39
Colorado	10	1,822	6.23
Underground	6	1,372	6.15
Surface	4	450	6.50
Illinois	32	4,218	5.99
Underground	19	3,772	6.13
Surface	13	446	4.92
Indiana	37	3,810	4.21
Underground	13	2,201	3.36
Surface	24	1,609	5.36
Kansas	2	10	3.86
Surface	2	10	3.86
Kentucky total	356	11,834	2.80
Underground	144	8,191	2.70
Surface	212	3,643	3.06
Kentucky (east)	323	7,566	2.23
Underground	123	4,349	1.89
Surface	200	3,217	2.69
Kentucky (west)	33	4,268	3.70
Underground	21	3,842	3.50
Surface	12	426	5.73
Louisiana	2	299	3.96
Surface	2	299	3.96
Maryland	21	386	2.36
Underground	3	167	1.83
Surface	18	219	2.82
Mississippi	2	324	5.71
Surface	2	324	5.71
Missouri	1	20	7.11
Surface	1	20	7.11
Montana	6	1,320	16.57
Underground	1	324	10.66
Surface	5	996	18.81
New Mexico	3	1,149	9.21
Underground	1	488	8.89
Surface	2	661	9.43
North Dakota	5	1,285	11.48
Surface	5	1,285	11.48
Ohio	38	2,923	3.38
Underground	14	1,997	3.43
Surface	24	926	3.25
Oklahoma	6	179	1.87
Underground	1	77	1.91
Surface	5	102	1.83
Pennsylvania total	300	7,938	3.52
Underground	78	5,821	4.02
Surface	222	2,117	1.93
Pennsylvania (anthracite)	99	956	0.98
Underground	17	85	0.60
Surface	82	871	1.01
Pennsylvania (bituminous)	201	6,982	3.83
Underground	61	5,736	4.07
Surface	140	1,246	2.58
Tennessee	10	222	1.85
Underground	4	158	1.73
Surface	6	64	2.30
Texas	16	2,806	7.22
Surface	16	2,806	7.22

Coal-producing state, region and mine type	Number of mining operations[a] 2014	Number of employees[b] 2014	Average production per employee hour (short tons)[c] 2014
Utah	17	1,393	5.97
Underground	13	1,330	6.13
Surface	4	63	3.32
Virginia	101	3,627	1.92
Underground	56	2,863	1.79
Surface	45	764	2.43
West Virginia total	288	18,330	2.69
Underground	155	14,338	2.53
Surface	133	3,992	3.24
West Virginia (northern)	46	5,888	3.70
Underground	26	5,677	3.71
Surface	20	211	3.30
West Virginia (southern)	242	12,442	2.22
Underground	129	8,661	1.75
Surface	113	3,781	3.24
Wyoming	18	6,624	28.62
Underground	1	315	4.39
Surface	17	6,309	30.05
Appalachia total	1,127	44,686	2.66
Underground	446	32,545	2.63
Surface	681	12,141	2.75
Appalachia central	676	23,857	2.17
Underground	312	16,031	1.79
Surface	364	7,826	2.94
Appalachia northern	405	17,135	3.53
Underground	121	13,662	3.78
Surface	284	3,473	2.45
Appalachia southern	46	3,694	1.88
Underground	13	2,852	1.84
Surface	33	842	2.02
Interior region total	133	16,018	4.98
Underground	55	9,974	4.37
Surface	78	6,044	6.05
Illinois basin	102	12,296	4.60
Underground	53	9,815	4.42
Surface	49	2,481	5.34
Other interior	31	3,722	6.35
Underground	2	159	1.26
Surface	29	3,563	6.61
Western region total	61	14,100	18.36
Underground	22	3,829	6.71
Surface	39	10,271	22.89
Powder River basin	16	6,592	30.55
Surface	16	6,592	30.55
Uinta basin	23	3,016	6.27
Underground	17	2,559	6.30
Surface	6	457	6.09
Other western	22	4,492	8.91
Underground	5	1,270	7.50
Surface	17	3,222	9.51
East of Mississippi River	1,231	57,306	3.12
Underground	499	42,360	3.07
Surface	732	14,946	3.27
West of Mississippi River	90	17,498	15.96
Underground	24	3,988	6.47
Surface	66	13,510	18.86
U.S. subtotal	**1,321**	**74,804**	**5.95**
Underground	523	46,348	3.35
Surface	798	28,456	10.42
Refuse recovery	33	127	13.21
U.S. total	**1,354**	**74,931**	**5.96**

PROCESSING AND TRANSPORTING COAL

Coal seams can contain noncoal materials, such as rock, ash, and other minerals. These impurities are removed at processing facilities (typically located at the

[a]Mining operations that consist of a mine and preparation plant or preparation plant processing both underground and surface coal are reported as two operations.
[b]Includes all employees engaged in production, processing, development, maintenance, repair shop, or yard work at mining operations, including office workers.
[c]Calculated by dividing total coal production by the total labor hours worked by all employees engaged in production, processing, development, maintenance, repair shop, or yard work at mining operations, including office workers.
Note: Excludes preparation plants with less than 5,000 employee hours per year, which are not required to provide data.

SOURCE: Adapted from "Table 21. Coal Productivity by State and Mine Type, 2014 and 2013," in *Annual Coal Report 2014*, U.S. Energy Information Administration, March 2016, http://www.eia.gov/coal/annual/pdf/acr.pdf (accessed August 15, 2016)

mines) to meet the requirements of the coal buyers. One of the targeted impurities is sulfur, which is found mostly in the form of pyrite, an iron sulfide mineral. Impurity removal helps improve coal's heat content, lowers transportation costs, and makes the coal burn cleaner—that is, it generates less air pollutants, particularly sulfur dioxide. Coal may be crushed, either before or after cleaning, for easier handling. It can also be pulverized into a fine dust.

Coal cleaning is not a perfect process; thus, some of the removed rock and mineral materials still contain enough hydrocarbons to make them useful combustible fuels. The EIA refers to these processing by-products as waste coal. Technological advances in combustion equipment have made waste coal a marketable energy product.

Cleaned coal is transported from mine sites to customer locations. In the United States the primary transportation modes are freight trains and, to a lesser extent, barges and trucks. Crushed coal can also be mixed with water and piped as a slurry to its destination.

DOMESTIC PRODUCTION

Traditional Coal

Table 4.2 shows domestic coal production between 1950 and 2015. During the 1950s and 1960s production hovered around 500 million tons (450 million t) per year. Demand for coal began increasing during the 1970s as a result of the oil embargo, which is described in Chapter 2. Domestic coal production rose over subsequent decades, reaching 1 billion tons (900 million t) per year by the early 1990s. Production has leveled off and even declined since then. In 2015 the United States produced 895.9 million tons (812.8 million t) of coal. Table 4.3 provides a breakdown of coal production by state and region. In 2015 Wyoming produced, by far, more coal than any other state, with 375.8 million tons (340.9 million t) and accounting for 42% of the total. Other major producing states included West Virginia, Kentucky, Illinois, Pennsylvania, and Montana. The western region produced the most coal in

TABLE 4.2

Coal production, trade, and consumption statistics, selected years 1950–2015

[Thousand short tons]

	Production[a]	Waste coal supplied[b]	Trade Imports	Trade Exports	Net imports[c]	Stock change[d,e]	Losses and unaccounted for[e,f]	Consumption
1950 Total	560,388	NA	365	29,360	−28,995	27,829	9,462	494,102
1955 Total	490,838	NA	337	54,429	−54,092	−3,974	−6,292	447,012
1960 Total	434,329	NA	262	37,981	−37,719	1,722	1,722	398,081
1965 Total	526,954	NA	184	51,032	−50,848	1,897	2,244	471,965
1970 Total	612,661	NA	36	71,733	−71,697	11,100	6,633	523,231
1975 Total	654,641	NA	940	66,309	−65,369	32,154	−5,522	562,640
1980 Total	829,700	NA	1,194	91,742	−90,548	25,595	10,827	702,730
1985 Total	883,638	NA	1,952	92,680	−90,727	−27,934	2,796	818,049
1990 Total	1,029,076	3,339	2,699	105,804	−103,104	26,542	−1,730	904,498
1995 Total	1,032,974	8,561	9,473	88,547	−79,074	−275	632	962,104
2000 Total	1,073,612	9,089	12,513	58,489	−45,976	−48,309	938	1,084,095
2001 Total	1,127,689	10,085	19,787	48,666	−28,879	41,630	7,120	1,060,146
2002 Total	1,094,283	9,052	16,875	39,601	−22,726	10,215	4,040	1,066,355
2003 Total	1,071,753	10,016	25,044	43,014	−17,970	−26,659	−4,403	1,094,861
2004 Total	1,112,099	11,299	27,280	47,998	−20,718	−11,462	6,887	1,107,255
2005 Total	1,131,498	13,352	30,460	49,942	−19,482	−9,702	9,092	1,125,978
2006 Total	1,162,750	14,409	36,246	49,647	−13,401	42,642	8,824	1,112,292
2007 Total	1,146,635	14,076	36,347	59,163	−22,816	5,812	4,085	1,127,998
2008 Total	1,171,809	14,146	34,208	81,519	−47,311	12,354	5,740	1,120,548
2009 Total	1,074,923	13,666	22,629	59,097	−36,458	39,668	14,985	997,478
2010 Total	1,084,368	13,651	19,353	81,716	−62,363	−13,039	182	1,048,514
2011 Total	1,095,628	13,088	13,088	107,259	−94,171	211	11,506	1,002,948
2012 Total	1,016,458	11,196	9,159	125,746	−116,586	6,902	14,980	889,185
2013 Total	984,842	11,279	8,906	117,659	−108,753	−38,525	1,451	924,442
2014 Total	1,000,049	12,090	11,350	97,257	−85,907	−2,601	11,101	917,731
2015 Total	895,936	F9,500	11,318	73,958	−62,640	45,035	−3,802	801,563

[a]Beginning in 2001, includes a small amount of refuse recovery (coal recaptured from a refuse mine and cleaned to reduce the concentration of noncombustible materials).

[b]Waste coal (including fine coal, coal obtained from a refuse bank or slurry dam, anthracite culm, bituminous gob, and lignite waste) consumed by the electric power and industrial sectors. Beginning in 1989, waste coal supplied is counted as a supply-side item to balance the same amount of waste coal included in Consumption.

[c]Net imports equal imports minus exports. A minus sign indicates exports are greater than imports.

[d]A negative value indicates a decrease in stocks and a positive value indicates an increase.

[e]In 1949, stock change is included in "Losses and Unaccounted for."

[f]The difference between calculated coal supply and disposition, due to coal quantities lost or to data reporting problems.

NA = Not available. F = Forecast.

Notes: Data values preceded by "F" are derived from the U.S. Energy Information Administration's Short-Term Integrated Forecasting System. Totals may not equal sum of components due to independent rounding. Geographic coverage is the 50 states and the District of Columbia.

SOURCE: Adapted from "Table 6.1. Coal Overview (Thousand Short Tons)," in *Monthly Energy Review: July 2016,* U.S. Energy Information Administration, July 2016, http://www.eia.gov/totalenergy/data/monthly/pdf/mer.pdf (accessed August 7, 2016)

TABLE 4.3

Coal production, by state and region, 2014 and 2015

[Thousands short tons]

Coal-producing region and state	Year to date 2015	Year to date 2014	Percent change
Alabama	13,016	16,363	−20.5
Alaska	1,193	1,502	−20.5
Arizona	6,805	8,051	−15.5
Arkansas	91	94	−2.7
Colorado	18,722	24,007	−22.0
Illinois	55,991	57,969	−3.4
Indiana	34,429	39,267	−12.3
Kansas	199	66	200.2
Kentucky total	61,331	77,335	−20.7
Eastern (Kentucky)	27,907	37,390	−25.4
Western (Kentucky)	33,424	39,945	−16.3
Louisiana	3,439	2,605	32.0
Maryland	2,149	1,978	8.7
Mississippi	3,143	3,737	−15.9
Missouri	138	363	−61.9
Montana	41,864	44,562	−6.1
New Mexico	19,341	21,963	−11.9
North Dakota	28,802	29,157	−1.2
Ohio	17,195	22,252	−22.7
Oklahoma	780	904	−13.7
Pennsylvania total	50,472	60,910	−17.1
Anthracite (Pennsylvania)	1,993	1,833	8.7
Bituminous (Pennsylvania)	48,479	59,076	−17.9
Tennessee	850	839	1.2
Texas	35,024	43,654	−19.8
Utah	14,825	17,934	−17.3
Virginia	13,450	15,059	−10.7
West Virginia total	95,523	112,187	−14.9
Northern (West Virginia)	47,648	48,858	−2.5
Southern (West Virginia)	47,875	63,329	−24.4
Wyoming	375,773	395,665	−5.0
Appalachia total	220,562	266,979	−17.4
Appalachia Central	90,082	116,617	−22.8
Appalachia Northern	117,464	133,998	−12.3
Appalachia Southern	13,016	16,363	−20.5
Interior Region total	166,660	188,604	−11.6
Illinois Basin	123,844	137,181	−9.7
Interior	42,816	51,423	−16.7
Western Region total	507,324	542,842	−6.5
Powder River Basin	398,577	418,156	−4.7
Uinta Region	32,168	40,122	−19.8
Western	76,579	84,563	−9.4
East of Mississippi River	347,549	407,897	−14.8
West of Mississippi River	546,996	590,528	−7.4
U.S. subtotal	**894,545**	**998,425**	**−10.4**
Refuse recovery	1,390	1,624	−14.4
U.S. total	**895,936**	**1,000,049**	**−10.4**

Note: Total may not equal sum of components because of independent rounding.

SOURCE: Adapted from "Table 2. Coal Production by State (Thousand Short Tons)," in *Quarterly Coal Report (Abbreviated) October–December 2015*, U.S. Energy Information Administration, April 2016, http://www.eia.gov/coal/production/quarterly/pdf/0121154q.pdf (accessed August 15, 2016)

TABLE 4.4

Productive capacity of coal mines, by state and type of mining, 2014

[Thousand short tons]

Coal-producing state	2014 Underground	2014 Surface	2014 Total
Alabama	13,915	5,530	19,445
Alaska	—	3,000	3,000
Arizona	—	8,500	8,500
Arkansas	240	—	240
Colorado	23,200	6,642	29,842
Illinois	68,336	8,008	76,344
Indiana	21,130	28,274	49,404
Kansas	—	65	65
Kentucky total	64,940	32,921	97,861
Kentucky (east)	23,700	25,651	49,351
Kentucky (west)	41,240	7,270	48,510
Louisiana	—	3,274	3,274
Maryland	837	1,874	2,711
Mississippi	—	8,700	8,700
Missouri	—	378	378
Montana	10,000	41,900	51,900
New Mexico	9,000	18,400	27,400
North Dakota	—	32,828	32,828
Ohio	22,293	23,037	45,330
Oklahoma	500	700	1,200
Pennsylvania total	56,699	10,914	67,613
Pennsylvania (anthracite)	101	3,339	3,440
Pennsylvania (bituminous)	56,598	7,575	64,173
Tennessee	641	311	952
Texas	—	45,824	45,824
Utah	22,313	2,000	24,313
Virginia	12,413	6,096	18,509
West Virginia total	98,157	40,665	138,822
West Virginia (northern)	53,574	1,474	55,049
West Virginia (southern)	44,583	39,190	83,773
Wyoming	5,000	484,262	489,262
U.S. total	**429,614**	**814,102**	**1,243,716**

— = No data reported.
Note: Excludes refuse recovery and mines producing less than 25,000 short tons, which are not required to provide data. Totals may not equal sum of components because of independent rounding.

SOURCE: Adapted from "Table 11. Productive Capacity of Coal Mines by State, 2014 and 2013," in *Annual Coal Report 2014*, U.S. Energy Information Administration, March 2016, http://www.eia.gov/coal/annual/pdf/acr.pdf (accessed August 15, 2016)

2015—507.3 million tons (460.2 million t)—which was more than half (57%) of the nation's total.

Table 4.4 shows the productive capacity of the nation's coal mines in 2014. This is the maximum amount of coal that could have been produced that year according to the mining companies. West Virginia had the largest underground capacity at 98.2 million tons (89.1 million t), while Wyoming had the largest surface capacity at 484.3 million tons (439.3 million t). Overall, domestic productive capacity totaled more than 1.2 trillion tons (1.1 trillion t). In *Annual Coal Report 2014* (March 2016, http://www.eia.gov/coal/annual/pdf/acr.pdf), the EIA indicates that 80.1% of U.S. coal mine capacity was used in 2014.

Until the 21st century bituminous coal was the most produced rank in the United States. (See Figure 4.2.) Sub-bituminous coal production began increasing during the early 1970s, and by around 2008 the two coal types were produced in near equal amounts. As shown in Figure 4.3 and Figure 4.4, in 2015 production by coal rank was:

- Subbituminous coal—428.2 million tons (388.4 million t) or 47.8% of the total

- Bituminous coal—394.9 million tons (358.2 million t) or 44.1% of the total

- Lignite—70.7 million tons (64.1 million t) or 7.9% of the total

FIGURE 4.2

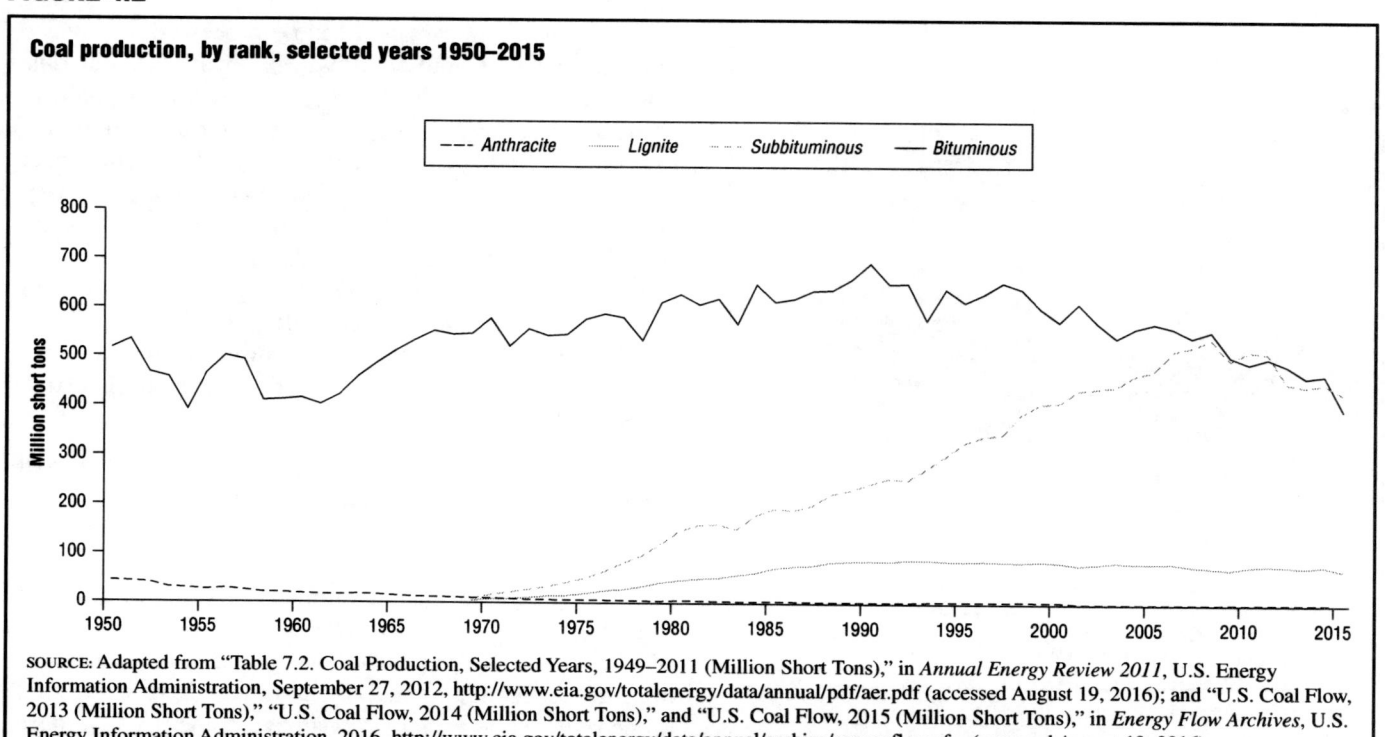

Coal production, by rank, selected years 1950–2015

Anthracite
Lignite
Subbituminous
Bituminous
Million short tons
800
700
600
500
400
300
200
100
0
1950
1955
1960
1965
1970
1975
1980
1985
1990
1995
2000
2005
2010
2015

SOURCE: Adapted from "Table 7.2. Coal Production, Selected Years, 1949–2011 (Million Short Tons)," in *Annual Energy Review 2011*, U.S. Energy Information Administration, September 27, 2012, http://www.eia.gov/totalenergy/data/annual/pdf/aer.pdf (accessed August 19, 2016); and "U.S. Coal Flow, 2013 (Million Short Tons)," "U.S. Coal Flow, 2014 (Million Short Tons)," and "U.S. Coal Flow, 2015 (Million Short Tons)," in *Energy Flow Archives*, U.S. Energy Information Administration, 2016, http://www.eia.gov/totalenergy/data/annual/archive/energyflow.cfm (accessed August 19, 2016)

FIGURE 4.3

Coal flow, 2015

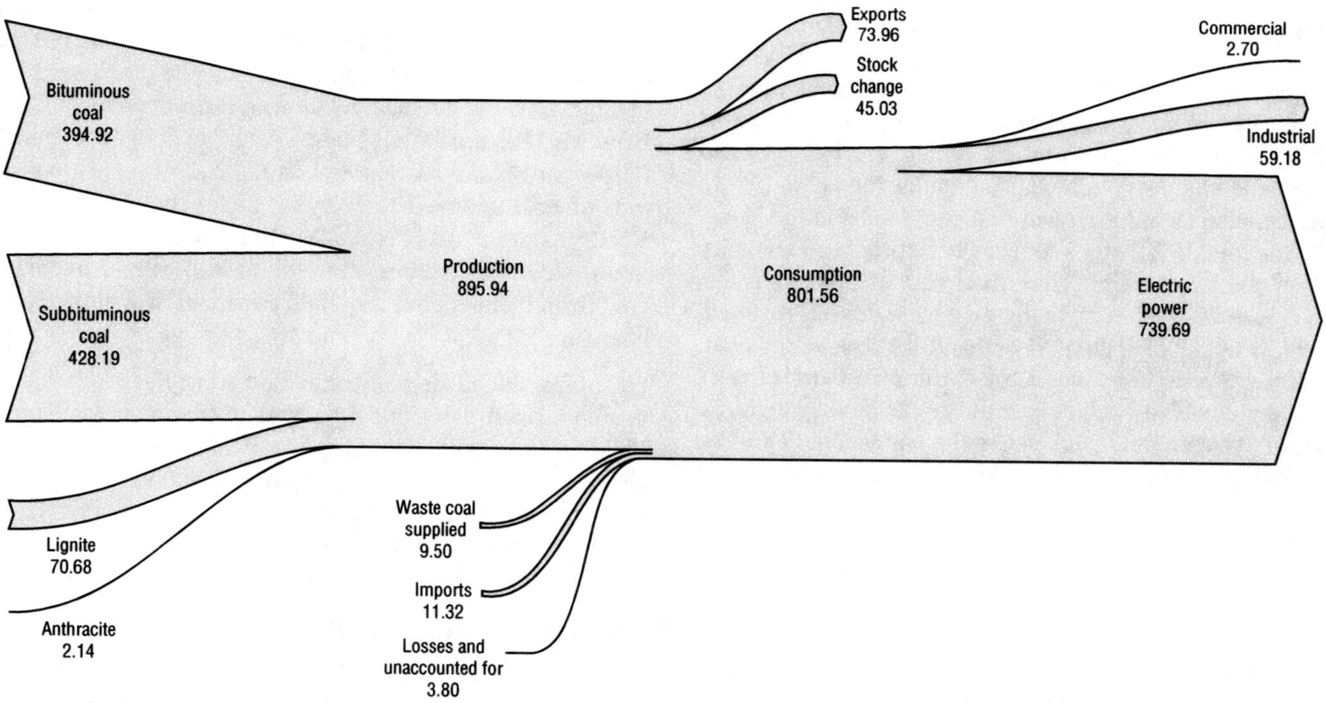

Bituminous coal 394.92
Subbituminous coal 428.19
Lignite 70.68
Anthracite 2.14
Production 895.94
Waste coal supplied 9.50
Imports 11.32
Losses and unaccounted for 3.80
Exports 73.96
Stock change 45.03
Consumption 801.56
Commercial 2.70
Industrial 59.18
Electric power 739.69

Notes: Production categories are estimated; all data are preliminary. Values are derived from source data prior to rounding for publication. Totals may not equal sum of components due to independent rounding.

SOURCE: "U.S. Coal Flow, 2015 (Million Short Tons)," in *Diagrams: Energy Flows*, U.S. Energy Information Administration, 2016, http://www.eia.gov/totalenergy/data/monthly/pdf/flow/coal.pdf (accessed August 15, 2016)

FIGURE 4.4

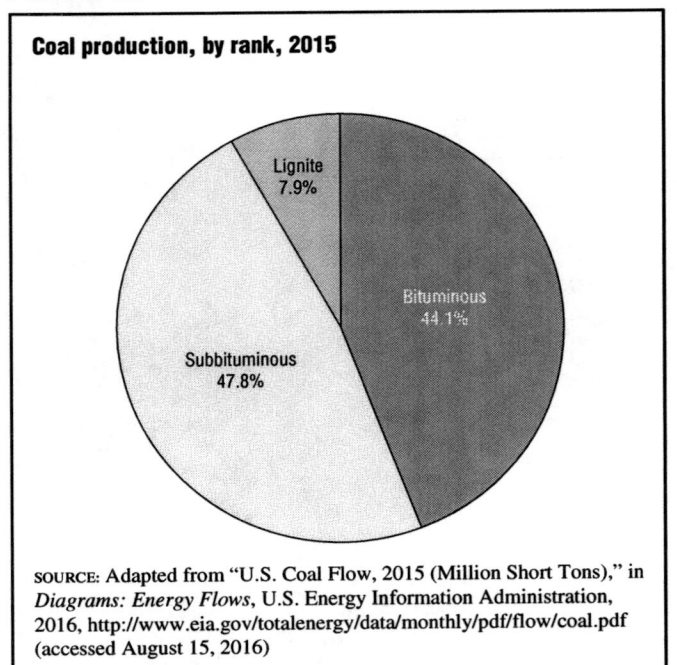

Coal production, by rank, 2015

Lignite 7.9%

Bituminous 44.1%

Subbituminous 47.8%

SOURCE: Adapted from "U.S. Coal Flow, 2015 (Million Short Tons)," in *Diagrams: Energy Flows*, U.S. Energy Information Administration, 2016, http://www.eia.gov/totalenergy/data/monthly/pdf/flow/coal.pdf (accessed August 15, 2016)

- Anthracite—2.1 million tons (1.9 million t) or 0.2% of the total

The EIA provides in *Annual Energy Review 2011* (September 2012, http://www.eia.gov/totalenergy/data/annual/pdf/aer.pdf) a historical production breakdown by mining method and location. During the 1970s surface mining first surpassed underground mining in terms of coal volume. Surface mining is easier, cheaper, and more efficient in terms of productivity than underground mining. Before 1999 most of the nation's coal was mined east of the Mississippi River. Miners had been digging deeper and deeper into the Appalachian Mountains for years before bulldozers began cutting open rich coal seams in the West. Since the mid-1990s more coal has been produced annually west of the Mississippi River than east of the river. The growth in coal production in the western states has resulted, in part, because of increased demand for low-sulfur coal, which is concentrated there. Low-sulfur coal burns cleaner than other coals and is less harmful to the environment. In addition, western coal is closer to the surface, so it can be extracted by surface mining, rather than by underground mining. Improved rail service has also made it easier to deliver coal mined in the western part of the country to electric power plants located in the eastern United States.

Waste Coal

As shown in Table 4.2, waste coal amounts have increased dramatically since 1990, when the EIA first began tracking this material. In 2015 mining operations supplied 9.5 million tons (8.6 million t) of waste coal to the electric power and industrial sectors. This value was down from 12.1 million tons (11 million t) in 2014.

Coal Products

Like crude oil, raw coal can be processed to produce other marketable commodities. For example, coal dust can be blended with binding agents, such as asphalt, to produce briquettes, pellets, or other materials with industrial uses. Coke is a high-value product made from coal at specialized facilities. The coal is heated to a high temperature to eliminate volatile impurities and fuse together certain carbon and ash materials within the coal. The result is a solid material with a high heat content of 24.8 million Btu per ton, according to the EIA (2016, http://www.eia.gov/tools/glossary/index.cfm?id=C). Coke is combusted as a fuel and used in certain industrial processes, particularly steelmaking.

Coal can also be processed into fuels called coal synfuels. These may be either liquid or gaseous and can be manufactured by subjecting extracted coal to high temperatures and pressures. Another method is called in situ (in place) coal gasification (ISCG) or underground coal gasification. ISCG processes burn coal while it is still in the ground to produce gas that can be pumped to the surface. Although such technologies have been tried in the past, modern innovations have made ISCG a more viable alternative for fuel production. It could conceivably produce huge amounts of energy from the earth's vast coal seams that are too deep to mine, under the oceans, or otherwise untapped because of technological or economic reasons. For example, in "Newly Discovered North Sea Coal 'Could Power Britain for Centuries'" (IBTimes.co.uk, March 30, 2014), Jack Moore notes that British researchers believe that trillions of tons of coal lying underneath the North Sea could be exploited using ISCG. Likewise, Neil Reynolds describes in "Cape Breton's Undersea Coal Field a Vein to Energy Wealth" (GlobeandMail.com, September 12, 2013) the billions of tons of coal believed to be lying under the waters of the North Atlantic near Nova Scotia, Canada. Traditional mining methods were used in the past to extract undersea coal from the area, but any future extraction will likely be based on ISCG.

Many ISCG demonstration projects have been conducted around the world to gather design data for larger-scale applications. As of September 2016, one of the most watched projects was the Swan Hills Synfuel project (http://swanhills-synfuels.com) in Alberta, Canada, which is scheduled to begin commercial operation in 2018.

DOMESTIC COAL CONSUMPTION

After rising for many decades, domestic coal consumption dipped dramatically during the latter part of the first decade of the 21st century. (See Figure 4.5.) As shown in Table 3.6 in Chapter 3, this period saw lowering natural gas prices, which made natural gas a more attractive fuel than coal to industrial users and electric power producers.

FIGURE 4.5

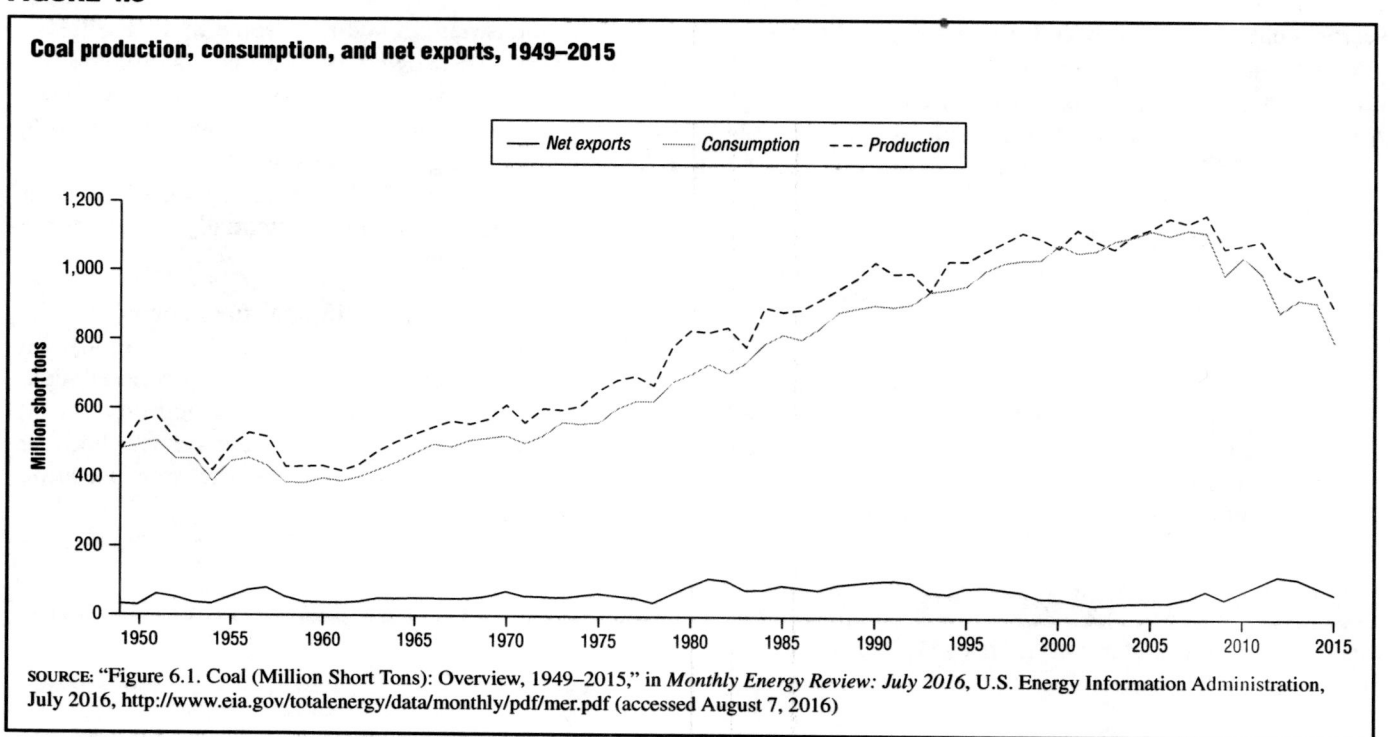

Coal production, consumption, and net exports, 1949–2015

SOURCE: "Figure 6.1. Coal (Million Short Tons): Overview, 1949–2015," in *Monthly Energy Review: July 2016*, U.S. Energy Information Administration, July 2016, http://www.eia.gov/totalenergy/data/monthly/pdf/mer.pdf (accessed August 7, 2016)

FIGURE 4.6

Coal consumption, by sector, 1949–2015

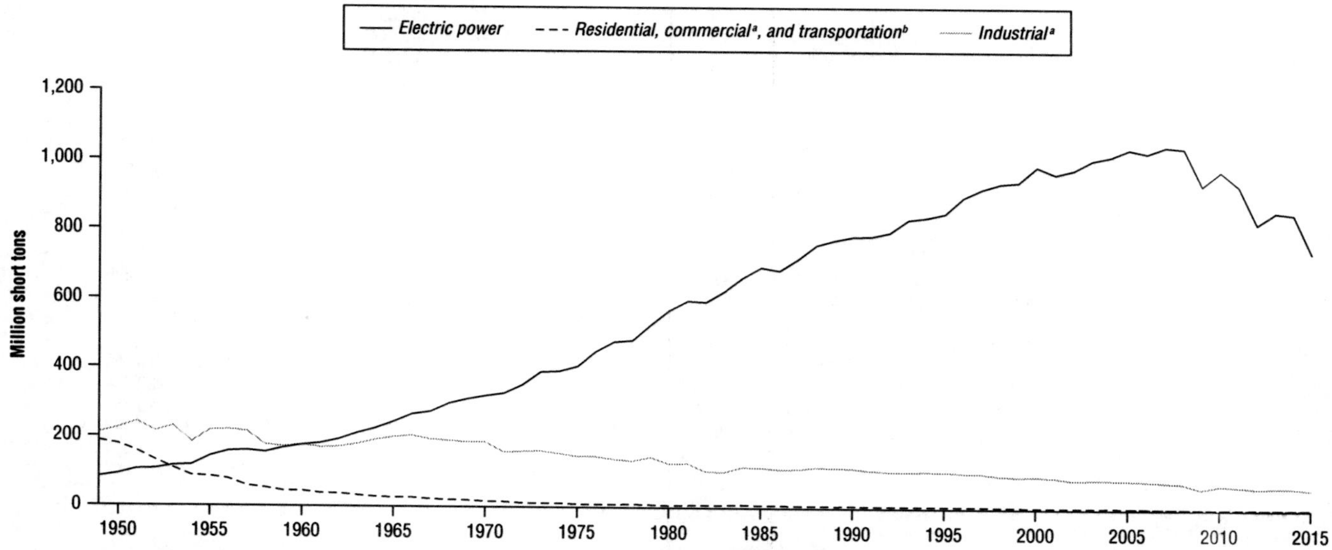

aIncludes combined-heat-and-power (CHP) plants and a small number of electricity-only-plants.
bFor 1978 forward, small amounts of transportation sector use are included in "Industrial."

SOURCE: "Figure 6.1. Coal (Million Short Tons): Consumption by Sector, 1949–2015," in *Monthly Energy Review: July 2016*, U.S. Energy Information Administration, July 2016, http://www.eia.gov/totalenergy/data/monthly/pdf/mer.pdf (accessed August 7, 2016)

Coal Consumption by Sector

Figure 4.6 provides a historical breakdown of coal consumption by sector. Since the early 1960s the electric power sector has been the dominant consumer of coal. In 2015 it used 739.7 million tons (671 million t) and accounted for 92% of total consumption, up from only

19% in 1950. (See Table 4.5.) In the electric power sector, coal is pulverized and either burned directly or gasified. Steam from boilers or the hot coal gases turn turbines, which power generators that create electricity. According to the EIA, in *Monthly Energy Review: July 2016*, coal-fired plants produced 1.3 trillion kilowatt-hours of electricity in 2015, or 34% of the nation's total net generation from the electric power sector. Net generation refers to the power available to the system—it does not include power used at the generating plants themselves.

The industrial sector was the second-largest coal consumer in 2015. (See Figure 4.6 and Table 4.5.) It used 59.2 million tons (53.7 million t), which was 7% of total consumption, down from 45% in 1950. Coal is used in many industrial applications, including the chemical,

cement, paper, synthetic fuels, metals, and food-processing industries. In addition, some industrial facilities burn coal in their own electricity plants or combined heat and power plants. As noted earlier, coal is also used to make coke and other products. As shown in Table 4.5, coke plants were large coal consumers during the 1950s and 1960s; however, the U.S. steel industry declined over subsequent decades, which substantially reduced the demand for coking coal.

Coal was once a significant fuel source in the residential and commercial sectors. (See Figure 4.6 and Table 4.5.) After the early 1950s, however, coal was replaced by oil, natural gas, and electricity. Thus, the residential and commercial sectors have become minor consumers of coal, as has the transportation sector.

TABLE 4.5

Coal consumption, by sector, selected years 1950–2015

[Thousand short tons]

		Commercial			End-use sectors — Industrial	Other industrial					Electric power sector[e, f]	Total
	Residential	CHP[a]	Other[b]	Total	Coke plants	CHP[c]	Non-CHP[d]	Total	Total	Transportation		
1950 Total	51,562	g	63,021	63,021	104,014	h	120,623	120,623	224,637	63,011	91,871	494,102
1955 Total	35,590	g	32,852	32,852	107,743	h	110,096	110,096	217,839	16,972	143,759	447,012
1960 Total	24,159	g	16,789	16,789	81,385	h	96,017	96,017	177,402	3,046	176,685	398,081
1965 Total	14,635	g	11,041	11,041	95,286	h	105,560	105,560	200,846	655	244,788	471,965
1970 Total	9,024	g	7,090	7,090	96,481	h	90,156	90,156	186,637	298	320,182	523,231
1975 Total	2,823	g	6,587	6,587	83,598	h	63,646	63,646	147,244	24	405,962	562,640
1980 Total	1,355	g	5,097	5,097	66,657	h	60,347	60,347	127,004	h	569,274	702,730
1985 Total	1,711	g	6,068	6,068	41,056	h	75,372	75,372	116,429	h	693,841	818,049
1990 Total	1,345	1,191	4,189	5,379	38,877	27,781	48,549	76,330	115,207	h	782,567[f]	904,498
1995 Total	755	1,419	3,633	5,052	33,011	29,363	43,693	73,055	106,067	h	850,230	962,104
2000 Total	454	1,547	2,126	3,673	28,939	28,031	37,177	65,208	94,147	h	985,821	1,084,095
2001 Total	481	1,448	2,441	3,888	26,075	25,755	39,514	65,268	91,344	h	964,433	1,060,146
2002 Total	533	1,405	2,506	3,912	23,656	26,232	34,515	60,747	84,403	h	977,507	1,066,355
2003 Total	551	1,816	1,869	3,685	24,248	24,846	36,415	61,261	85,509	h	1,005,116	1,094,861
2004 Total	512	1,917	2,693	4,610	23,670	26,613	35,582	62,195	85,865	h	1,016,268	1,107,255
2005 Total	378	1,922	2,420	4,342	23,434	25,875	34,465	60,340	83,774	h	1,037,485	1,125,978
2006 Total	290	1,886	1,050	2,936	22,957	25,262	34,210	59,472	82,429	h	1,026,636	1,112,292
2007 Total	353	1,927	1,247	3,173	22,715	22,537	34,078	56,615	79,331	h	1,045,141	1,127,998
2008 Total	i	2,021	1,485	3,506	22,070	21,902	32,491	54,393	76,463	h	1,040,580	1,120,548
2009 Total	i	1,798	1,412	3,210	15,326	19,766	25,549	45,314	60,641	h	933,627	997,478
2010 Total	i	1,720	1,361	3,081	21,092	24,638	24,650	49,289	70,381	h	975,052	1,048,514
2011 Total	i	1,668	1,125	2,793	21,434	22,319	23,919	46,238	67,671	h	932,484	1,002,948
2012 Total	i	1,450	595	2,045	20,751	20,065	22,773	42,838	63,589	h	823,551	889,185
2013 Total	i	1,356	595	1,951	21,474	19,761	23,294	43,055	64,529	h	857,962	924,442
2014 Total	i	1,063	824	1,887	21,297	19,076	23,870	42,946	64,243	h	851,602	917,731
2015 Total	i	861	F1,836	F2,697	F18,851	18,028	F22,297	F40,325	F59,176	h	739,689	801,563

[a]Commercial combined-heat-and-power (CHP) and a small number of commercial electricity-only plants, such as those at hospitals and universities.
[b]All commercial sector fuel use other than that in "Commercial CHP."
[c]Industrial combined-heat-and-power (CHP) and a small number of industrial electricity-only plants.
[d]All industrial sector fuel use other than that in "Coke Plants" and "Industrial CHP."
[e]The electric power sector comprises electricity-only and combined-heat-and-power (CHP) plants within the NAICS 22 category whose primary business is to sell electricity, or electricity and heat, to the public.
[f]Through 1988, data are for electric utilities only. Beginning in 1989, data are for electric utilities and independent power producers.
[g]Included in "Commercial Other."
[h]Included in "Industrial Non-CHP."
[i]Beginning in 2008, residential coal consumption data are no longer collected by the U.S. Energy Information Administration (EIA).
F = Forecast.
Notes: Data values preceded by "F" are derived from the U.S. Energy Information Administration's Short-Term Integrated Forecasting System. Totals may not equal sum of components due to independent rounding. Geographic coverage is the 50 states and the District of Columbia.

SOURCE: Adapted from "Table 6.2. Coal Consumption by Sector (Thousand Short Tons)," in *Monthly Energy Review: July 2016*, U.S. Energy Information Administration, July 2016, http://www.eia.gov/totalenergy/data/monthly/pdf/mer.pdf (accessed August 7, 2016)

COAL IMPORTS AND EXPORTS

As shown in Figure 4.5, domestic coal consumption was slightly lower than domestic production for most years dating back to 1949. As a result, the United States has exported small amounts of coal annually. (See Table 4.2.) In 2015 exports totaled 74 million tons (67.1 million t), which was considerably higher than many annual levels from the latter 20th century. According to the EIA, in *Quarterly Coal Report: October–December 2015* (August 2016, http://www.eia.gov/coal/production/quarterly/pdf/0121154q.pdf), the major destinations for U.S. coal in 2015 were:

- Netherlands—12.9 million tons (11.7 million t)

- India—6.4 million tons (5.8 million t)

- Brazil—6.3 million tons (5.7 million t)

- South Korea—6.1 million tons (5.6 million t)

- Canada—6 million tons (5.4 million t)

The United States has historically imported small amounts of coal each year. (See Table 4.2.) In 2015 imports totaled 11.3 million tons (10.3 million t). The EIA notes in *Quarterly Coal Report: October–December 2015* that more than three-fourths (79%) of the imported coal came from Colombia. Other source countries included Canada, Indonesia, and Venezuela.

THE DOMESTIC OUTLOOK

The EIA forecasts future energy production, consumption, and price data in *Annual Energy Outlook 2016 with Projections to 2040* (August 2016, https://www.eia.gov/forecasts/aeo/pdf/0383(2016).pdf). The agency considers various scenarios for future domestic coal demand. Table 4.6 shows the expected production levels through 2040 for a middle-of-the-road reference case. The EIA predicts that domestic coal production will decline over coming decades, dropping 1.2% between 2015 and 2040 due to decreasing domestic and world demand. As noted earlier, the electric power sector is, by far, the largest coal consumer. However, coal faces stiff competition from natural gas and renewable fuels in this sector over coming decades. In addition, domestic demand for coal has been and is expected to be muted by environmental laws such as the Mercury Air Toxics Standard (which took effect in 2015–16) and the Clean Power Plan (which is slated to take effect in 2022). Both laws are discussed in more detail in Chapter 8.

WORLD COAL PRODUCTION AND CONSUMPTION

The EIA provides in "International Energy Statistics" (2016, http://www.eia.gov/cfapps/ipdbproject/IEDIndex3.cfm?tid=1&pid=7&aid=1) data by country and region regarding production and consumption of energy resources. As of September 2016, complete data were available through 2012. Table 4.7 shows total coal production in 2012 for the world, by region, and for the top-20 producers. Total production was 8.7 billion tons (7.9 billion t). Asia and Oceania was the largest producing region, accounting for 5.8 billion tons (5.3 billion t), or 67% of world production. North America was second with 1.1 billion tons (1 billion t), or 13% of the total. China led all countries with 4 billion tons (3.7 billion t), or 46% of world production. The United States was second with 1 billion tons (921.7 million t), or 12% of the total, followed by India, Indonesia, and Australia.

The total world coal consumption in 2012 was 8.4 billion tons (7.7 billion t). (See Table 4.8.) China was the leading consumer, at 4.2 billion tons (3.8 billion t) and accounting for 49% of the world total. Other top consumers in 2012 included the United States, India, Russia, and Germany.

The International Energy Agency (IEA) is an independent member organization that focuses on energy issues. In the press release "Global Coal Demand Stalls

TABLE 4.6

Coal production, by region, 2015 and forecast through 2040

[Million short tons, unless otherwise noted]

Supply, disposition, and prices	2015	2020	2025	2030	2035	2040	2015–2040
Production*							
Appalachia	223	202	165	138	154	144	−1.7%
Interior	165	197	193	148	172	170	0.1%
West	484	473	408	378	335	329	−1.5%
East of the Mississippi	346	351	307	243	281	276	−0.9%
West of the Mississippi	526	521	460	422	380	367	−1.4%
Total	**873**	**872**	**766**	**664**	**661**	**643**	**−1.2%**

*Includes anthracite, bituminous coal, subbituminous coal, and lignite.
Note: Totals may not equal sum of components due to independent rounding.

SOURCE: Adapted from "Table 15. Coal Supply, Disposition, and Prices," in *Annual Energy Outlook 2016 Early Release*, U.S. Energy Information Administration, May 2016, https://www.eia.gov/forecasts/aeo/excel/aeotab_15.xlsx (accessed August 12, 2016)

TABLE 4.7

TABLE 4.8

World production of coal, by region and selected country, 2012

[Million short tons]

	2012
World	**8,695**
Regions	
Asia & Oceania	5,802
North America	1,107
Europe	774
Eurasia	607
Africa	295
Central & South America	110
Middle East	1
Countries	
China	4,025
United States	1,016
India	650
Indonesia	488
Australia	464
Russia	390
South Africa	286
Germany	217
Poland	158
Kazakhstan	139
Colombia	99
Turkey	77
Canada	73
Ukraine	71
Greece	68
Czech Republic	61
Vietnam	46
Korea, North	43
Serbia	42
Romania	38

SOURCE: Adapted from "Table. Total Primary Coal Production (Thousand Short Tons)," in *International Energy Statistics*, U.S. Energy Information Administration, 2016, http://www.eia.gov/cfapps/ipdbproject/iedindex3.cfm?tid=1&pid=7&aid=1&cid=regions&syid=2012&eyid=2012&unit=TST (accessed August 16, 2016)

World consumption of coal, by region and selected country, 2012

[Million short tons]

	2012
World	**8,449**
Regions	
Asia & Oceania	5,707
Europe	1,027
North America	956
Eurasia	465
Africa	221
Central & South America	52
Middle East	23
Countries	
China	4,151
United States	889
India	745
Russia	274
Germany	269
South Africa	206
Japan	202
Australia	151
Poland	147
Korea, South	138
Turkey	108
Kazakhstan	105
Ukraine	77
Taiwan	72
Greece	70
United Kingdom	70
Indonesia	66
Czech Republic	55
Canada	46
Serbia	43

SOURCE: Adapted from "Table. Total Coal Consumption (Thousand Short Tons)," in *International Energy Statistics*, U.S. Energy Information Administration, 2016, http://www.eia.gov/cfapps/ipdbproject/iedindex3.cfm?tid=1&pid=1&aid=2&cid=regions&syid=2012&eyid=2012&unit=TST (accessed August 16, 2016)

after More than a Decade of Relentless Growth" (December 18, 2015, http://www.iea.org/newsroomandevents/pressreleases/2015/december/global-coal-demand-stalls-after-more-than-a-decade-of-relentless-growth.html), the IEA summarizes its worldwide forecast for coal demand through 2020. Overall, the agency indicates that the coal industry "is facing huge pressures," primarily due to declining consumption in China. That nation accounted for half of the world's coal consumption in 2014; however, its economy is shifting away from dependence on energy-intensive industries and expanding electricity production from renewable resources. Outside of China, the IEA expects coal demand will increase "modestly" through 2020.

U.S. COAL PRICES

The EIA tracks and forecasts various types of coal prices, including the sales price at the coal mine mouth (the first point of sale) and the sales price at the point of delivery. Table 4.9 lists coal prices for 2015 and forecast through 2040. The prices are expressed in 2015 dollars (i.e., assuming that the value of the dollar remains constant at that level). In 2015 the average mine mouth price

was $33.80 per ton. The price is expected to decline 0.5% between 2015 and 2040. Overall, the average delivered price in 2015 was $45.85. It is predicted to increase 0.5% between 2015 and 2040.

In *Annual Coal Report 2014*, the EIA provides 2014 sales prices by rank as follows:

- Anthracite—$90.98 per ton
- Bituminous—$55.99 per ton
- Lignite—$19.44 per ton
- Subbituminous—$14.72 per ton

The average sales price in 2014 was $34.83 per ton. Surface-mined coal ($22.83 per ton) was far less expensive than underground-mined coal ($56.97 per ton).

Coal Pricing Factors

The pricing for coal, like for oil and natural gas, is dependent on various supply and demand factors and weather. Coal demand is particularly sensitive to weather conditions because the vast majority of production goes to electric power generation. Electricity demand varies strongly with outdoor temperature, given that heating and

TABLE 4.9

Coal prices, by type, 2015 and forecast through 2040

[Million short tons, unless otherwise noted]

Supply, disposition, and prices	2015	2020	2025	2030	2035	2040	2015–2040
Average minemouth price[a]							
(2015 dollars per short ton)	33.80	33.60	33.99	33.84	37.58	38.68	0.5%
Average	45.85	46.97	47.84	48.45	50.42	51.88	0.5%
Exports[b]	86.69	84.01	81.74	81.18	84.78	83.89	−0.1%

[a]Includes reported prices for both open market and captive mines. Prices weighted by production, which differs from average minemouth prices published in Energy Information Administration data reports where it is weighted by reported sales.
[b]Free-alongside-ship price at U.S. port of exit.
Note: Totals may not equal sum of components due to independent rounding. Data in 2015 dollars.

SOURCE: Adapted from "Table 15. Coal Supply, Disposition, and Prices," in *Annual Energy Outlook 2016 Early Release*, U.S. Energy Information Administration, May 2016, https://www.eia.gov/forecasts/aeo/excel/aeotab_15.xlsx (accessed August 12, 2016)

cooling homes and buildings are top electricity uses. Because the United States produces nearly all the coal it consumes, coal pricing in the United States is not dependent on foreign events and manipulation as is oil pricing.

As noted earlier, the electric power sector accounted for the vast majority of coal consumption in 2015. Thus, demand changes in that sector have a big impact on coal prices. Chapter 8 explains that natural gas is the chief competitor against coal in electricity production. When natural gas becomes cheaper than coal, the electric power sector uses more of its existing natural gas–burning units than its existing coal-burning units. This fuel switching greatly reduces the demand for coal and puts downward pressure on coal prices.

GOVERNMENT INTERVENTION. Coal pricing is also influenced by government actions. These include financial incentives, taxes, and regulations. Financial incentives put downward pressure on coal prices, whereas taxes and regulations push prices upward. The federal government and some state governments impose various kinds of taxes on domestically produced coal. The collected monies often go into trust funds that help offset some of the external costs of coal mining. (As is explained in Chapter 1, external costs are costs outside market costs.) The Black Lung Disability Fund has been operated since the late 1970s by the federal government and pays benefits under certain conditions to miners with black lung disease (a lung disease that is associated with coal mining). Federal and state taxes and fees are also used to clean up abandoned coal mines.

ENVIRONMENTAL ISSUES

Environmental concerns related to the coal industry primarily involve the mining and combustion stages. Surface mining strips away vegetation and soil, changing the landscape and producing vast amounts of dust and runoff contaminated with heavy metals. Although operating mines must implement control measures, there are thousands of abandoned coal mines across the country that pose a vexing environmental problem. Mountaintop mining in the Appalachian region of the eastern United States involves using explosives to blast away mountaintops and ridgelines to reach the coal seams underneath them. This method drastically alters the land and the natural stream flows in the area.

Coal is laden with heavy hydrocarbons and naturally occurring elements, such as mercury and sulfur. Combustion, even with pollution-control equipment, releases chemicals into the atmosphere that can negatively impact air and water quality, ecosystems, and human health. Huge amounts of ash and other waste by-products are produced that are often mixed with water as a slurry or sludge. Spills of these materials from pipes and ponds at power plants have flowed into nearby surface waters and contaminated them with toxic chemicals.

Coal combustion annually produces billions of tons of emissions of carbon dioxide, sulfur dioxide, and nitrogen oxides. The latter two gases are associated with air pollution problems, such as smog and acid rain (precipitation containing abnormally high levels of acids, particularly sulfuric acids). As is explained in Chapter 1, carbon emissions are blamed for enhancing global warming and related climate changes. Emissions from coal-fired power plants can also contain mercury, a toxin that settles in water bodies and is absorbed by fish and other aquatic creatures that humans ingest.

Fuel combustion is heavily regulated in the United States. Since 1970, when the Clean Air Act was passed, the government has imposed ever tighter restrictions on combustion emissions and invested money in making coal a cleaner burning fuel. For example, in 1984 Congress established the Clean Coal Technology program and directed the Department of Energy to administer projects designed to demonstrate more environmentally friendly and economically efficient coal uses. Mechanical and chemical control measures have been developed through industry and government investment that have substantially reduced the emissions from coal combustion and improved the nation's air quality.

Even stricter emissions standards have been implemented or proposed in the early 21st century. They include the Mercury and Air Toxics Standard and the Clean Power Plan, both of which are discussed in Chapter 8, along with pollution-control regulations and global warming mitigation techniques (such as carbon sequestration), which are related to electric power generation from coal.

CHAPTER 5
NUCLEAR ENERGY

During the early 20th century scientists succeeded in releasing energy that was bound up in the atom. Using a process called fission, they split apart the nucleus of a heavy atom (an atom containing many protons and neutrons) into two lighter nuclei. (See Figure 5.1.) The two resulting nuclei contained less mass than the original nucleus because some of the original atomic mass was converted into energy in the form of heat and radiation. Scientists knew that the key to harnessing this energy was setting up a chain reaction in which numerous heavy nuclei could be split apart in a confined space under controlled conditions. In 1942 the physicist Enrico Fermi (1901–1954) achieved this feat at the University of Chicago in Illinois by creating the first self-sustaining nuclear fission chain reaction. His work transformed energy production as the techniques were quickly refined to produce electricity using the heat that was generated during controlled fission reactions.

At first, nuclear power was hailed as a super energy source that could provide huge amounts of electricity without the need for burning air-polluting fossil fuels. Nuclear power's potential, however, has been tempered by the logistical, environmental, and safety considerations involved. Controlling chain reactions and disposing of the radioactive materials that result from them have proven to be massive challenges.

UNDERSTANDING NUCLEAR ENERGY

Radiation is a form of energy transfer that naturally results from the spontaneous emission of energy and/or high-energy particles from the nucleus of an atom. The earth is bombarded by radiation from the sun and other sources in outer space. In addition, many naturally radioactive elements, such as uranium, are found within the earth's crust and oceans. Scientists first produced nuclear energy by bombarding the nuclei of an isotope of uranium called uranium 235 (U-235). (Isotopes are atoms of an element that have the usual number of protons but different numbers of neutrons in their nuclei.)

Under proper conditions, the fission of a U-235 atom creates the needed cascading chain of nuclear reactions. If this series of reactions is regulated to occur slowly, as it is in nuclear power plants, the energy emitted can be captured for generating electricity. If this series of reactions is allowed to occur all at once, as in an atomic bomb, the energy emitted is explosive. (Plutonium 239 can also be used to generate a chain reaction similar to that of U-235.)

Figure 5.2 shows a pressurized-water nuclear reactor, the most common type of reactor in commercial use. Bombardment of uranium in the core of the reactor (shown as "1" in Figure 5.2) generates a nuclear reaction (fission) that produces heat. The heat from the reaction is carried away by water under high pressure ("2") to a steam generator ("3"). This heat vaporizes the water in the steam generator, producing steam. The steam is carried by a steamline ("4") to a turbine, making the attached generator spin, which produces electricity. The large cooling towers that are associated with nuclear plants cool the steam after it has run through the turbines. A boiling-water reactor works much the same way, except that the water surrounding the core boils and directly produces the steam, which is then piped to the turbine generator.

Commercial nuclear power reactors exclusively produce electrical power, which is measured by a basic unit called a watt. Because the watt is a relatively small unit, power plant capacities are typically measured in a multiple of watts, such as the kilowatt (10^3 watts), megawatt (MW; 10^6 watts), gigawatt (GW; 10^9), or terawatt (10^{12} watts). Electrical power production is often expressed in multiples of a kilowatt-hour (kWh; the amount of work done by a kilowatt over a period of one hour).

FIGURE 5.1

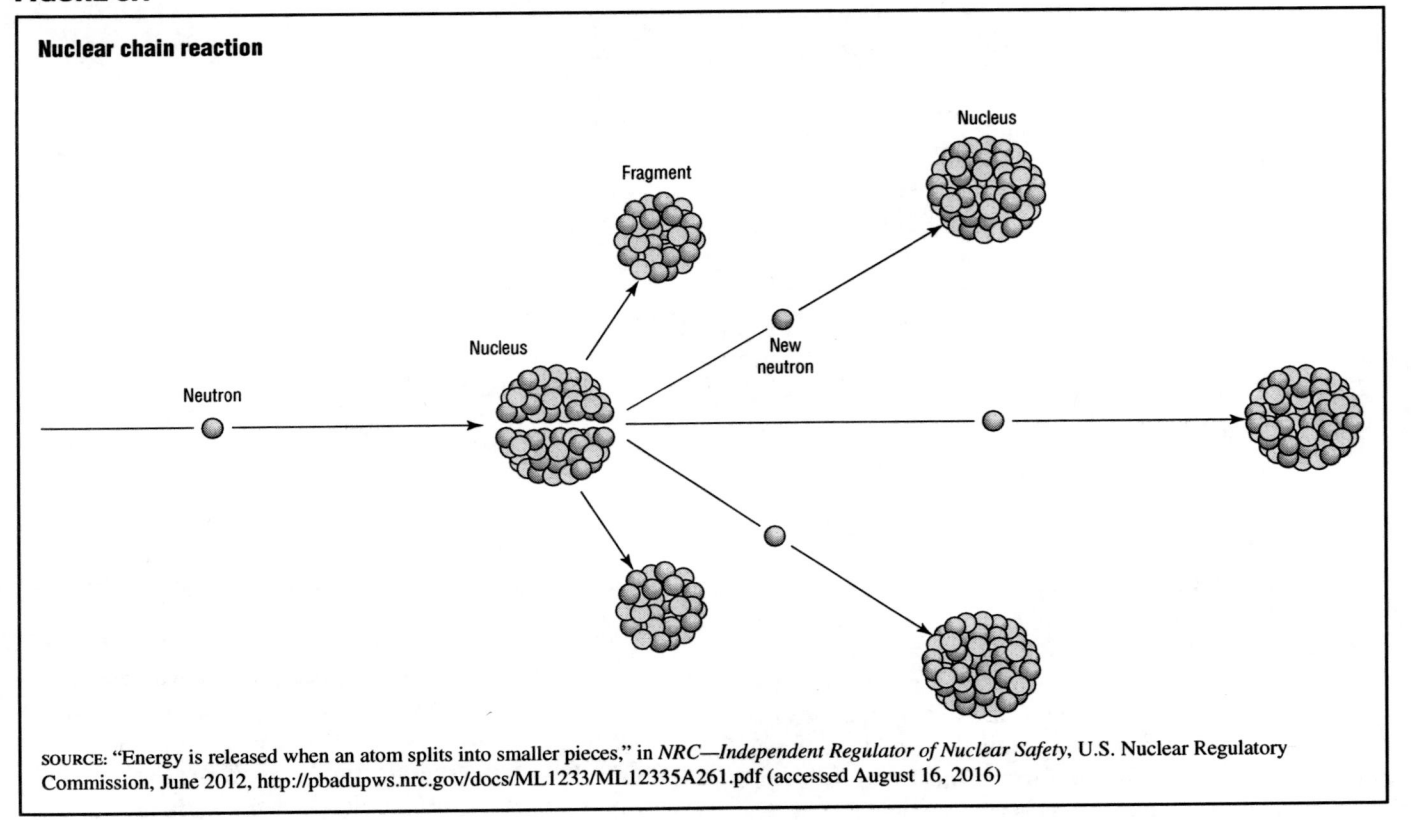

Nuclear chain reaction

SOURCE: "Energy is released when an atom splits into smaller pieces," in *NRC—Independent Regulator of Nuclear Safety*, U.S. Nuclear Regulatory Commission, June 2012, http://pbadupws.nrc.gov/docs/ML1233/ML12335A261.pdf (accessed August 16, 2016)

DOMESTIC URANIUM PRODUCTION, CONSUMPTION, AND PRICING

Uranium is a natural substance consisting almost entirely (greater than 99%) of U-238, which is not easily fissionable. Natural uranium contains only about 0.7% U-235 and a trace (extremely small) quantity of U-234. Uranium is present in low concentrations throughout the earth's soils, rocks, and water bodies. It is most highly concentrated in certain rock and mineral deposits called uranium ore. In "Nuclear Explained: Where Our Uranium Comes From" (July 20, 2016, http://www.eia.gov/energyexplained/index.cfm?page=nuclear_where), the U.S. Energy Information Administration (EIA) within the U.S. Department of Energy (DOE) explains that domestic uranium ore deposits are located primarily in the western United States. Uranium removal (recovery) from the deposits is regulated by the U.S. Nuclear Regulatory Commission (NRC).

Uranium Ore Recovery Methods

Uranium can be recovered by mining uranium ore from the ground. A typical uranium milling operation is shown in Figure 5.3. Mined ore is crushed and ground and then treated with liquid chemicals in a process called leaching. This separates the uranium from the other ore materials (or tailings). The uranium undergoes further chemical processing while the tailings go to disposal.

An alternative option for uranium recovery from ores is in situ (in place) leaching. (See Figure 5.4.) During in situ leaching a chemical solution is pumped through the underground ore deposits, and the separated uranium is pumped to the surface for processing.

Recovered uranium is processed into a powder called uranium concentrate, which has the chemical formula U_3O_8 (uranium oxide) and is commonly called yellowcake, although it may be yellow or brown in color.

Domestic Uranium Ore Mines and Production

The U.S. Environmental Protection Agency indicates in *Uranium Location Database Compilation* (August 2006, https://www.epa.gov/sites/production/files/2015-05/documents/402-r-05-009.pdf) that from the 1940s through the 1990s thousands of uranium ore mines operated in the United States, mostly in Arizona, Colorado, New Mexico, Utah, and Wyoming. Uranium ore is mined using mechanical methods that are similar to those used for other metal ores. A major difference is that uranium ore mining exposes workers to radioactivity. Uranium atoms naturally split by themselves at a slow rate, causing radioactive substances such as radon to accumulate slowly in the deposits.

According to the EIA, in *2015 Domestic Uranium Production Report* (May 2016, https://www.eia.gov/uranium/production/annual/pdf/dupr.pdf), only eight uranium

FIGURE 5.2

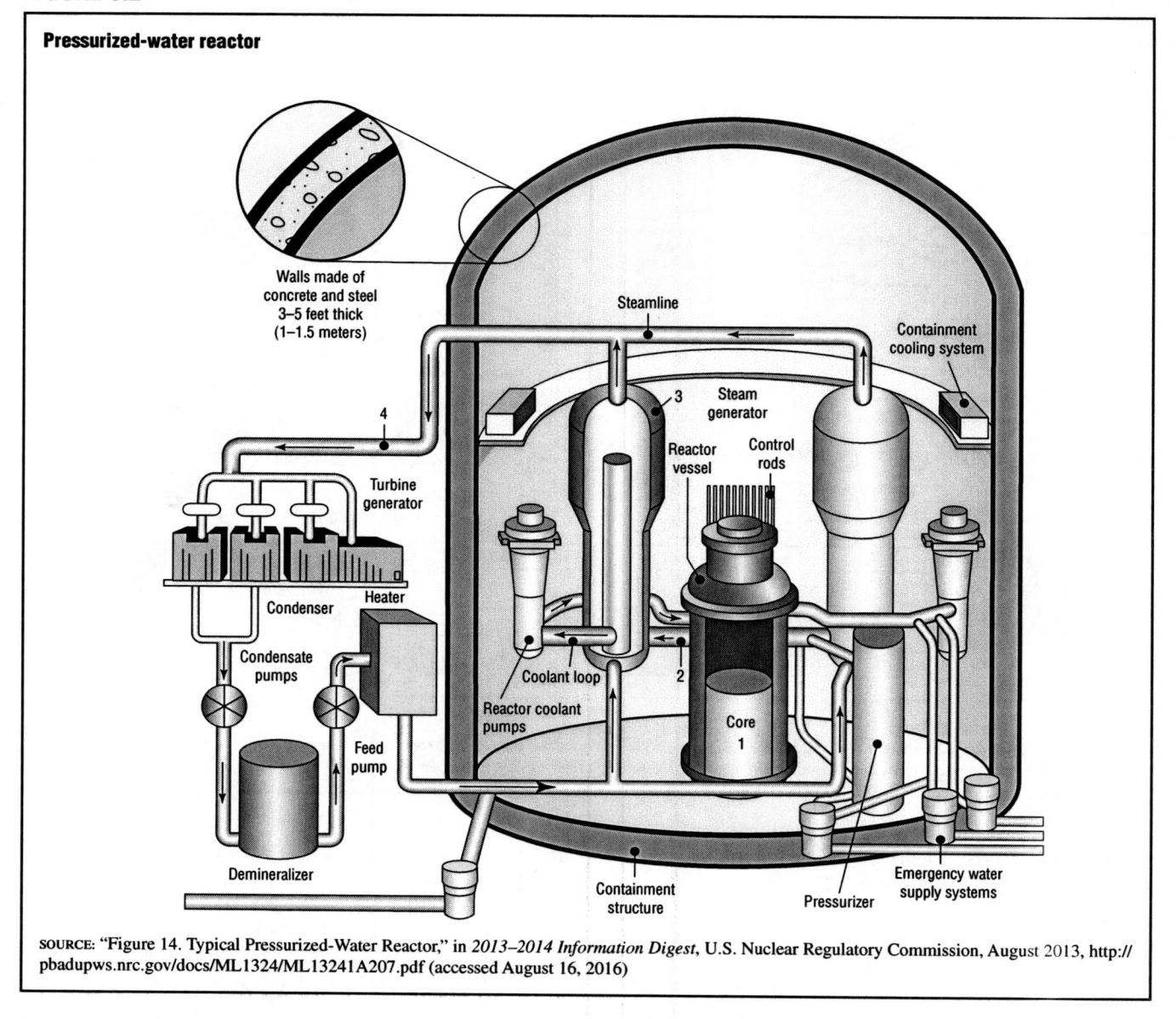

Pressurized-water reactor

Walls made of concrete and steel 3–5 feet thick (1–1.5 meters)

Steamline

Containment cooling system

3   Steam generator

Reactor vessel   Control rods

4

Turbine generator

Condenser   Heater

Condensate pumps

Coolant loop   2

Reactor coolant pumps

Core 1

Feed pump

Demineralizer

Containment structure   Pressurizer   Emergency water supply systems

SOURCE: "Figure 14. Typical Pressurized-Water Reactor," in *2013–2014 Information Digest*, U.S. Nuclear Regulatory Commission, August 2013, http://pbadupws.nrc.gov/docs/ML1324/ML13241A207.pdf (accessed August 16, 2016)

mines were in operation in the United States in 2015. One of the mines extracted ore and the other seven used in situ leaching. In addition, some uranium was recovered at other facilities from mining waste materials and by-products, such as mill tailings and mine water.

Uranium Consumption and Trade

Uranium has a variety of industrial applications. It is also used to produce nuclear weapons and as a fuel source for nuclear-powered submarines and ships. However, uranium is primarily used for electricity production. For this purpose yellowcake is made into a suitable fuel through processes called conversion and enrichment. During conversion, yellowcake is combined with fluorine to produce uranium hexafluoride (UF_6).

Nuclear reactor fuel requires a higher concentration of U-235 than what exists in natural uranium ore, yellowcake, or UF_6. These materials must be enriched to make the uranium more concentrated. According to the NRC, in "Uranium Enrichment" (July 19, 2016, http://www.nrc.gov/materials/fuel-cycle-fac/ur-enrichment.html), there are various means for enriching uranium; however, the gas centrifuge process is the primary method used in the United States. UF_6 gas is fed into a series of cylinders and rotated at high speed. The heavier molecules making up the enriched gas become concentrated near the outer wall of the apparatus and are removed. The enriched gas is then cooled and solidified for transport to fuel fabrication facilities. There, the solid UF_6 is vaporized and chemically transferred into uranium dioxide (UO_2) powder. (See Figure 5.5.) The powder is pressed into pellets that are stacked inside rods, which

FIGURE 5.3

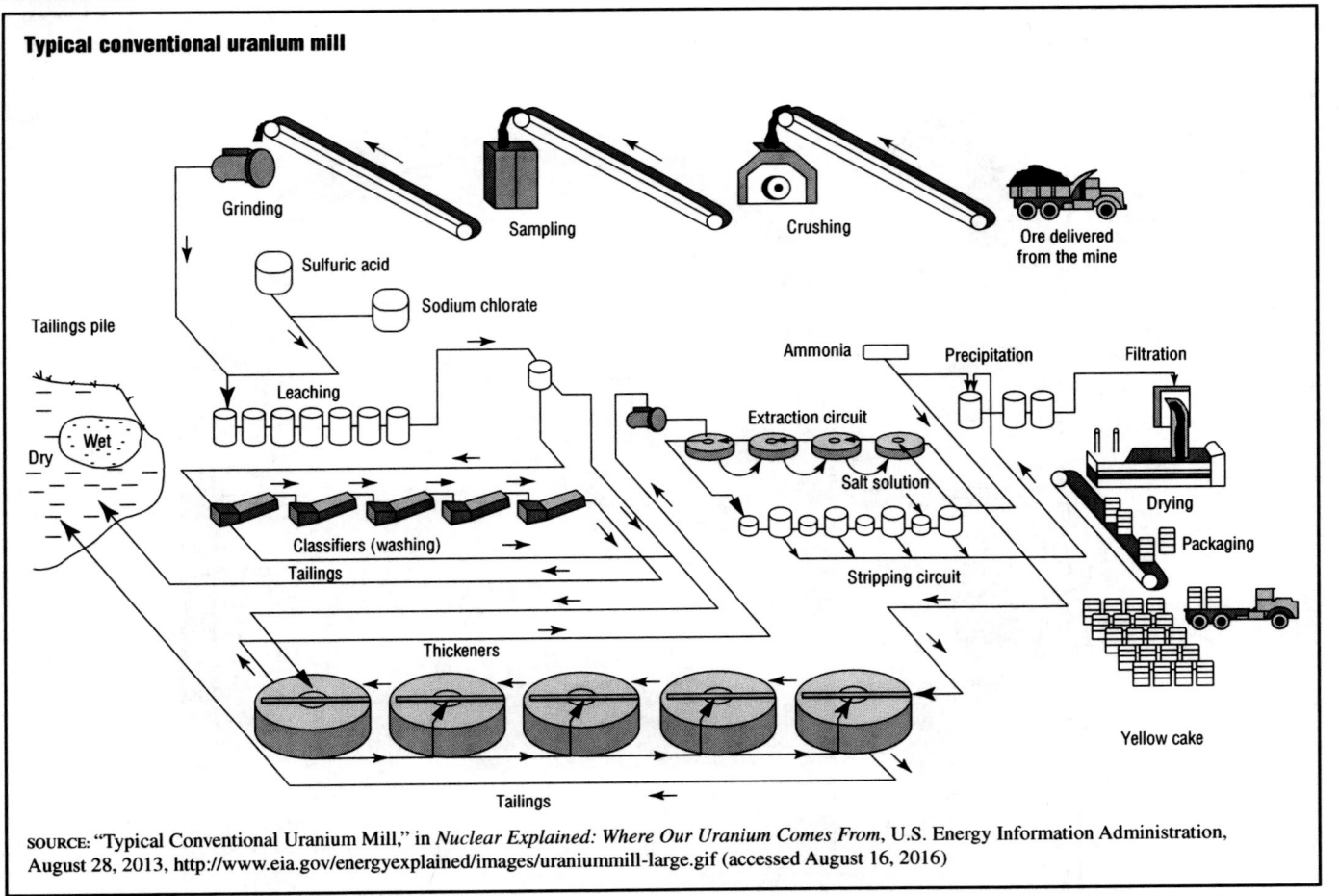

Typical conventional uranium mill

SOURCE: "Typical Conventional Uranium Mill," in *Nuclear Explained: Where Our Uranium Comes From*, U.S. Energy Information Administration, August 28, 2013, http://www.eia.gov/energyexplained/images/uraniummill-large.gif (accessed August 16, 2016)

are tubes about 12 feet (3.7 m) long. (See Figure 5.6.) Many rods (see "control rods" in Figure 5.2) are bundled together in assemblies, and hundreds of these assemblies make up the core of a nuclear reactor.

In "The U.S. Relies on Foreign Uranium, Enrichment Services to Fuel Its Nuclear Power Plants" (August 28, 2013, http://www.eia.gov/todayinenergy/detail.cfm?id=12731), the EIA notes that U.S. commercial nuclear power plants purchase uranium in three forms: U_3O_8, UF_6, and enriched uranium. These materials are referenced in terms of million pounds of U_3O_8 equivalent.

As noted earlier, domestic uranium production is very low. As a result, the United States has become heavily reliant on imported uranium. Table 5.1 lists U.S. uranium purchases for civilian nuclear power reactors between 1994 and 2015. Foreign-origin uranium made up the vast majority of the total. In 2015 U.S. nuclear power plants purchased 53.1 million pounds (24.1 million kg) of U_3O_8 equivalent of foreign-origin uranium. This accounted for 94% of the total 56.5 million pounds (25.6 million kg) purchased that year. Table 5.2 provides the amounts and prices for foreign-origin

uranium delivered between 2011 and 2015. Canada and Kazakhstan were the largest suppliers in 2015.

SECONDARY SOURCES. Nuclear power fuels are primarily produced from uranium taken from the ground (i.e., natural uranium) that is enriched to low levels. There are other methods that incorporate what are known as secondary sources of uranium: depleted uranium, highly enriched uranium (HEU), and reprocessed uranium. In addition, plutonium can be used as a nuclear power fuel.

Depleted uranium is a generic term for uranium that has been depleted of its U-235 content. It is a by-product of enrichment processes, such as the gas centrifuge process. In the United States depleted uranium is produced in the form of UF_6 gas in which U-238 has been highly concentrated. This isotope is not easily fissionable; thus, depleted uranium has long been considered a waste material called "tails." It could conceivably be re-enriched to provide suitable nuclear fuel. As of 2016, the United States did not conduct re-enrichment due to the high costs involved; however, higher uranium prices in the future could render the process economically viable.

The uranium meant for nuclear power production is enriched to a relatively low level of about 3% to 5% U-235 concentration. This is called low-enriched uranium (LEU). By contrast, HEU contains greater than 20% U-235. Nuclear weapons require uranium enriched to a very high level (in excess of 90% U-235). The U.S. stockpile of nuclear weapons is overseen by the DOE's National Nuclear Security Administration. In "U.S. HEU Disposition Program" (2016, http://nnsa.energy.gov/aboutus/ourprograms/dnn/fmd/heu), the National Nuclear Security Administration indicates that HEU can be chemically down-blended to LEU suitable for use in nuclear power plants. The process has been performed in the United States since the late 1990s using surplus HEU from dismantled U.S. nuclear weapons. The Nuclear Energy Institute notes in "Megatons to Megawatts Program Ends" (2016, http://www.nei.org/News-Media/Media-Room/Media-Briefings/Megatons-to-Megawatts-Program-Ends) that until 2013 Russian-supplied HEU was also used through a program called Megatons to Megawatts.

Plutonium, like uranium, is a radioactive metal. It is found in nature only in trace quantities. Plutonium can be created when uranium is subjected to fission, as in a nuclear power plant. Some other countries conduct reprocessing—that is, recover the still viable fuel (U-235 and any remaining plutonium) from the spent fuel rods. The United States has long rejected reprocessing, primarily because the technique separates plutonium from uranium. Plutonium can be used to build nuclear bombs.

Another option for nuclear power plant fuel is called mixed oxide (MOX). It contains a mixture of oxides, typically uranium mixed with plutonium, and could provide a means for the United States to dispose of its surplus plutonium. In 2007 construction began on a MOX facility near Augusta, Georgia. It was supposed to be operational by around 2015; however, schedule delays and cost overruns hampered the project's completion. The administration of

FIGURE 5.4

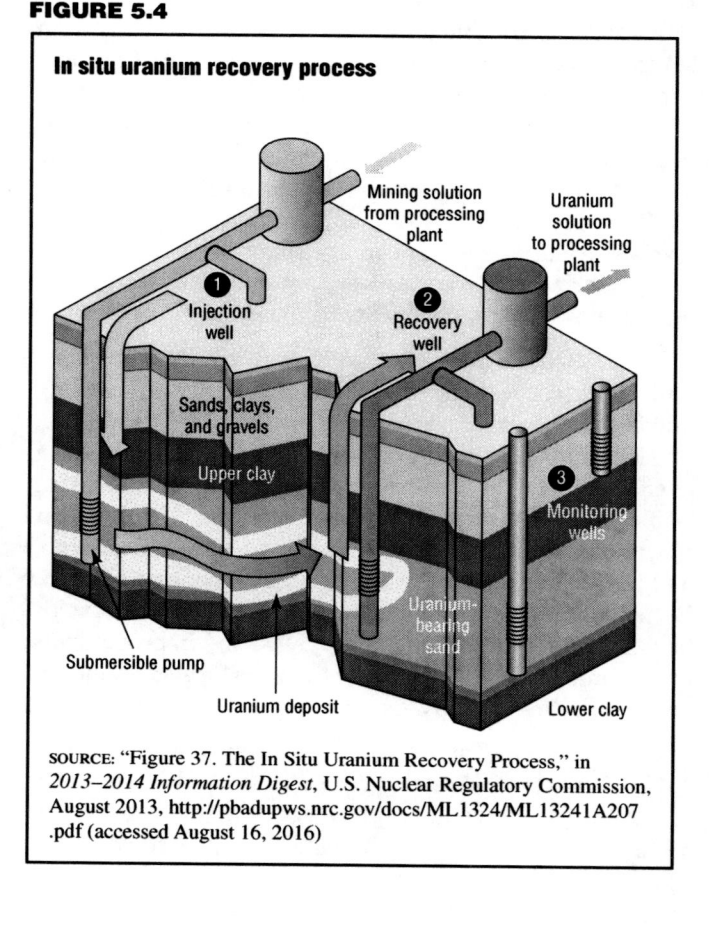

In situ uranium recovery process

Mining solution from processing plant

Uranium solution to processing plant

① Injection well

② Recovery well

③ Monitoring wells

Sands, clays, and gravels

Upper clay

Uranium-bearing sand

Submersible pump

Uranium deposit

Lower clay

SOURCE: "Figure 37. The In Situ Uranium Recovery Process," in *2013–2014 Information Digest*, U.S. Nuclear Regulatory Commission, August 2013, http://pbadupws.nrc.gov/docs/ML1324/ML13241A207.pdf (accessed August 16, 2016)

FIGURE 5.5

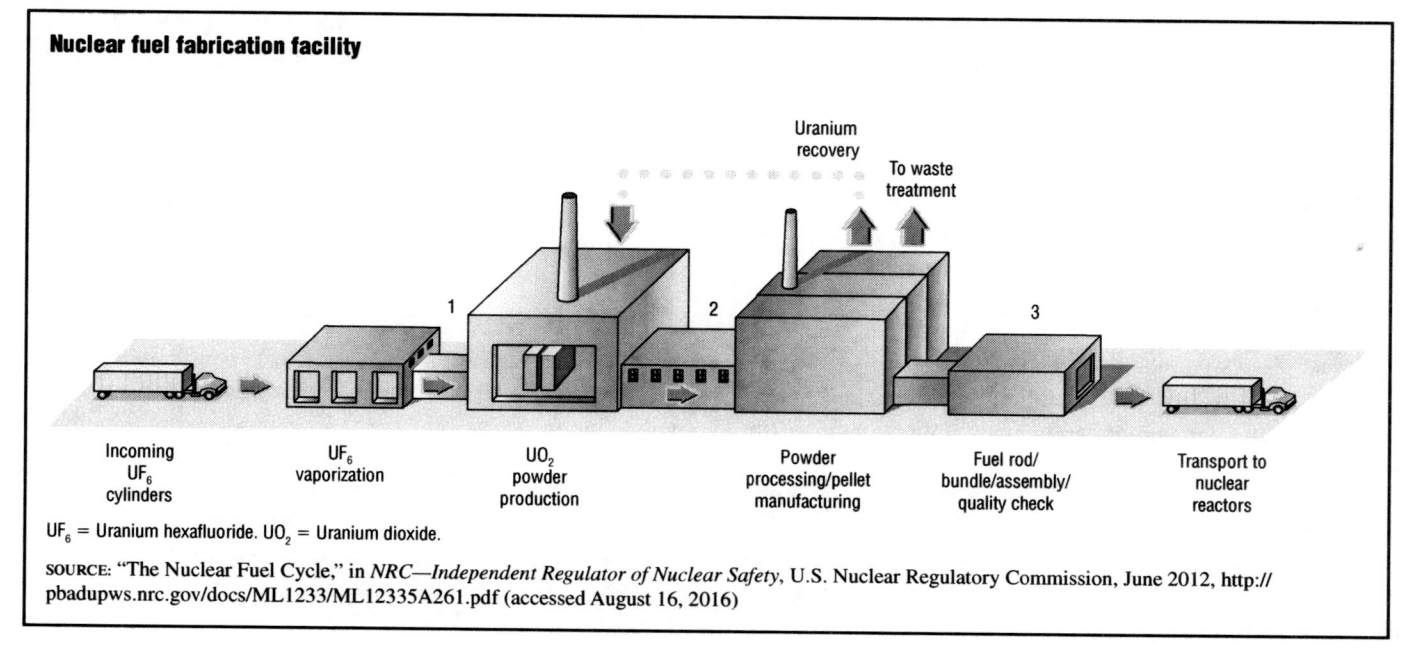

Nuclear fuel fabrication facility

Uranium recovery

To waste treatment

1 2 3

Incoming UF$_6$ cylinders

UF$_6$ vaporization

UO$_2$ powder production

Powder processing/pellet manufacturing

Fuel rod/bundle/assembly/quality check

Transport to nuclear reactors

UF$_6$ = Uranium hexafluoride. UO$_2$ = Uranium dioxide.

SOURCE: "The Nuclear Fuel Cycle," in *NRC—Independent Regulator of Nuclear Safety*, U.S. Nuclear Regulatory Commission, June 2012, http://pbadupws.nrc.gov/docs/ML1233/ML12335A261.pdf (accessed August 16, 2016)

FIGURE 5.6

Fuel rod containing uranium fuel pellets

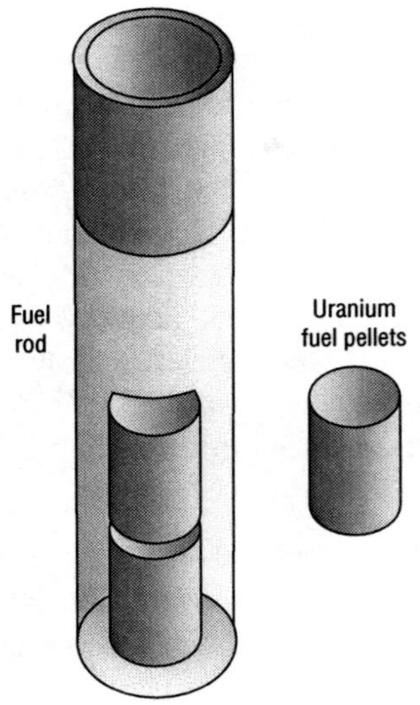

Fuel rod

Uranium fuel pellets

SOURCE: "Figure 43. Spent Fuel Generational and Storage after Use," in *2013–2014 Information Digest*, U.S. Nuclear Regulatory Commission, August 2013, http://www.nrc.gov/docs/ML1324/ML13241A207.pdf (accessed August 16, 2016)

President Barack Obama (1961–) also lost confidence in it. According to Vera Bergengruen and Sammy Fretwell, in "Obama Plans to Scrap MOX Plant; SC Leaders Livid" (State.com, February 9, 2016), President Obama's budget proposal for fiscal year 2017 (October 2016 through September 2017) calls for the project to be terminated by the DOE. As of September 2016, the DOE's budget had not been finalized, and the future of the MOX facility remained uncertain.

Uranium Prices

Table 5.3 shows the annual price per pound of U_3O_8 equivalent paid by U.S. civilian nuclear power plants between 1994 and 2015 for uranium from various sellers. In 2015 the average price of $44.13 per pound of U_3O_8 equivalent was down from its peak of $55.64 per pound of U_3O_8 equivalent in 2011. Overall, foreign-origin and U.S.-origin uranium were very similar in price in 2015.

DOMESTIC NUCLEAR ENERGY PRODUCTION

Table 5.4 shows the number of operable nuclear generating units in the United States dating back to the late 1950s. The number peaked in 1990 at 112 units and then declined. As of 2015, 99 nuclear generating units were operable. According to the NRC, in *2015–2016 Information Digest* (August 2015, http://www.nrc.gov/docs/ML1525/ML15254A321.pdf), the units were heavily concentrated in the eastern United States and mostly

used the pressurized-water type of reactor (the type illustrated in Figure 5.2).

The EIA notes in *Annual Energy Review 2011* (September 2012, http://www.eia.gov/totalenergy/data/annual/pdf/aer.pdf) that between 1980 and 2011 no new construction permits were issued for nuclear power plants in the United States. In addition, some plants were permanently shut down. The decline in nuclear power plants stems from several related issues. Financing is difficult to find, and construction has become more expensive, partly because of longer delays for licensing, but also because of regulations that were instituted following an accident at the Three Mile Island nuclear power plant in Pennsylvania in 1979, during which nuclear fuel overheated to dangerous levels. No large-scale releases or explosions resulted; however, much stricter controls were put into place to regulate nuclear power plant operations.

Although no new nuclear power plants have been built for decades, the output of electricity at existing plants has increased. A capacity factor is the proportion of electricity produced compared with what could have been produced at full-power operation. As shown in Table 5.4, the average capacity factor for U.S. nuclear power plants in 2015 was 92.2%, an all-time annual high, and far greater than the value of 55.9% reported in 1975. Better training for operators, longer operating cycles between refueling, and control-system improvements have contributed to increased plant performance and an increase in the capacity factor.

As shown in Table 5.4, nuclear power supplied only 1.4% of the total electricity generated in the United States in 1970. The percentage grew considerably during the 1970s and early to mid-1980s and then leveled off. (See Figure 5.7.) Nuclear power's share has hovered around 19% to 20% since 1990. (See Table 5.4.) Net electricity generation varied greatly from state to state in 2015. (See Figure 5.8.) Nineteen states, mostly in the interior west, generated no net electricity from nuclear power, while 18 others generated up to 29% of their electricity in this manner. Six states generated 30% to 39% of their electricity using nuclear power. Seven states—Connecticut, Illinois, New Hampshire, New Jersey, South Carolina, Vermont, and Virginia—generated at least 40% of their electricity using nuclear power in 2015.

OUTLOOK FOR DOMESTIC NUCLEAR ENERGY

As noted earlier, no new nuclear power units have been built in the United States in decades. However, some existing units increased their power production over their originally permitted levels. The NRC calls this uprating. In *2015–2016 Information Digest*, the commission notes that between 1977 and 2014 completed uprates resulted in 7,095 MW of additional electricity production. Between 2014 and 2019 the NRC projects that uprates will introduce another 580 MW.

TABLE 5.1

Uranium amounts purchased by owners and operators of U.S. civilian nuclear power reactors, 1994–2015

[Million pounds U₃O₈ equivalent]

Delivery year	Total purchased	Purchased from U.S. producers	Purchased from U.S. brokers and traders	Purchased from other owners and operators of U.S. civilian nuclear power reactors, other U.S. suppliers, (and U.S. government for 2007)[a]	Purchased from foreign suppliers	U.S.-origin uranium	Foreign-origin uranium	Spot contracts[b]	Short, medium, and long-term contracts[c]
1994	38.3	5.4	15.3	1.1	16.5	7.7	30.6	8.5	29.8
1995	43.4	5.3	16.2	0.6	21.4	5.2	38.2	13.6	29.8
1996	47.3	5.8	13.3	1.9	26.4	8.3	39.0	9.1	38.3
1997	42.0	5.7	9.9	3.0	23.4	8.1	33.9	5.5	36.5
1998	42.7	6.5	10.5	4.5	21.3	7.2	35.6	7.8	34.9
1999	47.9	5.2	10.4	5.6	26.8	11.4	36.5	8.0	40.0
2000	51.8	3.6	9.1	8.8	30.4	13.3	38.6	10.4	39.1
2001	55.4	2.3	11.7	11.4	30.0	13.2	42.2	14.4	40.0
2002	52.7	1.5	13.4	5.7	32.2	6.2	46.5	8.6	41.4
2003	56.6	0.6	10.5	8.3	37.2	10.2	46.4	8.2	46.7
2004	64.1	0	13.2	12.2	38.7	12.3	51.8	9.2	53.3
2005	65.7	d	10.4	d	39.4	11.0	54.7	6.9	58.8
2006	66.5	0	13.9	12.6	40.0	10.8	55.7	6.3	59.4
2007	51.0	0	9.8	7.6	33.5	4.0	47.0	6.6	43.7
2008	53.4	0.6	9.4	6.3	37.2	7.7	45.6	8.7	42.8
2009	49.8	d	11.1	d	36.8	7.1	42.8	8.1	41.0
2010	46.6	0.4	11.7	1.9	32.6	3.7	42.9	8.2	37.9
2011	54.8	0.6	14.8	1.1	38.4	5.2	49.6	12.0	42.3
2012	57.5	d	11.5	d	37.6	9.8	47.7	8.1	48.9
2013	57.4	d	12.8	d	37.4	9.5	47.9	11.3	46.1
2014	53.3	d	17.1	d	34.4	3.3	50.0	14.5	38.8
2015	56.5	1.5	13.9	3.0	38.2	3.4	53.1	11.3	43.2

[a]Includes purchases between owners and operators of U.S. civilian nuclear power reactors along with purchases from other U.S. suppliers which are U.S. converters, enrichers, and fabricators.
[b]Spot contract: A one-time delivery (usually) of the entire contract to occur within one year of contract execution (signed date).
[c]Short, medium, and long-term contracts: One or more deliveries to occur after a year following contract execution (signed date).
[d]Data withheld to avoid disclosure of individual company data.
Notes: "Other U.S. Suppliers" are U.S. converters, enrichers, and fabricators. Totals may not equal sum of components because of independent rounding.

SOURCE: "Table S1a. Uranium Purchased by Owners and Operators of U.S. Civilian Nuclear Power Reactors, 1994–2015," in *2015 Uranium Marketing Annual Report*, U.S. Energy Information Administration, May 2016, http://www.eia.gov/uranium/marketing/pdf/2015umar.pdf (accessed August 16, 2016)

The NRC lists in "Combined License Applications for New Reactors" (June 28, 2016, http://www.nrc.gov/reactors/new-reactors/col.html) the applications it has received for the construction and operation of nuclear power plants in the United States. These are called combined license (COL) applications. As of June 2016, 10 of the COL applications had been withdrawn or suspended for various reasons. Four other applications were under review, for a total of seven units in the following states: Florida (two sites with four units total), South Carolina (two units), and Virginia (one unit).

As of June 2016, the NRC had issued COL permits to four applicants for seven units:

• Detroit Edison Company for Fermi (Michigan), Unit 3

• Nuclear Innovation North America for South Texas Project, Units 3 and 4

• South Carolina Electric and Gas for Virgil C. Summer, Units 2 and 3

• Southern Nuclear Operating Company for Plant Vogtle (Georgia), Units 3 and 4

As of September 2016, none of the newly permitted units had begun operating.

The EIA predicts in *Annual Energy Outlook 2016 with Projections to 2040* (August 2016, https://www.eia.gov/forecasts/aeo/pdf/0383(2016).pdf) energy production in the future for various supply and demand scenarios. As shown in Figure 5.9, the agency forecasts that retirements in nuclear generating capacity will be larger than additions to the capacity through 2020. Figure 5.10 shows domestic electricity generation by fuel type between 2000 and 2015 and predicted through 2040. Nuclear energy generation is projected to continue to remain relatively flat through 2040. More information about projected future electricity supply and demand is included in Chapter 8.

WORLD NUCLEAR POWER PRODUCTION

The NRC notes in *2015–2016 Information Digest* that as of 2015, 438 nuclear power units were in operation in 29 countries. The nations with the most units were the United States (99), France (58), and Japan (43). Total world nuclear power production was 2.4 million

TABLE 5.2

Uranium purchased by owners and operators of U.S. civilian nuclear power reactors, by origin country, 2011–15

[Thousand pounds U₃O₈ equivalent; dollars per pound U₃O₈ equivalent]

Origin country	Deliveries in 2011		Deliveries in 2012		Deliveries in 2013		Deliveries in 2014		Deliveries in 2015	
	Purchases	Weighted-average price	Purchases	Weighted-average price	Purchases	Weighted-average price	Purchases	Weighted-average price	Purchases	Weighted-average price
Australia	6,001	57.47	6,724	51.17	10,741	49.92	10,511	48.03	9,678	44.16
Brazil	*	*	*	*	*	*	*	*	0	NA
Bulgaria	0	NA	0	NA	0	NA	0	NA	*	*
Canada	10,832	56.08	13,584	56.75	7,808	52.61	9,789	45.87	16,876	45.84
China	*	*	*	*	*	*	*	*	0	NA
Czech Republic	0	NA	0	NA	*	*	0	NA	0	NA
Germany	0	NA	0	NA	*	*	0	NA	0	NA
Hungary	0	NA	0	NA	*	*	0	NA	0	NA
Kazakhstan	9,728	53.71	6,234	51.69	6,454	46.73	12,032	44.47	10,723	42.82
Malawi	780	65.44	*	*	1,277	59.89	1,514	44.94	*	*
Namibia	6,199	56.74	5,986	54.56	5,677	49.78	4,603	45.54	3,456	48.57
Niger	1,744	54.38	2,133	50.45	1,666	51.26	1,316	42.86	922	39.74
Portugal	0	NA	0	NA	*	*	0	NA	0	NA
Russia	10,199	56.57	7,643	54.40	10,580	53.73	6,859	45.65	9,063	40.87
South Africa	1,524	53.62	1,243	56.45	186	46.72	938	43.71	826	37.64
Ukraine	*	*	*	*	0	NA	*	*	0	NA
United Kingdom	0	NA	0	NA	0	NA	*	*	0	NA
Uzbekistan	1,808	55.99	2,576	52.80	3,064	50.02	1,779	46.84	1,040	47.90
Unknown	0	NA	0	NA	*	*	*	*	*	*
Foreign total	**49,626**	**55.98**	**47,713**	**54.07**	**47,919**	**51.13**	**50,033**	**46.03**	**53,106**	**44.14**
United States	5,205	52.12	9,807	59.44	9,484	56.37	3,316	48.11	3,419	43.86
Total purchases	**54,831**	**55.64**	**57,520**	**54.99**	**57,403**	**51.99**	**53,349**	**46.16**	**56,524**	**44.13**

*Data withheld to avoid disclosure of individual company data.
NA = Not applicable.
Notes: Totals may not equal sum of components because of independent rounding. Weighted-average prices are not adjusted for inflation.

SOURCE: "Table 3. Uranium Purchased by Owners and Operators of U.S. Civilian Nuclear Power Reactors by Origin Country and Delivery Year, 2011–15," in *2015 Uranium Marketing Annual Report*, U.S. Energy Information Administration, May 2016, http://www.eia.gov/uranium/marketing/pdf/2015umar.pdf (accessed August 16, 2016)

gigawatt-hours (GWh) in 2015. The United States had the highest production, at 797,067 GWh. Other countries with substantial production included France, with 415,900 GWh, and Russia, with 169,049 GWh.

France produced 78% of its electricity from nuclear power in 2015, the largest percentage of any nation. Other major producers included Slovakia (57%) and Hungary (54%). The United States produced 19% of its electrical power using nuclear energy in 2015. Sixty-seven additional nuclear power units were under construction or on order worldwide in 2015. China was expected to install the most new units (24), followed by Russia (9 units) and India (6 units).

NUCLEAR SAFETY ISSUES

Safety is a concern in all energy industries, but the nuclear power industry has unique safety concerns. The consequences of a destructive accident or terrorist attack at a nuclear power plant could be quite calamitous due to radiation release. One troubling scenario involves a meltdown of the reactor core following the failure of the cooling system. In this event, all the control rods holding the uranium fuel get so hot they melt, releasing their radioactive contents. As shown in Figure 5.2, a typical

U.S. reactor is encased in a containment structure with walls that are made of concrete and steel several feet thick. Thus, a partial or even complete meltdown does not necessarily mean that radiation will escape from the reactor. It depends on the structural integrity of the containment walls.

Nuclear power has been generated commercially since only the late 1950s. Three major incidents, however, that have severely affected the industry's safety reputation have occurred in three different countries.

Three Mile Island

On March 28, 1979, the Three Mile Island nuclear facility near Harrisburg, Pennsylvania, was the site of the worst nuclear accident in U.S. history when one of its reactors overheated and suffered a partial meltdown. The emergency system was designed to dump water on the hot core of the reactor and spray water into the reactor building to stop the production of steam. During the accident, however, the valves leading to the emergency water pumps closed. Another valve was stuck in the open position, drawing water away from the core, which then became partially uncovered and began to melt.

TABLE 5.3

Prices for uranium purchased by owners and operators of U.S. civilian nuclear power reactors, 1994–2015

[Dollars per pound U_3O_8 equivalent]

Delivery year	Total purchased (weighted-average price)	Purchased from U.S. producers	Purchased from U.S. brokers and traders	Purchased from other owners and operators of U.S. civilian nuclear power reactors, other U.S. suppliers, (and U.S. government for 2007)[a]	Purchased from foreign suppliers	U.S.-origin uranium (weighted-average price)	Foreign-origin uranium (weighted-average price)	Spot contracts[b] (weighted-average price)	Short, medium, and long-term contracts[c] (weighted-average price)
1994	10.40	13.72	9.34	8.04	10.43	12.08	9.97	9.01	—
1995	11.25	14.84	9.83	12.52	11.40	14.20	10.84	10.30	—
1996	14.12	14.20	13.36	14.98	14.45	14.62	14.02	14.22	—
1997	12.88	13.60	12.31	[e]	12.91	12.78	12.78	11.61	—
1998	12.14	13.61	11.95	[e]	11.97	13.36	11.90	10.56	—
1999	11.63	13.93	11.54	[e]	11.47	13.37	11.47	9.52	—
2000	11.04	14.81	11.28	10.45	10.65	11.52	10.88	8.54	11.70
2001	10.15	13.26	10.44	9.98	9.86	10.50	10.05	7.92	10.96
2002	10.36	13.03	10.21	[e]	10.37	10.89	10.05	9.29	10.58
2003	10.81	14.17	11.05	10.16	10.82	10.81	10.81	10.10	10.94
2004	12.61	[d]	12.08	11.30	13.15	11.87	12.76	14.77	12.24
2005	14.36	[d]	13.76	14.70	14.70	15.11	14.21	20.04	13.70
2006	18.61	[d]	20.49	18.62	18.62	17.85	18.75	39.48	16.38
2007	32.78	[d]	34.10	32.36	32.36	28.89	33.05	88.25	24.45
2008	45.88	75.16	39.62	48.49	48.49	59.55	43.47	66.95	41.59
2009	45.86	[e]	41.88	46.68	46.68	48.92	45.35	46.45	45.74
2010	49.29	47.13	44.98	42.24	51.30	45.25	49.64	43.99	50.43
2011	55.64	58.12	53.29	52.50	56.60	52.12	55.98	54.69	55.90
2012	54.99	[e]	54.44		54.40	59.44	54.07	51.04	55.65
2013	51.99	[e]	54.44		51.93	56.37	51.13	43.83	54.00
2014	46.16	[e]	50.44		47.62	48.11	46.03	36.64	49.73
2015	44.13	52.35	44.67	31.31	44.66	43.86	44.14	36.80	46.04

[a]Includes purchases between owners and operators of U.S. civilian nuclear power reactors along with purchases from other U.S. suppliers which are U.S. converters, enrichers, and fabricators.
[b]Spot contract: A one-time delivery (usually) of the entire contract to occur within one year of contract execution (signed date).
[c]Short, medium, and long-term contracts: One or more deliveries to occur after a year following contract execution (signed date).
[d]Not applicable.
[e]Data withheld to avoid disclosure of individual company data.
[f]Not available.

Notes: "Other U.S. Suppliers" are U.S. converters, enrichers, and fabricators. Totals may not equal sum of components because of independent rounding. Weighted-average prices are not adjusted for inflation.

SOURCE: "Table S1b. Weighted-Average Price of Uranium Purchased by Owners and Operators of U.S. Civilian Nuclear Power Reactors, 1994–2015," in 2015 Uranium Marketing Annual Report, U.S. Energy Information Administration, May 2016, http://www.eia.gov/uranium/marketing/pdf/2015umar.pdf (accessed August 16, 2016)

TABLE 5.4

Nuclear power units and generation, selected years 1957–2015

	Total operable units[a, b]	Net summer capacity of operable units[b, c]	Nuclear electricity net generation	Nuclear share of electricity net generation	Capacity factor[d]
	Number	Million kilowatts	Million kilowatthours	Percent	Percent
1957 Total	1	0.055	10	(s)	NA
1960 Total	3	0.411	518	0.1	NA
1965 Total	13	0.793	3,657	0.3	NA
1970 Total	20	7.004	21,804	1.4	NA
1975 Total	57	37.267	172,505	9.0	55.9
1980 Total	71	51.810	251,116	11.0	56.3
1985 Total	96	79.397	383,691	15.5	58.0
1990 Total	112	99.624	576,862	19.0	66.0
1995 Total	109	99.515	673,402	20.1	77.4
2000 Total	104	97.860	753,893	19.8	88.1
2001 Total	104	98.159	768,826	20.6	89.4
2002 Total	104	98.657	780,064	20.2	90.3
2003 Total	104	99.209	763,733	19.7	87.9
2004 Total	104	99.628	788,528	19.9	90.1
2005 Total	104	99.988	781,986	19.3	89.3
2006 Total	104	100.334	787,219	19.4	89.6
2007 Total	104	100.266	806,425	19.4	91.8
2008 Total	104	100.755	806,208	19.6	91.1[d]
2009 Total	104	101.004	798,855	20.2	90.3
2010 Total	104	101.167	806,968	19.6	91.1
2011 Total	104	101.419[c]	790,204	19.3	89.1
2012 Total	104	101.885	769,331	19.0	86.1
2013 Total	100	99.240	789,016	19.4	89.9
2014 Total	99	98.569	797,166	19.5	91.7
2015 Total	99	98.729[E]	797,178	19.5	92.2[E]

[a]Total of nuclear generating units holding full-power licenses, or equivalent permission to operate, at end of period.
[b]At end of period.
[c]Beginning in 2011, monthly capacity values are estimated in two steps: 1) uprates and derates reported on Form EIA-860M are added to specific months; and 2) the difference between the resulting year-end capacity (from data reported on Form EIA-860M) and final capacity (reported on Form EIA-860) is allocated to the month of January.
[d]Beginning in 2008, capacity factor data are calculated using a new methodology.
E = Estimate. NA = Not available. (s) = Less than 0.05%.
Notes: Nuclear electricity net generation totals may not equal sum of components due to independent rounding. Geographic coverage is the 50 states and the District of Columbia.

SOURCE: Adapted from "Table 8.1. Nuclear Energy Overview," in *Monthly Energy Review: July 2016*, U.S. Energy Information Administration, July 2016, http://www.eia.gov/totalenergy/data/monthly/pdf/mer.pdf (accessed August 7, 2016)

The accident did not result in any deaths or injuries to plant workers or to people in the nearby community. On average, area residents were exposed to less radiation than that of a chest x-ray. Nevertheless, the incident raised concerns about nuclear safety, which resulted in more rigorous safety standards in the nuclear power industry. Antinuclear sentiment was fueled as well, heightening Americans' wariness of nuclear power as an energy source.

The damaged nuclear reactor at Three Mile Island was permanently shut down after it underwent cleanup. An undamaged reactor at the plant, however, continued to operate as of September 2016.

Chernobyl

On April 26, 1986, the most serious nuclear accident in history occurred at Chernobyl, a nuclear plant in what is now Ukraine (then part of the Soviet Union). At least 31 people died and hundreds were injured when one of the four reactors exploded during a badly run test. Millions of people were exposed to some levels of radiation when radioactive particles were released into the atmosphere. About 350,000 people were eventually evacuated from the area.

The cleanup was a huge project. Helicopters dropped tons of limestone, sand, clay, lead, and boron on the smoldering reactor to stop the radiation leakage and reduce the heat. Meanwhile, workers built a giant steel and cement sarcophagus to entomb the remains of the reactor and contain the radioactive waste.

The International Atomic Energy Agency indicates in *Chernobyl's Legacy: Health, Environmental and Socio-economic Impacts* (April 2006, http://www.iaea.org/sites/default/files/chernobyl.pdf) that about 1,000 people involved in the initial cleanup, including emergency workers and the military, received high doses of radiation. Eventually, more than 600,000 people were involved in decontamination and containment activities. The long-term effects of whatever exposure they received are being monitored.

Although some of the evacuated land in Chernobyl has been declared fit for habitation again, several areas

FIGURE 5.7

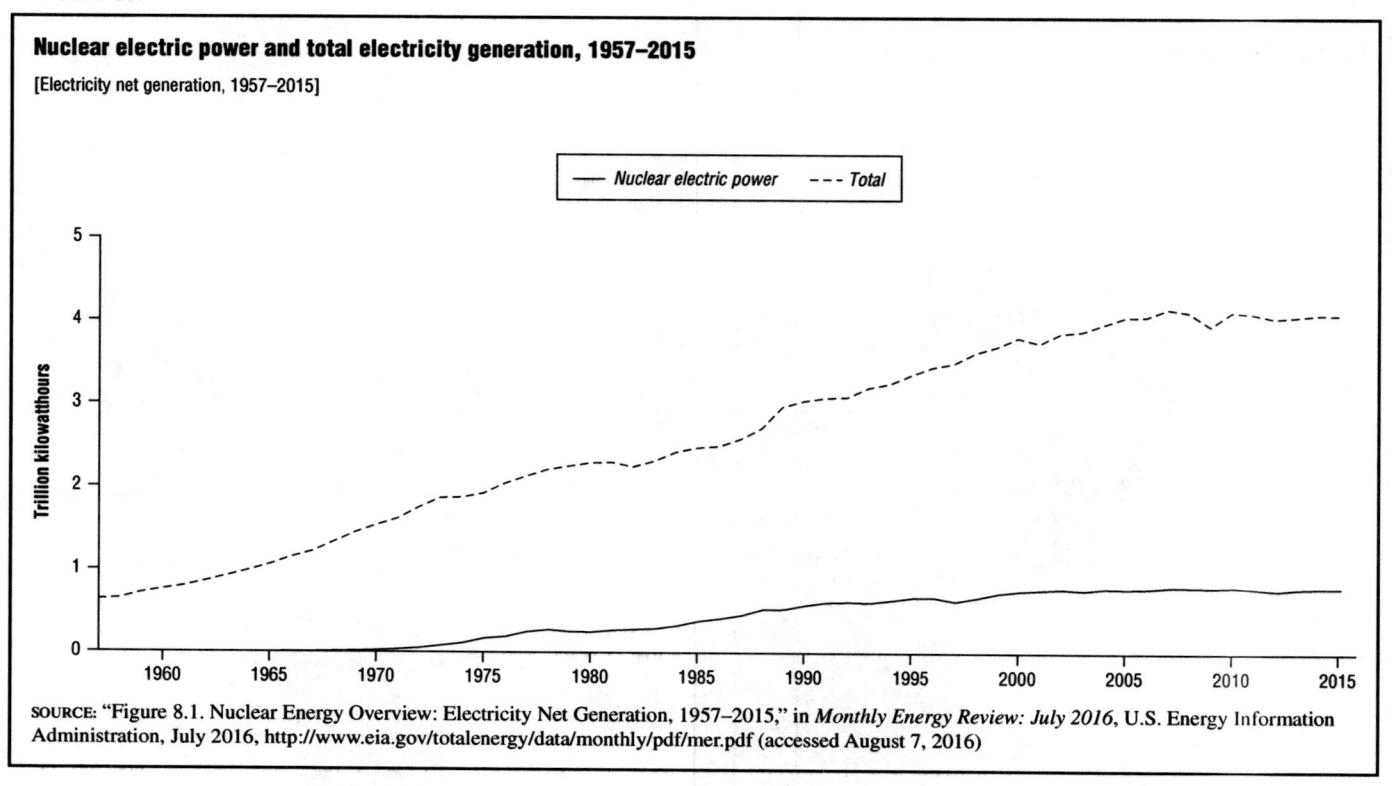

Nuclear electric power and total electricity generation, 1957–2015

[Electricity net generation, 1957–2015]

SOURCE: "Figure 8.1. Nuclear Energy Overview: Electricity Net Generation, 1957–2015," in *Monthly Energy Review: July 2016*, U.S. Energy Information Administration, July 2016, http://www.eia.gov/totalenergy/data/monthly/pdf/mer.pdf (accessed August 7, 2016)

that received heavy concentrations of radiation are expected to be closed for decades.

Fukushima Daiichi

On March 11, 2011, an underwater earthquake triggered a tsunami that flooded the northeastern coast of Japan and killed nearly 20,000 people. The Fukushima Daiichi nuclear power plant is located on the northeastern coast approximately 150 miles (240 km) north of Tokyo. Three of the plant's six reactors suffered meltdowns after their cooling systems became inoperable following the earthquake and tsunami. Over subsequent days the reactors were plagued by partial and complete meltdowns and small hydrogen gas explosions. Some radioactive gases were released into the atmosphere from the damaged containment structures. The overheated reactors were finally cooled with seawater to prevent further releases.

Kevin Krolicki reports in "Fukushima Radiation Higher than First Estimated" (Reuters.com, May 24, 2012) that more than a year after the accident occurred officials estimated that "the amount of radiation released in the first three weeks of the accident [was] about one-sixth the radiation released during the 1986 Chernobyl disaster." The Fukushima incident dampened the enthusiasm that had been building around the world for greater reliance on nuclear power. In *Annual Energy Outlook 2012* (June 2012, http://www.eia.gov/forecasts/aeo/pdf/0383(2012).pdf), the EIA notes "in the aftermath, governments in several countries that previously had planned

to expand nuclear capacity—including Japan, Germany, Switzerland, and Italy—reversed course." In fact, the agency notes that Germany decided to phase out all of its nuclear power by 2025.

The United States has continued to cautiously embrace nuclear power. The Fukushima accident did spur some changes in the U.S. nuclear power industry. The Nuclear Energy Institute explains in "Nuclear Industry Opens Memphis Response Center" (June 30, 2014, http://www.nei.org/News-Media/News/News-Archives/Nuclear-Industry-Opens-Memphis-Response-Center) that the industry has established a safety program that includes the positioning of emergency equipment at strategic locations around the country. As of September 2016, equipment such as portable backup generators, pumps, couplings, and hoses had been stationed in Phoenix, Arizona, and Memphis, Tennessee. The Nuclear Energy Institute notes the equipment can be transported "to any U.S. nuclear plant within 24 hours."

NUCLEAR WASTE ISSUES

Another safety (and environmental) issue related to nuclear power production is the creation of radioactive waste. Radioactive waste is produced at all stages of the nuclear fuel cycle, from the initial mining of the uranium to the final disposal of the spent fuel from the reactor. The term *radioactive waste* encompasses a broad range of material with widely varying characteristics. Some is

FIGURE 5.8

Net electricity generated by nuclear power in each state, June 2015

[Percent of total nuclear power generated]

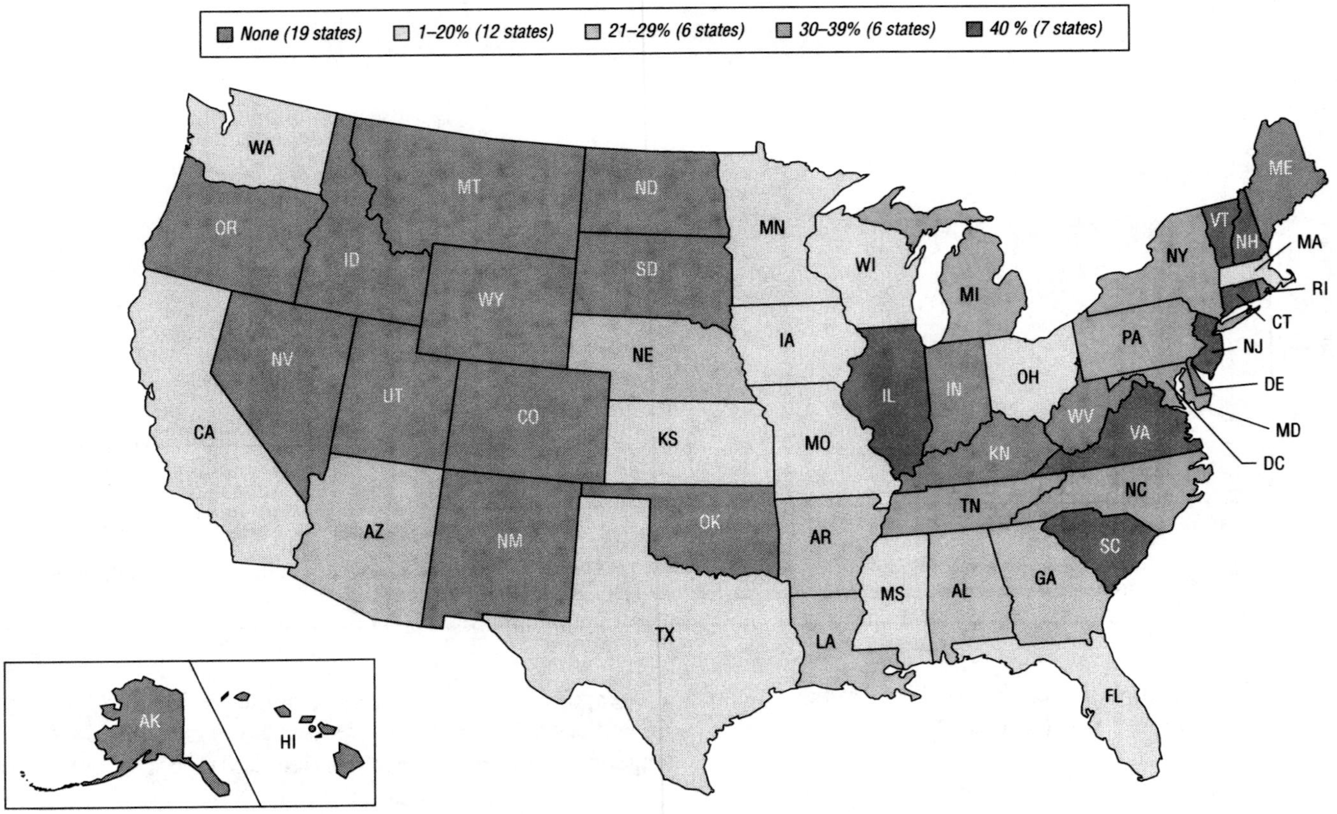

Legend: None (19 states) | 1–20% (12 states) | 21–29% (6 states) | 30–39% (6 states) | 40 % (7 states)

SOURCE: "Figure 12. Net Electricity Generated in Each State by Nuclear Power," in *2015–2016 Information Digest*, U.S. Nuclear Regulatory Commission, August 2015, http://www.nrc.gov/docs/ML1525/ML15254A321.pdf (accessed August 16, 2016)

barely radioactive and safe to handle, whereas other types are intensely hot and highly radioactive. Some waste decays to safe levels of radioactivity in a matter of days or weeks, whereas other types will remain dangerous for thousands of years.

Disposing of radioactive waste is unquestionably one of the major problems associated with the development of nuclear power. The highly toxic wastes must be isolated from the environment until the radioactivity decays to a safe level. That period can last from several years to several millennia, depending on the radioactivity of the waste. Although U.S. policy is based on the assumption that radioactive waste can be disposed of safely, new storage and disposal facilities for all types of radioactive waste have frequently been delayed or blocked by concerns about safety, health, and the environment.

Uranium Mill Tailings

Uranium mill tailings are sandlike wastes produced in uranium refining operations. Although they emit low levels of radiation, their large volume poses a hazard, particularly from radon emissions and groundwater contamination. Mill tailings are usually deposited in large piles next to the mill that processed the ore and must be covered to prevent radiation problems.

Low-Level Waste

Low-level waste (LLW) includes trash (such as wiping rags, swabs, and syringes), contaminated clothing (such as shoe covers and protective gloves), and hardware (such as luminous dials, filters, and tools). This waste comes from nuclear reactors, industrial users, government users (but not nuclear weapons sites), research universities, and medical facilities. In general, LLW decays relatively quickly (in 10 to 100 years). According to the NRC, in *2015–2016 Information Digest*, as of 2015 four licensed LLW facilities were operating in the United States: in Barnwell, South Carolina; in Richland, Washington; in Clive, Utah; and in Andrews, Texas.

FIGURE 5.9

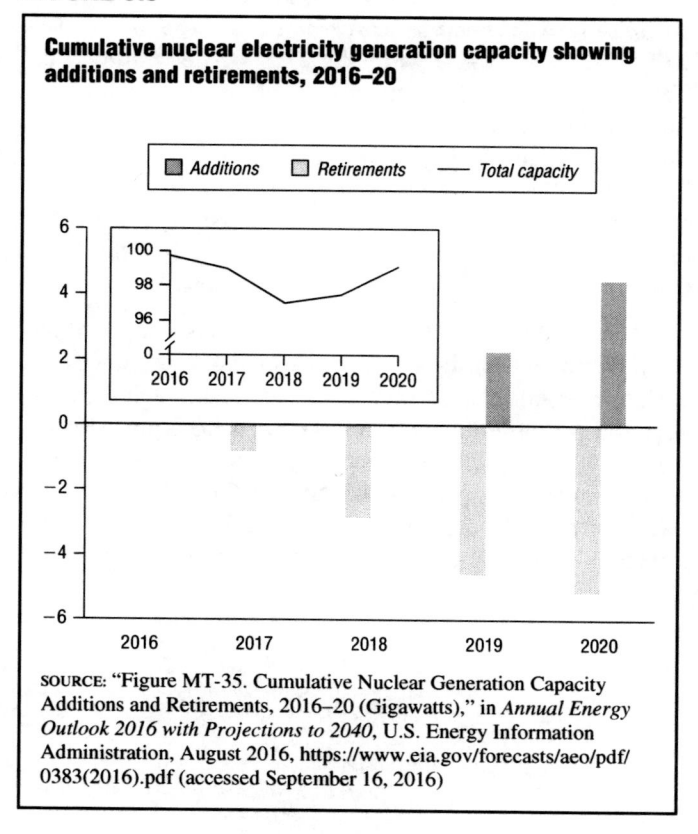

Cumulative nuclear electricity generation capacity showing additions and retirements, 2016–20

SOURCE: "Figure MT-35. Cumulative Nuclear Generation Capacity Additions and Retirements, 2016–20 (Gigawatts)," in *Annual Energy Outlook 2016 with Projections to 2040*, U.S. Energy Information Administration, August 2016, https://www.eia.gov/forecasts/aeo/pdf/0383(2016).pdf (accessed September 16, 2016)

FIGURE 5.10

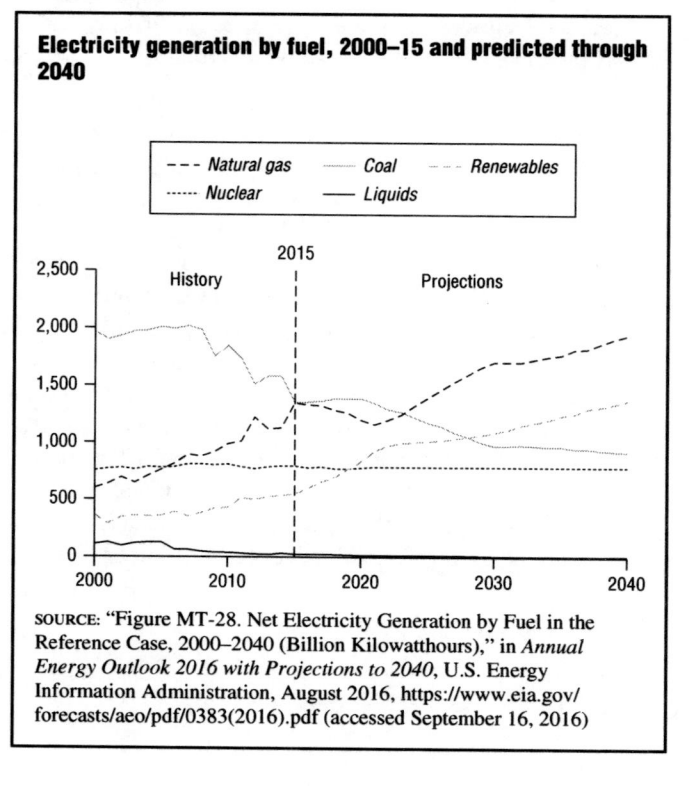

Electricity generation by fuel, 2000–15 and predicted through 2040

SOURCE: "Figure MT-28. Net Electricity Generation by Fuel in the Reference Case, 2000–2040 (Billion Kilowatthours)," in *Annual Energy Outlook 2016 with Projections to 2040*, U.S. Energy Information Administration, August 2016, https://www.eia.gov/forecasts/aeo/pdf/0383(2016).pdf (accessed September 16, 2016)

The Low-Level Radioactive Waste Policy Amendments Act of 1985 encouraged states to enter into compacts, which are legal agreements among states for low-level radioactive waste disposal. Each compact is responsible for the development of disposal capacity for the LLW generated within the compact; however, as of September 2016 new disposal sites had yet to be built. Nuclear power facilities that are located in compacts without existing LLW disposal sites must petition the compact to export their low-level radioactive waste to one of the four operating LLW disposal sites.

Spent Nuclear Fuel

Spent nuclear fuel is fuel that has exhausted its usefulness in a nuclear power reactor. It is called high-level waste because it is highly radioactive and requires very long containment times, typically thousands of years.

For decades the United States has pursued development of a national repository for its high-level wastes; however, finding a suitable site acceptable to all parties involved has proven impossible. In 1987 the federal government began investigating Yucca Mountain, a barren wind-swept mountain in the desert about 100 miles (161 km) northwest of Las Vegas, Nevada. The project was highly controversial from the start and was fought bitterly by the state of Nevada and environmentalists. After years of court challenges and political wrangling,

the Obama administration dropped the site in 2010 as a repository candidate.

Thus, as of September 2016 the United States had no central repository for spent nuclear fuel. The fuel continued to be stored either at the nuclear power plants that generated it or at other secure locations. The EIA indicates in "Spent Nuclear Fuel" (December 7, 2015, https://www.eia.gov/nuclear/spent_fuel/) that through June 2013, nearly 77,200 tons (70,000 t) of spent fuel had accumulated at these sites.

REPROCESSING SPENT NUCLEAR FUEL. As noted earlier, some other countries reprocess spent nuclear fuel to recycle uranium. Reprocessing also reduces the amount of spent fuel requiring disposal. The United States has rejected this approach because of the security dangers posed by plutonium. Currently, the plutonium within spent nuclear fuel in the United States is dispersed among large amounts of uranium and other contaminants, such as americium, curium, and neptunium. Thus, the plutonium is not a tempting target for terrorists or other parties seeking weapons-grade plutonium.

NUCLEAR POWER COST FACTORS

The commercial nuclear power industry is devoted entirely to electricity production. In the United States electricity is also produced by the combustion of fossil fuels, mainly coal and natural gas. Because electricity producers feed their electricity to the nation's electrical grid for consumption by consumers, it is difficult to distinguish between the prices for electricity produced from various fuel sources. However, there are specific supply and demand factors that affect nuclear power pricing.

Analysts agree that one cost differential between nuclear-based electricity and electricity from other sources is capital costs. Construction of a nuclear power plant is extremely expensive. Most of the United States' nuclear power plants were built decades ago. Thus, the high capital costs associated with building the reactors have long been absorbed by the industry and are not a significant factor in current pricing. The same holds true for initial licensing costs and other costs that are incurred before plants begin operating. Nuclear power plant operators also incur fuel, operating, and maintenance costs. Fuel costs can vary considerably from year to year as shown in Table 5.3. For decades, the nuclear power industry had to pay into the Nuclear Waste Fund, which is administered by the federal government. According to

Kim Cawley of the Congressional Budget Office, in *Testimony: The Federal Government's Responsibilities and Liabilities under the Nuclear Waste Policy Act* (December 3, 2015, https://www.cbo.gov/sites/default/files/114th-congress-2015-2016/reports/51035-Nuclear Waste_Testimony.pdf), the fund was established by law in 1983; collections were halted, however, in 2014 after nuclear power industry groups successfully sued the federal government. As of September 30, 2015, the fund had accrued $41.9 billion in fees and interest.

The Nuclear Waste Fund was an expense imposed by the government on the nuclear power industry; however, the government has also taken actions to financially support and promote the industry. These actions help lower the production price of electricity that is generated by nuclear power. Chapter 1 describes the federal tax breaks, research and development funds, and other types of financial assistance that are provided to energy suppliers.

CHAPTER 6
RENEWABLE ENERGY

Renewable energy is energy that is virtually unlimited. As is explained in Chapter 1, under the right circumstances renewable energy sources are constantly produced and can be tapped again and again by humans without eliminating them. Examples include flowing water, wood, wind, biologically based waste materials, sunlight, and geothermal energy (i.e., the heat stored beneath the earth's crust).

Until the early 1970s most Americans were content to rely on fossil fuels for their energy needs. However, an embargo on imported oil ended this carefree approach. Throughout the United States people waited in line to fill their gas tanks—in some places gasoline was rationed—and lower heat settings for offices and homes were encouraged. In a country where mobility and convenience were highly valued, the 1970s oil crisis was a shock to the system. Developing alternative sources of energy to supplement and perhaps eventually replace fossil fuels suddenly became important. Over the following decades financial incentives and technological advancements helped alternative energy providers build their industries.

Renewable energy sources are relative newcomers to the energy marketplace and, in many cases, must compete directly with fossil fuels for consumers. This is a difficult task. The systems and infrastructure for fossil fuel production and delivery have long been in place, and Americans are accustomed to them. As a result, renewables must overcome logistical, technological, and economical challenges to get to consumers.

It is also important to understand that although renewables begin as natural sources, they may be heavily processed before they actually provide energy to consumers. Industrial processing requires energy—that is, it has an energy price. For example, chipping wood into small pieces so it is easier to burn is energy intensive. Likewise, converting crops, such as corn, into liquid fuel is a highly industrial process. Because U.S. industry is heavily dependent on fossil fuels, the reality is that fossil fuels

are burned during the processing of many renewable sources. This energy price has to be considered when evaluating the relative advantages and disadvantages of alternative fuels.

As noted in previous chapters, fossil fuels are forecast to maintain their prominent role as energy sources for decades to come. Even so, renewable sources have carved out a niche in the market, and that niche seems destined to grow.

MARKET FACTORS

The renewables market is driven by concerns about energy production from nuclear energy and fossil fuels. One major concern relates to environmental impacts. Nuclear power generates radioactive waste that can be hazardous for thousands of years. The combustion of fossil fuels releases emissions that degrade air quality and contribute to global warming and climate change. Renewable fuels do not generate radioactive waste. The noncombustible renewables (solar, wind, tides, hydropower, and geothermal) do not emit the air pollutants that are associated with fossil fuels. The combustible renewables, by virtue of their organic makeup, do contribute such emissions, but to a lesser extent than fossil fuels. Energy self-sufficiency is another concern that drives interest in renewable fuels because they can be produced domestically.

Although environmental impacts and self-sufficiency are powerful motivators for developing alternative fuels, both concerns pale in comparison to economic considerations. Many renewable energy source technologies are relatively immature and still in the research and development (R&D) stage. As such, they are more expensive to produce commercially than fossil fuels. When fossil fuels drop in price, interest wanes in the business world for developing alternative fuels because there is less profit to be made. In addition, the impetus for renewables development declines when "new" domestic sources of fossil fuels become available. As is described in Chapters 2 and 3, domestic production of oil and natural gas from unconventional geological sources, such as shale and tar sands, has skyrocketed. These sources will likely help keep domestic fossil fuel prices low, further damaging the economic competitiveness of renewables.

Renewable Energy Providers

Renewable energy is a focus of investment for companies both large and small. Large energy companies may operate renewables facilities themselves or invest in smaller renewables companies. Chapter 2 describes the so-called supermajor fossil fuel companies that are collectively dubbed "Big Oil." One of these companies is Total, which is based in France. SunPower Inc. is a solar energy provider headquartered in California. According to SunPower, in *SunPower Annual Report 2015* (March 2015, http://files.shareholder.com/down loads/SPWR/2878952645x0x881825/44C08D50-3E90-49A6-A4AE-1D8F5B17869A/SunPower_2015_Annual _Report.pdf), the company has been majority owned by Total since 2011. Chevron (2016, https://www.chevron .com/stories/geothermal-energy), another of the Big Oil companies, indicates that it is "one of the world's leading producers of geothermal energy."

Smaller players in the fossil fuel industry, such as Valero Energy Corporation, have invested heavily in the production of transportation fuels, such as ethanol, which are derived from corn and other biological sources. According to Valero (https://www.valero.com/en-us/ AboutValero/CompanyHistory), in 2015 it was one of the largest ethanol producers in the United States. In addition, the company (2015, https://www.valero.com/en-us/About Valero/Renewables) notes that it has teamed with Darling Ingredients Inc. to produce renewable (or green) diesel fuel from recycled animal fat and used cooking oil.

Excluding ethanol and other biofuels, renewable energy sources are almost entirely devoted to electricity generation. The federal government, by virtue of its control of large hydropower dams, is the leading provider of renewables-derived electricity. Electric utilities, both public owned and investor owned, use renewable sources to varying degrees. For example, Ceres and Clean Edge are nonprofit organizations devoted to sustainability. In June 2016 the two organizations published a report rating the nation's largest investor-owned electric utilities in terms of their renewables utilization. In *Benchmarking Utility Clean Energy Deployment: 2016* (June 2016, http://www.ceres.org/resources/reports/clean-energy-utility -benchmarking-report-2016/view), Ceres and Clean Edge note that Sempra Energy (which operates San Diego Gas and Electric) used renewable sources for 36.5% of the electricity it sold in 2014. Other major providers of renewables-derived electricity included PG&E, Edison International, and Xcel Energy. The electric power sector also includes independent power producers. NRG Energy, Inc. (2016, http://www.nrg.com/renewables/pro jects/generation/), the nation's largest independent power producer as of 2016, operates dozens of power plants that are fueled by solar and wind in addition to its fossil fuel– fired fleet.

Government Involvement

When interest in developing renewable energy sources became keen during the 1970s, the government began providing financial support to the fledgling industry. As is described in Chapter 1, the federal government uses a variety of incentives to encourage domestic energy development. Figure 1.14 in Chapter 1 shows the costs of energy-related tax preferences between 1985 and 2015. The fossil fuel industry has historically been the major beneficiary; preferences for the renewable energy industry, however, began increasing dramatically during the first decade of the 21st century. Legislative changes, particularly the Energy Policy Act of 2005, helped turn the focus toward renewables.

As is shown in Table 1.6 in Chapter 1, the federal government gave $15.8 billion in total energy-related tax preferences in fiscal year (FY) 2015. (The federal government's fiscal year runs from October to September; thus, FY 2015 covered October 1, 2014, to September 30, 2015.) Renewable energy enjoyed around $7.7 billion in tax preferences in FY 2015, or 49% of the total. As is noted in Chapter 1, however, most renewable energy provisions are temporary, whereas those given to fossil fuels and nuclear energy are mostly permanent.

Critics complain that the incentives granted to the renewable energy sector pale in comparison with the many billions of dollars that have been pumped into the fossil fuel industry for nearly a century. Government support is particularly important during the initial R&D stages of an industry. The fossil fuel industry is extremely mature, whereas the renewables industry is still largely doing initial R&D tasks. (It should be noted that this is not true for the hydroelectric sector, which has operated for many decades.) Some analysts believe the government should provide more funding support for renewables at this crucial time in their development and make their tax preferences permanent to boost the competitiveness of the industry.

As noted earlier, government entities are substantial suppliers of renewable energy through their role as electricity utility operators. As is explained in Chapter 8, the U.S. electric power sector includes power plants that are owned and operated by municipalities, federal agencies (such as the Bonneville Power Administration), and federally owned corporations (such as the Tennessee Valley Authority).

The government also supports renewables development through mandates and standards. For example, the Energy Independence and Security Act of 2007 includes a Renewable Fuels Standard that mandates the use of specified amounts of biofuels by 2022. This standard will be explained in more detail later in this chapter. State governments also issue renewables mandates. The U.S. Energy Information Administration (EIA) indicates in *Annual Energy Outlook 2016 with Projections to 2040* (https://www.eia.gov/forecasts/aeo/pdf/0383(2016).pdf) that as of August 2016, 29 states and the District of Columbia had mandatory (enforceable) renewable portfolio standards or similar laws. The agency notes that "under such standards, each state determines its own levels of renewable generation, eligible technologies, and noncompliance penalties." For example, California requires that renewables account for 50% of electricity sales in the state by 2030.

THE EXECUTIVE BRANCH. As is described in Chapter 1, President Barack Obama (1961–) has championed renewable energy usage as part of his "all-of-the-above" energy policy. One major driver is concern about the contribution of fossil fuel combustion to global warming and climate change. Congress has proved reluctant to pass laws that could encumber the nation's oil and gas industry and hence boost usage of renewable fuels. As a result, Obama has furthered his renewables agenda by taking actions that affect the executive branch (the offices and agencies under the control of the president). For example, in "Advancing American Energy" (2016, https://www.whitehouse.gov/energy/securing-american-energy), the White House indicates that the U.S. Department of Defense has committed to deploying 3 gigawatts of renewable energy on military installations by 2025. Agencies such as the U.S. Department of the Interior's Bureau of Land Management (BLM) control huge swaths of government-owned land in the West. As of August 2016, the BLM (http://www.blm.gov/wo/st/en/prog/energy/renewable_energy/Renewable_Energy_Projects _Approved_to_Date.html) had allowed dozens of companies to develop utility-scale renewable energy projects on public lands under its control. The projects rely on solar, wind, or geothermal resources.

The U.S. Environmental Protection Agency (EPA) encourages use of renewables-derived electricity through its Green Power Partnership program. In "Green Power Partnership National Top 100" (July 25, 2016, https://www.epa.gov/greenpower/green-power-partnership-national-top-100), the EPA ranks 100 of its commercial partners in terms of their usage of renewables-derived electricity. As of July 2016, the top-five companies were Intel Corporation, Microsoft Corporation, Kohl's Department Stores, Cisco Systems, Inc., and Google Inc. The 100 companies obtained green power from numerous providers, including utilities and independent power producers. In addition, some of them generated their own green power on-site. The EPA (April 19, 2016, https://www.epa.gov/greenpower/green-power-leadership-awards#current-winners) also annually recognizes green power suppliers. The winners of the agency's 2015 Green Power Supplier Award were 3Degrees, Renewable Choice Energy, and Silicon Valley Power.

PRODUCTION AND CONSUMPTION

Figure 6.1 shows total U.S. energy consumption by major energy source between 1949 and 2015. Historically, fossil fuels have dominated domestic consumption. As shown in Table 1.2 in Chapter 1, renewable sources accounted for 9.7 quadrillion British thermal units (Btu) of consumption in 2015, or 11% of the total of 88.1 quadrillion Btu. In 2015 hydroelectric power was the most consumed renewable source, followed by biofuels and wood. (See Figure 6.2 and Table 6.1.) The EIA puts wood and biofuels together with waste under the biomass category. (Waste refers to municipal solid waste from biogenic [biologically derived] sources, landfill gas, sludge waste, agricultural by-products [such as stalks and husks], and other biologically based waste.) Biomass is either directly combustible or is used to produce other combustible fuels, such as ethanol and biodiesel. As indicated in Figure 6.3, biomass and hydroelectric power have been the two most commonly used renewables for decades. Biomass consumption has increased noticeably since around 2000.

Figure 6.4 provides a breakdown of renewables consumption in 2015 by end-use sectors. The electric power sector accounted for 5.1 quadrillion Btu, which was more than half (53%) of the total consumption of 9.6 quadrillion Btu. The industrial and transportation sectors were the next biggest consumers of renewable energy sources in 2015. The residential and commercial sectors were much smaller users.

Biomass Energy

Biomass provided 4.7 quadrillion Btu in 2015, or 49% of the total renewables consumed. (See Table 6.1.) Biofuels were the largest biomass source providing 2.1 quadrillion Btu, or nearly half (46%) of the biomass total. They were followed by wood (2 quadrillion Btu, or 43% of the biomass total) and waste (0.5 quadrillion Btu, or 11% of the biomass total).

The biofuels category includes fuel ethanol and biodiesel. Fuel ethanol is ethanol intended for fuel use, rather than for human consumption. Fuel ethanol is denatured (made unfit for human consumption) by the addition of petroleum products. Fuel ethanol can be manufactured from various vegetative feedstocks, including starchy/sugary crops, such as corn (which is primarily used in the United States), and cellulosic sources, such as trees and grasses.

FIGURE 6.1

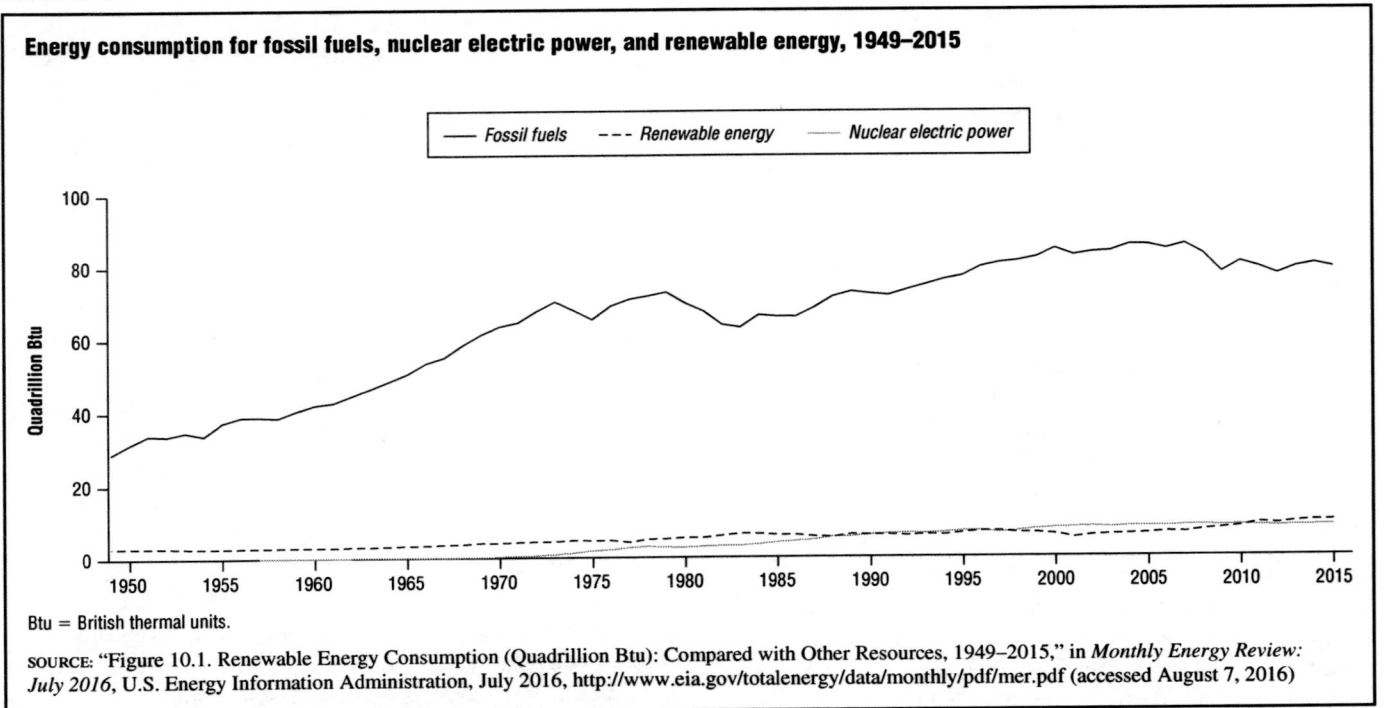

Energy consumption for fossil fuels, nuclear electric power, and renewable energy, 1949–2015

Btu = British thermal units.

SOURCE: "Figure 10.1. Renewable Energy Consumption (Quadrillion Btu): Compared with Other Resources, 1949–2015," in *Monthly Energy Review: July 2016*, U.S. Energy Information Administration, July 2016, http://www.eia.gov/totalenergy/data/monthly/pdf/mer.pdf (accessed August 7, 2016)

FIGURE 6.2

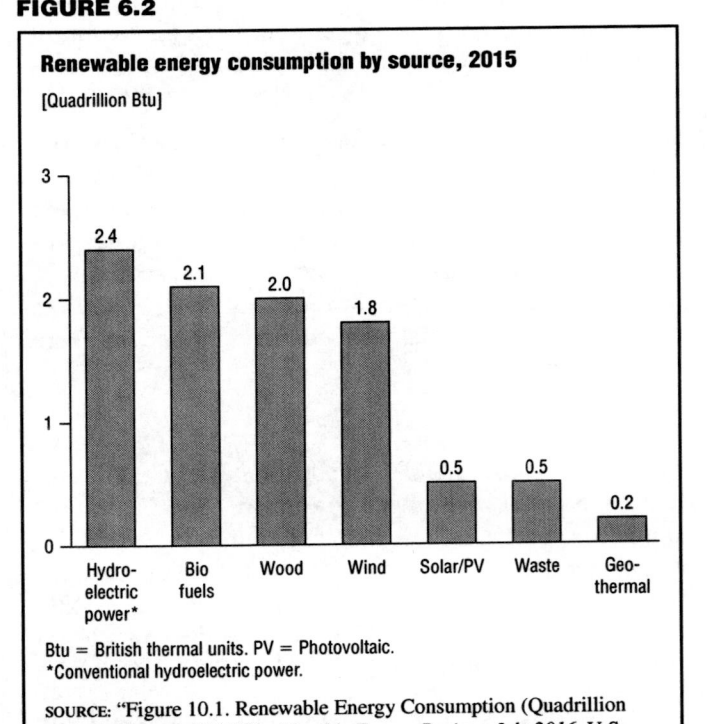

Renewable energy consumption by source, 2015

[Quadrillion Btu]

Btu = British thermal units. PV = Photovoltaic.
*Conventional hydroelectric power.

SOURCE: "Figure 10.1. Renewable Energy Consumption (Quadrillion Btu): By Source, 2015," in *Monthly Energy Review: July 2016*, U.S. Energy Information Administration, July 2016, http://www.eia.gov/totalenergy/data/monthly/pdf/mer.pdf (accessed August 7, 2016)

Fuel ethanol can be blended at low concentrations into motor gasoline. For example, gasohol is a gasoline blend that contains up to 10% fuel ethanol by volume and can be used just like gasoline in conventional vehicles. At high concentrations, ethanol is blended with gasoline to make fuels that are suitable only for specially designed vehicles called alternative-fuel vehicles. For example, E85 is the short name for a fuel that contains 85% ethanol and 15% motor gasoline. Biodiesel is a fuel made from biological sources, such as soybeans or animal fats, and is used in vehicles that ordinarily run on petroleum-derived diesel fuel.

As shown in the footnotes for Table 6.1, annual domestic production equals annual domestic consumption for all renewables except biofuels. Biofuels are heavily processed, and some losses and coproducts result during processing. In addition, the United States imports and exports small amounts of biofuels. In 2015 fuel ethanol feedstocks (corn and other biomass inputs) totaled 1,998 trillion Btu. (See Table 6.2.) Losses and coproducts totaled 774 trillion Btu. After denaturant addition, the heat content of the final product was 1,254 trillion Btu. Overall, fuel ethanol production in 2015 was 14.8 billion gallons (56 billion L), whereas consumption was 13.9 billion gallons (52.8 billion L). Consumption of fuel ethanol increased dramatically during the first decade of the 21st century.

As shown in Table 6.3, biodiesel production totaled 1.3 billion gallons (4.8 billion L) in 2015, whereas consumption was nearly 1.5 billion gallons (5.6 billion L). The consumption of biodiesel was only around 300 million gallons (1.1 billion L) from 2007 to 2010 and then grew considerably.

TABLE 6.1

Renewable energy production and consumption by major source, selected years 1949–2015

[Trillion Btu]

	Production[a]			Consumption								
	Biomass		Total renewable energy[d]	Hydroelectric power[e]	Geo-thermal[f]	Solar/PV[g]	Wind[h]	Biomass				Total renewable energy
	Biofuels[b]	Total[c]						Wood[i]	Waste[j]	Biofuels[k]	Total	
1950 Total	NA	1,562	2,978	1,415	NA	NA	NA	1,562	NA	NA	1,562	2,978
1955 Total	NA	1,424	2,784	1,360	NA	NA	NA	1,424	NA	NA	1,424	2,784
1960 Total	NA	1,320	2,928	1,608	(s)	NA	NA	1,320	NA	NA	1,320	2,928
1965 Total	NA	1,335	3,396	2,059	2	NA	NA	1,335	NA	NA	1,335	3,396
1970 Total	NA	1,431	4,070	2,634	6	NA	NA	1,429	2	NA	1,431	4,070
1975 Total	NA	1,499	4,687	3,155	34	NA	NA	1,497	2	NA	1,499	4,687
1980 Total	NA	2,475	5,428	2,900	53	NA	NA	2,474	2	NA	2,475	5,428
1985 Total	93	3,016	6,084	2,970	97	(s)	(s)	2,687	236	93	3,016	6,084
1990 Total	111	2,735	6,041	3,046	171	59	29	2,216	408	111	2,735	6,041
1995 Total	198	3,099	6,558	3,205	152	69	33	2,370	531	200	3,101	6,560
2000 Total	233	3,006	6,104	2,811	164	66	57	2,262	511	236	3,008	6,106
2001 Total	254	2,624	5,164	2,242	164	64	70	2,006	364	253	2,622	5,163
2002 Total	308	2,705	5,734	2,689	171	63	105	1,995	402	303	2,701	5,729
2003 Total	401	2,805	5,946	2,793	173	62	113	2,002	401	403	2,806	5,948
2004 Total	486	2,996	6,067	2,688	178	63	142	2,121	389	498	3,008	6,079
2005 Total	561	3,101	6,226	2,703	181	63	178	2,137	403	574	3,114	6,239
2006 Total	716	3,212	6,594	2,869	181	68	264	2,099	397	766	3,262	6,645
2007 Total	970	3,472	6,520	2,446	186	76	341	2,089	413	983	3,485	6,533
2008 Total	1,374	3,868	7,206	2,511	192	89	546	2,059	435	1,357	3,851	7,189
2009 Total	1,570	3,953	7,641	2,669	200	98	721	1,931	452	1,553	3,936	7,624
2010 Total	1,868	4,316	8,112	2,539	208	126	923	1,981	468	1,821	4,270	8,066
2011 Total	2,029	4,501	9,155	3,103	212	171	1,168	2,010	462	1,933	4,405	9,059
2012 Total	1,929	4,406	8,813	2,629	212	227	1,340	2,010	467	1,892	4,369	8,777
2013 Total	1,981	4,647	9,330	2,562	214	305	1,601	2,170	496	2,007	4,673	9,356
2014 Total	2,103	4,849	9,678	2,467	214	420	1,728	2,230	516	2,067	4,812	9,641
2015 Total	2,161	4,715	9,694	2,389	224	550	1,816	2,040	514	2,142	4,696	9,675

[a]Production equals consumption for all renewable energy sources except biofuels.
[b]Total biomass inputs to the production of fuel ethanol and biodiesel.
[c]Wood and wood-derived fuels, biomass waste, and total biomass inputs to the production of fuel ethanol and biodiesel.
[d]Hydroelectric power, geothermal, solar thermal/photovoltaic, wind, and biomass.
[e]Conventional hydroelectricity net generation.
[f]Geothermal electricity net generation, and geothermal heat pump and direct use energy.
[g]Solar thermal and photovoltaic (PV) electricity net generation, and solar thermal direct use energy.
[h]Wind electricity net generation.
[i]Wood and wood-derived fuels.
[j]Municipal solid waste from biogenic sources, landfill gas, sludge waste, agricultural byproducts, and other biomass. Through 2000, also includes non-renewable waste (municipal solid waste from non-biogenic sources, and tire-derived fuels).
[k]Fuel ethanol (minus denaturant) and biodiesel consumption, plus losses and co-products from the production of fuel ethanol and biodiesel.
NA = Not available. (s) = Less than 0.5 trillion Btu.
Notes: Most data for the residential, commercial, industrial, and transportation sectors are estimates. Totals may not equal sum of components due to independent rounding. Geographic coverage is the 50 states and the District of Columbia. Btu = British thermal units. PV = Photovoltaic.

SOURCE: Adapted from "Table 10.1 Renewable Energy Production and Consumption by Source (Trillion Btu)," in *Monthly Energy Review: July 2016*, U.S. Energy Information Administration, July 2016, http://www.eia.gov/totalenergy/data/monthly/pdf/mer.pdf (accessed August 7, 2016)

GOVERNMENT INVOLVEMENT. Growth in biofuels consumption has been driven largely by government mandates for biofuels use. Janet McGurty and Matthew Robinson report in "Analysis: U.S. Government Mandate or No, Fuel Ethanol Is Here to Stay" (Reuters.com, August 24, 2012) that in 1990 the Clean Air Act was amended to require the motor gasoline industry to sell reformulated gasoline that burns cleaner (i.e., produces less air pollutants) than regular gasoline. Reformulated gasoline burns cleaner because it contains an oxygenate additive. Fuel ethanol has become the primary oxygenate used to produce reformulated gasoline.

The Energy Independence and Security Act of 2007 includes a Renewable Fuel Standard that mandates biofuel use. Specifically, the Renewable Fuel Standard requires that by 2022 U.S. refineries will blend 36 billion gallons (136.3 billion L) of biofuels into their transportation fuel annually. Figure 6.5 shows the total amount required each year through 2022 and the required breakdown by renewable fuel. When the law was passed it was expected that cellulosic biofuel use would grow dramatically during the second decade of the 21st century and the early 2020s; this view, however, is now considered overly optimistic. In *Testimony: The Renewable Fuel Standard: Issues for 2015 and Beyond* (November 3, 2015, https://www.cbo.gov/sites/default/files/114th-congress-2015-2016/reports/50944-RenewableFuelStandard.pdf), Terry Dinan of the Congressional Budget Office notes that "fuel suppliers have had trouble meeting the annual requirements for cellulosic biofuels because making such fuels is complex, capital-intensive, and

FIGURE 6.3

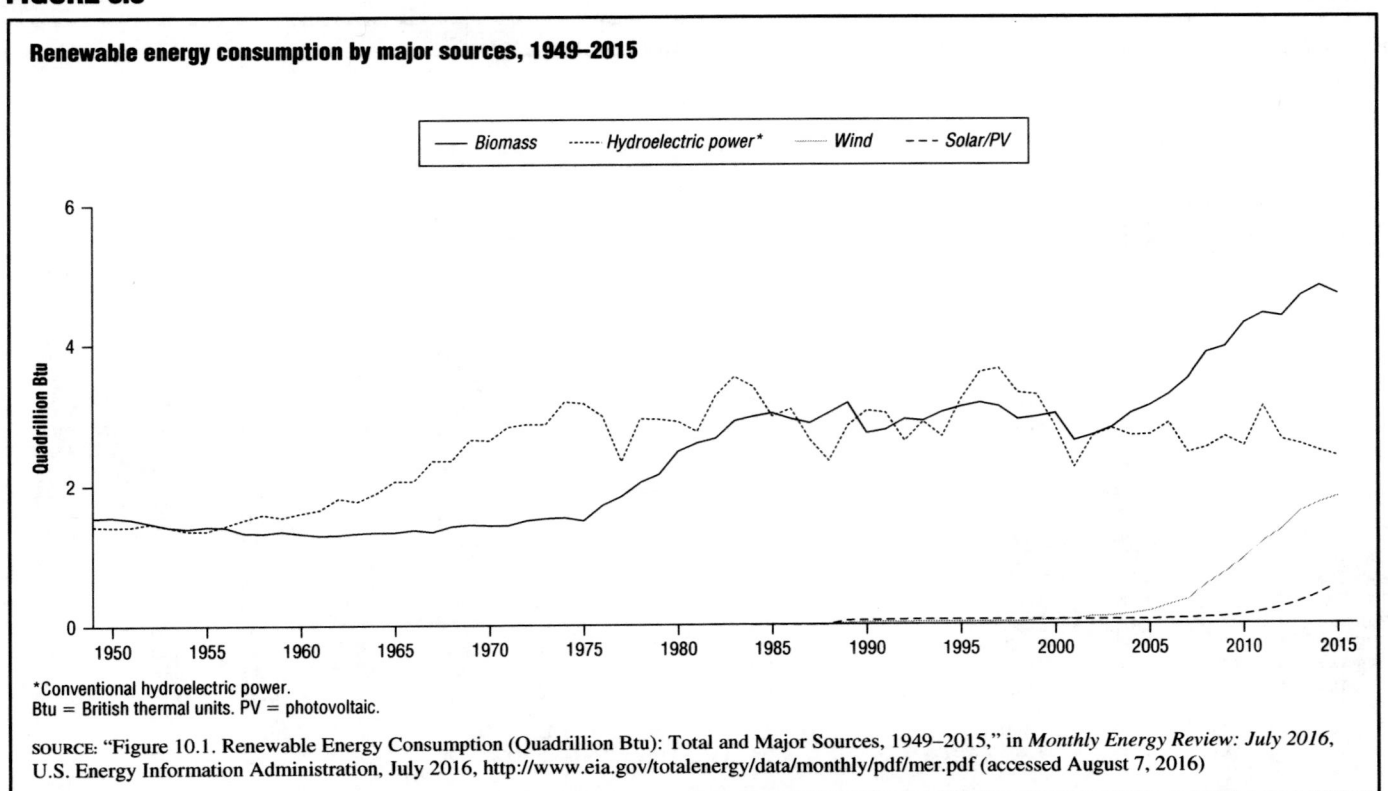

Renewable energy consumption by major sources, 1949–2015

*Conventional hydroelectric power.
Btu = British thermal units. PV = photovoltaic.

SOURCE: "Figure 10.1. Renewable Energy Consumption (Quadrillion Btu): Total and Major Sources, 1949–2015," in *Monthly Energy Review: July 2016,*
U.S. Energy Information Administration, July 2016, http://www.eia.gov/totalenergy/data/monthly/pdf/mer.pdf (accessed August 7, 2016)

FIGURE 6.4

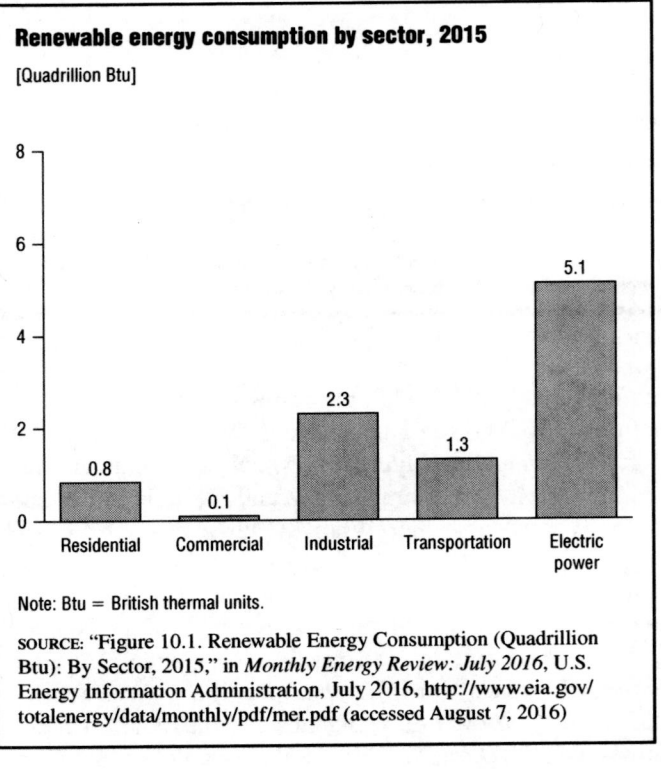

Renewable energy consumption by sector, 2015

[Quadrillion Btu]

Note: Btu = British thermal units.

SOURCE: "Figure 10.1. Renewable Energy Consumption (Quadrillion Btu): By Sector, 2015," in *Monthly Energy Review: July 2016,* U.S. Energy Information Administration, July 2016, http://www.eia.gov/totalenergy/data/monthly/pdf/mer.pdf (accessed August 7, 2016)

costly." Meanwhile, there are practical limits on the amount of ethanol that can be blended into gasoline, particularly for older vehicles. These issues pose significant challenges to the future success of the Renewable Fuel Standard mandates.

As is explained in Chapter 1, energy producers, including the biomass industries, benefit from financial incentives that are provided by the federal government. Government incentives for fuel ethanol production have long been controversial because corn is a food crop. Critics fear that strong demand for corn-derived fuel ethanol since 1990 has driven up prices for food corn for humans, pets, and livestock. At the end of 2011 the federal government let a long-standing subsidy for corn ethanol expire. The article "Congress Ends Era of Ethanol Subsidies" (NPR.org, January 3, 2012) notes that the subsidy had been in place for three decades and amounted to around $20 billion in total.

ENVIRONMENTAL ISSUES. In general, biomass sources are hailed as more environmentally friendly than fossil fuels. However, the use of biomass is not without environmental problems. Deforestation can occur from widespread use of wood, especially if forests are clear-cut, which can result in soil erosion and mudslides. In addition, burning biomass produces air emissions that degrade air quality. Although biomass is less energy intensive (has a lower heat content) than fossil fuels, the combustion of any carbon-containing fuel releases carbon into the atmosphere that contributes to problems with global warming and climate change.

TABLE 6.2

Fuel ethanol production and consumption, selected years 1981–2015

	Feedstock[a]	Losses and co-products[b]	Denaturant[c]	Production[d]			Trade[d] Net imports[e]	Stocks[d, f]	Stock change[d, g]	Consumption[d]			Consumption minus denaturant[h]
	TBtu	TBtu	Mbbl	Mbbl	MMgal	TBtu	Mbbl	Mbbl	Mbbl	Mbbl	MMgal	TBtu	TBtu
1981 Total	13	6	40	1,978	83	7	NA	NA	NA	1,978	83	7	7
1985 Total	93	42	294	14,693	617	52	NA	NA	NA	14,693	617	52	51
1990 Total	111	49	356	17,802	748	63	NA	NA	NA	17,802	748	63	62
1995 Total	198	86	647	32,325	1,358	115	387	2,186	−207	32,919	1,383	117	114
2000 Total	233	99	773	38,627	1,622	138	116	3,400	−624	39,367	1,653	140	137
2001 Total	253	108	841	42,028	1,765	150	315	4,298	898	41,445	1,741	148	144
2002 Total	307	130	1,019	50,956	2,140	182	306	6,200	1,902	49,360	2,073	176	171
2003 Total	400	168	1,335	66,772	2,804	238	292	5,978	−222	67,286	2,826	240	233
2004 Total	482	201	1,621	81,058	3,404	289	3,542	6,002	24	84,576	3,552	301	293
2005 Total	550	227	1,859	92,961	3,904	331	3,234	5,563	−439	96,634	4,059	344	335
2006 Total	683	280	2,326	116,294	4,884	414	17,408	8,760	3,197	130,505	5,481	465	453
2007 Total	907	368	3,105	155,263	6,521	553	10,457	10,535	1,775	163,945	6,886	584	569
2008 Total	1,286	518	4,433	221,637	9,309	790	12,610	14,226	3,691	230,556	9,683	821	800
2009 Total	1,503	602	5,688	260,424	10,938	928	4,720	16,594	2,368	262,776	11,037	936	910
2010 Total	1,823	726	6,506	316,617	13,298	1,127	−9,115	17,941	1,347	306,155	12,858	1,090	1,061
2011 Total	1,904	754	6,649	331,646	13,929	1,181	−24,365	18,238	297	306,984	12,893	1,093	1,065
2012 Total	1,801	709	6,264	314,714	13,218	1,120	−5,891	20,350	2,112	306,711	12,882	1,092	1,064
2013 Total	1,805	707	6,181	316,493	13,293	1,126	−5,761	16,424	−3,926	314,658	13,216	1,120	1,092
2014 Total	1,938	755	6,476	340,781	14,313	1,212	−18,371	18,739	2,315	320,095	13,444	1,139	1,111
2015 Total	1,998	774	6,641	352,520	14,806	1,254	−17,924	21,438	2,699	331,897	13,940	1,181	1,152

[a]Total corn and other biomass inputs to the production of undenatured ethanol used for fuel ethanol.
[b]Losses and co-products from the production of fuel ethanol. Does not include natural gas, electricity, and other non-biomass energy used in the production of fuel ethanol—these are included in the industrial sector consumption statistics for the appropriate energy source.
[c]The amount of denaturant in fuel ethanol produced.
[d]Includes denaturant.
[e]Through 2009, data are for fuel ethanol imports only; data for fuel ethanol exports are not available. Beginning in 2010, data are for fuel ethanol imports minus fuel ethanol (including industrial alcohol) exports.
[f]Stocks are at end of period.
[g]A negative value indicates a decrease in stocks and a positive value indicates an increase.
[h]Consumption of fuel ethanol minus denaturant.
NA = Not available.
Notes: Mbbl = thousand barrels. MMgal = million U.S. gallons. TBtu = trillion Btu. Fuel ethanol data in thousand barrels are converted to million gallons by multiplying by 0.042, and are converted to Btu by multiplying by the approximate heat content of fuel ethanol. Through 1980, data are not available. For 1981–1992, data are estimates. For 1993–2008, only data for feedstock, losses and co-products, and denaturant are estimates. Beginning in 2009, only data for feedstock, and losses and co-products, are estimates. Totals may not equal sum of components due to independent rounding. Geographic coverage is the 50 states and the District of Columbia.

SOURCE: Adapted from "Table 10.3. Fuel Ethanol Overview," in *Monthly Energy Review: July 2016*, U.S. Energy Information Administration, July 2016, http://www.eia.gov/totalenergy/data/monthly/pdf/mer.pdf (accessed August 7, 2016).

Hydropower

Hydropower provided 2.4 quadrillion Btu in 2015, or 25% of the renewables total of 9.7 quadrillion Btu. (See Table 6.1.)

For decades, hydropower has been used in the United States to generate electricity. Hydropower facilities convert the energy of flowing water into mechanical energy, turning turbines to create electricity. In "Hydroelectric Power Resources Form Regional Clusters" (June 10, 2011, http://www.eia.gov/todayinenergy/detail.cfm?id=1750), the EIA divides hydropower into two broad categories: conventional and nonconventional.

Conventional hydropower plants use either flowing water (a run-of-river plant) or water backed up behind a dam (a storage plant) to produce electricity. A run-of-river plant produces electricity as river flows allow. The flows can be quite variable and depend heavily on weather events, such as rainfall and snowmelt. By contrast, a storage plant relies on a dam to create an ever-ready reservoir of water that can be tapped as needed.

(See Figure 6.6.) The dam creates a height from which water can flow at a fast rate. When the water reaches the power plant at the bottom of the dam, it pushes the turbine blades that are attached to the electrical generator. Whenever power is needed, the valves are opened, the moving water spins the turbines, and the generator produces electricity.

There are various nonconventional hydropower means for generating electricity. The most common method is called pumped storage. In these systems water is pumped from a low elevation to a high elevation within the plant during times of low demand for electricity. In essence, some of the water that has already been used to generate electricity is reused. Because pumping is an energy-intensive process, more energy can be used during the pumping than is generated from the pumped water.

There are hundreds of conventional and pumped-storage hydroelectric plants around the United States. (The EIA provides a map of their locations in "Hydroelectric Power Resources Form Regional Clusters.")

TABLE 6.3

Biodiesel production, trade, and consumption, 2001–15

	Feedstock[a] TBtu	Losses and co-products[b] TBtu	Production Mbbl	Production MMgal	Production TBtu	Trade Imports Mbbl	Trade Exports Mbbl	Net imports[c] Mbbl	Stocks[d] Mbbl	Stock change[e] Mbbl	Consumption Mbbl	Consumption MMgal	Consumption TBtu	Other renewable fuels TBtu
2001 Total	1	(s)	204	9	1	81	41	40	NA	NA	244	10	1	NA
2002 Total	1	(s)	250	10	1	197	57	140	NA	NA	390	16	2	NA
2003 Total	2	(s)	338	14	2	97	113	−17	NA	NA	322	14	2	NA
2004 Total	4	(s)	666	28	4	101	128	−27	NA	NA	639	27	3	NA
2005 Total	12	(s)	2,162	91	12	214	213	1	NA	NA	2,163	91	12	NA
2006 Total	32	(s)	5,963	250	32	1,105	856	250	NA	NA	6,213	261	33	NA
2007 Total	63	1	11,662	490	62	3,455	6,696	−3,241	NA	NA	8,422	354	45	NA
2008 Total	88	1	16,145	678	87	7,755	16,673	−8,918	NA	NA	7,228	304	39	NA
2009 Total	67	1	12,281	516	66	1,906	6,546	−4,640	711	711	7,663[f]	322	41	(s)
2010 Total	44	1	8,177	343	44	564	2,588	−2,024	672	−39	6,192	260	33	(s)
2011 Total	125	2	23,035	967	123	890	1,799	−908	2,005	1,028[g]	21,099	886	113	(s)
2012 Total	128	2	23,588	991	126	853	3,056	−2,203	1,984	−20	21,406	899	115	3
2013 Total	176	2	32,368	1,359	173	8,152	4,675	3,477	3,810	1,825	34,020	1,429	182	24
2014 Total	165	2	30,452	1,279	163	4,578	1,974	2,604	3,131	−679	33,735	1,417	181	18
2015 Total	163	2	30,064	1,263	161	7,957	2,093	5,864	3,815	779[h]	35,149	1,476	188	25

[a]Total vegetable oil and other biomass inputs to the production of biodiesel—calculated by multiplying biodiesel production by 5.433 million Btu per barrel.
[b]Losses and co-products from the production of biodiesel. Does not include natural gas, electricity, and other non-biomass energy used in the production of biodiesel—these are included in the industrial sector consumption statistics for the appropriate energy source.
[c]Net imports equal imports minus exports.
[d]Stocks are at end of period. Through 2010, includes stocks at bulk terminals only. Beginning in 2011, includes stocks at bulk terminals and biodiesel production plants.
[e]A negative value indicates a decrease in stocks and a positive value indicates an increase.
[f]In 2009, because of incomplete data coverage and differing data sources, a "Balancing Item" amount of 733 thousand barrels (653 thousand barrels in January 2009; 80 thousand barrels in February 2009) is used to balance biodiesel supply and disposition.
[g]Derived from the final 2010 stocks value for bulk terminals and biodiesel production plants (977 thousand barrels), not the final 2010 value for bulk terminals only (672 thousand barrels) that is shown under "Stocks."
[h]Derived from the preliminary 2014 stocks value (3,036 thousand barrels), not the final 2014 value (3,131 thousand barrels) that is shown under "Stocks."
NA = Not available. (s) = Less than 0.5 trillion Btu and greater than −0.5 trillion Btu.
Notes: Mbbl = thousand barrels. MMgal = million U.S. gallons. TBtu = trillion Btu. Biodiesel data in thousand barrels are converted to million gallons by multiplying by 0.042, and are converted to Btu by multiplying by 5.359 million Btu per barrel (the approximate heat content of biodiesel. Through 2000, data are not available. Beginning in 2001, data not from U.S. Energy Information Administration (EIA) surveys are estimates. Totals may not equal sum of components due to independent rounding. Geographic coverage is the 50 states and the District of Columbia.

SOURCE: Adapted from "Table 10.4. Biodiesel and Other Renewable Fuels Overview," in *Monthly Energy Review: July 2016*, U.S. Energy Information Administration, July 2016, http://www.eia.gov/totalenergy/data/monthly/pdf/mer.pdf (accessed August 7, 2016)

They are heavily concentrated in the river valleys of the central Atlantic states, the Pacific Northwest, and California. Most of the dams were built decades ago as part of massive federal programs designed to decrease flooding and provide freshwater supplies and electricity to the public. The EIA indicates in "Hydropower Explained: Where Hydropower Is Generated" (May 29, 2015, http://www.eia.gov/energyexplained/index.cfm?page=hydropower_where) that more than half of the U.S. hydroelectric capacity is concentrated in Washington, Oregon, and California. In *State Electricity Profiles* (March 24, 2016, http://www.eia.gov/electricity/state/), the agency ranks the largest hydroelectric facilities around the country based on their net summer generation capacity in 2014. The five largest facilities were:

- Grand Coulee (Washington)—7,079 megawatts (MW)
- Bath County (Virginia)—3,003 MW
- Chief Joseph (Washington)—2,456 MW
- Robert Moses Niagara (New York)—2,439 MW
- John Day (Oregon)—2,160 MW

The Bath County facility in Virginia is the only pumped-storage facility among the top-five generators. The Grand Coulee facility in Washington is particularly notable because it was not only the nation's largest hydropower generator but also the nation's largest electricity generator overall in 2014.

According to the EIA, in *Monthly Energy Review: July 2016* (July 2016, http://www.eia.gov/totalenergy/data/monthly/archive/00351607.pdf), conventional hydroelectric power accounted for 251.2 billion kilowatt-hours (kWh), or 6% of the total 4,087.4 billion kWh of U.S. electricity production in 2015. Among the renewable sources used for electricity production, hydropower was the dominant source. As shown in Table 6.1 and Table 6.4, nearly all (2,376 trillion Btu) of the 2,389 trillion Btu of hydropower consumed in 2015 was consumed by the electric power sector.

The federal government is the nation's leading provider of hydroelectric power. The Tennessee Valley Authority and the Power Marketing Administration are federally owned corporations that have long provided

FIGURE 6.5

Past use and future requirements of the Renewable Fuel Standard

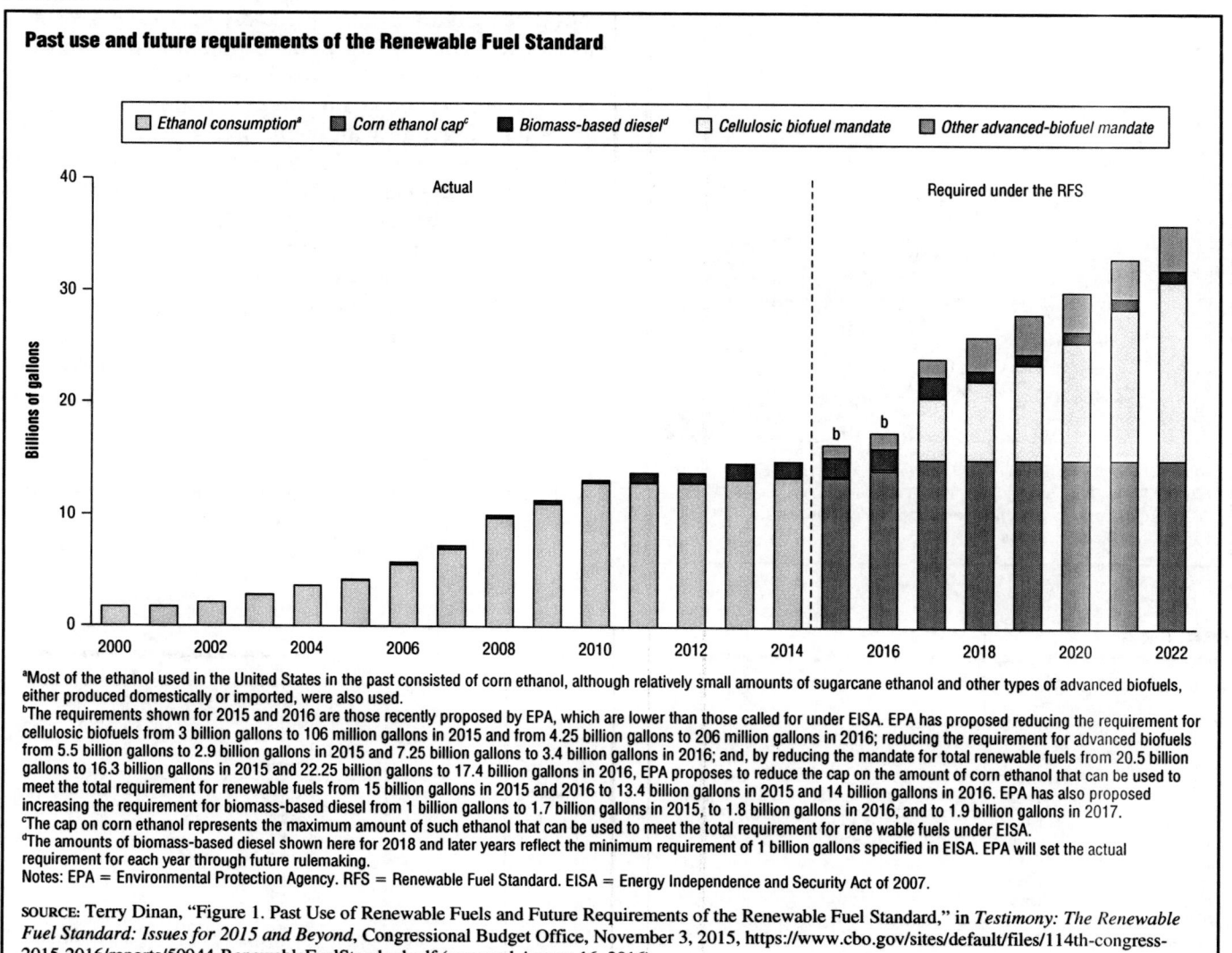

[Legend: Ethanol consumption[a] Corn ethanol cap[c] Biomass-based diesel[d] Cellulosic biofuel mandate Other advanced-biofuel mandate]

[a]Most of the ethanol used in the United States in the past consisted of corn ethanol, although relatively small amounts of sugarcane ethanol and other types of advanced biofuels, either produced domestically or imported, were also used.

[b]The requirements shown for 2015 and 2016 are those recently proposed by EPA, which are lower than those called for under EISA. EPA has proposed reducing the requirement for cellulosic biofuels from 3 billion gallons to 106 million gallons in 2015 and from 4.25 billion gallons to 206 million gallons in 2016; reducing the requirement for advanced biofuels from 5.5 billion gallons to 2.9 billion gallons in 2015 and 7.25 billion gallons to 3.4 billion gallons in 2016; and, by reducing the mandate for total renewable fuels from 20.5 billion gallons to 16.3 billion gallons in 2015 and 22.25 billion gallons to 17.4 billion gallons in 2016, EPA proposes to reduce the cap on the amount of corn ethanol that can be used to meet the total requirement for renewable fuels from 15 billion gallons in 2015 and 2016 to 13.4 billion gallons in 2015 and 14 billion gallons in 2016. EPA has also proposed increasing the requirement for biomass-based diesel from 1 billion gallons to 1.7 billion gallons in 2015, to 1.8 billion gallons in 2016, and to 1.9 billion gallons in 2017.

[c]The cap on corn ethanol represents the maximum amount of such ethanol that can be used to meet the total requirement for rene wable fuels under EISA.

[d]The amounts of biomass-based diesel shown here for 2018 and later years reflect the minimum requirement of 1 billion gallons specified in EISA. EPA will set the actual requirement for each year through future rulemaking.

Notes: EPA = Environmental Protection Agency. RFS = Renewable Fuel Standard. EISA = Energy Independence and Security Act of 2007.

SOURCE: Terry Dinan, "Figure 1. Past Use of Renewable Fuels and Future Requirements of the Renewable Fuel Standard," in *Testimony: The Renewable Fuel Standard: Issues for 2015 and Beyond*, Congressional Budget Office, November 3, 2015, https://www.cbo.gov/sites/default/files/114th-congress-2015-2016/reports/50944-RenewableFuelStandard.pdf (accessed August 16, 2016)

hydroelectricity to consumers in the south-central and western United States, respectively.

ENVIRONMENTAL ISSUES. Hydroelectric power dams have greatly disrupted natural water flows because they are so large. The structures also impede the migration paths of aquatic creatures, and their spinning turbines can kill and injure creatures unable to escape the blades. Although modern dams typically include fish ladders (stepping-stone waterfalls that provide fish a pathway up and over dam structures), the dams still negatively affect aquatic life by altering natural water flows and temperatures.

Wind Energy

Winds are created by the uneven heating of the atmosphere by the sun, the irregularities of the earth's surface, and the rotation of the planet. They are strongly influenced by bodies of water, weather patterns, vegetation, and other factors. The natural power of wind energy

is collected by wind turbines, which resemble airplane propellers. The turbines convert wind energy to mechanical energy and finally to electrical energy. Figure 6.7 shows a wind turbine in which the blades rotate around a horizontal axis. Other types feature vertically aligned blades. Wind turbines are usually clustered on wind farms that may feature dozens or hundreds of individual wind turbines. The most favorable locations for wind turbines are in mountain passes and offshore along coastlines, where wind speeds are generally highest and most consistent.

Wind energy provided 1.8 quadrillion Btu in 2015, or 19% of the total renewables consumed. (See Table 6.1.) Wind was a small energy provider through the 1990s; after the turn of the 21st century, consumption began to grow dramatically. As shown in Table 6.1 and Table 6.4, the electric power sector accounted for nearly all of wind power consumption in 2015.

FIGURE 6.6

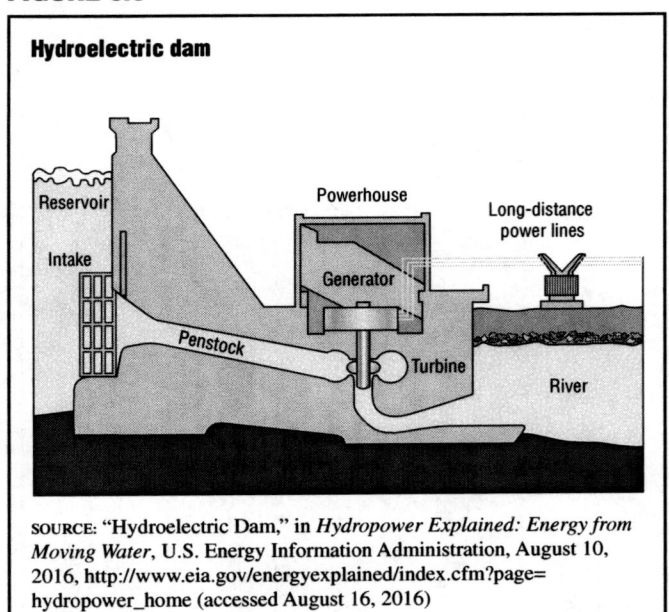

Hydroelectric dam

Reservoir

Intake

Penstock

Powerhouse

Generator

Turbine

Long-distance power lines

River

SOURCE: "Hydroelectric Dam," in *Hydropower Explained: Energy from Moving Water*, U.S. Energy Information Administration, August 10, 2016, http://www.eia.gov/energyexplained/index.cfm?page= hydropower_home (accessed August 16, 2016)

ENVIRONMENTAL ISSUES. In general, wind energy is considered environmentally friendly because it does not involve fuel combustion. Some people find the whirring noise of wind turbines annoying and object to clusters of wind turbines in mountain passes and along shorelines, where they interfere with scenic views. Environmentalists also point out that wind turbines are responsible for the loss of thousands of birds and bats that inadvertently fly into the blades. Birds frequently use windy passages in their travel patterns. Nevertheless, wind farms do not emit climate-altering carbon dioxide and other pollutants, respiratory irritants, or radioactive waste. Furthermore, because wind farms do not require water to operate, they are especially well suited to semiarid and arid regions.

Solar Energy

Solar energy, which comes from the sun, is a renewable, widely available energy source that does not generate pollution or radioactive waste. Nonetheless, converting

TABLE 6.4

Renewable energy consumption by electric power sector, by source, selected years 1950–2015

[Trillion Btu]

	Hydroelectric power[a]	Geothermal[b]	Solar/PV[c]	Wind[d]	Biomass Wood[e]	Biomass Waste[f]	Biomass Total	Total
1950 Total	1,346	NA	NA	NA	5	NA	5	1,351
1955 Total	1,322	NA	NA	NA	3	NA	3	1,325
1960 Total	1,569	(s)	NA	NA	2	NA	2	1,571
1965 Total	2,026	2	NA	NA	3	NA	3	2,031
1970 Total	2,600	6	NA	NA	1	2	4	2,609
1975 Total	3,122	34	NA	NA	(s)	2	2	3,158
1980 Total	2,867	53	NA	NA	3	2	4	2,925
1985 Total	2,937	97	(s)	(s)	8	7	14	3,049
1990 Total	3,014	161	4	29	129	188	317	3,524
1995 Total	3,149	138	5	33	125	296	422	3,747
2000 Total	2,768	144	5	57	134	318	453	3,427
2001 Total	2,209	142	6	70	126	211	337	2,763
2002 Total	2,650	147	6	105	150	230	380	3,288
2003 Total	2,749	146	5	113	167	230	397	3,411
2004 Total	2,655	148	6	142	165	223	388	3,339
2005 Total	2,670	147	6	178	185	221	406	3,406
2006 Total	2,839	145	5	264	182	231	412	3,665
2007 Total	2,430	145	6	341	186	237	423	3,345
2008 Total	2,494	146	9	546	177	258	435	3,630
2009 Total	2,650	146	9	721	180	261	441	3,967
2010 Total	2,521	148	12	923	196	264	459	4,064
2011 Total	3,085	149	17	1,167	182	255	437	4,855
2012 Total	2,606	148	40	1,339	190	262	453	4,586
2013 Total	2,529	151	83	1,600	207	262	470	4,833
2014 Total	2,454	151	165	1,726	251	279	530	5,026
2015 Total	2,376	159	246	1,814	246	274	520	5,116

[a]Conventional hydroelectricity net generation.
[b]Geothermal electricity net generation.
[c]Solar thermal and photovoltaic (PV) electricity net generation.
[d]Wind electricity net generation.
[e]Wood and wood-derived fuels.
[f]Municipal solid waste from biogenic sources, landfill gas, sludge waste, agricultural byproducts, and other biomass. Through 2000, also includes non-renewable waste (municipal solid waste from non-biogenic sources, and tire-derived fuels).
NA = Not available. (s) = Less than 0.5 trillion Btu. Btu = British thermal units.
Notes: The electric power sector comprises electricity-only and combined-heat-and-power (CHP) plants within the NAICS 22 category whose primary business is to sell electricity, or electricity and heat, to the public. Totals may not equal sum of components due to independent rounding. Geographic coverage is the 50 states and the District of Columbia.

SOURCE: Adapted from "Table 10.2c. Renewable Energy Consumption: Electric Power Sector (Trillion Btu)," in *Monthly Energy Review: July 2016*, U.S. Energy Information Administration, July 2016, http://www.eia.gov/totalenergy/data/monthly/pdf/mer.pdf (accessed August 7, 2016)

FIGURE 6.7

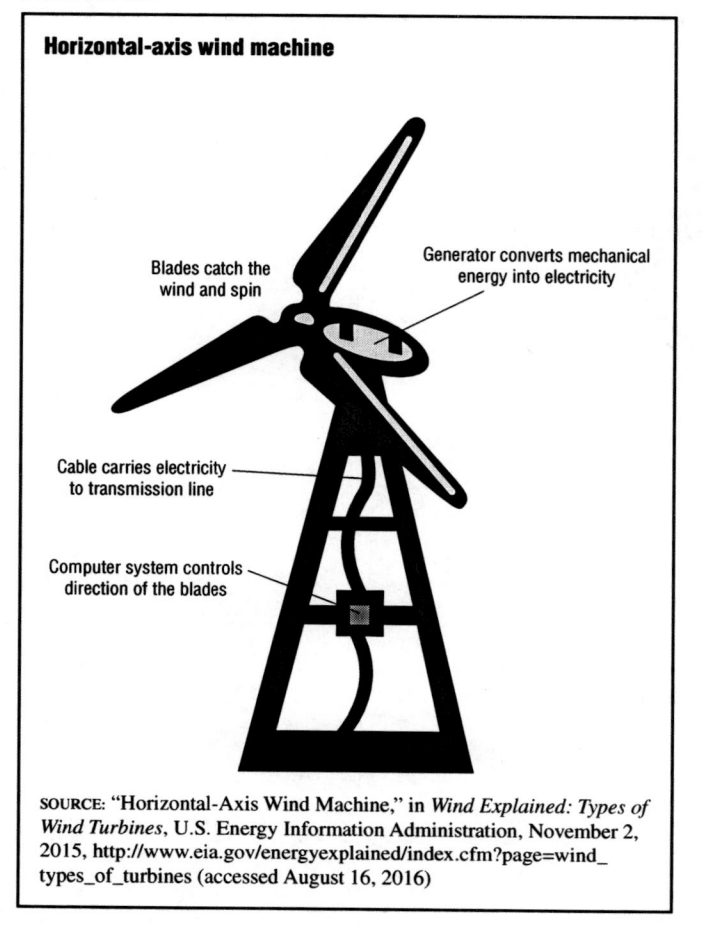

Horizontal-axis wind machine

Blades catch the wind and spin

Generator converts mechanical energy into electricity

Cable carries electricity to transmission line

Computer system controls direction of the blades

SOURCE: "Horizontal-Axis Wind Machine," in *Wind Explained: Types of Wind Turbines*, U.S. Energy Information Administration, November 2, 2015, http://www.eia.gov/energyexplained/index.cfm?page=wind_types_of_turbines (accessed August 16, 2016)

solar energy to electricity on a commercial scale has proved to be technologically and economically challenging.

There are two main types of solar systems: passive and active. In both systems the conversion of solar energy into a form of power is made at the site where it is used.

Passive solar energy systems, such as greenhouses or windows with a southern exposure, use heat flow, evaporation, or other natural processes to collect and transfer heat. They are considered to be the least costly and least difficult solar systems to implement.

Active solar systems require collectors and storage devices as well as motors, pumps, and valves to operate the systems that transfer heat. Some collectors consist of an absorbing plate that transfers the sun's heat to a working fluid (liquid or gas). Photovoltaic cells (which are combined to form solar rooftop panels or collectors) convert sunlight directly to electricity without the use of mechanical generators. Photovoltaic cells do not have moving parts, are easy to install, and require little maintenance. The use of photovoltaic cells is expanding around the world. Because they contain no turbines or other moving parts, operating costs are low and maintenance is minimal. Above all, the fuel source (sunshine) is free and plentiful under the right weather conditions. The main disadvantage of photovoltaic cell systems is the high initial cost, although prices have fallen considerably. Toxic materials are often used in the construction of the cells, but researchers are investigating new materials, recycling, and disposal.

Solar/photovoltaic energy accounted for 550 trillion Btu of consumption in 2015, or 6% of total domestic renewables consumption. (See Table 6.1.) According to the EIA, in *Monthly Energy Review: July 2016*, the residential sector consumed 298 trillion Btu of the total, followed by 246 trillion Btu by the electric power sector. This consumption was small in comparison to that of some competing renewable sources.

Geothermal Energy

Geothermal energy is the natural, internal heat of the earth trapped in rock formations deep underground. Only a fraction of it can be extracted, usually through large fractures in the earth's crust. Hot springs, geysers, and fumaroles (holes in or near volcanoes from which vapor escapes) are the most easily exploitable sources. Geothermal reservoirs provide hot water or steam that can be used for heating buildings and processing food. Pressurized hot water or steam can also be directed toward turbines, which spin, generating electricity for residential and commercial customers.

Geothermal energy has been a very slow growing source of renewable energy. Greater use is limited by geological constraints. Geothermal energy is usable only when it is concentrated in one spot—in this case, in what is known as a thermal reservoir. Most of the known reservoirs for geothermal power in the United States are located west of the Mississippi River, and the highest-temperature geothermal resources occur for the most part west of the Rocky Mountains.

Geothermal consumption was 224 trillion Btu in 2015, or 2% of the renewables total. (See Table 6.1.) The vast majority of the consumption (159 quadrillion Btu, or 71%) was by the electric power sector. (See Table 6.4.)

DOMESTIC OUTLOOK FOR RENEWABLES

The EIA predicts in *Annual Energy Outlook 2016 with Projections to 2040* domestic capacity and electricity generation by renewable sources in 2040 using 2015 levels as a baseline. The amounts shown in Table 6.5 are for net summer capacity and generation. According to the EIA (2016, http://www.eia.gov/tools/glossary/index.cfm?id=N), net summer capacity is the maximum output of the generating equipment during the peak summer demand time (between June 1 and September 30) less any capacity used by the generating station itself.

TABLE 6.5

Renewable energy generating capacity and generation, 2015 and predicted for 2040

[Gigawatts, unless otherwise noted]

Net summer capacity and generation	2015	2020	2025	2030	2035	2040	2015–2040
Electric power sector[a]							
Net summer capacity							
Conventional hydroelectric power	79.24	79.78	79.98	80.05	80.13	80.40	0.1%
Geothermal[b]	2.50	3.10	4.46	5.63	6.73	7.20	4.3%
Municipal waste[c]	3.82	3.85	3.85	3.85	3.85	3.85	0.0%
Wood and other biomass[d]	3.40	3.55	3.55	3.55	3.67	4.07	0.7%
Solar thermal	2.04	2.49	2.49	2.49	2.49	2.49	0.8%
Solar photovoltaic[e]	11.71	25.49	52.48	67.62	117.56	155.56	10.9%
Wind	74.38	120.39	141.33	142.00	142.55	145.75	2.7%
Offshore wind	0.00	0.03	0.03	0.03	0.03	0.03	—
Total electric power sector capacity	**177.10**	**238.68**	**288.19**	**305.23**	**357.01**	**399.36**	**3.3%**
Generation (billion kilowatthours)							
Conventional hydroelectric power	245.48	292.73	293.72	294.24	294.79	296.25	0.8%
Geothermal[b]	16.68	21.48	32.62	42.27	51.38	55.53	4.9%
Biogenic municipal waste[e]	19.41	20.93	20.76	20.76	21.67	21.85	0.5%
Wood and other biomass	6.16	9.40	13.08	14.84	13.78	17.66	4.3%
Dedicated plants	5.43	8.74	12.42	14.15	13.07	16.98	4.7%
Cofiring	0.73	0.66	0.66	0.69	0.71	0.68	−0.3%
Solar thermal	3.31	4.49	4.55	4.63	4.71	4.80	1.5%
Solar photovoltaic[e]	18.82	47.81	107.47	143.46	256.25	345.03	12.3%
Wind	187.54	364.46	449.93	453.10	455.97	468.32	3.7%
Offshore wind	0.00	0.10	0.10	0.10	0.10	0.10	—
Total electric power sector generation	**497.40**	**761.39**	**922.23**	**973.40**	**1,098.65**	**1,209.53**	**3.6%**
End-use sectors[g]							
Net summer capacity							
Conventional hydroelectric power	0.28	0.28	0.28	0.28	0.28	0.28	0.0%
Geothermal	0.00	0.00	0.00	0.00	0.00	0.00	—
Municipal waste[h]	0.58	0.58	0.58	0.58	0.58	0.58	0.0%
Biomass	4.71	4.74	4.87	5.00	5.01	5.04	0.3%
Solar photovoltaic[e]	11.19	28.66	40.96	55.14	71.54	88.30	8.6%
Wind	1.59	2.33	2.38	2.60	2.89	3.20	2.8%
Total end-use sector capacity	**18.35**	**36.59**	**49.06**	**63.60**	**80.30**	**97.41**	**6.9%**
Generation (billion kilowatthours)							
Conventional hydroelectric power	1.32	1.32	1.32	1.32	1.32	1.32	0.0%
Geothermal	0.00	0.00	0.00	0.00	0.00	0.00	—
Municipal waste[h]	4.10	4.10	4.10	4.10	4.10	4.10	0.0%
Biomass	25.96	25.89	26.61	27.35	27.41	27.58	0.2%
Solar photovoltaic[e]	15.49	40.23	58.07	78.73	102.69	127.23	8.8%
Wind	2.09	3.05	3.13	3.46	3.88	4.34	3.0%
Total end-use sector generation	**48.96**	**74.60**	**93.23**	**114.97**	**139.41**	**164.58**	**5.0%**
All sectors							
Net summer capacity							
Conventional hydroelectric power	79.52	80.05	80.25	80.33	80.41	80.68	0.1%
Geothermal	2.50	3.10	4.46	5.63	6.73	7.20	4.3%
Municipal waste	4.40	4.43	4.43	4.43	4.43	4.43	0.0%
Wood and other biomass[d]	8.11	8.29	8.42	8.55	8.68	9.11	0.5%
Solar[e]	24.95	56.65	95.94	125.25	191.59	246.36	9.6%
Wind	75.97	122.75	143.74	144.63	145.47	148.98	2.7%
Total capacity, all sectors	**195.45**	**275.27**	**337.25**	**368.83**	**437.30**	**496.77**	**3.8%**
Generation (billion kilowatthours)							
Conventional hydroelectric power	246.80	294.05	295.04	295.56	296.12	297.57	0.8%
Geothermal	16.68	21.48	32.62	42.27	51.38	55.53	4.9%
Municipal waste	23.51	25.03	24.87	24.86	25.78	25.96	0.4%
Wood and other biomass	32.12	35.29	39.69	42.20	41.20	45.24	1.4%
Solar[e]	37.62	92.52	170.10	226.82	363.65	477.06	10.7%
Wind	189.63	367.61	453.15	456.66	459.95	472.75	3.7%
Total generation, all sectors	**546.36**	**835.99**	**1,015.46**	**1,088.37**	**1,238.06**	**1,374.11**	**3.8%**

In 2040 wind is expected to be the largest renewable energy source for electricity generation, providing 468.4 billion kilowatt-hours (39% of the total) from onshore and offshore resources. (See Table 6.5.) Solar is projected to be the second-largest energy source, with 349.8 billion kilowatt-hours (29% of the total) from thermal and photovoltaic resources. As shown in Figure 6.8, electricity generation from solar power in residential and commercial buildings is expected to soar through 2040.

TABLE 6.5

Renewable energy generating capacity and generation, 2015 and predicted for 2040 [CONTINUED]

[Gigawatts, unless otherwise noted]

aIncludes electricity-only and combined heat and power plants that have a regulatory status.
bIncludes both hydrothermal resources (hot water and steam) and near-field enhanced geothermal systems (EGS). Near-field EGS potential occurs on known hydrothermal sites, however this potential requires the addition of external fluids for electricity generation and is only available after 2025.
cIncludes municipal waste, landfill gas, and municipal sewage sludge. Incremental growth is assumed to be for landfill gas facilities. All municipal waste is included, although a portion of the municipal waste stream contains petroleum-derived plastics and other non-renewable sources.
dFacilities co-firing biomass and coal are classified as coal.
eDoes not include off-grid photovoltaics (PV). Based on annual PV shipments from 1989 through 2014, EIA estimates that as much as 274 megawatts of remote electricity generation PV applications (i.e., off-grid power systems) were in service in 2014, plus an additional 573 megawatts in communications, transportation, and assorted other non-grid-connected, specialized applications. The approach used to develop the estimate, based on shipment data, provides an upper estimate of the size of the PV stock, including both grid-based and off-grid PV. It will overestimate the size of the stock, because shipments include a substantial number of units that are exported, and each year some of the PV units installed earlier will be retired from service or abandoned.
fIncludes biogenic municipal waste, landfill gas, and municipal sewage sludge. Incremental growth is assumed to be for landfill gas facilities. Only biogenic municipal waste is included. The U.S. Energy Information Administration estimates that in 2014 approximately 7 billion kilowatthours of electricity were generated from a municipal waste stream containing petroleum-derived plastics and other non-renewable sources.
gIncludes combined heat and power plants and electricity-only plants in the commercial and industrial sectors that have a non-regulatory status; and small on-site generating systems in the residential, commercial, and industrial sectors used primarily for own-use generation, but which may also sell some power to the grid.
hIncludes municipal waste, landfill gas, and municipal sewage sludge. All municipal waste is included, although a portion of the municipal waste stream contains petroleum-derived plastics and other non-renewable sources.
— = Not applicable.
Note: Totals may not equal sum of components due to independent rounding.

SOURCE: Adapted from "Table 16. Renewable Energy Generating Capacity and Generation," in *Annual Energy Outlook 2016 Early Release*, U.S. Energy Information Administration, May 2016, https://www.eia.gov/forecasts/aeo/excel/aeotab_16.xlsx (accessed August 12, 2016)

FIGURE 6.8

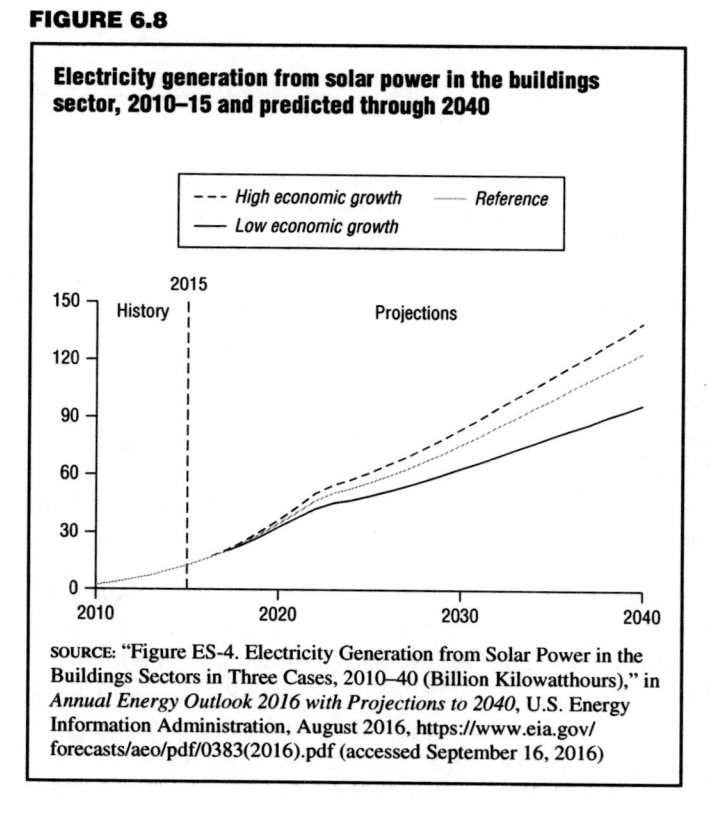

Electricity generation from solar power in the buildings sector, 2010–15 and predicted through 2040

SOURCE: "Figure ES-4. Electricity Generation from Solar Power in the Buildings Sectors in Three Cases, 2010–40 (Billion Kilowatthours)," in *Annual Energy Outlook 2016 with Projections to 2040*, U.S. Energy Information Administration, August 2016, https://www.eia.gov/forecasts/aeo/pdf/0383(2016).pdf (accessed September 16, 2016)

World Production, Consumption, and Outlook

The EIA states in *International Energy Outlook 2016* (May 2016, http://www.eia.gov/forecasts/ieo/pdf/0484(2016).pdf) that "with government policies and incentives promoting the use of nonfossil energy sources in many countries, renewable energy is the world's fastest-growing source of energy, at an average rate of 2.6%/year, while nuclear energy use increases by 2.3%/year, and natural gas use increases by 1.9%/year." Figure 6.9 provides EIA estimates of world energy consumption by fuel type between 1990 and 2012 and predicted through 2040. Renewables consumption is forecast to increase dramatically, from around 60 quadrillion Btu in 2012 to around 140 quadrillion Btu in 2040. The Clean Power Plan (CPP), which would limit carbon emissions from some U.S. power plants, is projected to provide a very minor boost to renewables consumption beginning in the 2020s. The CPP is described in detail in Chapter 8. Figure 6.10 shows EIA estimates of world net electricity generation by fuel source in 2012 and predicted for 2020 to 2040. Assuming that the CPP is not implemented, renewable sources are expected to account for 29% of total generation in 2040, up from 22% in 2012.

Figure 6.11 shows EIA projections for world electricity generation from renewable energy sources broken down by country membership in the Organisation for Economic Co-operation and Development (OECD). The OECD is a collection of dozens of mostly Western nations (including the United States) that are devoted to global economic development. The EIA indicates that around 4.6 trillion kWh were generated from renewables in 2012. By 2040 the value is expected to reach nearly 11 trillion kWh. Most of the growth is expected from non-OECD members using hydropower resources. Many developing nations see hydropower as an effective means of supplying power to growing populations. These massive public works projects usually require huge amounts of money—most of it borrowed from the developed world. Hydroelectric dams, however, are considered worth the cost and potential environmental threats because they bring cheap electric power to the citizenry.

FIGURE 6.9

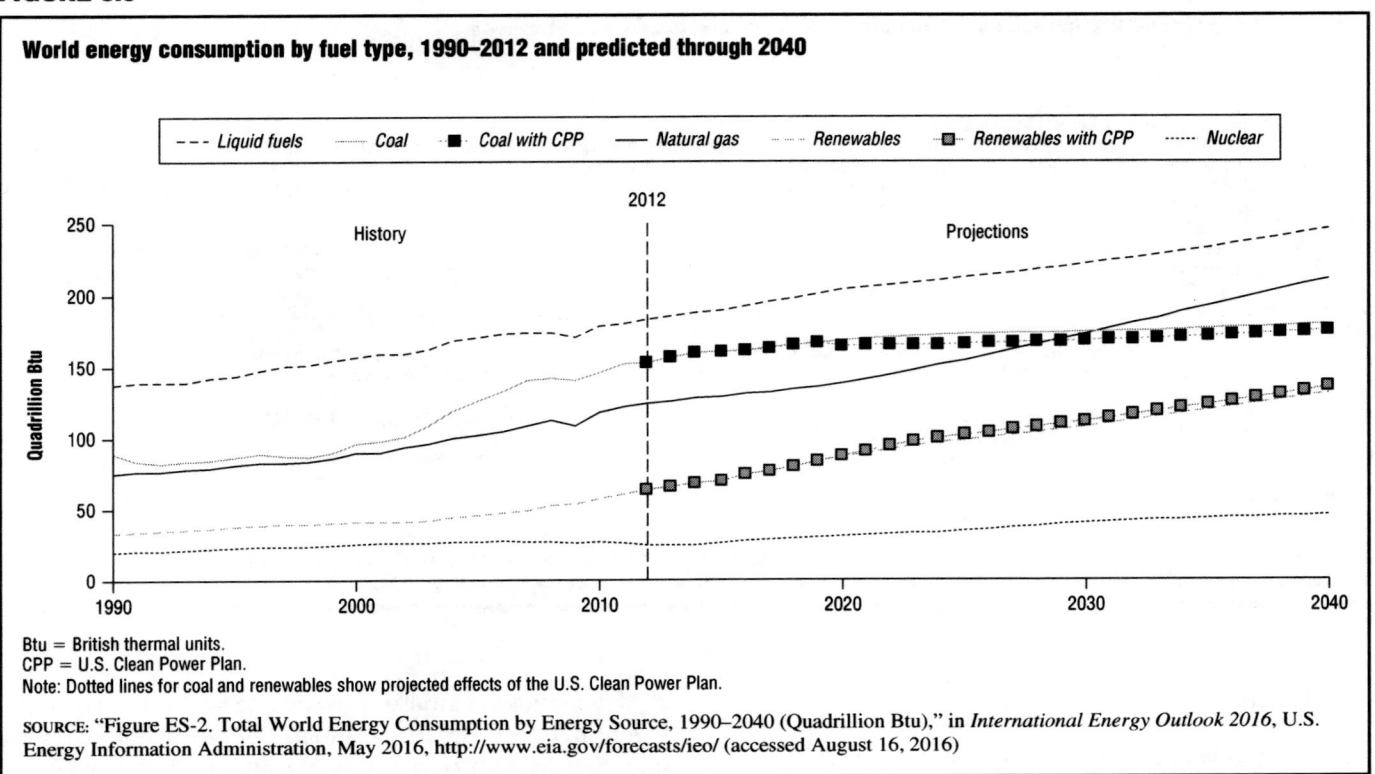

World energy consumption by fuel type, 1990–2012 and predicted through 2040

Btu = British thermal units.
CPP = U.S. Clean Power Plan.
Note: Dotted lines for coal and renewables show projected effects of the U.S. Clean Power Plan.

SOURCE: "Figure ES-2. Total World Energy Consumption by Energy Source, 1990–2040 (Quadrillion Btu)," in *International Energy Outlook 2016*, U.S. Energy Information Administration, May 2016, http://www.eia.gov/forecasts/ieo/ (accessed August 16, 2016)

FIGURE 6.10

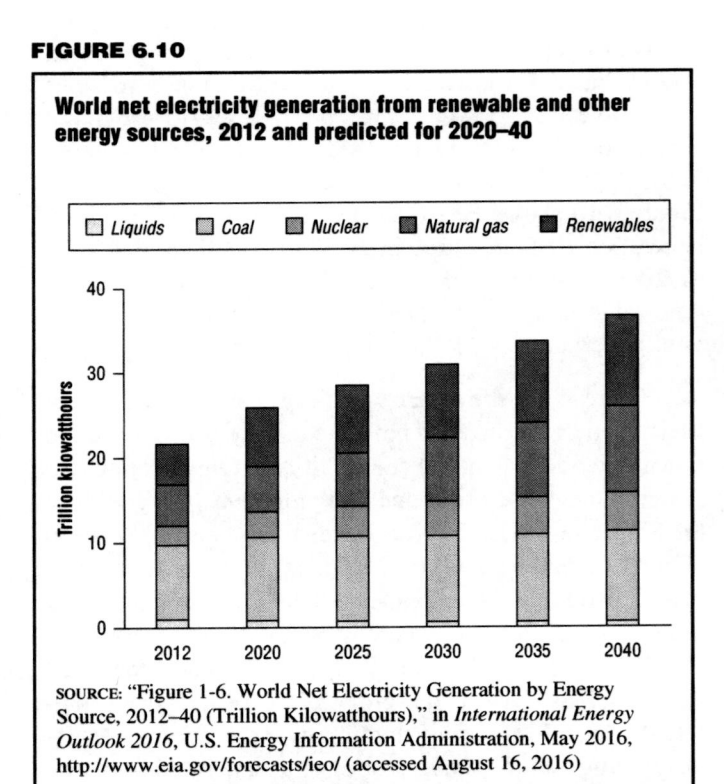

World net electricity generation from renewable and other energy sources, 2012 and predicted for 2020–40

SOURCE: "Figure 1-6. World Net Electricity Generation by Energy Source, 2012–40 (Trillion Kilowatthours)," in *International Energy Outlook 2016*, U.S. Energy Information Administration, May 2016, http://www.eia.gov/forecasts/ieo/ (accessed August 16, 2016)

The Chinese government has constructed the world's largest dam, the Three Gorges Dam, on the Yangtze River in Hubei Province. Five times the size of the Hoover Dam in the United States, the Three Gorges Dam is 607 feet (185 m) tall and 7,575 feet (2,309 m) in length. One decade after the project was launched in 1993, the dam began generating power. The article "China's Three Gorges Dam Reaches Operating Peak" (BBC.com, July 5, 2012) indicates that the dam reached its full operating peak in July 2012, after its 32nd, and final, generator began operating. The addition boosted the dam's generating capacity to 22.5 gigawatts, or around 11% of China's total hydropower capacity at that time. The article notes that the dam cost approximately $40 billion to construct and displaced more than 1 million people from the Yangtze River basin.

Several international organizations are devoted to promoting the use of renewable energy sources. In April 2014 the United Nations (http://www.un.org/apps/news/story.asp?NewsID=47537#.U8q97p5dWrY) launched the initiative Decade of Sustainable Energy for All (2014–2024). The organization notes the initiative has three goals: "Ensuring universal access to modern energy services, doubling the global rate of improvement in energy efficiency and sharing renewable energy globally." The International Renewable Energy Agency (2016, http://www.irena.org/Menu/index.aspx?PriMenuID=13&mnu=Pri) is an intergovernmental membership organization that "encourages governments to adopt enabling policies for renewable energy investments, provides practical tools and policy advice to accelerate renewable energy deployment, and facilitates knowledge sharing

FIGURE 6.11

World net electricity generation from renewable energy sources, by country classification, 2012 and predicted for 2040

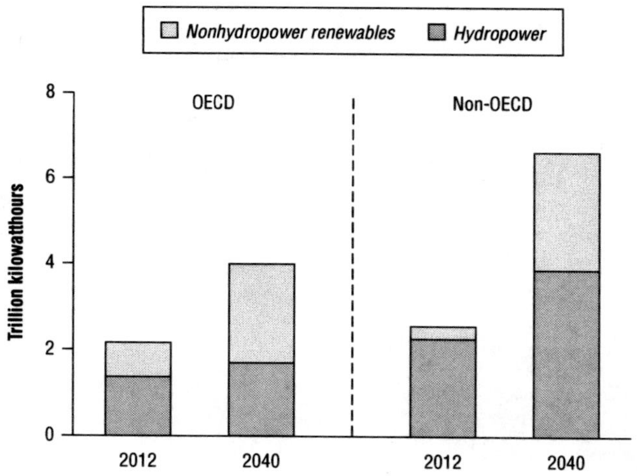

OECD = Office of Environment Compliance and Documentation.

SOURCE: "Figure 1-7. World Net Electricity Generation from Renewable Energy Sources, 2012 and 2040 (Trillion Kilowatthours)," in *International Energy Outlook 2016*, U.S. Energy Information Administration, May 2016, http://www.eia.gov/forecasts/ieo/ (accessed August 16, 2016)

and technology transfer to provide clean, sustainable energy for the world's growing population." It is headquartered in Abu Dhabi in the United Arab Emirates.

RENEWABLE INNOVATIONS FOR THE FUTURE

As of September 2016, numerous other renewable energy sources and technologies were being investigated for their potential to provide thermal power and/or electricity generation. Some innovative projects had reached the commercial stage. For example, in 2012 the Ocean Renewable Power Company (http://www.orpc.co/content.aspx?p=h3jCHHn6gcg%3d) began operating the first commercial tidal power system to be connected to the U.S. electricity grid. The system is located in the Bay of Fundy between Maine and Canada. It uses the tidal movement of the sea as it ebbs and flows to generate power. According to Ocean Renewable, 100 billion tons (91 billion t) of water flow in and out of the bay each day with the changing of the tides.

Other renewable energy sources of interest include:

- Wave energy—ocean wave power plants capture energy directly from wind-driven surface waves or from pressure changes below the surface to generate electricity.

- Ocean thermal energy conversion—this source uses the temperature difference between warm surface water and the cooler water in the ocean's depths to power a heat engine into producing electricity. Ocean thermal energy conversion systems can be installed on ships, barges, or offshore platforms with underwater cables that transmit electricity to shore.

- Hydrogen—hydrogen is the lightest and most abundant chemical element, and an interesting fuel from an environmental point of view. Its combustion produces only water vapor, and it is entirely carbon free. Three-quarters of the mass of the universe is hydrogen, so in theory the supply is ample. Nonetheless, the combustible form of hydrogen is a gas and is not found in nature. It must be made from other energy sources, such as fossil fuels. Hydrogen can be split from water, but the processes are either quite costly, require a great deal of energy, or both.

CHAPTER 7
ENERGY RESERVES—OIL, GAS, COAL, AND URANIUM

Energy resources are not the same as energy reserves. Energy resources are all deposits that exist, whereas energy reserves have a much narrower definition. Energy reserves are deposits about which some specific information is known or can be estimated. Reserves are quantified using specific criteria that are technologically and/or economically based. One problem is that there are many different terms used by U.S. government agencies to refer to reserves, such as *proved, unproved, technically recoverable, undiscovered, conventional,* and *continuous.* Thus, one must be careful to specify what types of reserves are being discussed. At the federal level, there are two primary agencies that estimate and publish energy reserve amounts:

- U.S. Geological Survey (USGS)—according to the USGS, in "About the Energy Resources Program" (May 5, 2016, http://energy.usgs.gov/GeneralInfo/AbouttheEnergyProgram.aspx), its Energy Resources Program "conducts research and assessments on the location, quantity, and quality of mineral and energy resources, including the economic and environmental effects of resource extraction and use."

- U.S. Energy Information Administration (EIA) within the U.S. Department of Energy—the EIA collects data about reserves from a variety of sources, including other federal and state agencies, industry, and academia.

OIL AND NATURAL GAS

As explained in earlier chapters, the United States is highly dependent on oil and natural gas as energy sources. Combined, these two fuels accounted for 63.7 quadrillion British thermal units (Btu) of the United States' 97.5 quadrillion Btu primary energy consumption in 2015, or 65% of the total. (See Table 1.3 in Chapter 1.) Thus, sufficient domestic reserves of these fuels are vitally important to the nation's economic well-being.

PROVED RESERVES

In *U.S. Crude Oil and Natural Gas Proved Reserves, 2014* (November 2015, http://www.eia.gov/naturalgas/crudeoilreserves/pdf/usreserves.pdf), the EIA defines proved reserves as "estimated volumes of hydrocarbon resources that analysis of geologic and engineering data demonstrates with reasonable certainty are recoverable under existing economic and operating conditions." This definition encompasses both technical and economic considerations. Proved reserves are not simply deposits that are technically viable to extract, they must also be economically viable to extract. Changing economic conditions affect proved reserves estimates in that rising market prices push proved reserves estimates upward, whereas falling market prices push estimates downward.

The EIA provides reserves estimates for crude oil and lease condensate and for total natural gas. As is noted in Chapter 2, lease condensate is a liquid recovered from natural gas at the well (the extraction point) and is generally blended with crude oil for refining.

According to the EIA, proved reserves of the fuels at year-end 2014 were:

- Crude oil and lease condensate—39.9 billion barrels (see Table 7.1)

- Total natural gas—388.8 trillion cubic feet (tcf; 11 trillion cubic m [tcm]) (see Table 7.2)

Figure 7.1 shows historical data for proved U.S. reserves of crude oil and lease condensate dating back to 1984. The total fell from around 30 billion barrels during the early 1980s to 21 billion barrels in 2008. Subsequent estimates indicate far greater reserve amounts. The uptick since 2008 reflects substantial additional reserves estimated for onshore reservoirs in the lower 48 states. Figure 7.2 shows proved reserves volumes in 2014 by geographical area. Texas had the largest volume (14,058 million barrels), followed by North Dakota (6,045 million barrels),

TABLE 7.1

Proved reserves of crude oil and lease condensate, 2004–14

[Million barrels]

Year	Adjustments	Net revisions	Revisions[a] and adjustments	Net of sales[b] and acquisitions	Extensions	New field discoveries	New reservoir discoveries in old fields	Total[c] discoveries	Estimated production	Proved[d] reserves 12/31	Change from prior year
Crude oil and lease condensate (million barrels)											
2004	80	444	524	37	731	36	159	926	2,001	22,592	−514
2005	237	558	795	327	946	209	57	1,212	1,907	23,019	427
2006	109	43	152	189	685	38	62	785	1,834	22,311	−708
2007	21	1,275	1,296	44	865	81	87	1,033	1,872	22,812	501
2008	318	−2,189	−1,871	187	968	166	137	1,271	1,845	20,554	−2,258
2009	46	2,008	2,054	95	1,305	141	95	1,541	1,929	22,315	1,761
2010	188	1,943	2,131	667	1,766	124	169	2,059	1,991	25,181	2,866
2011	207	1,414	1,621	537	3,107	481	88	3,676	2,065	28,950	3,769
2012	137	912	1,049	415	5,191	55	129	5,375	2,386	33,403	4,453
2013	−595	545	−50	389	4,973	191	343	5,507	2,729	36,520	3,117
2014	440	416	856	353	5,021	164	219	5,404	3,200	39,933	3,413

[a]Revisions and adjustments = Col. 1 + Col. 2.
[b]Net of sales and acquisitions = acquisitions − sales.
[c]Total discoveries = Col. 5 + Col. 6 + Col. 7.
[d]Proved reserves = Col. 10 from prior year + Col. 3 + Col. 4 + Col. 8 − Col. 9.
Notes: Old means discovered in a prior year. New means discovered during the report year. One barrel = 42 U.S. gallons. The production estimates in this table are based on data reported on Form EIA-23L, Annual Survey of Domestic Oil and Gas Reserves. They may differ slightly from the official U.S. EIA production data for crude oil and lease condensate for 2014 contained in the Petroleum Supply Annual 2014, DOE/EIA-0340(14).

SOURCE: Adapted from "Table 5. Total U.S. Proved Reserves of Crude Oil and Lease Condensate, Crude Oil, and Lease Condensate, 2004–14 (Million Barrels)," in *U.S. Crude Oil and Natural Gas Proved Reserves, 2014*, U.S. Energy Information Administration, November 2015, http://www.eia.gov/naturalgas/crudeoilreserves/pdf/usreserves.pdf (accessed August 17, 2016)

TABLE 7.2

Proved reserves of wet natural gas, 2001–14

[Billion cubic feet]

Year	Adjustments	Net revisions	Revisions[a] and adjustments	Net of sales[b] and acquisitions	Extensions	New field discoveries	New reservoir discoveries in old fields	Total[c] discoveries	Estimated production	Proved[d] reserves 12/31	Change from prior year
Total natural gas (billion cubic feet)											
2001	1,849	−2,438	−589	2,715	17,183	3,668	2,898	23,749	20,642	191,743	5,233
2002	4,006	1,038	5,044	428	15,468	1,374	1,752	18,594	20,248	195,561	3,818
2003	2,323	−1,715	608	1,107	17,195	1,252	1,653	20,100	20,231	197,145	1,584
2004	170	825	995	1,975	19,068	790	1,244	21,102	20,017	201,200	4,055
2005	1,693	2,715	4,408	2,674	22,069	973	1,243	24,285	19,259	213,308	12,108
2006	946	−2,099	−1,153	3,178	22,834	425	1,197	24,456	19,373	220,416	7,108
2007	990	15,936	16,926	452	28,255	814	1,244	30,313	20,318	247,789	27,373
2008	271	−3,254	−2,983	937	27,800	1,229	1,678	30,707	21,415	255,035	7,246
2009	5,923	−1,899	4,024	−222	43,500	1,423	2,656	47,579	22,537	283,879	28,844
2010	1,292	4,055	5,347	2,766	46,283	895	1,701	48,879	23,224	317,647	33,768
2011	2,715	−112	2,603	3,298	47,635	987	1,260	49,882	24,621	348,809	31,162
2012	−810	45,614	−46,424	−1,859	47,053	780	408	48,241	26,097	322,670	−26,139
2013	693	2,794	3,487	1,287	51,074	263	1,680	53,017	26,467	353,994	31,324
2014	4,905	984	5,889	6,565	47,071	671	2,745	50,487	28,094	388,841	34,847

[a]Revisions and adjustments = Col. 1 + Col. 2.
[b]Net of sales and acquisitions = acquisitions − sales.
[c]Total discoveries = Col. 5 − Col. 6 + Col. 7.
[d]Proved reserves = Col. 10 from prior year + Col. 3 + Col. 4 + Col. 8 − Col. 9.
Notes: Old means discovered in a prior year. New means discovered during the report year. The production estimates in this table are based on data reported on Form EIA-23L, Annual Survey of Domestic Oil and Gas Reserves. They may differ slightly from the official U.S. EIA production data for wet and dry natural gas for 2014 contained in the Natural Gas Annual 2014, DOE/EIA-0131(14). Natural gas is measured at 60 degrees Fahrenheit and atmospheric pressure base of 14.73 pounds per square inch absolute (psia).

SOURCE: "Table 9. U.S. Proved Reserves of Total Natural Gas, Wet after Lease Separation, 2001–14 (Billion Cubic Feet)," in *U.S. Crude Oil and Natural Gas Proved Reserves, 2014*, U.S. Energy Information Administration, November 2015, http://www.eia.gov/naturalgas/crudeoilreserves/pdf/usreserves.pdf (accessed August 17, 2016)

the Gulf of Mexico federal offshore area (4,704 million barrels), California (2,874 million barrels), and Alaska (2,857 million barrels).

Historical proved reserves data for wet natural gas are shown in Figure 7.3. The overall U.S. total was relatively flat or slightly declining from 1980 through

FIGURE 7.1

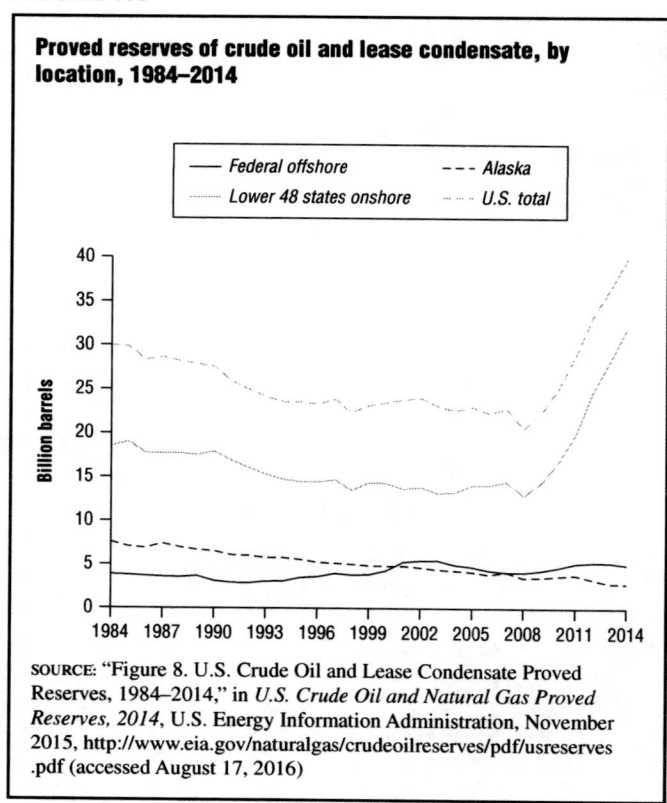

Proved reserves of crude oil and lease condensate, by location, 1984–2014

SOURCE: "Figure 8. U.S. Crude Oil and Lease Condensate Proved Reserves, 1984–2014," in *U.S. Crude Oil and Natural Gas Proved Reserves, 2014*, U.S. Energy Information Administration, November 2015, http://www.eia.gov/naturalgas/crudeoilreserves/pdf/usreserves.pdf (accessed August 17, 2016)

the 1990s. A tremendous upswing then occurred. Proved reserves increased from around 175 tcf (5 tcm) in 1999 to nearly 389 tcf (11 tcm) in 2014. All of the increase was due to greater proved reserves in natural gas reservoirs in the lower 48 states. Figure 7.4 shows proved reserves of wet natural gas in 2014 by geographical area. Texas had the largest volume, at 105,955 billion cubic feet (bcf; 3,000 billion cubic m [bcm]). Pennsylvania was the second largest, at 60,443 bcf (1,711.6 bcm), followed by Oklahoma, at 34,319 bcf (971.8 bcm); West Virginia, at 31,153 bcf (882.2 bcm); and Wyoming, at 28,787 bcf (815.2 bcm).

The calculations involved in estimating proved reserves of the two fuels between 2004 and 2014 are shown in Table 7.1 and Table 7.2. The EIA notes that "reserves estimates change from year to year as new discoveries are made, as existing fields are more thoroughly appraised, as existing reserves are produced, and as prices and technologies change."

Some of the terms listed in Table 7.1 and Table 7.2 require more explanation. The column labeled "Total discoveries" is the sum of the columns labeled "Extensions," "New field discoveries," and "New reservoir discoveries in old fields." The EIA states that extensions are "additions to reserves that result from additional drilling and exploration in previously discovered reservoirs." As shown in Table 7.1 and

Table 7.2, extensions have accounted for the vast majority of total fuel discoveries.

The EIA indicates that recent reserves gains reflect higher estimates for unconventional geological sources (e.g., shale and tight formations) that have low permeability—meaning that liquids and gases do not flow easily through them. These sources are described in detail in Chapter 2 for oil and Chapter 3 for natural gas. Technological advancements, such as horizontal drilling and hydraulic fracturing, have allowed operators greater access to fuels that are trapped in these formerly inaccessible geological sources.

TECHNICALLY RECOVERABLE RESOURCES

Technically recoverable resources (TRR) are energy resources that are technically recoverable; however, it may or may not be economically viable to recover them. The EIA explains in *Assumptions to the Annual Energy Outlook 2015* (September 2015, http://www.eia.gov/forecasts/aeo/assumptions/pdf/0554(2015).pdf) that TRR is "a common measure of the long-term viability of U.S. domestic crude oil and natural gas as an energy source." The EIA uses TRR estimates to forecast future domestic oil and natural gas production.

TRR include both proved reserves (as defined earlier) and unproved resources, which the EIA says include resources that have been confirmed by exploratory drilling and undiscovered resources (i.e., those assumed to be present based on geological information). TRR estimates are highly uncertain and change as new data are collected and analyzed. EIA estimates of U.S. TRR in 2013 were:

- Crude oil and lease condensate—259.8 billion barrels
- Dry natural gas—2,276.5 tcf (64.5 tcm)

It should be noted that the EIA does not include in its TRR estimates any oil and natural gas resources that are located in areas in which drilling is officially prohibited or drilling leases are not expected to be issued.

Off-Limit Areas

As of September 2016, there were several areas around the United States that were off-limits for oil and natural gas drilling for various reasons. Perhaps the most well-known (and most controversial) area is the Arctic National Wildlife Refuge (ANWR) in Alaska. The state's northern region, or North Slope, has long been a prolific production area for oil and natural gas. However, for decades the adjacent ANWR has been closed by federal law to oil and natural gas development. This 19-million-acre (7.7-million-ha) area of pristine wilderness lies along the Alaskan-Canadian border. The USGS believes that there are substantial volumes of oil and natural gas beneath ANWR. Oil from the North Slope is transported via the Trans-Alaska Pipeline System to the port city of Valdez in

FIGURE 7.2

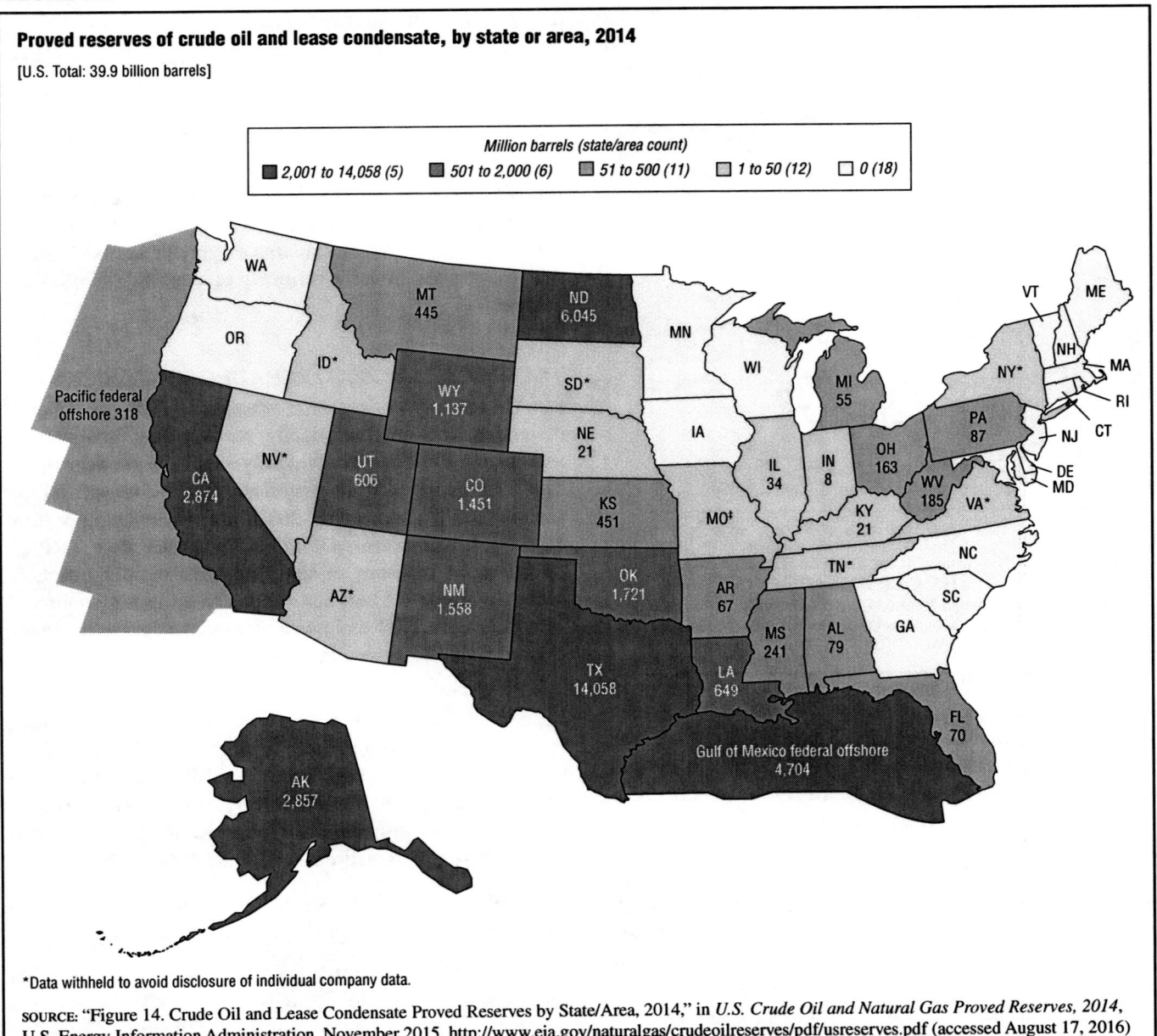

Proved reserves of crude oil and lease condensate, by state or area, 2014

[U.S. Total: 39.9 billion barrels]

Million barrels (state/area count)

■ 2,001 to 14,058 (5)   ■ 501 to 2,000 (6)   ■ 51 to 500 (11)   □ 1 to 50 (12)   □ 0 (18)

WA

MT 445

ND 6,045

MN

VT   ME

OR

ID*

SD*

WI

NH

MA

NY*

Pacific federal offshore 318

WY 1,137

NE 21

IA

MI 55

PA 87

RI

NJ   CT

NV*

UT 606

CO 1,451

IL 34

IN 8

OH 163

WV 185

DE MD

CA 2,874

KS 451

MO‡

KY 21

VA*

NC

AZ*

NM 1,558

OK 1,721

AR 67

TN*

SC

MS 241

AL 79

GA

TX 14,058

LA 649

FL 70

AK 2,857

Gulf of Mexico federal offshore 4,704

*Data withheld to avoid disclosure of individual company data.

SOURCE: "Figure 14. Crude Oil and Lease Condensate Proved Reserves by State/Area, 2014," in *U.S. Crude Oil and Natural Gas Proved Reserves, 2014*, U.S. Energy Information Administration, November 2015, http://www.eia.gov/naturalgas/crudeoilreserves/pdf/usreserves.pdf (accessed August 17, 2016)

southern Alaska. Over the years there have been numerous calls (mostly from Republican politicians) for ANWR to be opened to oil and natural gas drilling. However, as of September 2016, no federal legislation had been passed that would permit such development.

As is explained in Chapter 1, the federal and state governments control resource leases for public lands within their jurisdictions, including offshore areas. Although oil and natural gas drilling are prolific in the Gulf of Mexico, the same is not true for areas offshore the Atlantic and Pacific coasts. For decades, these areas have been off-limits to resource development. New offshore drilling along the West Coast was banned by the

federal government and the coastal states decades ago. In 2010 President Barack Obama (1961–) announced a controversial plan to open the Atlantic Outer Continental Shelf to drilling. However, the plan was put on hold only months later after the BP (formerly British Petroleum) oil spill occurred in the Gulf of Mexico. (See Chapter 2 for a description of the spill and its aftermath.) Thus, as of September 2016, no new oil and natural gas leases were in effect within U.S. waters off the Atlantic and Pacific coasts. In addition, the federal government's lease sale schedule through 2022 (2016, http://www.boem.gov/2017-2022-Lease-Sale-Schedule/) showed no lease sales planned for the Atlantic or Pacific coasts.

FIGURE 7.3

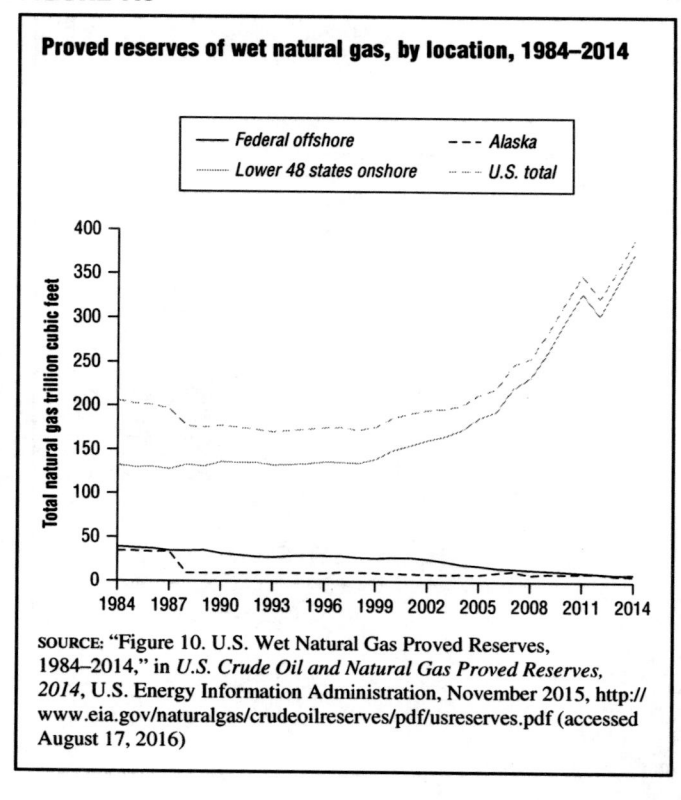

Proved reserves of wet natural gas, by location, 1984–2014

— Federal offshore   - - - Alaska
········· Lower 48 states onshore   -··- U.S. total

SOURCE: "Figure 10. U.S. Wet Natural Gas Proved Reserves, 1984–2014," in *U.S. Crude Oil and Natural Gas Proved Reserves, 2014*, U.S. Energy Information Administration, November 2015, http://www.eia.gov/naturalgas/crudeoilreserves/pdf/usreserves.pdf (accessed August 17, 2016)

Exploration and Development

Finding oil and natural gas usually takes two steps. First, geological and geophysical exploration identifies areas where oil and natural gas are most likely to be found. Much of this exploration is seismic, in which shock waves are used to determine the formations below the surface of the earth. Different rock formations transmit shock waves at different velocities, so they help determine if the geological features most often associated with oil and natural gas accumulations are present. After the seismic testing has been completed—and if it has been successful—exploratory wells are drilled.

In *Annual Energy Review 2011* (September 2012, http://www.eia.gov/totalenergy/data/annual/pdf/aer.pdf), the EIA notes that exploratory wells are drilled for three purposes: to find crude oil or natural gas in an area previously considered to be unproductive, to find a new reservoir in a field that has previously produced crude oil or natural gas in another reservoir, and to extend the limit of a crude oil or natural gas reservoir that has previously been productive. By contrast, the agency indicates that development wells are drilled within proved areas of reservoirs to depths that are known to be productive. Figure 7.5 shows the number of wells drilled by fuel type between 1949 and 2010. It also shows the number of wells that were dry. Overall, the majority of the exploratory and development wells were successful.

COAL

Coal supplied 15.6 quadrillion Btu of the United States' 97.5 quadrillion Btu primary energy consumption in 2015, or 16% of the total. (See Table 1.3 in Chapter 1.) The different ranks of coal (anthracite, bituminous coal, subbituminous coal, and lignite) and the different types of coal mining are described in detail in Chapter 4. The EIA measures three categories of coal reserves (see Table 7.3):

- Demonstrated reserve base (DRB)—coal known from publicly available data to be mapped to measured and indicated degrees of accuracy and found at depths and in coal-bed thicknesses considered technologically minable at the time of determinations

- Estimated recoverable reserves—DRB coal considered recoverable after excluding coal estimated to be unavailable because of land use restrictions and after applying assumed mining recovery rates

- Recoverable reserves at producing mines—the quantity of coal that can be recovered (i.e., mined) from existing coal reserves at reporting mines

In 2014 the nation's total DRB was 478.4 billion tons (434 billion t). (See Table 7.3.) Most of the DRB requires underground mining, rather than surface mining, to be extracted. The five states with the largest DRB quantities in 2014 were:

- Montana—118.7 billion tons (107.7 billion t)
- Illinois—103.8 billion tons (94.2 billion t)
- Wyoming—59 billion tons (53.5 billion t)
- West Virginia—30.9 billion tons (28 billion t)
- Kentucky—28.4 billion tons (25.8 billion t)

URANIUM

As is explained in Chapter 5, uranium is the resource used to produce nuclear power for electricity generation. Nuclear electric power supplied 8.3 quadrillion Btu of the United States' 97.5 quadrillion Btu primary energy consumption in 2015, or 9% of the total. (See Table 1.3 in Chapter 1.)

The world's natural uranium supply is enormous because the element is present at low levels throughout the earth's crust and oceans. Uranium is most highly concentrated in uranium ores, which are mined as described in Chapter 5. The recovered uranium is processed into a powder called yellowcake, which has the chemical formula U_3O_8.

In *2015 Domestic Uranium Production Report* (May 2016, http://www.eia.gov/uranium/production/annual/pdf/dupr.pdf), the EIA provides U.S. uranium reserve estimates at year-end 2015. (See Table 7.4). These are the amounts believed to be present at 75 mines and

FIGURE 7.4

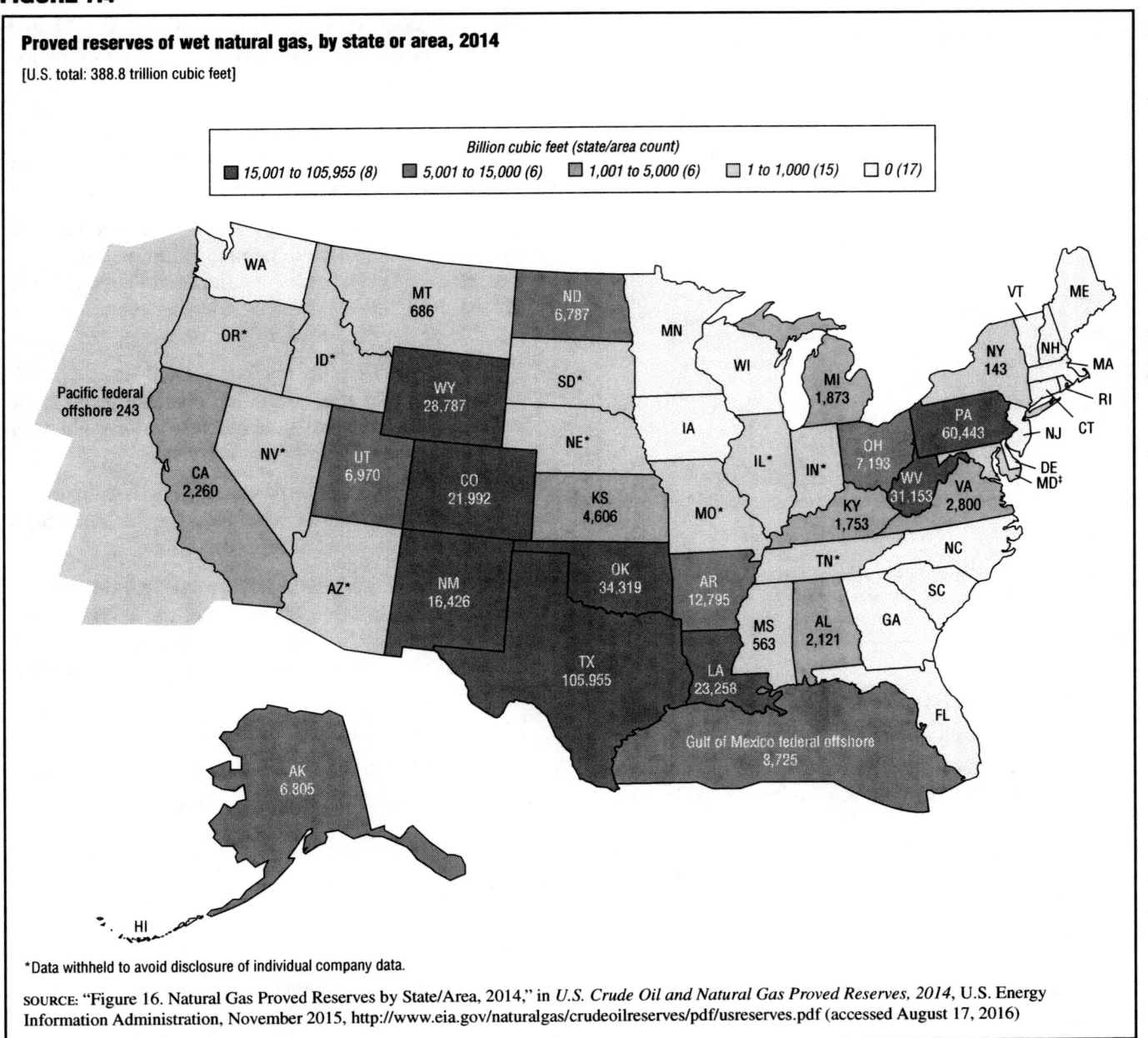

Proved reserves of wet natural gas, by state or area, 2014

[U.S. total: 388.8 trillion cubic feet]

*Data withheld to avoid disclosure of individual company data.

SOURCE: "Figure 16. Natural Gas Proved Reserves by State/Area, 2014," in *U.S. Crude Oil and Natural Gas Proved Reserves, 2014*, U.S. Energy Information Administration, November 2015, http://www.eia.gov/naturalgas/crudeoilreserves/pdf/usreserves.pdf (accessed August 17, 2016)

properties that could be extracted at various cost levels. Overall, the total reserves were estimated at 361.8 million pounds (164.1 million kg) of U_3O_8.

Besides uranium ores, natural uranium can also be extracted from so-called unconventional sources, which are described by Susan Hall and Margaret Coleman in *Critical Analysis of World Uranium Resources* (2013, http://pubs.usgs.gov/sir/2012/5239/sir2012-5239.pdf). These sources include seawater (which has not yet been commercially exploited due to high costs) and deposits of phosphate rock, lignite, and black shale. These deposits are found around the world (including in the United States) and have provided uranium in the past under favorable economic conditions. Hall and Coleman note,

"The extraction of uranium from phosphates is receiving the most attention, because it can potentially tap into a vast resource." Technical innovations have improved the cost effectiveness of uranium extraction from phosphate deposits. The United States, in particular, contains uranium-rich phosphate deposits in Florida. (See Figure 7.6.)

INTERNATIONAL RESERVES

When considering energy reserves outside of the United States, it is important to understand that many different terms are used internationally to refer to reserve volumes and to categorize them based on technological and economic criteria.

FIGURE 7.5

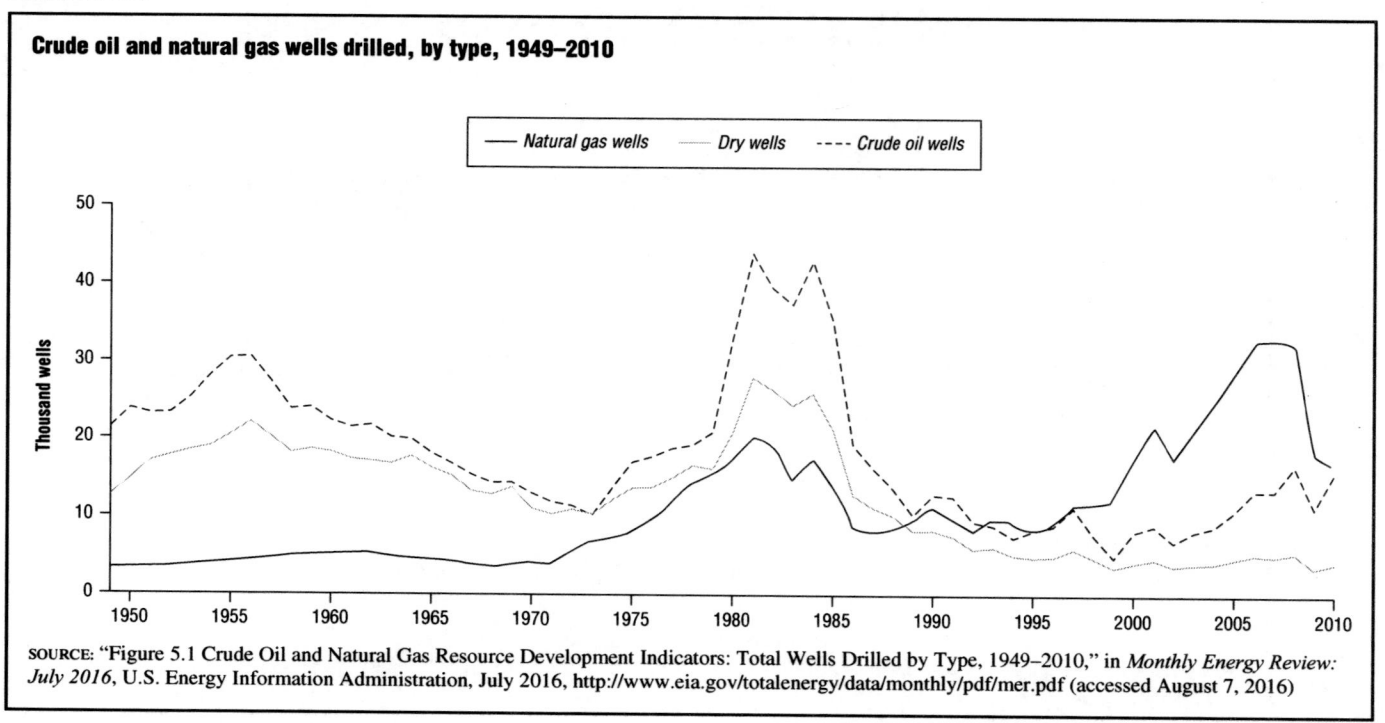

Crude oil and natural gas wells drilled, by type, 1949–2010

SOURCE: "Figure 5.1 Crude Oil and Natural Gas Resource Development Indicators: Total Wells Drilled by Type, 1949–2010," in *Monthly Energy Review: July 2016*, U.S. Energy Information Administration, July 2016, http://www.eia.gov/totalenergy/data/monthly/pdf/mer.pdf (accessed August 7, 2016)

The EIA provides worldwide estimates of proved reserves of several fuels through its "International Energy Statistics" (http://www.eia.gov/cfapps/ipdbproject/IEDIndex3.cfm). However, data are not available for all fuels, countries, or regions for every year.

Crude Oil and Natural Gas

According to the EIA (2016, http://www.eia.gov/cfapps/ipdbproject/IEDIndex3.cfm?tid=5&pid=57&aid=6), world proved reserves of crude oil totaled 1.7 trillion barrels in 2014. A total for 2015 was not available as of September 2016; however, the countries with the largest reserves in 2015 were Venezuela (298 billion barrels), Saudi Arabia (268 billion barrels), Canada (172 billion barrels), Iran (158 billion barrels), and Iraq (144 billion barrels).

The EIA (2016, http://www.eia.gov/cfapps/ipdbproject/IEDIndex3.cfm?tid=3&pid=3&aid=6) indicates that proved reserves of natural gas totaled 6,973 tcf (197.5 tcm) in 2014. A total for 2015 was not available as of September 2016; however, the countries with the largest reserves in 2015 were Russia (1,688 tcf [47.8 tcm]), Iran (1,201 tcf [34 tcm]), Qatar (872 tcf [24.7 tcm]), the United States (the 2015 value was unavailable; the 2014 value was 338 tcf [9.6 tcm]), and Saudi Arabia (294 tcf [8.3 tcm]).

Coal

As of September 2016, the EIA (http://www.eia.gov/cfapps/ipdbproject/IEDIndex3.cfm?tid=1&pid=7&aid=6) reported worldwide proved recoverable reserves of coal

for 2011. The total was 979.8 billion tons (888.9 billion t). The largest reserves were held by the United States (258.6 billion tons [234.6 billion t]), Russia (173.1 billion tons [157 billion t]), China (126.2 billion tons [114.5 billion t]), Australia (84.2 billion tons [76.4 billion t]), and India (66.8 billion tons [60.6 billion t]).

Uranium

The Organisation for Economic Co-operation and Development (OECD) is a collection of dozens of mostly Western nations (including the United States) that are devoted to global economic development. Every two years the OECD's Nuclear Energy Agency, in collaboration with the International Atomic Energy Agency, publishes a report on the worldwide uranium industry. As of September 2016, the most recent report was *Uranium 2014: Resources, Production and Demand* (September 2014, https://www.oecd-nea.org/ndd/pubs/2014/7209-uranium-2014.pdf). The Nuclear Energy Agency and the International Atomic Energy Agency estimate total world identified uranium resources between 6.5 million and 8.4 million tons (5.9 million and 7.6 million t) of contained uranium metal in 2013.

As is explained in Chapter 5, nuclear fuel can also be made from plutonium (a by-product of uranium fission), from the by-products and waste materials resulting from uranium mining and processing, and from uranium that was originally processed for use in nuclear weapons. These are considered secondary uranium sources. They are used to meet uranium demand

TABLE 7.3

Coal reserves, by type and mining method, by state, 2014

[Million short tons]

Coal-resource state	Underground-minable coal			Surface-minable coal			Total		
	Recoverable reserves at producing mines	Estimated recoverable reserves	Demonstrated reserve base	Recoverable reserves at producing mines	Estimated recoverable reserves	Demonstrated reserve base	Recoverable reserves at producing mines	Estimated recoverable reserves	Demonstrated reserve base
Alabama	213	399	791	16	2,222	3,119	228	2,621	3,911
Alaska	[a]	2,335	5,423	53	483	668	53	2,818	6,091
Arizona				216	[a]	[a]	216	[a]	[a]
Arkansas	25	126	271	[a]	101	144	25	228	416
Colorado	207	5,766	10,987	126	3,742	4,756	333	9,508	15,743
Georgia	[a]	1	2	[a]	1	2	[a]	2	4
Idaho	[a]	2	4				[a]	2	4
Illinois	2,426	27,729	87,294	37	10,035	16,489	2,463	37,764	103,783
Indiana	295	3,515	8,486	351	286	490	646	3,801	8,976
Iowa	[a]	807	1,732	[a]	320	457	[a]	1,127	2,189
Kansas		[a]		[b]	679	970	[a]	679	970
Kentucky total	767	6,845	15,915	122	7,230	12,520	889	14,075	28,435
Kentucky (east)	293	317	568	66	5,003	8,960	360	5,320	9,528
Kentucky (west)	474	6,528	15,347	55	2,227	3,560	529	8,755	18,907
Louisiana		[a]		92	283	382	92	283	382
Maryland	8	307	561	14	31	45	22	338	606
Michigan	[a]	55	123	[a]	3	5	[a]	58	128
Mississippi	[a]	689	1,479	698	3,154	4,506	698	3,843	5,985
Missouri				1	858	858	1	858	858
Montana	240	35,889	70,891	618	38,666	47,839	858	74,555	118,730
New Mexico	16	2,749	6,043	169	4,048	5,782	186	6,797	11,826
North Carolina	[a]	5	11				[a]	5	11
North Dakota				1,003	6,657	8,726	1,003	6,657	8,726
Ohio	332	7,585	17,240	47	3,705	5,661	379	11,290	22,901
Oklahoma	8	570	1,223	1	220	314	9	790	1,537
Oregon	[a]	6	15	[a]	2	3	[a]	9	17
Pennsylvania total	1,088	10,232	22,326	167	973	4,134	1,256	11,205	26,460
Pennsylvania (anthracite)	1	340	3,841	121	418	3,337	122	757	7,178
Pennsylvania (bituminous)	1,087	9,892	18,485	46	555	797	1,133	10,448	19,283
South Dakota				[b]	277	366	1	277	366
Tennessee	1	273	497	[a]	171	252	1	443	749
Texas				703	9,169	11,911	703	9,169	11,911
Utah	95	2,332	4,757	2	210	265	97	2,542	5,023
Virginia	230	491	874	23	306	477	253	796	1,351
Washington		674	1,332	[a]	6	8	[a]	681	1,340
West Virginia total	1,554	14,778	27,689	475	2,013	3,190	2,028	16,790	30,879
West Virginia (northern)	937	NA	NA	7	NA	NA	943	NA	NA
West Virginia (southern)	617	NA	NA	468	NA	NA	1,085	NA	NA
Wyoming	35	22,918	42,441	6,878	13,683	16,525	6,913	36,601	58,966
U.S. total	**7,542**	**147,079**	**328,410**	**11,810**	**108,676**	**150,005**	**19,351**	**255,755**	**478,415**

TABLE 7.3

Coal reserves, by type and mining method, by state, 2014 [CONTINUED]

[Million short tons]

ᵃNo data reported.
ᵇValue is less than 0.5 of the table metric.
EIA = Energy Information Administration. NA = Not available.
Notes: Recoverable coal reserves at producing mines represent the quantity of coal that can be recovered (i.e. mined) from existing coal reserves at reporting mines. EIA's estimated recoverable reserves include the coal in the demonstrated reserve base considered recoverable after excluding coal estimated to be unavailable due to land use restrictions, and after applying assumed mining recovery rates. This estimate does not include any specific economic feasibility criteria. The effective date for the demonstrated reserve base, as customarily worded, is "Remaining as of January 1, 2015." These data are contemporaneous with the Recoverable Reserves at Producing Mines, customarily presented as of the end of the reporting year's mining, that is in this case, December 31, 2014. The demonstrated reserve base includes publicly available data on coal mapped to measured and indicated degrees of accuracy and found at depths and in coalbed thicknesses considered technologically minable at the time of determinations. All reserve expressions exclude silt, culm, refuse bank, slurry dam, and dredge operations. Reserves at Producing Mines exclude mines producing less than 25,000 short tons, which are not required to provide reserves data.

SOURCE: "Table 15. Recoverable Coal Reserves at Producing Mines, Estimated Recoverable Reserves, and Demonstrated Reserve by Mining Method, 2014 (Million Short Tons)," in *Annual Coal Report 2014*, U.S. Energy Information Administration, March 2016, http://www.cia.gov/coal/annual/pdf/acr.pdf (accessed August 15, 2016)

TABLE 7.4

Uranium reserves, year-end 2014 and year-end 2015

[Million pounds U$_3$O$_8$]

Uranium reserve estimates[a] by mine and property status, mining method, and state(s)	End of 2014			End of 2015		
	Forward cost[b]					
	$0 to $30 per pound	$0 to $50 per pound	$0 to $100 per pound	$0 to $30 per pound	$0 to $50 per pound	$0 to $100 per pound
Properties with exploration completed, exploration continuing, and only assessment work	W	W	154.6	24.3	W	151.6
Properties under development for production and development drilling	W	38.2	W	W	38.2	W
Mines in production	W	19.2	W	W	16.4	W
Mines closed temporarily, closed permanently, and mined out	W	W	W	W	W	135.2
Total	**45.3**	**163.5**	**359.3**	**66.2**	**165.8**	**361.8**
In-situ leach mining	W	W	150.8	W	W	148.6
Underground and open pit mining	W	W	208.5	W	W	213.2
Total	**45.3**	**163.5**	**359.3**	**66.2**	**165.8**	**361.8**
Arizona, New Mexico and Utah	0	W	212.3	0	W	212.0
Colorado, Nebraska and Texas	W	W	40.3	W	39.2	44.3
Wyoming	W	W	106.8	W	W	105.6
Total	**45.3**	**163.5**	**359.3**	**66.2**	**165.8**	**361.8**

[a]Reserve estimates on 75 mines and properties for end of 2014 and on 70 mines and properties for end of 2015. These uranium reserve estimates cannot be compared with the much larger historical data set of uranium reserves that were published in the July 2010 report U.S. Uranium Reserves Estimates Reserves, as reported here, do not necessarily imply compliance with U.S. or Canadian government definitions for purposes of investment disclosure.
[b]Forward cost: The operating and capital costs still to be incurred in the production of uranium from in-place reserves. By using forward costing, estimates for reserves for ore deposits in differing geological settings and status of development can be aggregated and reported for selected cost categories. Included are costs for labor, materials, power and fuel, royalties, payroll taxes, insurance, and applicable general and administrative costs. Excluded from forward cost estimates are prior expenditures, if any, incurred for property acquisition, exploration, mine development, and mill construction, as well as income taxes, profit, and the cost of money. Forward costs are neither the full costs of production nor the market price at which the uranium, when produced, might be sold.
W = Data withheld to avoid disclosure of individual company data.
Note: Totals may not equal sum of components because of independent rounding. U$_3$O$_8$ = uranium oxide.

SOURCE: "Table 10. Uranium Reserve Estimates at the End of 2014 and 2015," in *2015 Domestic Uranium Production Report*, U.S. Energy Information Administration, May 2016, http://www.eia.gov/uranium/production/annual/pdf/dupr.pdf (accessed August 17, 2016)

to various degrees around the world. In *Critical Analysis of World Uranium Resources*, the USGS and EIA note that secondary sources (including Russian and U.S. government stockpiles of natural uranium) accounted for 25% of the world's uranium production in 2010.

FIGURE 7.6

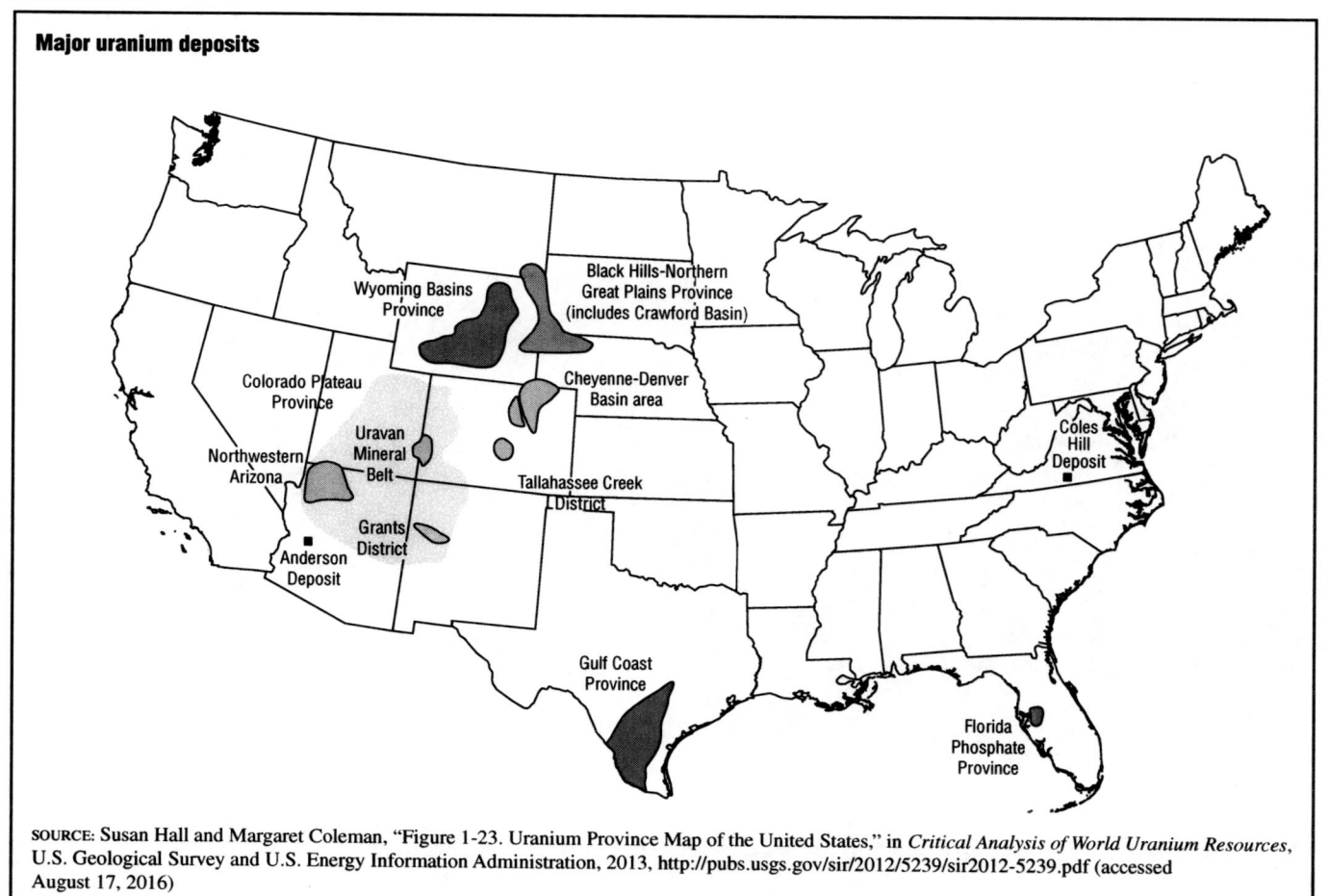

Major uranium deposits

SOURCE: Susan Hall and Margaret Coleman, "Figure 1-23. Uranium Province Map of the United States," in *Critical Analysis of World Uranium Resources*, U.S. Geological Survey and U.S. Energy Information Administration, 2013, http://pubs.usgs.gov/sir/2012/5239/sir2012-5239.pdf (accessed August 17, 2016)

CHAPTER 8
ELECTRICITY

In 1879 Thomas Alva Edison (1847–1931) flipped the first switch to light Menlo Park, New Jersey. Since that time the use of electrical power has become nearly universal in the United States. Electricity is not really an energy source but an energy carrier, because it is generated using primary energy sources, such as fossil fuels. As such, electricity supplies and pricing are highly dependent on the economic factors underlying the fuels and processes that are used to generate electricity. Likewise, the electric power sector is the focal point for environmental concerns that are associated with combusting or otherwise using primary energy sources to produce electricity.

UNDERSTANDING ELECTRICITY

Electricity results from the interaction of charged particles, such as electrons (negatively charged subatomic particles) and protons (positively charged subatomic particles). For example, static electricity is caused by friction: when one material rubs against another, it transfers charged particles. The zap people might feel and the spark people might see when they drag their feet on a carpet and then touch a metal doorknob demonstrate static electricity—electrons being transferred between a hand and the doorknob.

Generating Electricity

As is noted in Chapter 1, electricity is not a primary energy source because energy is required to produce electricity. In the United States most electric power is produced by burning fossil fuels. The resulting heat turns water into steam, which can be used as a working fluid to turn the blades of a turbine. The hot gases from the burning fuels can also be used for this purpose. In either case, the turbine rotates a magnet that is nestled within or around coiled wire, which generates an electric current in the wire. Thus, heat is a primary factor in the operation of these plants. The same is true for nuclear power plants. They rely on the heat that is released from splitting uranium atoms apart to produce steam. (See Chapter 5.) Thermally derived electricity is also obtained from burning wood or waste, from geothermal reservoirs, and through some solar (sunlight-based) systems. These renewable energy sources are described in Chapter 6.

There are also nonthermal means for producing electricity. The most common is hydropower, which is described in Chapter 6. Hydropower relies on water (rather than on steam or hot gases) to be the working fluid that turns turbines. Wind is the working fluid that turns turbines at wind farms. Lastly, some solar systems turn sunlight directly into electrical current using crystalline materials.

Overall, the vast majority of electricity generation methods operated in the United States are thermally based—that is, they convert heat energy to mechanical energy to electrical energy. This conversion process is inherently inefficient because large amounts of energy are lost along the way.

Measuring Electricity

Electric current is the flow of electric charge; it is measured in amperes (amps). Electrical power is the rate at which energy is transferred by electric current. A watt is the standard measure of electrical power, named after the Scottish engineer James Watt (1736–1819). A watt is a very small unit of measure, so electrical power is typically measured in multiples of the watt, such as the kilowatt (kW; 1,000 watts), the megawatt (MW; 1 million watts), or the gigawatt (GW; 1 billion watts). Electrical work is usually measured using the kilowatt-hour (kWh), which is the work done by 1 kW acting for one hour. A 1,000-kW generator running at full capacity for one hour supplies 1,000 kWh of power. That generator operating continuously for an entire year produces nearly 8.8 million kWh of electricity (1,000 kW × 24 hours per day × 365 days per year).

Electric Power System/Electrical Grid

An electric power system, or electrical grid, is a network that connects the locations of electrical power

FIGURE 8.1

Transmission and distribution of electricity

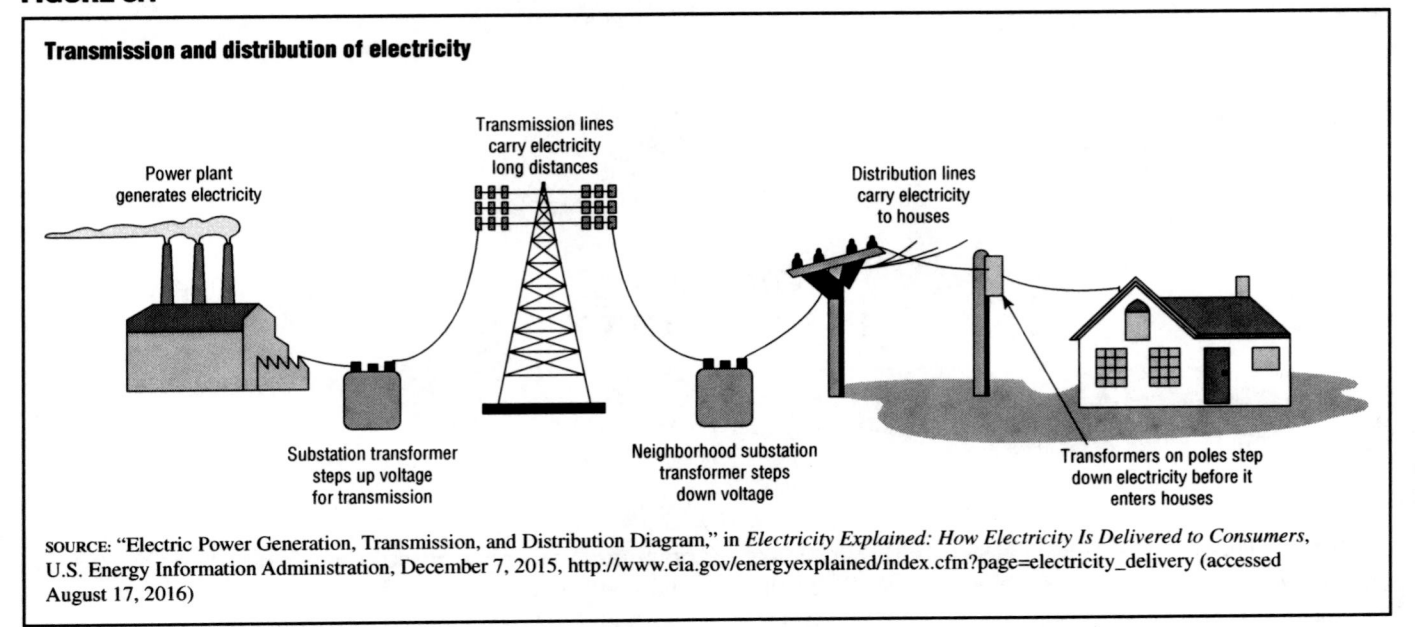

SOURCE: "Electric Power Generation, Transmission, and Distribution Diagram," in *Electricity Explained: How Electricity Is Delivered to Consumers,* U.S. Energy Information Administration, December 7, 2015, http://www.eia.gov/energyexplained/index.cfm?page=electricity_delivery (accessed August 17, 2016)

generation with the locations of electrical power consumption. Figure 8.1 illustrates the components of a simple electric system. Power plants generate electricity, which is raised to a high voltage for transmission. Voltage is a complicated concept, but basically raising the voltage improves the energy efficiency (i.e., reduces losses) as the transmission lines carry electricity over long distances. The voltage is stepped down (lowered) somewhat before the electricity goes onto the distribution lines that deliver it to neighborhoods, shopping centers, and other clusters of users. Then the voltage is stepped down again for delivery to individual homes and businesses. It should be noted that some industrial facilities can take their electricity at higher voltages than what is delivered to residential and commercial customers.

Electricity is generated and distributed around the country by numerous individual utilities and companies. In "What Is the Electric Power Grid and What Are Some Challenges It Faces?" (December 22, 2015, http://www.eia.gov/energy_in_brief/article/power_grid.cfm), the U.S. Energy Information Administration (EIA), a division of the U.S. Department of Energy, notes that the United States includes more than 7,200 electric power plants and generating facilities, 2,000 electric distribution utilities, and 300,000 miles (483,000 km) of transmission and distribution lines. There is no single national grid. The 48 contiguous states have three grids:

- Eastern Interconnection—east of the Rocky Mountains
- Western Interconnection—from the Pacific Ocean to the Rocky Mountains
- Texas Interconnected System—most of Texas

The EIA explains that "these systems operate independently of each other for the most part, although there

are limited links between them." Within the grids, substations connect the pieces of the system together, and energy control centers coordinate the operation of all the components. At the federal level the interstate transmission of electricity is regulated by the Federal Energy Regulatory Commission (FERC). The Energy Policy Act of 2005 gave FERC the authority to certify a single organization to enforce mandatory electric reliability standards that are applicable to much of the industry. FERC certified the North American Electric Reliability Corporation for this purpose. It is a nonprofit organization responsible for ensuring the reliability of the electric power system throughout most of Canada and the United States and parts of northern Mexico.

DOMESTIC PRODUCTION AND CONSUMPTION

Electricity is produced on demand (i.e., as it is needed). However, consumer demand varies constantly as people turn on and off air conditioners, light switches, appliances, and other electrical devices. In "Electricity Explained: Factors Affecting Electricity Prices" (April 29, 2015, http://www.eia.gov/energyexplained/index.cfm?page=electricity_factors_affecting_prices), the EIA indicates that electricity demand on a daily basis is usually highest in the afternoon and early evening. On a seasonal basis, demand is highest during the summer.

There are no large-scale means by which electricity can be efficiently stored for later use. This deficiency profoundly affects the electric power sector and the economics of electricity because it means the system as a whole has to be ready for peak demand at all times. In general, the power industry operates two kinds of generating capacity: baseload and peaking. The EIA explains in

"Electric Generators' Roles Vary Due to Daily and Seasonal Variation in Demand" (June 8, 2011, http://www.eia.gov/todayinenergy/detail.cfm?id=1710) that "baseload capacity runs around the clock when it is not down for maintenance. Peaking capacity runs a few times a year for short periods to help electricity systems meet peak demand."

The nation's electricity production has increased over the decades, but its growth has slowed recently. As shown in Table 8.1, net generation (which excludes the electricity used by power plants themselves) increased from 334 billion kWh in 1950 to 4,087 billion kWh in 2015. The vast majority of the nation's electricity is generated by the electric power sector; however, some industrial and commercial facilities operate their own power plants. Electricity produced by these facilities is called direct-use or self-generated electricity. Table 8.1 indicates that very small amounts of electricity are imported or exported across U.S. borders.

Production Sources

Figure 8.2 shows net electricity generation by source between 1949 and 2015. Coal has historically been the largest source. In 2015 it accounted for 1,356.1 billion kWh, or 33% of the total net generation. Natural gas was a very close second, at 1,335.1 billion kWh, which was also 33% of the total. These were followed by nuclear power, at 797.2 billion kWh (20%); renewable energy sources, at 570.6 billion kWh (14%); and petroleum, at 28.4 billion kWh (0.7%). According to the EIA, in *Monthly Energy Review: July 2016* (July 2016, http://www .eia.gov/totalenergy/data/monthly/archive/00351607.pdf), other gases derived from fossil fuels accounted for a minute fraction of the total production.

Coal was long the fuel of choice because, as is explained in Chapter 4, it is abundant domestically and relatively low priced. Nuclear power began playing a larger role during the 1980s, but its use has been rather flat since the late 1990s. (See Figure 8.2.) The biggest movement in fuels has been by natural gas. During the second decade of the 21st century, coal use dropped dramatically, and natural gas use soared due to various technological, economic, and legislative factors.

The EIA indicates in "Most Electric Generating Capacity Additions in the Last Decade Were Natural Gas–Fired" (July 5, 2011, http://www.eia.gov/todayinenergy/detail.cfm?id=2070) that more than 80% of total generation capacity additions made between 2000 and 2010 were natural gas–fired. This growth reflects market changes that began during the late 1980s:

- Decreasing natural gas prices and increasing domestic supplies.
- Increasing availability of combined-cycle units, which are more efficient than steam-only units. As noted

earlier, the working fluid that turns a turbine can be hot gases or steam. In a combined-cycle plant, both types of turbines are used, in that hot gases leaving one turbine are used to heat water to produce steam to turn another turbine.

- Repeal of provisions contained in a 1978 law that "discouraged" the use of natural gas for electricity generation.

In addition, natural gas became a favored fuel for power generation because it was cheaper and faster to construct natural gas–fired plants than coal-fired plants.

It is important to understand that fossil fuel–fired power plants do not necessarily use a single fuel for all of their capacity. For example, a plant might use natural gas for its baseload capacity and petroleum for its peaking capacity.

Consumption

Figure 8.3 shows retail electricity sales for various economic sectors. The residential sector was the largest user in 2015, at 1,399.9 billion kWh. It was followed closely by the commercial sector, at 1,358.4 billion kWh, and the industrial sector, at 958.6 billion kWh. The transportation sector was a very small electricity consumer in 2015, accounting for only 7.7 billion kWh.

From 1949 to the mid-1980s the industrial sector was the largest consumer of electricity in the United States, and its usage rate grew quickly. (See Figure 8.3.) That growth slowed through the 1990s, and during the first decade of the 21st century industrial consumption was flat to slightly declining. Meanwhile, residential and commercial consumption continued to grow.

Losses

As noted earlier, energy is lost when thermal energy is converted to mechanical energy and then to electrical energy. Conversion losses are significant. Figure 8.4 shows an energy balance for electricity flows in 2015. Nearly 38.9 quadrillion British thermal units (Btu) of energy was input to electricity generation; however, 24.1 quadrillion Btu (62%) of it was lost during conversion, leaving 14.7 quadrillion Btu of gross generation. An additional 0.99 quadrillion Btu was lost during transmission and distribution of the net generated electricity. Overall, 25.1 quadrillion Btu, or 65% of the incoming energy, was lost.

Scientists have developed materials called superconductors that transmit electricity with virtually no losses. In 2008 a superconductor-based transmission cable was installed by Long Island Power Authority in New York. The Department of Energy notes in "Long Island HTS Power Cable: Project Fact Sheet" (May 16, 2008, http://energy.gov/sites/prod/files/oeprod/DocumentsandMedia/LIPA__5_16_08.pdf) that it is "the first ever installation of a superconductor cable in a live grid and at transmission

TABLE 8.1

Electricity generation, trade, losses, and end uses, selected years 1950–2015

[Billion kilowatthours]

Year	Net generation[a] — Electric power sector[b]	Commercial sector[c]	Industrial sector[d]	Total	Trade — Imports[e]	Exports[e]	Net imports[e]	T&D losses[f] and unaccounted for[g]	End use — Retail sales[h]	Direct use[i]	Total
1950 Total	329	NA	5	334	2	(s)	2	44	291	NA	291
1955 Total	547	NA	3	550	5	(s)	4	58	497	NA	497
1960 Total	756	NA	4	759	5	1	5	76	688	NA	688
1965 Total	1,055	NA	3	1,058	4	4	(s)	104	954	NA	954
1970 Total	1,532	NA	3	1,535	6	4	2	145	1,392	NA	1,392
1975 Total	1,918	NA	3	1,921	11	5	6	180	1,747	NA	1,747
1980 Total	2,286	NA	3	2,290	25	4	21	216	2,094	NA	2,094
1985 Total	2,470	NA	3	2,473	46	5	41	190	2,324	NA	2,324
1990 Total	2,901	6	131[c]	3,038	18	16	2	203	2,713	125	2,837
1995 Total	3,194	8	151	3,353	43	4	39	229	3,013	151	3,164
2000 Total	3,638	8	157	3,802	49	15	34	244	3,421	171	3,592
2001 Total	3,580	8	149	3,737	39	16	22	202	3,394	163	3,557
2002 Total	3,698	8	153	3,858	37	16	21	248	3,465	166	3,632
2003 Total	3,721	7	155	3,883	30	24	6	228	3,494	168	3,662
2004 Total	3,808	8	154	3,971	34	23	11	266	3,547	168	3,716
2005 Total	3,902	8	145	4,055	44	19	25	269	3,661	150	3,811
2006 Total	3,908	8	148	4,065	43	24	18	266	3,670	147	3,817
2007 Total	4,005	8	143	4,157	51	20	31	298	3,765	126	3,890
2008 Total	3,974	8	137	4,119	57	24	33	286	3,734	132	3,866
2009 Total	3,810	8	132	3,950	52	18	34	261	3,597	127	3,724
2010 Total	3,972	9	144	4,125	45	19	26	264	3,755	132	3,887
2011 Total	3,948	10	142	4,100	52	15	37	255	3,750	133	3,883
2012 Total	3,890	11	146	4,048	59	12	47	263	3,695	138	3,832
2013 Total	3,904	12	150	4,066	69	11	58	256	3,725	143	3,868
2014 Total	3,937	13	144	4,094	69	13	53	244	3,765	139	3,903
2015 Total	3,931	13	144	4,087	76	9	66	291	3,725	139[E]	3,863

[a] Electricity net generation at utility-scale facilities. Does not include estimated distributed solar photovoltaic generation, which was 10 billion kilowatthours in 2014 and 12 billion kilowatthours in 2015.
[b] Electricity-only and combined-heat-and-power (CHP) plants within the NAICS 22 category whose primary business is to sell electricity, or electricity and heat, to the public. Through 1988, data are for electric utilities only; beginning in 1989, data are for electric utilities and independent power producers.
[c] Commercial combined-heat-and-power (CHP) and commercial electricity-only plants.
[d] Industrial combined-heat-and-power (CHP) and industrial electricity-only plants. Through 1988, data are for industrial hydroelectric power only.
[e] Electricity transmitted across U.S. borders. Net imports equal imports minus exports.
[f] Transmission and distribution losses (electricity losses that occur between the point of generation and delivery to the customer).
[g] Data collection frame differences and nonsampling error.
[h] Electricity retail sales to ultimate customers by electric utilities and, beginning in 1996, other energy service providers.
[i] Use of electricity that is 1) self-generated, 2) produced by either the same entity that consumes the power or an affiliate, and 3) used in direct support of a service or industrial process located within the same facility or group of facilities that house the generating equipment. Direct use is exclusive of station use.
E = Estimate. NA = Not available. (s) = Less than 0.5 billion kilowatthours.
Notes: Totals may not equal sum of components due to independent rounding. Geographic coverage is the 50 states and the District of Columbia. T&D = transmission and distribution.

SOURCE: Adapted from "Table 7.1. Electricity Overview (Billion Kilowatthours)," in *Monthly Energy Review: July 2016*, U.S. Energy Information Administration, July 2016, http://www.eia.gov/totalenergy/data/monthly/pdf/mer.pdf (accessed August 7, 2016).

FIGURE 8.2

Electricity net generation, by source, 1949–2015

[Total (all sectors), major sources, 1949–2015]

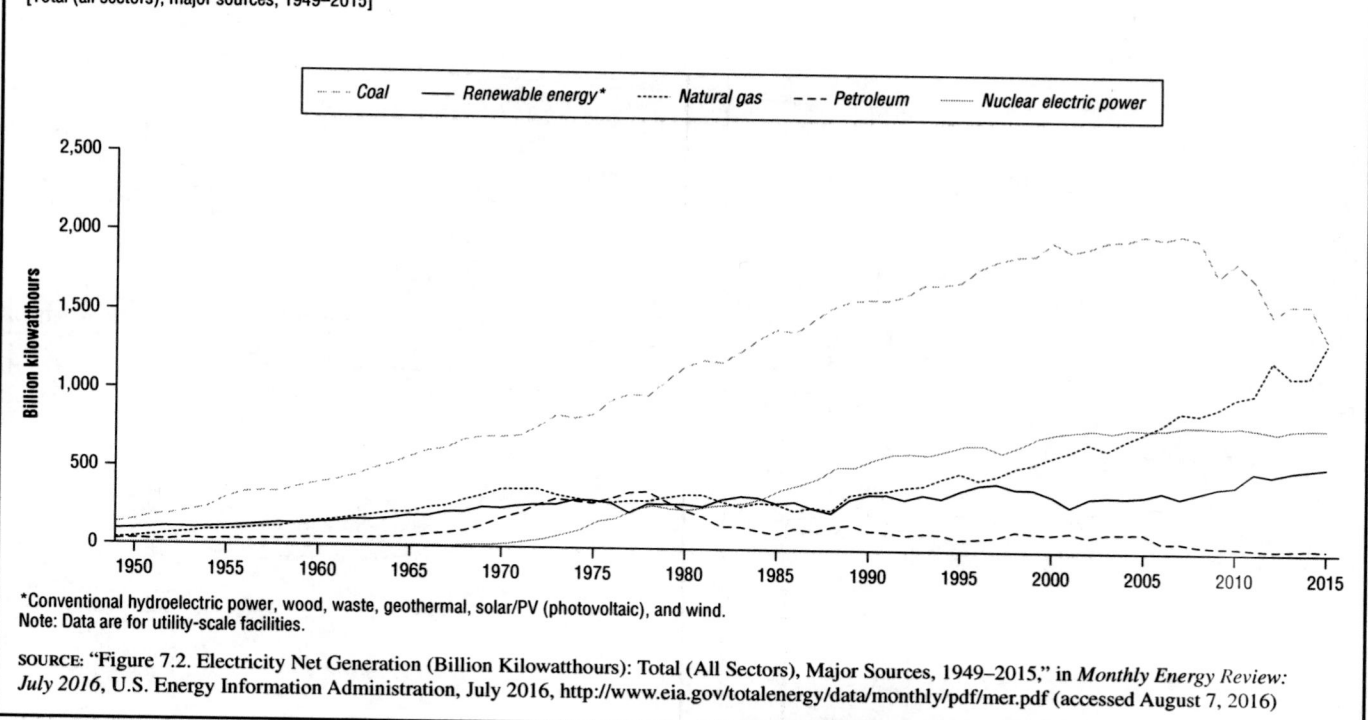

*Conventional hydroelectric power, wood, waste, geothermal, solar/PV (photovoltaic), and wind.
Note: Data are for utility-scale facilities.

SOURCE: "Figure 7.2. Electricity Net Generation (Billion Kilowatthours): Total (All Sectors), Major Sources, 1949–2015," in *Monthly Energy Review: July 2016*, U.S. Energy Information Administration, July 2016, http://www.eia.gov/totalenergy/data/monthly/pdf/mer.pdf (accessed August 7, 2016)

FIGURE 8.3

Retail electricity sales, by end-use sector, 1949–2015

[Retail sales^a by sector, 1949–2015]

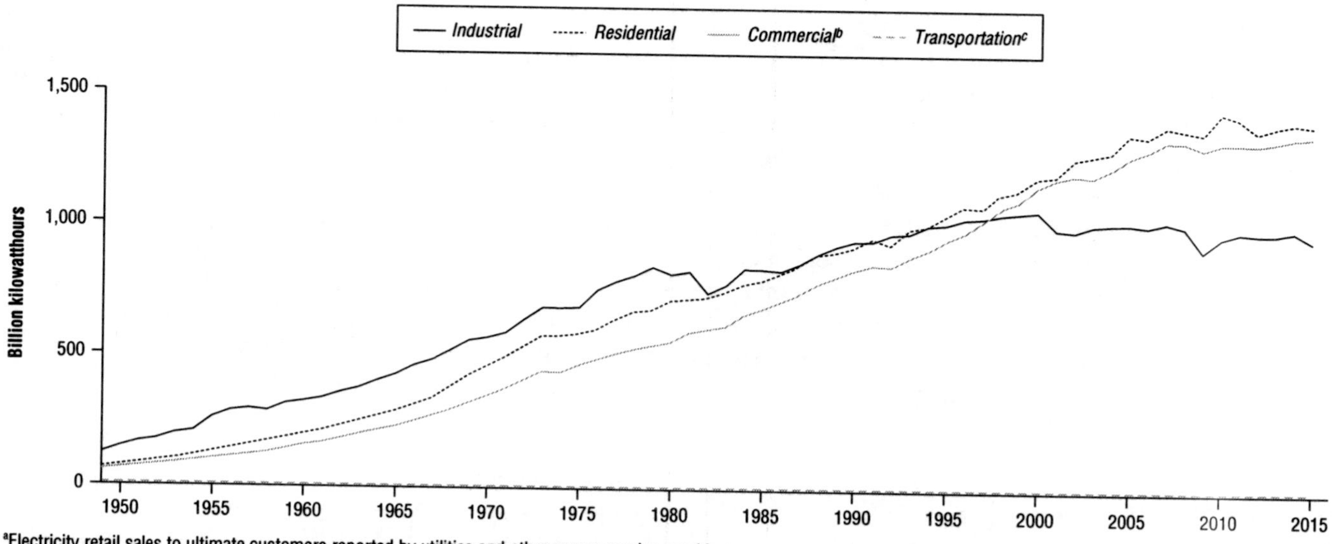

aElectricity retail sales to ultimate customers reported by utilities and other energy service providers.
bCommercial sector, including public street and highway lighting, interdepartmental sales, and other sales to public authorites.
cTransportation sector, including sales to railroads and railways.

SOURCE: "Figure 7.6. Electricity End Use (Billion Kilowatthours): Retail Sales by Sector, 1949–2015," in *Monthly Energy Review: July 2016*, U.S. Energy Information Administration, July 2016, http://www.eia.gov/totalenergy/data/monthly/pdf/mer.pdf (accessed August 7, 2016)

FIGURE 8.4

Electricity flow, 2015

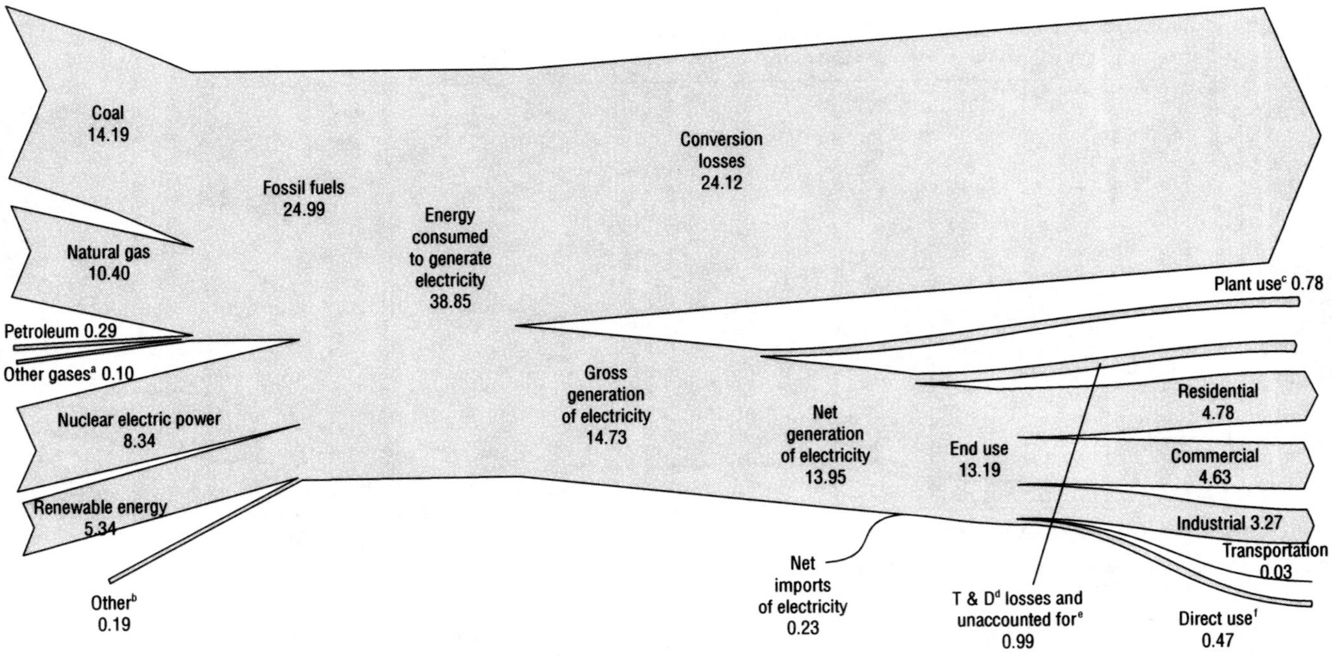

ᵃBlast furnace gas and other manufactured and waste gases derived from fossil fuels.
ᵇBatteries, chemicals, hydrogen, pitch, purchased steam, sulfur, miscellaneous technologies, and non-renewable waste (municipal solid waste from nonbiogenic sources, and tire-derived fuels).
ᶜElectric energy used in the operation of power plants.
ᵈTransmission and distribution losses (electricity losses that occur between the point of generation and delivery to the customer).
ᵉData collection frame differences and nonsampling error.
ᶠUse of electricity that is 1) self-generated, 2) produced by either the same entity that consumes the power or an affiliate, and 3) used in direct support of a service or industrial process located within the same facility or group of facilities that house the generating equipment. Direct use is exclusive of station use.
Notes: Data are preliminary. Net generation of electricity includes pumped storage facility production minus energy used for pumping. Values are derived from source data prior to rounding for publication. Totals may not equal sum of components due to independent rounding. Btu = British thermal units.

SOURCE: "U.S. Electricity Flow, 2015 (Quadrillion Btu)," in *Diagrams: Energy Flows*, U.S. Energy Information Administration, 2016, http://www.eia.gov/totalenergy/data/monthly/pdf/flow/electricity.pdf (accessed August 17, 2016)

voltages." The cable is cooled by liquid nitrogen to a temperature of −321 degrees Fahrenheit (−196 Celsius). According to Heiko Thomas et al., in "Superconducting Transmission Lines—Sustainable Electric Energy Transfer with Higher Public Acceptance?" (*Renewable and Sustainable Energy Reviews*, vol. 55, March 2016), superconductor cables were being installed or were under construction or development at a dozen other power facilities around the world as of 2016. The relatively high costs of the cables, compared with conventional power lines, are expected to decrease over time as superconducting materials become more commercially available.

ELECTRICITY PRICES

Figure 8.5 shows the average retail prices of electricity by sector between 1960 and 2015. Retail prices were rather flat during the 1960s and early 1970s and then climbed steeply over the next decade. Price trends varied by sector through the end of the century, but were generally flat to slightly increasing. The main exception was in the industrial sector, which saw its prices slightly decline. During the first decade of the 21st century, prices began creeping upward again. The prices shown in Figure 8.5 are nominal, meaning they do not account for the effects of inflation. By contrast, real prices assume that the value of a dollar is constant over time. Thus, changes reflect actual market variations and not inflationary effects. Table 8.2 shows real prices for residential electricity between 1960 and 2015. Real electricity prices for this sector declined through 2004 and then fluctuated through 2015.

Pricing Factors

In "Factors Affecting Electricity Prices," the EIA notes that electricity prices are affected by fuel costs, power plant construction and maintenance costs, and transmission and distribution line costs. Weather also plays a factor. As noted earlier, electricity usage is higher during the summer than during other seasons. Hot

FIGURE 8.5

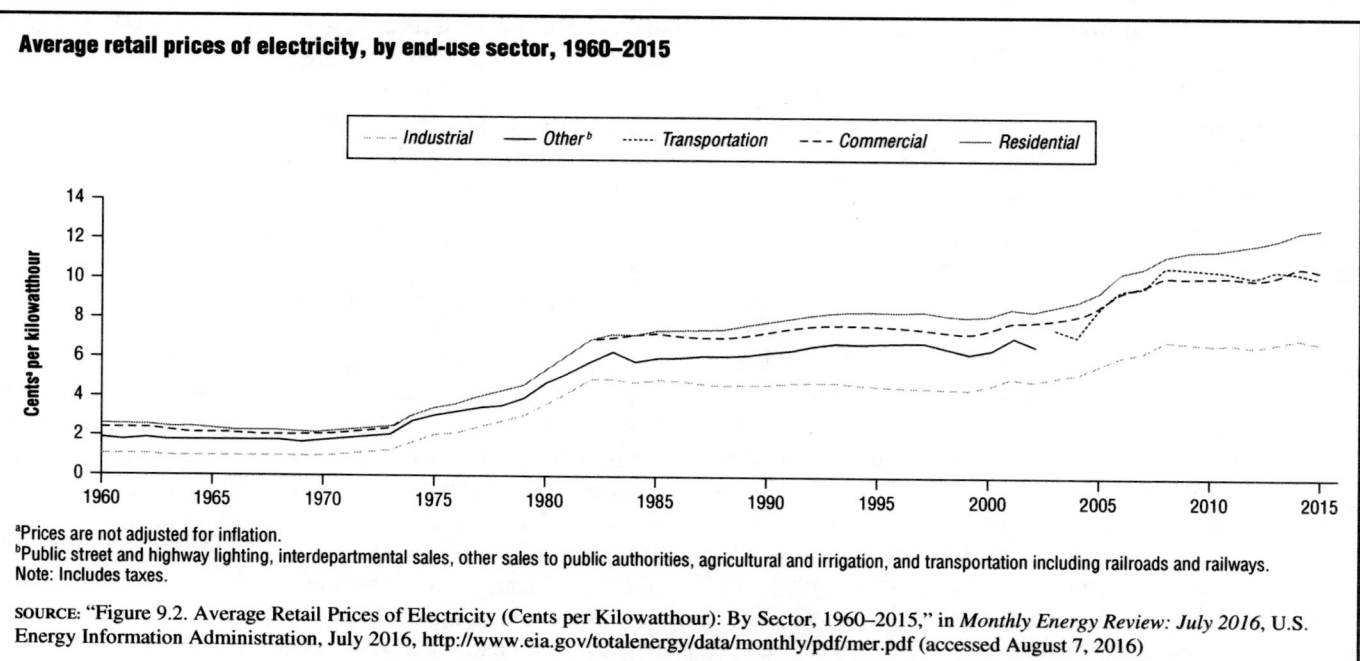

Average retail prices of electricity, by end-use sector, 1960–2015

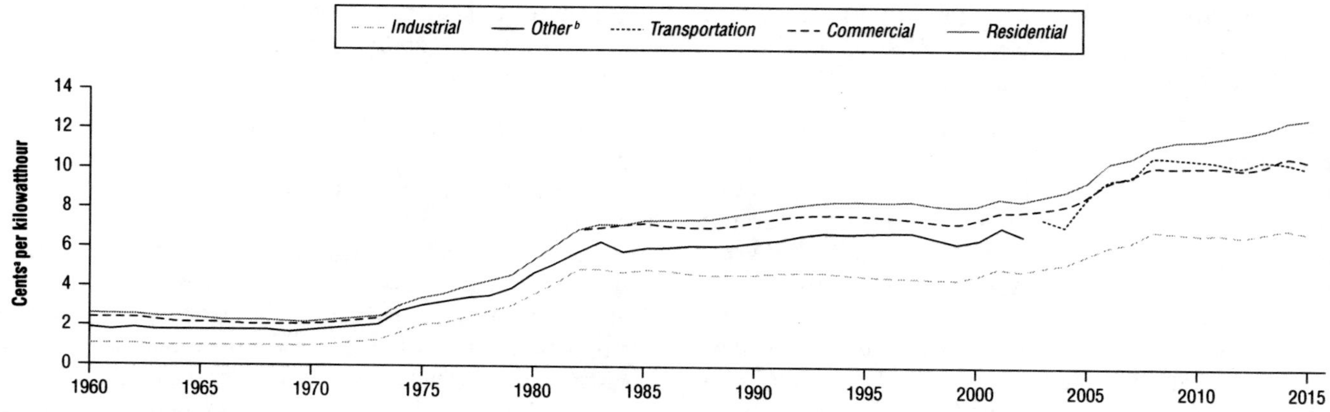

Industrial
Other[b]
Transportation
Commercial
Residential
Cents[a] per kilowatthour
14
12
10
8
6
4
2
0
1960
1965
1970
1975
1980
1985
1990
1995
2000
2005
2010
2015

[a]Prices are not adjusted for inflation.
[b]Public street and highway lighting, interdepartmental sales, other sales to public authorities, agricultural and irrigation, and transportation including railroads and railways.
Note: Includes taxes.

SOURCE: "Figure 9.2. Average Retail Prices of Electricity (Cents per Kilowatthour): By Sector, 1960–2015," in *Monthly Energy Review: July 2016*, U.S. Energy Information Administration, July 2016, http://www.eia.gov/totalenergy/data/monthly/pdf/mer.pdf (accessed August 7, 2016)

TABLE 8.2

Real (inflation-adjusted) costs of electricity to residential customers, selected years 1960–2015

	Residential electricity*	
	Cents per kilowatthour	Dollars per million Btu
1960 Average	8.80	25.74
1965 Average	7.60	22.33
1970 Average	5.70	16.62
1975 Average	6.50	19.07
1980 Average	6.60	19.21
1985 Average	6.87	20.13
1990 Average	5.99	17.56
1995 Average	5.51	16.15
2000 Average	4.79	14.02
2001 Average	4.84	14.20
2002 Average	4.69	13.75
2003 Average	4.74	13.89
2004 Average	4.74	13.89
2005 Average	4.84	14.18
2006 Average	5.16	15.12
2007 Average	5.14	15.05
2008 Average	5.23	15.33
2009 Average	5.37	15.72
2010 Average	5.29	15.51
2011 Average	5.21	15.27
2012 Average	5.17	15.17
2013 Average	5.21	15.26
2014 Average	5.29	15.50
2015 Average	5.35	15.67

Btu = British thermal units.
*Includes taxes.
Notes: Geographic coverage is the 50 states and the District of Columbia.

SOURCE: Adapted from "Table 1.6. Cost of Fuels to End Users in Real (1982–1984) Dollars," in *Monthly Energy Review: July 2016*, U.S. Energy Information Administration, July 2016, http://www.eia.gov/totalenergy/data/monthly/pdf/mer.pdf (accessed August 7, 2016)

summer weather can greatly increase the demand for electricity for air conditioning and drive up prices. Lastly, electricity prices are affected by government regulations and policies, which will be explained later in this chapter.

The prices that are paid by electricity consumers vary by economic sector. According to the EIA, residential and commercial customers pay the most for electricity because delivery to them is the most expensive. By contrast, industrial customers pay the least because they purchase electricity in large amounts and because many industrial facilities do not require their electricity to be stepped down by transformers—that is, their systems can handle electricity at higher voltages than what is delivered to commercial and residential customers.

The EIA indicates in "State Electricity Profiles" (March 24, 2016, http://www.eia.gov/electricity/state) that electricity prices vary considerably state by state. For example, in 2014 the average price was only 7.1 cents per kWh in Washington, but 33.4 cents per kWh in Hawaii. Pricing differences between states are due to various factors, including the number and type of power plants in an area, the availability and price of fuel in local markets, and government regulations and policies that affect pricing.

GOVERNMENT INTERVENTION. Electricity is considered to be a vital resource for the public. Hence, for decades the government heavily controlled the nation's electricity markets to ensure that this resource was widely available at relatively low costs. As a result, local utility companies developed monopolies in that each company had market control over a specified geographical area. During the 1970s and 1980s the federal government began experimenting with deregulation (breaking up government-supported monopolies). The idea was that competition would keep electricity prices low.

In the electric power sector deregulation has meant allowing consumers to purchase electricity from competing sellers but still receive delivery over existing power lines that are maintained by a local utility. The overall process is known as restructuring. In 1978 Congress passed the Public Utilities Regulatory Policies Act, which required utilities to buy electricity from private companies when doing so was cheaper than building their own power plants. The Energy Policy Act of 1992 gave other electricity generators greater access to the market, which enhanced the states' ability to restructure their systems. Widespread debates occurred regarding regulatory, economic, energy, and environmental policies. State public utility commissions conducted proceedings and crafted rules that were related to competition.

California was a leader in deregulation during the mid-1990s. However, during the summer of 2000 the state experienced rolling electrical blackouts, and electricity bills doubled for many customers. Fearful of similar blackouts and price spikes, most other states slowed or stopped their efforts to deregulate their electricity markets. As a result, as of September 2016 few states had deregulated their electricity markets to any degree. Northeastern states had most fully deregulated, and Texas had competitive markets in most, but not all, of its major cities. However, it is difficult to determine how deregulation has affected electricity pricing because so many different variables are at work.

In the United States the electric power sector includes government entities, such as municipally owned utilities. In addition, the federal government generates electricity for consumers through federally owned corporations, such as the Tennessee Valley Authority. Electricity is also generated by independent power producers (IPPs). In "NRG-GenOn Acquisition Plan Would Create the Largest Independent Power Producer" (September 6, 2012, http://www.eia.gov/todayinenergy/detail.cfm?id=7850), the EIA defines IPPs as "unregulated entities providing electricity into a wholesale electricity market or to another company that provides distribution to the ultimate customers." In 2012 NRG Energy, Inc., merged with GenOn Energy, Inc., and became the largest IPP in the nation. As of September 2016, NRG Energy (http://maps.nrg.com/) had dozens of generating plants around the country.

The EIA explains in *Electric Power Annual 2014* (February 2016, http://www.eia.gov/electricity/annual/pdf/epa.pdf) that electric utilities generated 2,382 million megawatt-hours in 2014, or 58% of the total 4,093

million megawatt-hours generated by the domestic electric power sector. IPPs accounted for 1,404 million megawatt-hours, or 34% of the total. The remaining 8% of the total was provided by a variety of sources including combined heat and power plants, which typically provide heat to nearby industrial facilities and also provide electricity to the nation's electrical grid.

As is described in Chapter 1, the federal government supports the electric power sector via financial incentives, such as tax breaks and subsidies. Whereas these measures put downward pressure on electricity prices, other government activities tend to push prices upward. The primary example is the regulation of emissions and discharges from fuel combustion. As noted earlier, the electric power sector is the biggest end user of coal in the United States. However, coal-fired power plants have been under increasing pressure to reduce their emissions of air pollutants. For example, the Mercury Air Toxics Standard took effect in 2015–16. As of 2016, the Clean Power Plan rule, which is described later in this chapter, was slated to take effect in 2022 and impose new limits on carbon emissions from power plants. Overall, tightening standards have forced coal-fired power plants to invest in better control technologies and/or use coal that contains lower sulfur contents. Pollution-control technologies, in particular, can be very expensive.

Additionally, the government has been spearheading a modernization of the nation's electricity system through its Smart Grid initiative. In "Smart Grid" (2016, http://energy.gov/oe/services/technology-development/smart-grid), the Department of Energy's Office of Electricity Delivery and Energy Reliability states that "'Smart grid' generally refers to a class of technology [that] people are using to bring utility electricity delivery systems into the 21st century, using computer-based remote control and automation. These systems are made possible by two-way communication technology and computer processing that has been used for decades in other industries." Modernizing the grid is expected to reap numerous energy-saving benefits and reduce carbon emissions, as shown in Figure 8.6. A more flexible grid will allow consumers greater access to environmentally friendly (or green) power generated with renewable energy sources, such as wind and solar. The most visible Smart Grid innovation has been so-called smart meters, which have been installed at millions of homes and businesses. These computerized meters directly communicate power usage to utility companies and consumers.

Smart Grid projects have been funded by a substantial investment of taxpayer dollars. The administration of President Barack Obama (1961–) notes in *A Policy Framework for the 21st Century Grid: A Progress Report* (February 2013, http://www.whitehouse.gov/sites/default/files/microsites/ostp/2013_nstc_grid.pdf) that $4.5 billion was provided by the American Recovery and Reinvestment Act of 2009. That amount was matched with like funds from the

FIGURE 8.6

Expected benefits from the Smart Grid

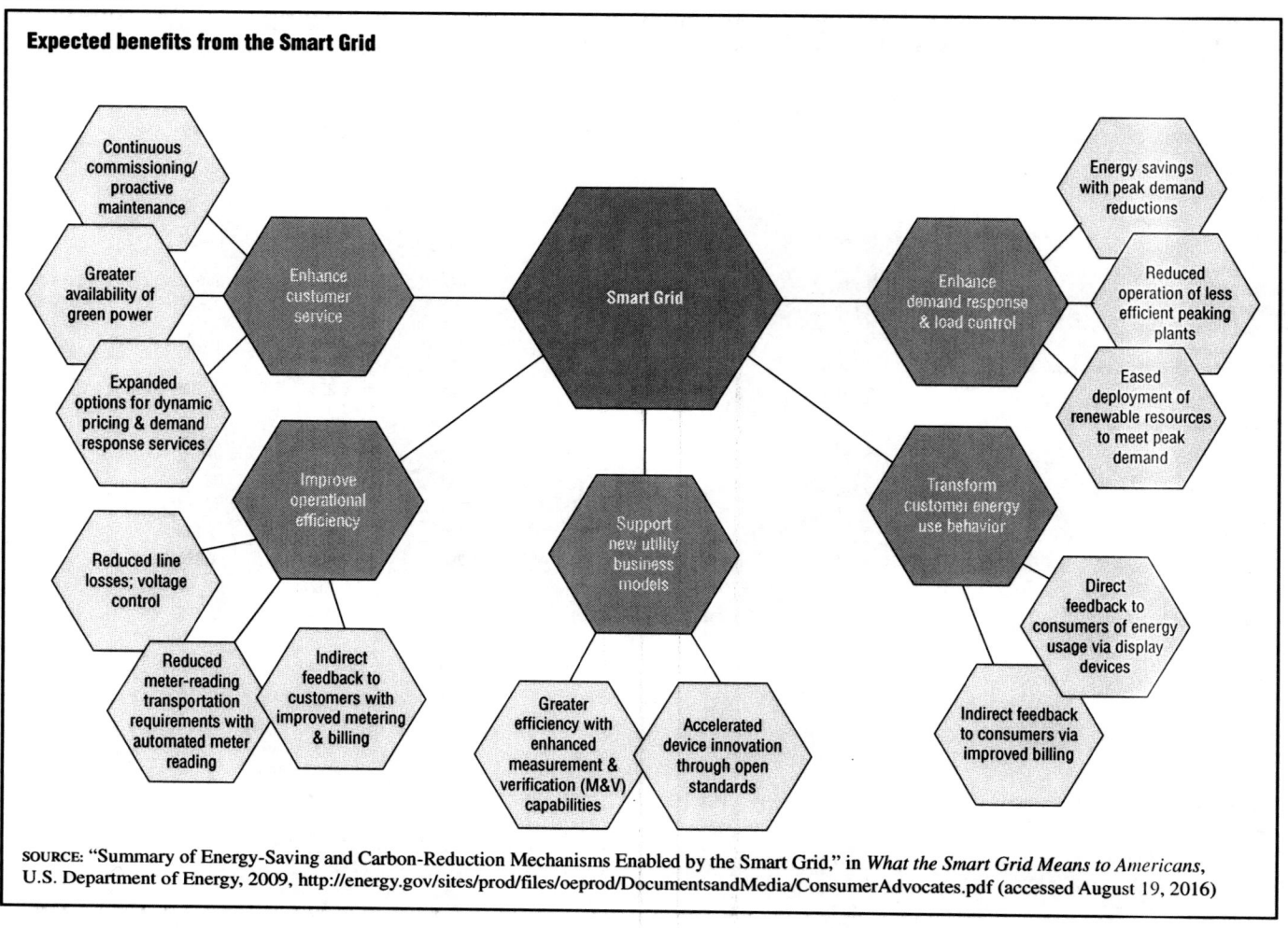

SOURCE: "Summary of Energy-Saving and Carbon-Reduction Mechanisms Enabled by the Smart Grid," in *What the Smart Grid Means to Americans*, U.S. Department of Energy, 2009, http://energy.gov/sites/prod/files/oeprod/DocumentsandMedia/ConsumerAdvocates.pdf (accessed August 19, 2016)

power industry. The Smart Grid initiative is a long-term project that will take years—perhaps decades—to implement across the nation's vast electrical network. Ultimately, it is expected to make the grid more reliable, efficient, and cost effective and empower consumers to make better energy use decisions. In addition, safeguards are being included to help protect the grid from cyberattacks by terrorists or unfriendly foreign governments.

Mohana Ravindranath describes in "As Smart-Grid Funding Winds Down, Energy Leaders Assess Progress" (WashingtonPost.com, February 23, 2014) some of the challenges facing the Smart Grid initiative. They include consumer resistance to change and a lack of universal standards that would ensure interoperability and communication between different electronic systems. Future funding for continued modernization is also a concern given the high costs involved.

THE DOMESTIC OUTLOOK

In *Annual Energy Outlook 2016 with Projections to 2040* (August 2016, https://www.eia.gov/forecasts/aeo/pdf/0383(2016).pdf), the EIA predicts future domestic electricity generation through 2040 for various scenarios. One of them is called the reference case, which the EIA notes "assumes that current laws and regulations affecting the energy sector are largely unchanged throughout the projection period (including the implication that laws which include sunset dates are no longer in effect at the time of those sunset dates)."

As shown in Table 8.3, the agency predicts for the reference case that natural gas will supply 1,618 billion kWh in 2040, or 36% of total net electricity generation. It will be followed by renewable sources, at 1,205 billion kWh, or 27% of the total. Coal (884 billion kWh) and nuclear power (789 billion kWh) will provide 20% and 18%, respectively, of the total. Petroleum and other sources will make up the remainder. Overall, fossil fuels are forecast to account for just over half (56%) of electricity generation in 2040 in the reference case.

Figure 8.7 shows EIA projections through 2040 by fuel category for the reference case and for an extended policies case. The latter case assumes that federal tax credits available in 2015 for renewable electricity

TABLE 8.3

Electricity generation by fuel, 2015 and predicted for selected years 2020–40

[Billion kilowatthours, unless otherwise noted]

Supply, disposition, prices, and emissions	2015	2020	2025	2030	2035	2040	2015–2040
Net generation by fuel type							
Electric power sector[a]							
Power only[b]							
Coal	1,320	1,355	1,145	938	928	884	−1.6%
Petroleum	23	13	11	9	8	7	−4.6%
Natural gas[c]	1,114	947	1,129	1,412	1,460	1,618	1.5%
Nuclear power	798	777	789	789	789	789	0.0%
Pumped storage/other[d]	3	3	3	3	3	3	0.1%
Renewable sources[e]	493	757	918	969	1,094	1,205	3.6%
Distributed generation (natural gas)	0	0	1	1	1	2	—
Total	**3,751**	**3,853**	**3,996**	**4,121**	**4,284**	**4,508**	**0.7%**
Combined heat and power[f]							
Coal	23	21	21	21	21	21	−0.4%
Petroleum	1	1	1	1	1	1	0.0%
Natural gas	136	143	143	147	142	139	0.1%
Renewable sources	4	4	4	4	4	4	0.1%
Total	**164**	**168**	**169**	**173**	**169**	**165**	**0.0%**
Total net electric power sector generation	**3,915**	**4,021**	**4,165**	**4,294**	**4,452**	**4,673**	**0.7%**
Less direct use	18	18	17	17	17	17	−0.1%
Net available to the grid	**3,897**	**4,004**	**4,148**	**4,276**	**4,435**	**4,656**	**0.7%**
End-use sector[g]							
Coal	12	12	13	13	13	14	0.6%
Petroleum	2	1	1	1	1	2	−0.4%
Natural gas	99	111	124	143	165	183	2.5%
Other gaseous fuels[h]	11	21	21	21	21	21	2.5%
Renewable sources[i]	49	75	93	115	139	165	5.0%
Other[j]	3	3	3	3	3	3	0.0%
Total end-use sector net generation	**176**	**223**	**255**	**296**	**343**	**387**	**3.2%**
Less direct use	127	181	210	246	286	324	3.8%
Total sales to the grid	**49**	**42**	**45**	**51**	**57**	**63**	**1.0%**
Total net electricity generation by fuel							
Coal	1,355	1,388	1,179	972	962	919	−1.5%
Petroleum	26	15	13	11	10	9	−4.0%
Natural gas	1,348	1,201	1,396	1,702	1,768	1,942	1.5%
Nuclear power	798	777	789	789	789	789	0.0%
Renewable sources[e, i]	546	836	1,015	1,088	1,238	1,374	3.8%
Other[k]	17	27	27	27	27	27	1.8%
Total net electricity generation	**4,090**	**4,244**	**4,420**	**4,590**	**4,795**	**5,060**	**0.9%**
Net generation to the grid	**3,946**	**4,046**	**4,193**	**4,327**	**4,492**	**4,719**	**0.7%**
Net imports	**57**	**57**	**58**	**50**	**46**	**43**	**−1.1%**
Electricity sales by sector							
Residential	1,402	1,395	1,393	1,416	1,457	1,523	0.3%
Commercial	1,360	1,374	1,425	1,491	1,562	1,647	0.8%
Industrial	959	1,059	1,145	1,166	1,197	1,249	1.1%
Transportation	9	13	23	32	40	45	6.7%
Total	**3,729**	**3,841**	**3,986**	**4,105**	**4,256**	**4,464**	**0.7%**
Direct use	144	199	227	263	303	341	3.5%
Total electricity use	**3,873**	**4,039**	**4,213**	**4,368**	**4,559**	**4,805**	**0.9%**
End-use prices							
(2015 cents per kilowatthour)							
Residential	12.4	12.9	13.2	13.4	13.2	13.0	0.2%
Commercial	10.5	10.7	10.9	11.0	10.7	10.5	0.0%
Industrial	6.9	7.1	7.3	7.5	7.3	7.2	0.2%
Transportation	10.1	11.3	12.3	12.7	12.4	12.1	0.7%
All sectors average	**10.3**	**10.5**	**10.7**	**10.9**	**10.6**	**10.5**	**0.1%**

generation sources (such as wind) will be extended through 2040 and that the Clean Power Plan rule will become more stringent during the 2030s. In both cases, the EIA anticipates that during the 2020s natural gas will replace coal as the nation's largest energy source for electricity generation.

TABLE 8.3

Electricity generation by fuel, 2015 and predicted for selected years 2020–40 [CONTINUED]

[Billion kilowatthours, unless otherwise noted]

Supply, disposition, prices, and emissions	2015	2020	2025	2030	2035	2040	2015–2040
(nominal cents per kilowatthour)							
Residential	12.4	14.2	16.2	18.2	19.9	21.9	2.3%
Commercial	10.5	11.9	13.4	14.9	16.2	17.6	2.1%
Industrial	6.9	7.9	9.0	10.2	11.1	12.2	2.3%
Transportation	10.1	12.5	15.1	17.2	18.8	20.4	2.9%
All sectors average	**10.3**	**11.6**	**13.1**	**14.7**	**16.1**	**17.6**	**2.2%**
Prices by service category							
(2015 cents per kilowatthour)							
Generation	6.4	6.4	6.8	7.3	6.8	6.6	0.1%
Transmission	1.1	1.2	1.2	1.3	1.3	1.3	0.7%
Distribution	2.8	3.0	2.7	2.3	2.6	2.6	−0.3%
(nominal cents per kilowatthour)							
Generation	6.4	7.0	8.4	9.9	10.3	11.1	2.2%
Transmission	1.1	1.3	1.5	1.7	1.9	2.2	2.8%
Distribution	2.8	3.3	3.3	3.2	3.9	4.4	1.8%
Electric power sector emissions[a]							
Sulfur dioxide (million short tons)	3.57	1.20	1.07	0.77	0.84	0.79	−5.9%
Nitrogen oxide (million short tons)	1.41	1.16	1.00	0.91	0.90	0.88	−1.9%
Mercury (short tons)	23.74	5.55	4.62	3.76	3.82	3.57	−7.3%

[a]Includes electricity-only and combined heat and power plants that have a regulatory status.
[b]Includes plants that only produce electricity and that have a regulatory status.
[c]Includes electricity generation from fuel cells.
[d]Includes non-biogenic municipal waste. The U.S. Energy Information Administration estimates that in 2014 approximately 7 billion kilowatthours of electricity were generated from a municipal waste stream containing petroleum-derived plastics and other non-renewable sources.
[e]Includes conventional hydroelectric, geothermal, wood, wood waste, biogenic municipal waste, landfill gas, other biomass, solar, and wind power.
[f]Includes combined heat and power plants whose primary business is to sell electricity and heat to the public (i.e., those that report North American Industry Classification System code 22 or that have a regulatory status).
[g]Includes combined heat and power plants and electricity-only plants in the commercial and industrial sectors that have a non-regulatory status; and small on-site generating systems in the residential, commercial, and industrial sectors used primarily for own-use generation, but which may also sell some power to the grid.
[h]Includes refinery gas and still gas.
[i]Includes conventional hydroelectric, geothermal, wood, wood waste, all municipal waste, landfill gas, other biomass, solar, and wind power.
[j]Includes batteries, chemicals, hydrogen, pitch, purchased steam, sulfur, and miscellaneous technologies.
[k]Includes pumped storage, non-biogenic municipal waste, refinery gas, still gas, batteries, chemicals, hydrogen, pitch, purchased steam, sulfur, and miscellaneous technologies.
Note: Totals may not equal sum of components due to independent rounding.

SOURCE: Adapted from "Table 8. Electricity Supply, Disposition, Prices, and Emissions," in *Annual Energy Outlook 2016 Early Release*, U.S. Energy Information Administration, May 2016, https://www.eia.gov/forecasts/aeo/excel/aeotab_8.xlsx (accessed August 12, 2016)

WORLD ELECTRICITY PRODUCTION AND CONSUMPTION

Net electricity generation worldwide totaled 21.6 trillion kWh in 2012. (See Table 8.4.) Coal provided 8.6 trillion kWh, or 40% of the total. It was followed by natural gas, at 4.8 trillion kWh (22% of the total); renewable sources, at 4.7 trillion kWh (22%); nuclear energy, at 2.3 trillion kWh (11%); and petroleum and other liquids at 1.1 trillion kWh (5%).

The EIA examines and predicts electricity generation for countries that are and are not members of the Organisation for Economic Co-operation and Development (OECD). The OECD is a collection of dozens of mostly Western nations that are devoted to global economic development. As shown in Table 8.4, the total net electricity generation in 2012 was slightly higher for non-members (11.3 trillion kWh) than for OECD members (10.2 trillion kWh). OECD members are expected to make small gains (up 1.2% annually) in electricity generation through 2040. Most of this growth will be from

renewables and natural gas. Nonmember electricity generation is projected to grow 2.5% annually through 2040 with gains across most fuel categories. The largest increase (5.7%) is predicted for nuclear power generation due primarily to huge capacity additions in China. (See Figure 8.8.) Table 8.4 also shows the minor effects the EIA expects the Clean Power Plan rule will have on world electricity generation in the future. It would slightly dampen use of fossil fuels by 2040 in favor of greater use of renewable sources.

ENVIRONMENTAL ISSUES

The primary environmental issues involved with electricity generation relate to the underlying fuels and methods that are used to generate power. These issues are briefly described for natural gas in Chapter 3, for coal in Chapter 4, for nuclear power in Chapter 5, and for hydropower and other renewables in Chapter 6.

The electric power sector is regulated for environmental compliance, particularly in regards to air emissions.

FIGURE 8.7

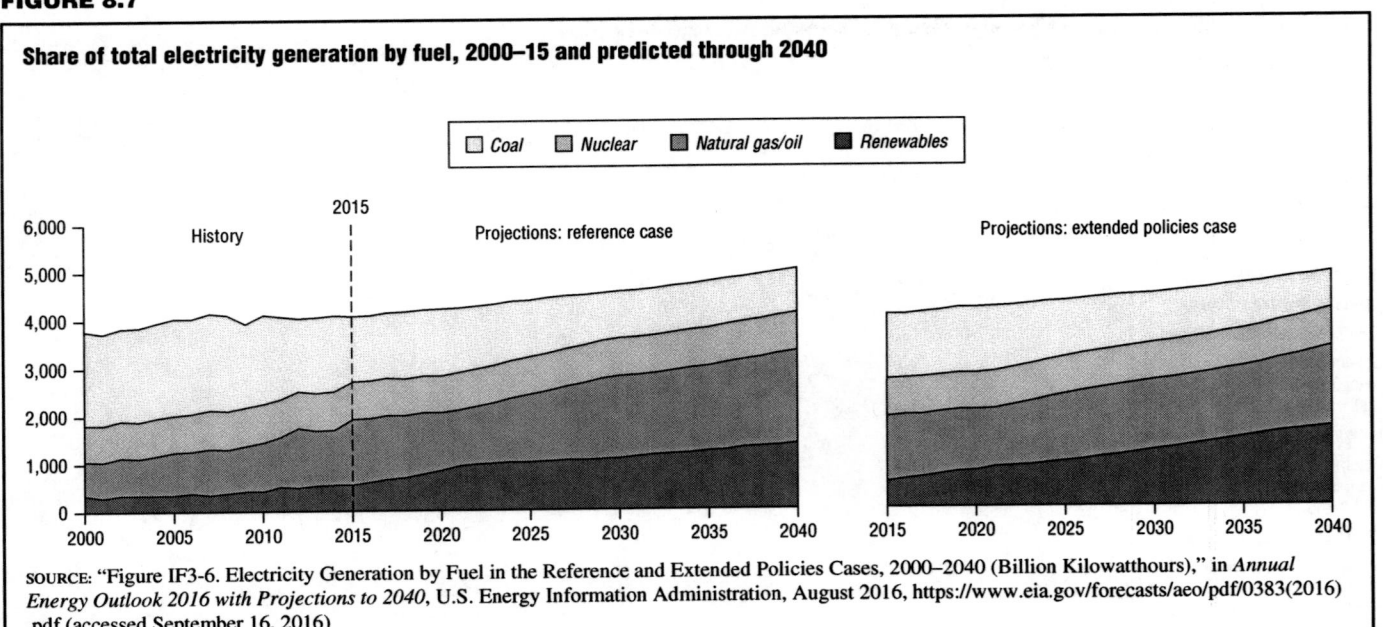

Share of total electricity generation by fuel, 2000–15 and predicted through 2040

Legend: ☐ Coal ▦ Nuclear ▨ Natural gas/oil ■ Renewables

History | 2015 | Projections: reference case | Projections: extended policies case

SOURCE: "Figure IF3-6. Electricity Generation by Fuel in the Reference and Extended Policies Cases, 2000–2040 (Billion Kilowatthours)," in *Annual Energy Outlook 2016 with Projections to 2040*, U.S. Energy Information Administration, August 2016, https://www.eia.gov/forecasts/aeo/pdf/0383(2016).pdf (accessed September 16, 2016)

TABLE 8.4

World net electricity generation, by country category and energy source, 2012, and predicted through 2040

[Trillion kilowatthours]

Energy source by region	2012	2020	2025	2030	2035	2040	Average annual percent change, 2012–40
OECD	**10.2**	**11.3**	**12.0**	**12.6**	**13.3**	**14.2**	**1.2**
Petroleum and other liquids	0.4	0.2	0.1	0.1	0.1	0.1	−4.1
Natural gas	2.6	2.6	3.0	3.5	4.0	4.5	2.0
Coal	3.2	3.4	3.4	3.3	3.3	3.3	0.0
Nuclear	1.9	2.1	2.2	2.3	2.3	2.2	0.7
Renewables	2.2	3.0	3.2	3.4	3.7	4.0	2.2
OECD with CPP	**10.2**	**11.3**	**11.8**	**12.5**	**13.2**	**14.0**	**1.1**
Petroleum and other liquids	0.4	0.2	0.1	0.1	0.1	0.1	−4.2
Natural gas	2.6	2.9	3.1	3.5	3.9	4.4	1.9
Coal	3.2	3.0	2.8	2.8	2.8	2.8	−0.5
Nuclear	1.9	2.1	2.2	2.3	2.3	2.2	0.6
Renewables	2.2	3.0	3.6	3.8	4.1	4.4	2.6
Non-OECD	**11.3**	**14.4**	**16.4**	**18.2**	**20.2**	**22.3**	**2.5**
Petroleum and other liquids	0.7	0.6	0.6	0.5	0.5	0.5	−1.5
Natural gas	2.2	2.6	3.3	4.0	4.8	5.6	3.4
Coal	5.4	6.3	6.7	6.8	7.0	7.3	1.1
Nuclear	0.5	0.9	1.2	1.7	2.0	2.3	5.7
Renewables	2.6	3.9	4.7	5.3	6.0	6.6	3.5
Total world	**21.6**	**25.8**	**28.4**	**30.8**	**33.6**	**36.5**	**1.9**
Petroleum and other liquids	1.1	0.9	0.7	0.6	0.6	0.6	−2.2
Natural gas	4.8	5.3	6.3	7.5	8.8	10.1	2.7
Coal	8.6	9.7	10.1	10.1	10.3	10.6	0.8
Nuclear	2.3	3.1	3.4	3.9	4.3	4.5	2.4
Renewables	4.7	6.9	7.9	8.7	9.6	10.6	2.9
Total world with CPP	**21.6**	**25.7**	**28.2**	**30.7**	**33.5**	**36.3**	**1.9**
Petroleum and other liquids	1.1	0.9	0.7	0.6	0.6	0.6	−2.2
Natural gas	4.8	5.5	6.4	7.5	8.8	10.0	2.6
Coal	8.6	9.4	9.5	9.6	9.8	10.2	0.6
Nuclear	2.3	3.1	3.4	3.9	4.2	4.5	2.3
Renewables	4.7	6.9	8.3	9.1	10.1	11.1	3.1

OECD = Organisation for Economic Cooperation and Development. CPP = U.S. Clean Power Plan.

SOURCE: "Table 5-1. OECD and Non-OECD Net Electricity Generation by Energy Source, 2012–40 (Trillion Kilowatthours)," in *International Energy Outlook 2016*, U.S. Energy Information Administration, May 2016, http://www.eia.gov/forecasts/ieo/ (accessed August 16, 2016)

FIGURE 8.8

World net electricity generation from nuclear power, by country or country category, 2012, and predicted for 2040

[Gigawatts]

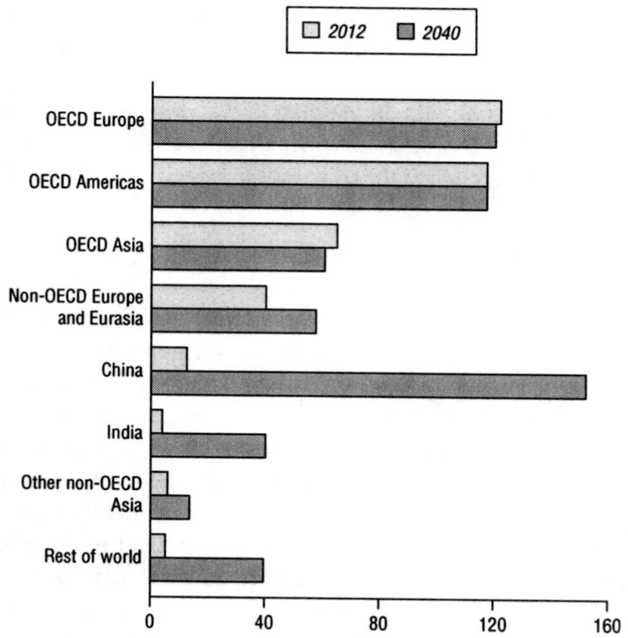

OECD = Organisation for Economic Cooperation and Development.

SOURCE: "Figure 1.8. World Nuclear Electricity Generation Capacity by Region, 2012 and 2040 (Gigawatts)," in *International Energy Outlook 2016*, U.S. Energy Information Administration, May 2016, http://www.eia.gov/forecasts/ieo/ (accessed August 16, 2016)

The combustion of coal, natural gas, and petroleum produces air contaminants, such as sulfur dioxide and carbon dioxide. Coal is especially troublesome because it burns "dirtier" than its counterparts. As shown in Figure 8.2, the United States has long been dependent on coal for its electricity generation. According to the U.S. Environmental Protection Agency (EPA), in "Cleaner Power Plants" (June 10, 2016, https://www.epa.gov/mats/cleaner-power-plants), power plants account for at least half of the nation's emissions of certain regulated pollutants:

- Acid gases—77%

- Arsenic—62%

- Sulfur dioxide—60%

- Mercury—50%

Coal-fired power plants are the main culprit when it comes to air emissions from the electric power industry. For example, in "How Much Carbon Dioxide Is Produced When Different Fuels Are Burned?" (June 14, 2016, https://www.eia.gov/tools/faqs/faq.cfm?id=73&t=11), the EIA indicates that coal combustion produces nearly twice as much carbon dioxide as natural gas combustion to generate the same amount of energy.

Since the Clean Air Act (CAA) was first passed in 1963, the United States has substantially improved its air quality by lowering contaminant emissions from multiple sources. This has been achieved through various programs that target particular pollutants or problems, such as acid rain. The EPA and state environmental agencies require certain emitters to take operational measures and use pollutant control equipment to reduce harmful emissions. For example, coal-burning power plants may be required to burn low-sulfur coal or install expensive scrubbers to wash sulfur and other contaminants from their emissions before discharging them to the air. These requirements have not been applied evenly across the industry because the CAA distinguishes between existing electric generating units (EGUs) and new EGUs. Over the decades many existing EGUs have been exempted from meeting some new and stricter air quality standards through a policy known as "grandfathering."

In 1977, when the CAA was substantially amended to tighten air quality standards on new EGUs, most of the nation's existing EGUs burned coal. These grandfathered EGUs were not required to meet the stricter standards unless and until they made certain major modifications to their infrastructure. It was assumed that the existing EGUs would inevitably make such modifications and hence lose their grandfathered status. However, this has not been the case. Although many companies have since made modifications to their existing EGUs, they have argued in court that the modifications are not major enough to trigger the stricter standards. Numerous court battles have taken place over this highly politicized issue. When government agencies sue power companies over grandfathering disputes, they are praised by environmentalists but derided by critics for waging a "war" on coal—a domestically produced fuel that is important to the nation's economy.

In 2011 the EPA and the states of Pennsylvania and New York sued the Homer City Generating Station, a large coal-fired power plant in Pennsylvania. In "Homer City Plant Sued on Emissions" (Post-Gazette.com, January 7, 2011), David Templeton and Don Hopey report the plant was constructed in 1969 with two EGUs. A third EGU was later added, and it was equipped with a scrubber as required for new units. However, the two original EGUs were operated for decades without scrubbers because they were able to meet their laxer emissions standards using other means. In the lawsuit, the EPA, Pennsylvania, and New York accused the plant of making major modifications to the two old units during the 1990s and failing to install scrubbers to meet the stricter standards that should have been triggered. However, a judge tossed out the case arguing that too much time had passed since the modifications were made. Environmentalists were sorely disappointed because the Homer City plant was alleged to be one of the nation's dirtiest power plants.

Meanwhile, in late 2011 the EPA finalized new regulations called the Mercury and Air Toxics Standards (MATS). In "Cleaner Power Plants," the agency notes, "These standards level the playing field so that all plants will have to limit their emissions of mercury as newer plants already do." MATS went into effect in 2015–16 and can be met via use of scrubbers or other specialized equipment. In addition, in 2014 the EPA won a favorable ruling from the U.S. Supreme Court regarding the agency's plan to tighten restrictions on traditional air pollutants, such as sulfur dioxide. The power plant industry, led by the owners of the Homer City plant, had bitterly fought against the new regulations. However, in *Environmental Protection Agency et al. v. EME Homer City Generation, L.P. et al.* (No. 12-1182 [2014]), the court cleared the way for the agency to proceed with its Cross-State Air Pollution Rule (https://www3.epa.gov/airtransport/CSAPR/index.html).

Installing scrubbers or other pollution control equipment, particularly at old power plants, is expensive. In addition, coal has become less economically attractive for power generation. Natural gas has surged in popularity due to domestic abundance and low prices. As a result, some power companies have chosen to retire old coal-fired EGUs rather than renovate them. This was not the case at the Homer City plant. Randy Wells reports in "Upgrade to Power Plant Seen as Boon" (IndianaGazette.com, January 11, 2012) that the plant's owners decided to install scrubbers on the two old EGUs to keep them operating.

Historically, CAA regulations have not covered carbon dioxide, which is believed to be a major contributor to global warming and associated climate change. As is noted in Chapter 1, President Obama's energy policy focuses heavily on reducing U.S. carbon emissions. A fierce political debate has raged in the United States over what, if any, action the nation should take in this regard. Critics believe that limiting carbon emissions will place an unreasonable financial burden on the electric power industry and irreparably harm the U.S. economy. In March 2012 the EPA first proposed limiting carbon emissions from newly constructed power plants. The agency revamped and reissued its proposal several times and published a final rule in August 2015. Months later, in October 2015, the EPA also finalized the Clean Power Plan rule. It would apply to existing power plants beginning in 2022.

The EPA explains in "Fact Sheet: Clean Power Plan by the Numbers" (July 14, 2016, https://www.epa.gov/cleanpowerplan/fact-sheet-clean-power-plan-numbers) that the new regulations would help lower carbon emissions from the electric power sector by 32% by 2030 compared with 2005 levels. In addition, they would reduce emissions of soot- and smog-forming contaminants by more than 20% by 2030. The EPA estimates that compliance with the new regulations could cost the power industry as much as $8.4 billion by 2030. Benefits, however, could total up to $54 billion in 2030 because of reduced climate effects and public health improvements from cleaner air. The electric power industry (particularly the coal-burning sector) and its political champions have been staunchly opposed to the regulations, which they see as unnecessarily burdensome, and have fought them in court. In February 2016 the U.S. Supreme Court suspended enforcement of the Clean Power Plan rule pending a review by a lower court of the issues involved. That review by the U.S. Court of Appeals for the District of Columbia Circuit was scheduled to begin in late September 2016. Regardless of the outcome, analysts believe the case will come before the U.S. Supreme Court again. Thus, the status of the Clean Power Plan rule as of September 2016 was uncertain.

CHAPTER 9
ENERGY CONSERVATION

The word *conservation* has different meanings depending on the context in which it is used. When referring to a resource, such as energy, to conserve means to use less of the resource. Of course, energy is a vital resource to a modern society with a growing population and a growing economy. It is a difficult proposition to use less energy and keep growing. Nevertheless, energy conservation is a national goal for the United States. For example, the government uses a variety of measures to pressure or encourage energy users to reduce their consumption of petroleum because large amounts of crude oil have to be imported from the Middle East, a region that is riddled with political insecurity and a history of poor relations with the United States. Another motivator for energy conservation lies in environmental concerns about energy sources. Historically, the government has focused on air pollutants, such as sulfur dioxide, that result from the combustion of fossil fuels and are known to damage ecosystems and human health. During the 20th century the world became aware of global warming. Scientists believe that the release of large amounts of carbon into the atmosphere has caused the earth's atmosphere to warm unnaturally. (Carbon-containing gases are also known as greenhouse gases.) Anthropogenic (human-caused) warming is occurring at an alarming rate and is precipitating climate and ecosystem changes around the world. Concern about global warming has become a new, and powerful, impetus for reducing fossil fuel combustion.

NATIONAL ENERGY CONSERVATION

At first glance, it appears that the United States has not been successful at conserving energy. Domestic energy consumption increased from 34.6 quadrillion British thermal units (Btu) in 1950 to 97.5 quadrillion Btu in 2015, an increase of 182%. (See Table 1.3 in Chapter 1.) However, this trend is not unexpected, given that the U.S. population and economy grew tremendously during this period.

National energy efficiency can be measured using two indicators. The first is energy consumption per capita (per person). According to the U.S. Energy Information Administration (EIA) within the U.S. Department of Energy (DOE), in *Monthly Energy Review: July 2016* (July 2016, http://www.eia.gov/totalenergy/data/monthly/archive/00351607.pdf), energy consumption per capita grew from 227 million Btu in 1950 to 303 million Btu in 2015, a 33% increase. Thus, energy consumption per capita grew much slower than did total energy consumption.

A second indicator of efficiency is energy consumption per dollar of gross domestic product (GDP; the total market value of final goods and services that are produced within an economy in a given year). The GDP is a measure of national economic well-being; a growing GDP over time indicates a growing and thriving economy. As shown in Figure 9.1, U.S. primary energy consumption per real dollar of GDP decreased from around 16,000 Btu in 1949 to around 6,000 Btu in 2015, a decrease of 63%.

Clearly, the United States improved its energy efficiency to a great extent between 1949 and 2015. These gains were achieved to varying degrees across all sectors: electric power, transportation, industrial, residential, and commercial. In *Monthly Energy Review: July 2016*, the EIA provides the following breakdown of the nation's 97.5 quadrillion Btu consumption of primary energy in 2015:

- Electric power sector—38.1 quadrillion Btu (39% of the total)

- Transportation sector—27.6 quadrillion Btu (28% of the total)

- Industrial sector—21.2 quadrillion Btu (22% of the total)

- Residential sector—6.5 quadrillion Btu (7% of the total)

- Commercial sector—4.1 quadrillion Btu (4% of the total)

FIGURE 9.1

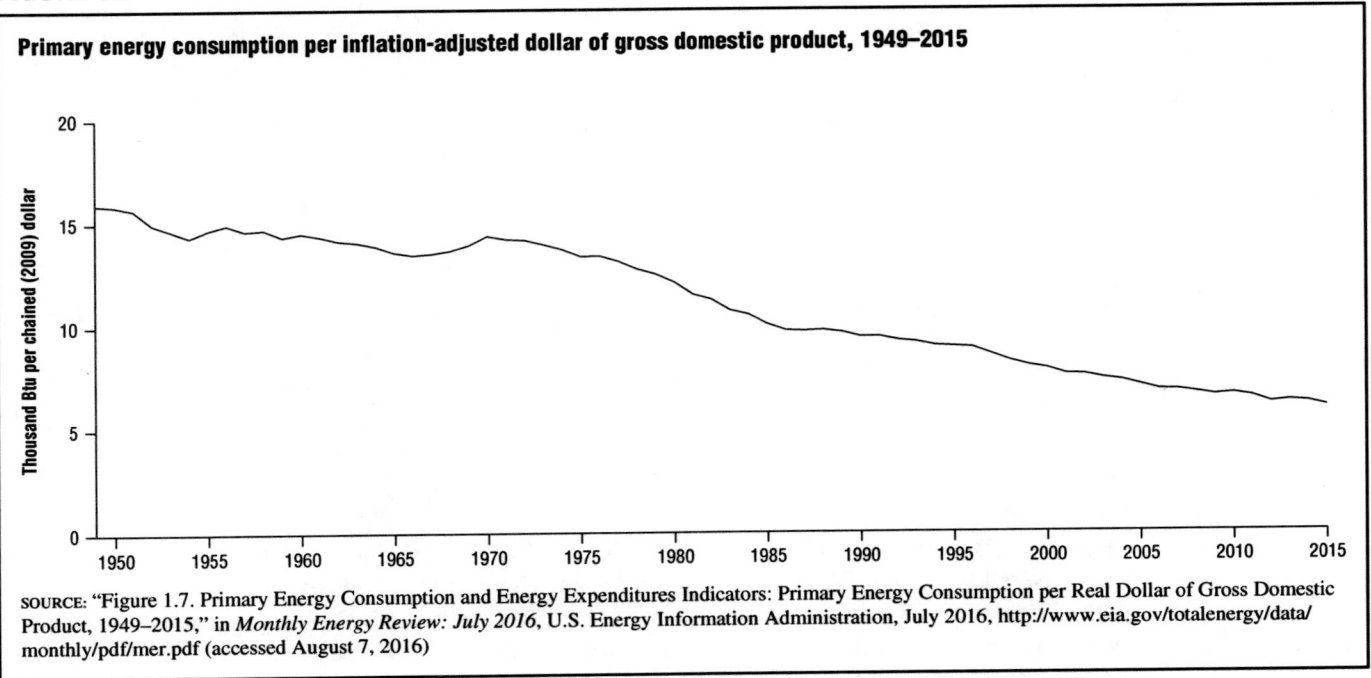

Primary energy consumption per inflation-adjusted dollar of gross domestic product, 1949–2015

SOURCE: "Figure 1.7. Primary Energy Consumption and Energy Expenditures Indicators: Primary Energy Consumption per Real Dollar of Gross Domestic Product, 1949–2015," in *Monthly Energy Review: July 2016*, U.S. Energy Information Administration, July 2016, http://www.eia.gov/totalenergy/data/monthly/pdf/mer.pdf (accessed August 7, 2016)

THE ELECTRIC POWER SECTOR

The electric power sector was the largest consumer of primary energy in 2015, accounting for 39% of the total. As is explained in Chapter 8, the sector used fossil fuels for around two-thirds of electricity generation that year (33% each from coal and natural gas, and less than 1% from petroleum and miscellaneous fossil fuel gases). Nuclear energy accounted for another 20% and renewable sources for 14% of the total. The EIA notes that net electricity generation increased from 334 billion kilowatt-hours (kWh) in 1950 to 4,087 billion kWh in 2015. (See Table 8.1 in Chapter 8.) Electricity demand has been driven by growing consumption in the residential, commercial, and industrial sectors.

The electric power sector experiences huge energy losses between inputs and outputs. As is explained in Chapter 8, around 65% of the incoming energy in 2015 was lost during generation. The sector has focused its conservation efforts on enhancing the efficiency of individual power plants and their systems. One innovation is the combined-cycle power plant, which reuses the heat leaving one turbine to boil water into steam to turn another turbine. Efficiency gains such as this have allowed the industry to generate more power using less fuel. In addition, the sector as a whole has enhanced its efficiency over time by retiring older less-efficient plants and equipment in favor of newer models.

THE TRANSPORTATION SECTOR

The U.S. transportation system plays a central role in the economy and is a major energy consumer. As noted earlier, the transportation sector accounted for 28% of total primary energy consumption in 2015. As is explained in Chapter 1, this sector's energy consumption is for vehicles whose primary purpose is transporting people and/or goods from place to place. Transportation vehicles include automobiles; trucks; buses; motorcycles; trains, subways, and other rail vehicles; aircraft; and ships, barges, and other waterborne vehicles. According to the EIA, in *Monthly Energy Review: July 2016*, Americans used 27.6 quadrillion Btu of energy for transportation in 2015, of which petroleum accounted for 25.4 quadrillion Btu, or 92% of the total.

Historical petroleum consumption by sector is shown in Figure 2.16 in Chapter 2. Between 1949 and 2015 petroleum usage by the industrial, residential and commercial, and electric power sectors was flat to declining. In contrast, petroleum consumption by the transportation sector grew from 3.4 million barrels per day (mbpd) in 1950 to 13.8 mbpd in 2015, a 306% increase. In part, this growth was due to an increasing population and more vehicles on the road. In addition, vehicle types changed dramatically during this period. The DOE's Oak Ridge National Laboratory indicates in *Transportation Energy Data Book, Edition 34* (2015, http://cta.ornl.gov/data/tedb34/Edition34_Full_Doc.pdf) that in 1975 cars had an 80.7% market share. By 2014 that percentage had dropped to 61.3% as sport-utility vehicles, minivans, and pickup trucks dominated the market. As shown in Figure 9.2, vehicles with long wheelbases have inherently poorer fuel economy than vehicles with short wheelbases. As is explained in Chapter 2, oil prices were historically low from the mid-1980s through the end of the 1990s.

FIGURE 9.2

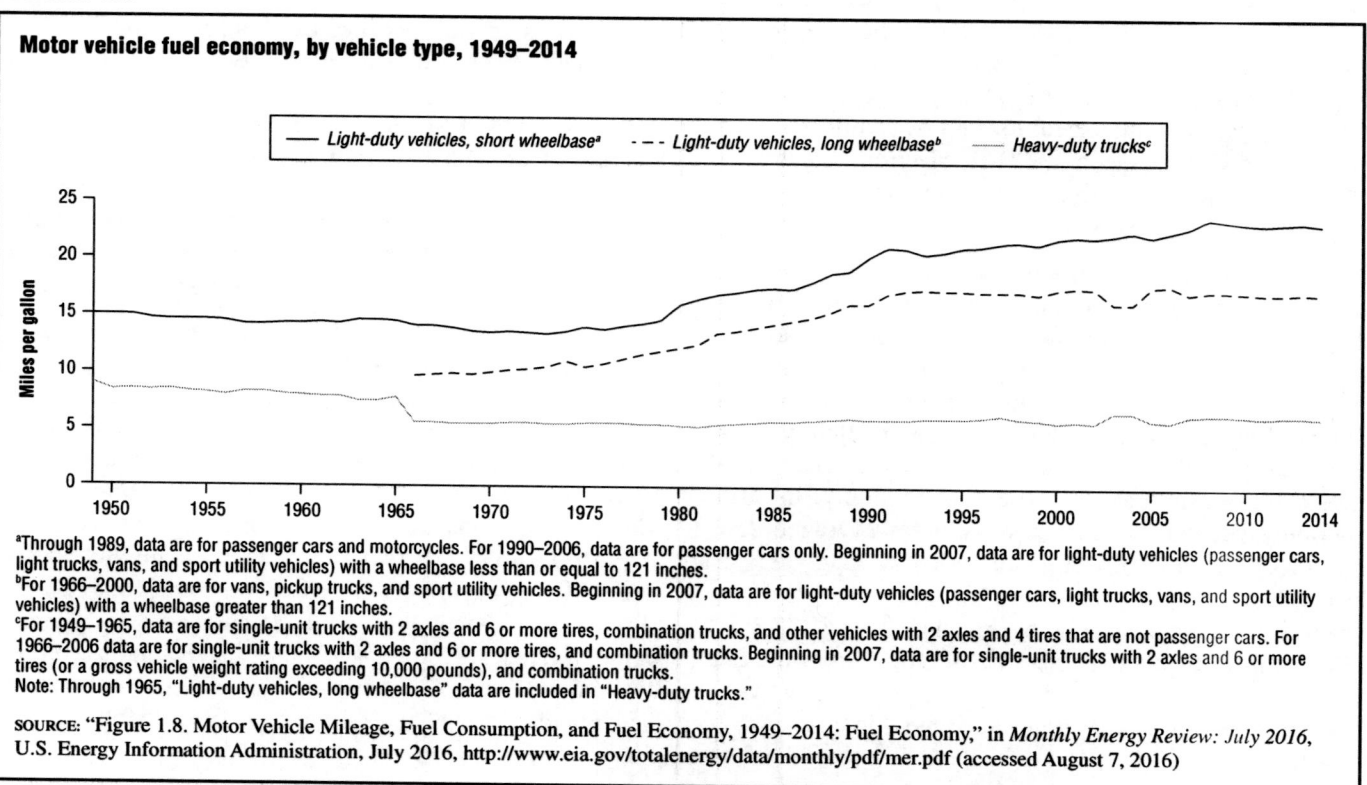

Motor vehicle fuel economy, by vehicle type, 1949–2014

— Light-duty vehicles, short wheelbase[a]   - - - Light-duty vehicles, long wheelbase[b]   ······ Heavy-duty trucks[c]

[a]Through 1989, data are for passenger cars and motorcycles. For 1990–2006, data are for passenger cars only. Beginning in 2007, data are for light-duty vehicles (passenger cars, light trucks, vans, and sport utility vehicles) with a wheelbase less than or equal to 121 inches.
[b]For 1966–2000, data are for vans, pickup trucks, and sport utility vehicles. Beginning in 2007, data are for light-duty vehicles (passenger cars, light trucks, vans, and sport utility vehicles) with a wheelbase greater than 121 inches.
[c]For 1949–1965, data are for single-unit trucks with 2 axles and 6 or more tires, combination trucks, and other vehicles with 2 axles and 4 tires that are not passenger cars. For 1966–2006 data are for single-unit trucks with 2 axles and 6 or more tires, and combination trucks. Beginning in 2007, data are for single-unit trucks with 2 axles and 6 or more tires (or a gross vehicle weight rating exceeding 10,000 pounds), and combination trucks.
Note: Through 1965, "Light-duty vehicles, long wheelbase" data are included in "Heavy-duty trucks."

SOURCE: "Figure 1.8. Motor Vehicle Mileage, Fuel Consumption, and Fuel Economy, 1949–2014: Fuel Economy," in *Monthly Energy Review: July 2016*, U.S. Energy Information Administration, July 2016, http://www.eia.gov/totalenergy/data/monthly/pdf/mer.pdf (accessed August 7, 2016)

During this period Americans bought and drove larger vehicles to satisfy their personal preferences. This highlights the huge influence that market prices have on consumer demand and shows how difficult it can be to get consumers to conserve oil by their own accord.

Government Intervention

Chapter 2 describes the energy crisis (actually an oil crisis) that stunned the nation during the early 1970s. The political and economic consequences of the United States' dependence on foreign oil spurred government actions to reduce domestic oil consumption, particularly in the transportation sector. In *Saving Energy in U.S. Transportation* (July 1994, http://govinfo.library.unt .edu/ota/Ota_1/DATA/1994/9432.PDF), the Office of Technology Assessment lists the types of conservation measures that government entities have used over the years:

- Require vehicles to have higher fuel economy

- Design highways to optimize traffic flow and reduce fuel consumption

- Impose higher taxes on petroleum fuels and/or low-fuel-economy vehicles

- Use tax credits and subsidies to support research and development devoted to petroleum conservation

- Pass regulations requiring stricter inspection and maintenance programs for vehicles

- Encourage carpooling and working from home

- Add and improve mass transit options

- Mandate the use of alternative-fuel (nonpetroleum) vehicles and alternative fuels

- Offer tax credits and other financial incentives to encourage petroleum conservation by consumers

Not all the measures are mutually supportive. For example, efforts to promote a freer flow of automobile traffic, such as high-occupancy vehicle lanes or free parking for carpools, may sabotage efforts to shift travelers to mass transit or reduce trip lengths and frequency.

FUEL ECONOMY STANDARDS. Of all the measures that the federal government uses to enhance oil conservation, the most well-known and perhaps most controversial are fuel economy standards. These standards represent a high level of government intervention in private markets. In 1975 the Energy Policy and Conservation Act set the initial Corporate Average Fuel Economy (CAFE) standards; since then, the standards have been modified numerous times.

The first CAFE standards required domestic automakers to increase the average mileage of new cars sold to 27.5 miles per gallon (mpg; 8.6 L/100 km) by 1985. Manufacturers could still sell large, less-efficient cars, but to meet the average fuel efficiency rates, they also had to sell smaller, more efficient cars. Automakers that failed to meet each year's standards were fined; those that managed to surpass the rates earned credits they could use in years when they fell below the requirements. Even while keeping some models relatively large and roomy, the manufacturers managed to improve mileage with innovations such as electronic fuel injection, which supplied fuel to an automotive engine more efficiently than its predecessor, the carburetor.

Over the decades more demanding CAFE standards have helped raise the national average fuel economy. As shown in Figure 9.2, highway vehicles are divided by duty and wheelbase. Light-duty vehicles include cars, sport-utility vehicles, and minivans, while heavy-duty vehicles include tractor trailers, buses, and delivery vans. Historically, light-duty vehicles with short wheelbases have achieved the best (highest) fuel economy. In 2014 light-duty vehicles with short wheelbases averaged 23.2 mpg (10.1 L/100 km), compared with 17.1 mpg (13.8 L/100 km) for light-duty vehicles with long wheelbases. By contrast, heavy-duty trucks averaged 6.3 mpg (37.3 L/100 km) in 2014. In 2010 new CAFE standards were the first to be attribute-based, meaning that they vary depending on specific vehicle attributes, in this case a vehicle's footprint (i.e., the surface area between all of its wheels). Thus, attribute-based CAFE standards vary by vehicle model.

In the press release "Obama Administration Finalizes Historic 54.5 MPG Fuel Efficiency Standards" (http://www.whitehouse.gov/the-press-office/2012/08/28/obama-administration-finalizes-historic-545-mpg-fuel-efficiency-standard), the White House notes that in August 2012 the administration of President Barack Obama (1961–) finalized fuel economy standards that will require model year 2025 cars and light-duty trucks to achieve the equivalent of 54.5 mpg (4.3 L/100 km).

THE INDUSTRIAL SECTOR

The industrial sector operates facilities and equipment that are devoted to producing, processing, or assembling goods. As is noted in Chapter 1, the major energy uses by this sector are for process heat and for cooling and powering machinery. The sector was the third-largest consumer of primary energy in 2015, accounting for 22% of the total. Natural gas and petroleum were the major energy sources used by the sector in 2015. (See Figure 1.5 in Chapter 1.) Electricity, coal, and renewable sources played smaller roles. The annual energy consumption increased dramatically between 1949 and 1970, but has been relatively flat since then. The industrial sector has reduced its energy usage through efficiency improvements to machines and processes. Another major component of industrial energy conservation has been the on-site production of combined heat and power (CHP).

Combined Heat and Power

Many industrial facilities use both heat and electricity in their processes. The electricity can be purchased from a local utility, while fuel can be purchased and burned on-site to produce heat, for example, to boil water to make steam. Great efficiency gains can be achieved by performing both these tasks on-site through a CHP plant. A CHP plant is basically a small power plant that burns fuel to generate electricity; the leftover heat can be used to boil water for steam or for other industrial purposes.

In August 2012 President Obama issued the executive order "Accelerating Investment in Industrial Energy Efficiency" (http://www.whitehouse.gov/the-press-office/2012/08/30/executive-order-accelerating-investment-industrial-energy-efficiency), which set a national goal of achieving 40 gigawatts of new CHP capacity over the coming decade. The EIA indicates in *Annual Energy Outlook 2016 with Projections to 2040* (http://www.eia.gov/forecasts/aeo/pdf/0383(2016).pdf) that as of August 2016, 11 states (Arizona, Connecticut, Maine, Michigan, New Hampshire, New York, North Carolina, Pennsylvania, Vermont, Washington, and Wisconsin) included CHP options in their mandatory (enforceable) renewable portfolio standards or similar laws.

THE RESIDENTIAL AND COMMERCIAL SECTORS

The residential and commercial sectors are often lumped together in discussions of energy conservation because their energy consumption is similar. The primary energy uses for both sectors are for space heating, water heating, air conditioning, lighting, refrigeration, cooking, and running appliances and other equipment.

As noted earlier, the two sectors combined accounted for 11% of primary energy consumption in 2015. Figure 1.4 and Figure 1.6 in Chapter 1 indicate that the sectors mainly consumed natural gas and electricity in 2015. Petroleum, coal, and renewable energy sources were minor energy sources. As shown in both figures, the overall energy consumption for both sectors increased between 1949 and 2015, especially for electricity. Natural gas consumption has been relatively flat for several decades. Figure 8.3 in Chapter 8 shows that the residential and commercial sectors were the largest users of electricity in 2015, accounting for 2,758 billion kWh, or 74% of total electricity retail sales.

Total energy use in these two sectors has increased over the years because the number of people, households, and offices has increased. In addition, people are using ever larger amounts of electronic gadgets, such as computers, printers, televisions, and copiers. However, increased energy demand has been offset somewhat by efficiency gains in equipment and in building efficiency. Also, many people have migrated to the South and West, where their combined use of heating and cooling has generally been lower than in other parts of the country.

Efficiency Gains

Energy conservation in buildings in both the residential and commercial sectors has improved considerably since the early 1980s. Among the techniques for reducing energy use are advanced window designs, "daylighting" (letting light in from the outside by adding a skylight or building a large building around an atrium), solar water heating, landscaping, and planting trees. Residential energy conservation is enhanced by building more efficient new housing and appliances, improving energy efficiency in existing housing, and building more multifamily units.

Efforts to enhance building energy efficiency are driven by various factors, including the desire of building owners to reduce their energy costs. The government also plays a role. The American Recovery and Reinvestment Act, which was passed in 2009, included billions of taxpayer dollars for grants and other programs devoted to improving the energy efficiency of residences and commercial and government buildings. In February 2011 President Obama (http://www.whitehouse.gov/the-press-office/2011/ 02/03/president-obama-s-plan-win-future-making-american-businesses-more-energy) launched his Better Buildings Initiative with the goal of making commercial and industrial buildings 20% more energy efficient by 2020. It was later expanded to include multifamily housing and government buildings. In "Fact Sheet: Administration Announces New Actions and Progress Made to Make American Buildings More Efficient and Save Businesses and Households on Their Energy Bills" (May 11, 2016, https://www.whitehouse .gov/the-press-office/2016/05/11/fact-sheet-administration-announces-new-actions-and-progress-made-make), the White House notes that more than 750 organizations around the country were participating in the initiative as of 2016 and more than $10 billion in public- and private-sector money had been committed to energy efficiency projects. In addition, six companies and five government entities (including the state of Delaware) had improved their energy efficiency by at least 20% in five years.

APPLIANCES AND LIGHTING. In 1987 Congress passed the National Appliance Energy Conservation Act, which gave the DOE the authority to formulate minimum efficiency requirements for 13 classes of consumer products. It can also revise and update these standards as technologies and economic conditions change. Energy efficiency has increased for all major household appliances but most dramatically for refrigerators and freezers because of better insulation, motors, and compressors. In addition, efficiency labels are now required on appliances, which makes purchasing efficient models easier for consumers.

The Energy Independence and Security Act of 2007 mandated the gradual phasing out of many incandescent lightbulbs. These bulbs feature a wire filament that generates light and heat when an electric current passes through it. They have been in use for decades and are far less efficient than more modern designs, such as compact fluorescent lightbulbs, halogen bulbs, and light-emitting diode bulbs. The EPA provides in "Energy Independence and Security Act of 2007 (EISA): Frequently Asked Questions" (2011, http://www.energystar.gov/ia/products/lighting/cfls/ downloads/EISA_Backgrounder_FINAL_4-11_EPA.pdf? 6bd2-3775) the phaseout schedule and lists the types of incandescent bulbs affected. As of January 1, 2014, the domestic manufacture of 100-watt, 75-watt, 60-watt, and 40-watt incandescent lightbulbs had been discontinued.

TAX PREFERENCES. As is shown in Table 1.6 in Chapter 1, the federal government supplied $2.7 billion in tax preferences for energy efficiency in fiscal year 2015. The largest amount within the energy efficiency category was $1.2 billion, which was directed at incorporating energy-efficiency improvements into existing homes. Overall, the federal government's tax preferences devoted to energy efficiency accounted for 17% of the total amount allocated to energy that year. (See Figure 1.15 in Chapter 1.)

THE DOMESTIC OUTLOOK

U.S. total energy consumption is expected to increase at an average annual rate of 0.4% between 2015 and 2040. (See Table 1.8 in Chapter 1.) Increases in demand are projected to be offset in part by efficiency gains. In *Annual Energy Outlook 2016 with Projections to 2040*, the EIA predicts that federal and state mandates and incentives will continue to push more efficient technologies and processes. Energy consumption per capita and energy consumption per dollar of GDP are expected to decrease through 2040 even as the nation's population, GDP, and total energy consumption increase. The EIA mentions several factors that it believes will contribute to energy efficiency through 2040, including efficiency gains in appliances, retirement of older less-efficient power plants, and stricter environmental regulations.

INTERNATIONAL COMPARISONS OF CONSERVATION EFFORTS

The International Energy Agency (IEA; http://www .iea.org/about/) is an independent member organization devoted to energy issues. As of 2016, it had 29 member countries, including the United States and other developed nations. The IEA, like many international organizations, uses the unit tonne of oil equivalent (toe) when discussing large energy amounts. One toe is the amount of energy released when 1 tonne (1.1 ton) of oil is burned. Different kinds of oil have varying heat contents, so the exact conversion factors used can vary by organization.

In *Key World Energy Statistics: 2016* (September 2016, http://www.iea.org/publications/freepublications/

publication/KeyWorld2016.pdf), the IEA compares countries based on their total primary energy supply (TPES). As noted earlier, one indicator of a country's energy efficiency is the amount of energy it consumes per capita. According to the IEA, worldwide energy supply per capita in 2014 was 1.89 toe per person. The values for some major countries were as follows: United States (6.94 toe/capita), Russian Federation (4.94), and China (2.24).

Another measure of national energy efficiency is the amount of energy a country consumes for every dollar of goods and services it produces. According to the IEA, the world had 0.19 TPES per dollar (in 2010 U.S. dollars) of GDP in 2014. The United States had 0.14 TPES per dollar (in 2010 U.S. dollars) of GDP, compared with 0.42 TPES per dollar for the Russian Federation and 0.37 TPES per dollar for China.

ENERGY CONSERVATION AND GLOBAL WARMING
Greenhouse Gases

The EPA publishes an annual report on the nation's emissions of greenhouse gases (gases that contribute to global warming). For comparison, the EPA converts the emission amounts of different gases from different sources into units of teragrams of carbon dioxide equivalent (Tg CO_2 Eq.). The agency indicates in *Inventory of U.S. Greenhouse Gas Emissions and Sinks: 1990–2014* (April 15, 2016, https://www.epa.gov/sites/production/files/2016-04/documents/us-ghg-inventory-2016-main-text.pdf) that energy accounted for almost all of U.S. greenhouse gas emissions between 1990 and 2014. (See Figure 9.3.) As shown in Figure 9.4, fossil fuel combustion was, by far, the leading source of the emissions within the energy sector. Figure 9.5 provides a breakdown of the carbon flows for fossil fuels in 2014. Most of the emissions resulted from combustion; small amounts occurred when fossil fuels were used for nonenergy purposes, for example, as feedstock for products such as plastics or asphalt. Overall, the combustion emissions by fossil fuel were:

- Petroleum—2,128 Tg CO_2 Eq., or 39% of the total
- Coal—1,654 Tg CO_2 Eq., or 30% of the total
- Natural gas—1,427 Tg CO_2 Eq., or 26% of the total

As shown in Figure 9.4, 83.6% of U.S. greenhouse gas emissions in 2014 were energy-related emissions. Nearly all of these emissions were carbon dioxide

FIGURE 9.3

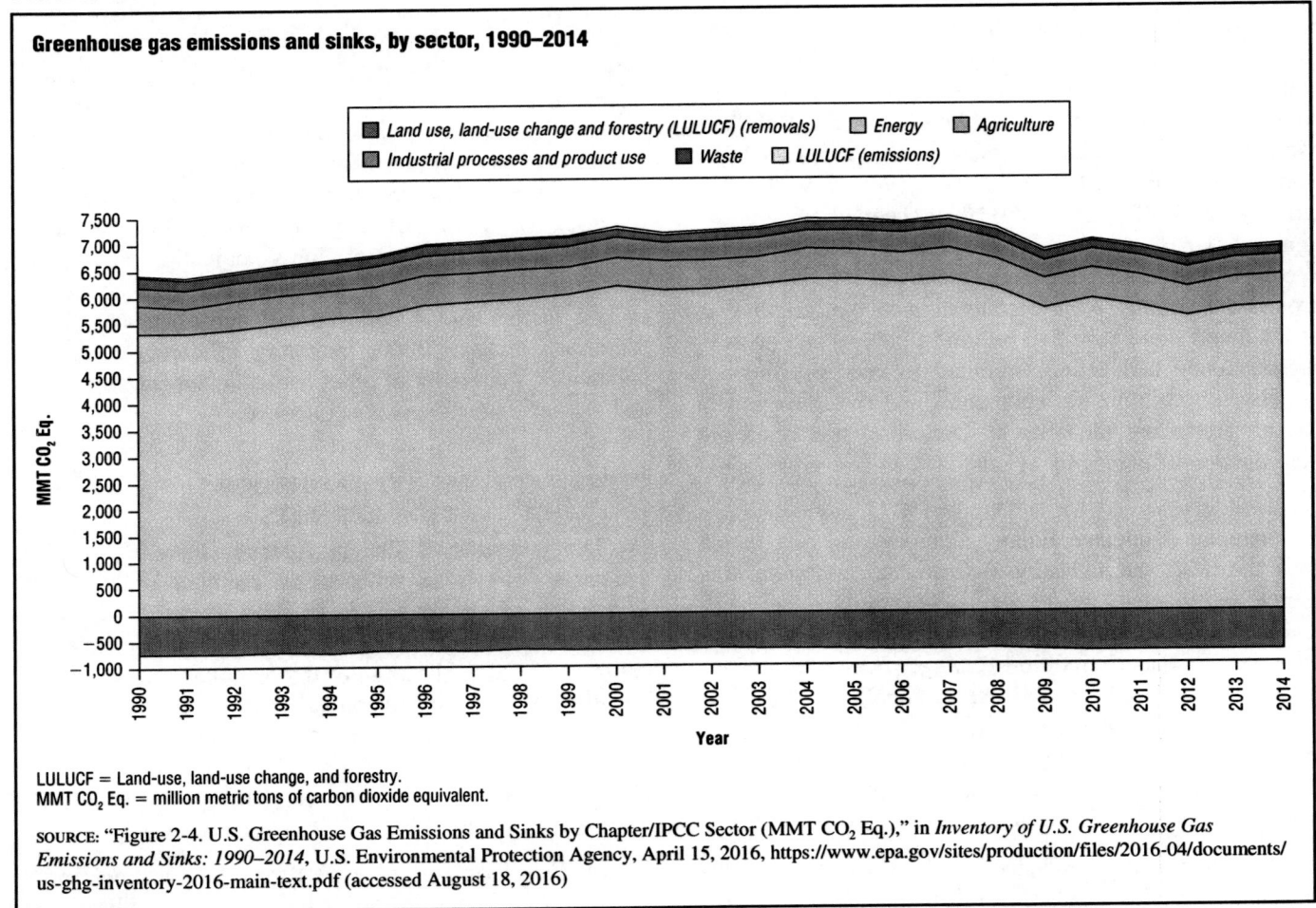

Greenhouse gas emissions and sinks, by sector, 1990–2014

LULUCF = Land-use, land-use change, and forestry.
MMT CO$_2$ Eq. = million metric tons of carbon dioxide equivalent.

SOURCE: "Figure 2-4. U.S. Greenhouse Gas Emissions and Sinks by Chapter/IPCC Sector (MMT CO$_2$ Eq.)," in *Inventory of U.S. Greenhouse Gas Emissions and Sinks: 1990–2014*, U.S. Environmental Protection Agency, April 15, 2016, https://www.epa.gov/sites/production/files/2016-04/documents/us-ghg-inventory-2016-main-text.pdf (accessed August 18, 2016)

FIGURE 9.4

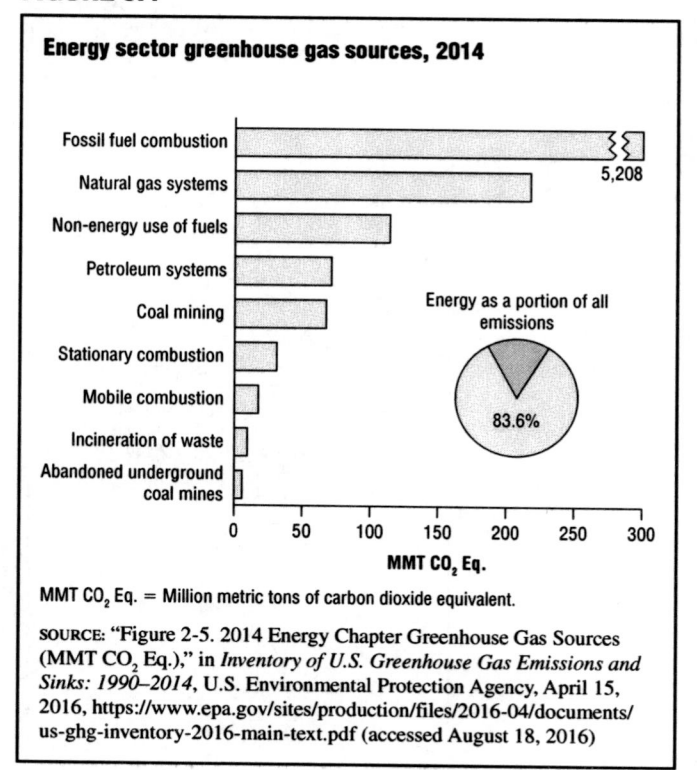

Energy sector greenhouse gas sources, 2014

Energy as a portion of all emissions

83.6%

MMT CO$_2$ Eq. = Million metric tons of carbon dioxide equivalent.

SOURCE: "Figure 2-5. 2014 Energy Chapter Greenhouse Gas Sources (MMT CO$_2$ Eq.)," in *Inventory of U.S. Greenhouse Gas Emissions and Sinks: 1990–2014*, U.S. Environmental Protection Agency, April 15, 2016, https://www.epa.gov/sites/production/files/2016-04/documents/us-ghg-inventory-2016-main-text.pdf (accessed August 18, 2016)

emissions from fossil fuel combustion. Table 9.1 and Figure 9.6 provide breakdowns of U.S. energy-related carbon dioxide emissions by major fuel and economic sector, respectively, between 1973 and 2015. In 2015 petroleum accounted for more of the carbon dioxide emissions (2,518 million tons [2,284 million t]) than did coal (1,638 million tons [1,486 million t]) or natural gas (1,631 million tons [1,480 million t]). The breakdown in Figure 9.6 is for primary energy consumers. It should be noted that emissions from energy consumption in the electric power sector are allocated to the end-use sectors in proportion to each sector's share of total electricity retail sales.

The U.S. government has focused much of its greenhouse gas reduction efforts on the electric power and transportation sectors because they are such large emitters.

THE ELECTRIC POWER SECTOR. Table 9.2 provides a historical breakdown of carbon dioxide emissions from energy consumption by the electric power sector. Coal has historically accounted for the vast majority of the emissions. In 2015 coal emissions from the electric power sector totaled 1,491 million tons (1,353 million t), or 71% of the sector's total of 2,115 million tons (1,919 million t). Environmental concerns about coal-fired power plants are discussed at length in Chapter 8. That chapter also notes that in August 2015 the EPA finalized regulations limiting carbon emissions from

newly constructed power plants. In October 2015 the agency finalized similar limits on existing power plants through its Clean Power Plan rule. This rule, however, met with fierce resistance and was challenged in court. As of September 2016, its status was uncertain.

THE TRANSPORTATION SECTOR. Table 9.3 provides a historical breakdown of carbon dioxide emissions from energy consumption by the transportation sector. Petroleum has historically accounted for the vast majority of the emissions. In 2015 petroleum emissions from the transportation sector totaled 2,001 million tons (1,815 million t), or 97% of the sector's total of 2,059 million tons (1,868 million t). Among petroleum products, motor gasoline was responsible for most of the emissions. As noted earlier, ever-tighter CAFE standards have been implemented by the federal government over the decades to improve the nation's average fuel economy (miles per gallon of motor fuel). In 2010 and 2012 the EPA issued companion standards limiting carbon dioxide emissions from new vehicles. Under these standards, model year 2025 automobiles are required to have an average fuel economy of 56.2 mpg (4.2 L/100 km) and emit no more than 143 grams of carbon dioxide per mile.

In 2011 the EPA and the National Highway Traffic Safety Administration within the U.S. Department of Transportation finalized the first fuel economy and carbon dioxide emissions limits for non-light-duty highway vehicles, such as large pickup trucks, tractor trailers, and buses, for 2014 to 2018. The agencies indicate in *EPA and NHTSA Adopt Standards to Reduce Greenhouse Gas Emissions and Improve Fuel Efficiency of Medium- and Heavy-Duty Vehicles for Model Year 2018 and Beyond* (https://www3.epa.gov/otaq/climate/documents/420f16044.pdf) that in August 2016 the standards were extended to 2027. Not all the standards apply to all vehicle types, and the standards vary based on vehicle attributes, such as engine classifications.

The Domestic Outlook

The EIA predicts in *Annual Energy Outlook 2016 with Projections to 2040* domestic energy-related carbon dioxide emissions through 2040 for various scenarios. (See Figure 9.7.) The agency notes that the reference scenario is a "business-as-usual trend estimate, given known technology and technological and demographic trends." The extended policies scenario assumes that the government will put into place more extensive subsidies and tax credits and continue to tighten equipment and building efficiency and fuel economy standards. Both scenarios present a decreasing outlook for energy-related carbon dioxide emissions through 2030. Beyond that point, emissions are expected to continue to decline for the extended policies scenario, but flatten and grow slightly for the reference scenario.

FIGURE 9.5

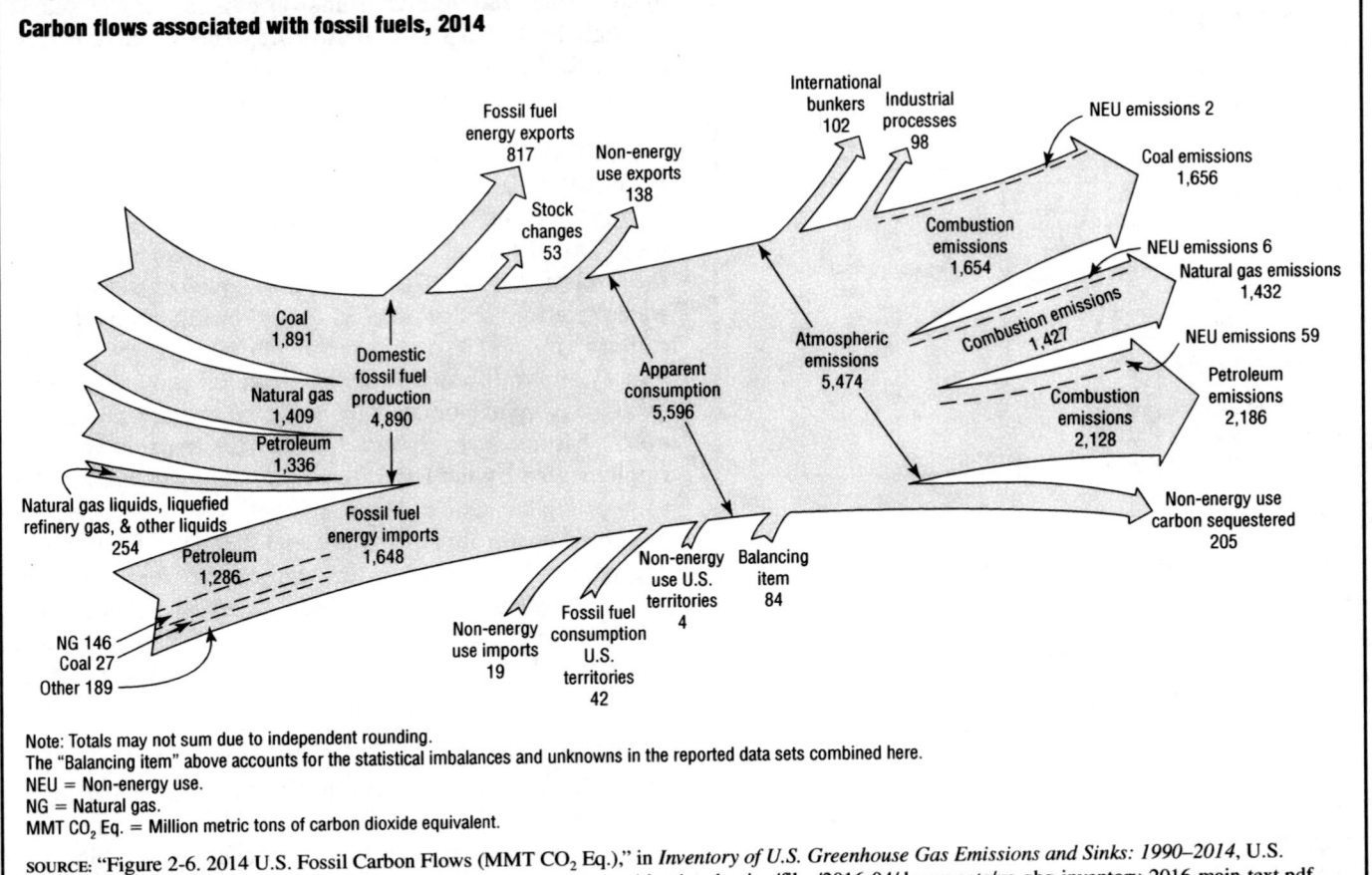

Carbon flows associated with fossil fuels, 2014

Note: Totals may not sum due to independent rounding.
The "Balancing item" above accounts for the statistical imbalances and unknowns in the reported data sets combined here.
NEU = Non-energy use.
NG = Natural gas.
MMT CO_2 Eq. = Million metric tons of carbon dioxide equivalent.

SOURCE: "Figure 2-6. 2014 U.S. Fossil Carbon Flows (MMT CO_2 Eq.)," in *Inventory of U.S. Greenhouse Gas Emissions and Sinks: 1990–2014*, U.S. Environmental Protection Agency, April 15, 2016, https://www.epa.gov/sites/production/files/2016-04/documents/us-ghg-inventory-2016-main-text.pdf (accessed August 18, 2016)

The Worldwide Outlook

As noted in previous chapters, worldwide energy production is highly dependent on fossil fuel combustion, particularly in developing countries, such as China and India. Therefore, world energy-related carbon dioxide emissions are expected to continue to increase through 2040. (See Figure 9.8.) The EIA predicts in *International Energy Outlook 2016* (May 2016, http://www.eia.gov/forecasts/ieo/pdf/0484(2016).pdf) that worldwide emissions will grow from 35.6 billion tons (32.3 billion t) in 2012 to 47.6 billion tons (43.2 billion t) in 2040, an increase of 34%. Most of the carbon dioxide emissions in 2040 are expected to be from the use of coal for energy production. The combustion of liquid fuels (such as petroleum) and natural gas are predicted to cause lower emissions in comparison to coal. Coal emissions skyrocketed during the first decade of the 21st century and through 2012. This was due in large part to extensive coal consumption in China. (See Figure 9.9.) However, as Chinese coal consumption peaks and levels off in the early 2020s, carbon dioxide emissions associated with coal are projected to grow less quickly, as shown in Figure 9.8.

INTERNATIONAL EFFORTS TO CURB CARBON EMISSIONS. Concern about global warming has spurred many efforts by diplomats and politicians to draw up agreements that would bind countries to certain carbon emissions limits or reductions over time. These efforts date back to 1988, when the United Nations (UN) established the Intergovernmental Panel on Climate Change (IPCC), a group of hundreds of the world's leading scientists. Since that time the IPCC has issued several reports (http://www.ipcc.ch/publications_and_data/publications _and_data_reports.htm) on its findings, including the causes and consequences of global warming and climate change. In addition, it has continually urged governments to move quickly with policies to protect the planet. This has proved to be a near impossible task.

In 1997 the UN convened a 160-nation conference on global warming in Kyoto, Japan, to develop a treaty on climate change that would place binding caps on industrial emissions. The resulting agreement, known as the Kyoto Protocol, bound industrialized nations to reducing their emissions of six greenhouse gases by 2012 to below 1990 levels. The United States refused to be a party to the Kyoto Protocol mostly because the protocol did not apply

TABLE 9.1

Carbon dioxide emissions from energy consumption, by source, selected years 1973–2015

[Million metric tons of carbon dioxide[a]]

									Petroleum					
	Coal[b]	Natural gas[c]	Aviation gasoline	Distillate fuel oil[d]	Jet fuel	Kerosene	LPG[e]	Lubricants	Motor gasoline[f]	Petroleum coke	Residual fuel oil	Other[g]	Total	Total[h, i]
1973 Total	1,207	1,178	6	480	155	32	92	13	911	54	508	100	2,350	4,735
1975 Total	1,181	1,046	5	443	146	24	82	11	911	51	443	97	2,212	4,439
1980 Total	1,436	1,061	4	446	156	24	87	13	900	49	453	142	2,275	4,771
1985 Total	1,638	926	3	445	178	17	87	12	930	54	216	93	2,036	4,600
1990 Total	1,821	1,024	3	470	223	6	67	13	988	70	220	127	2,187	5,039
1995 Total	1,913	1,183	3	498	222	8	80	13	1,045	76	152	121	2,216	5,323
1996 Total	1,995	1,204	3	524	232	9	86	12	1,063	79	152	139	2,300	5,510
1997 Total	2,040	1,210	3	534	234	10	87	13	1,075	80	142	145	2,323	5,584
1998 Total	2,064	1,189	2	537	238	12	82	14	1,107	93	158	128	2,372	5,635
1999 Total	2,062	1,193	3	555	245	11	90	14	1,128	96	148	133	2,422	5,688
2000 Total	2,155	1,243	3	579	254	10	97	14	1,136	86	163	118	2,459	5,868
2001 Total	2,088	1,188	2	597	243	11	88	13	1,152	89	144	135	2,474	5,761
2002 Total	2,095	1,227	2	586	237	6	91	12	1,183	96	125	130	2,470	5,804
2003 Total	2,136	1,193	2	610	231	8	87	11	1,187	96	138	142	2,513	5,853
2004 Total	2,160	1,200	2	632	240	10	87	12	1,210	107	155	144	2,598	5,970
2005 Total	2,182	1,183	2	639	246	10	84	12	1,209	106	165	143	2,617	5,993
2006 Total	2,147	1,167	2	645	240	8	80	11	1,217	106	122	152	2,584	5,910
2007 Total	2,172	1,241	2	647	238	5	83	12	1,211	100	128	150	2,576	6,001
2008 Total	2,140	1,248	2	610	226	2	79	11	1,143	93	110	132	2,409	5,809
2009 Total	1,876	1,225	2	559	204	3	78	10	1,129	87	90	112	2,273	5,386
2010 Total	1,986	1,286	2	585	210	3	79	11	1,112	82	93	122	2,299	5,582
2011 Total	1,876	1,305	2	599	209	2	78	10	1,078	79	79	117	2,252	5,445
2012 Total	1,657	1,363	2	574	206	1	81	9	1,071	79	65	113	2,200	5,232
2013 Total	1,718	1,400	2	581	210	1	88	10	1,087	77	56	119	2,231	5,360
2014 Total	1,713	1,434	2	614	216	1	83	10	1,095	76	45	110	2,252	5,411
2015 Total	1,486	1,480	1	604	226	1	82	11	1,123	77	46	115	2,284	5,262

[a]Metric tons of carbon dioxide can be converted to metric tons of carbon equivalent by multiplying by 12/44.
[b]Includes coal coke net imports.
[c]Natural gas, excluding supplemental gaseous fuels.
[d]Distillate fuel oil, excluding biodiesel.
[e]Liquefied petroleum gases.
[f]Finished motor gasoline, excluding fuel ethanol.
[g]Aviation gasoline blending components, crude oil, motor gasoline blending components, pentanes plus, petrochemical feedstocks, special naphthas, still gas, unfinished oils, waxes, and miscellaneous petroleum products.
[h]Includes electric power sector use of geothermal energy and non-biomass waste.
[i]Excludes emissions from biomass energy consumption.
Notes: Data are estimates for carbon dioxide emissions from energy consumption, including the nonfuel use of fossil fuels. Data exclude emissions from biomass energy consumption. Totals may not equal sum of components due to independent rounding. Geographic coverage is the 50 states and the District of Columbia.

SOURCE: Adapted from "Table 12.1. Carbon Dioxide Emissions from Energy Consumption by Source (Million Metric Tons of Carbon Dioxide)," in *Monthly Energy Review: July 2016*, U.S. Energy Information Administration, July 2016, http://www.eia.gov/totalenergy/data/monthly/pdf/mer.pdf (accessed August 7, 2016)

to developing nations such as China. Some of the nations covered by the agreement found it impossible to meet their limits, sometimes by wide margins. International meetings convened since the late 1990s have struggled to develop new agreements that are acceptable to developed and developing nations alike.

In December 2015, however, a UN Climate Change Conference held in Paris resulted in an international agreement that included pledges to cut carbon emissions by 2030. In "Breakthrough as US and China Agree to Ratify Paris Climate Deal" (Guardian.com, September 3, 2016), Tom Phillips, Fiona Harvey, and Alan Yuhas indicate that the agreement "must be ratified by 55 countries, representing 55% of global emissions, in order to come into force." That outcome seemed much more likely in early September 2016, after the United States and China agreed to ratify the accord. The decision for the United States was made by President Obama. Nevertheless, with a new presidential administration taking office in January 2017, it was unclear as of September 2016 if the new administration would also agree to abide by the agreement.

FIGURE 9.6

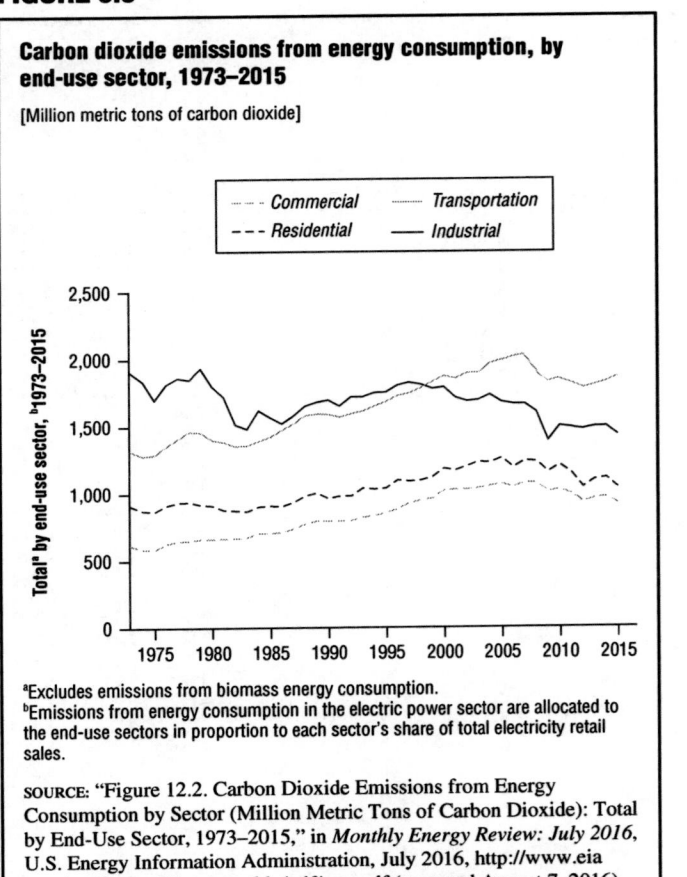

Carbon dioxide emissions from energy consumption, by end-use sector, 1973–2015

[Million metric tons of carbon dioxide]

Legend:
- Commercial
- Residential
- Transportation
- Industrial

(y-axis: Total[a] by end-use sector,[b] 1973–2015; values 0, 500, 1,000, 1,500, 2,000, 2,500; x-axis: 1975, 1980, 1985, 1990, 1995, 2000, 2005, 2010, 2015)

[a]Excludes emissions from biomass energy consumption.
[b]Emissions from energy consumption in the electric power sector are allocated to the end-use sectors in proportion to each sector's share of total electricity retail sales.

SOURCE: "Figure 12.2. Carbon Dioxide Emissions from Energy Consumption by Sector (Million Metric Tons of Carbon Dioxide): Total by End-Use Sector, 1973–2015," in *Monthly Energy Review: July 2016*, U.S. Energy Information Administration, July 2016, http://www.eia .gov/totalenergy/data/monthly/pdf/mer.pdf (accessed August 7, 2016)

TABLE 9.2

Carbon dioxide emissions from energy consumption by the electric power sector, selected years 1973–2015

[Million metric tons of carbon dioxide[a]]

	Coal	Natural gas[b]	Petroleum Distillate fuel oil[c]	Petroleum Petroleum coke	Petroleum Residual fuel oil	Petroleum Total	Geothermal	Non-biomass waste[d]	Total[e]
1973 Total	812	199	20	2	254	276	NA	NA	1,286
1975 Total	824	172	17	(s)	231	248	NA	NA	1,244
1980 Total	1,137	200	12	1	194	207	NA	NA	1,544
1985 Total	1,367	166	6	1	79	86	NA	NA	1,619
1990 Total	1,548	176	7	3	92	102	(s)	6	1,831
1995 Total	1,661	228	8	8	45	61	(s)	10	1,960
1996 Total	1,752	205	8	8	50	66	(s)	10	2,033
1997 Total	1,797	219	8	10	56	75	(s)	10	2,101
1998 Total	1,828	248	10	13	82	105	(s)	10	2,192
1999 Total	1,836	260	10	11	76	97	(s)	10	2,204
2000 Total	1,927	281	13	10	69	91	(s)	10	2,310
2001 Total	1,870	290	12	11	79	102	(s)	11	2,273
2002 Total	1,890	306	9	18	52	79	(s)	13	2,288
2003 Total	1,931	278	12	18	69	98	(s)	11	2,319
2004 Total	1,943	297	8	22	69	99	(s)	11	2,350
2005 Total	1,984	319	8	24	69	101	(s)	11	2,416
2006 Total	1,954	338	5	21	28	55	(s)	12	2,358
2007 Total	1,987	372	6	17	31	54	(s)	11	2,425
2008 Total	1,959	362	5	15	19	39	(s)	12	2,373
2009 Total	1,741	373	5	13	14	33	(s)	11	2,158
2010 Total	1,828	399	6	14	12	32	(s)	11	2,270
2011 Total	1,723	409	5	14	7	26	(s)	11	2,170
2012 Total	1,511	493	4	9	6	19	(s)	11	2,034
2013 Total	1,571	444	4	13	6	23	(s)	11	2,050
2014 Total	1,569	444	6	12	7	26	(s)	11	2,050
2015 Total	1,353	530	5	11	7	24	(s)	11	1,919

[a]Metric tons of carbon dioxide can be converted to metric tons of carbon equivalent by multiplying by 12/44.
[b]Natural gas, excluding supplemental gaseous fuels.
[c]Distillate fuel oil, excluding biodiesel.
[d]Municipal solid waste from non-biogenic sources, and tire-derived fuels. Through 1994, also includes blast furnace gas, and other manufactured and waste gases derived from fossil fuels.
[e]Excludes emissions from biomass energy consumption.
NA = Not available. (s) = Less than 0.5 million metric tons.
Notes: Data are estimates for carbon dioxide emissions from energy consumption. Data exclude emissions from biomass energy consumption. Totals may not equal sum of components due to independent rounding. Geographic coverage is the 50 states and the District of Columbia.

SOURCE: Adapted from "Table 12.6. Carbon Dioxide Emissions from Energy Consumption: Electric Power Sector (Million Metric Tons of Carbon Dioxide)," in *Monthly Energy Review: July 2016*, U.S. Energy Information Administration, July 2016, http://www.eia.gov/totalenergy/data/monthly/pdf/mer.pdf (accessed August 7, 2016)

TABLE 9.3

Carbon dioxide emissions from energy consumption by the transportation sector, selected years 1973–2015

[Million metric tons of carbon dioxide[a]]

			Petroleum										
	Coal	Natural gas[b]	Aviation gasoline	Distillate fuel oil[c]	Jet fuel	LPG[d]	Lubricants	Motor gasoline[e]	Residual fuel oil	Total	Retail electricity[f]	Total[g]
1973 Total	(s)	39	6	163	152	3	6	886	57	1,273	2	1,315
1975 Total	(s)	32	5	155	145	3	6	889	56	1,258	2	1,292
1980 Total	h	34	4	204	155	1	6	881	110	1,363	2	1,400
1985 Total	h	28	3	232	178	2	6	908	62	1,391	3	1,421
1990 Total	h	36	3	268	223	1	7	967	80	1,548	3	1,588
1995 Total	h	38	3	307	222	1	6	1,029	72	1,640	3	1,681
1996 Total	h	39	3	327	232	1	6	1,047	67	1,683	3	1,725
1997 Total	h	41	3	341	234	1	6	1,057	56	1,700	3	1,744
1998 Total	h	35	2	352	238	1	7	1,090	53	1,743	3	1,782
1999 Total	h	36	3	365	245	1	7	1,115	52	1,789	3	1,828
2000 Total	h	36	3	377	254	1	7	1,122	70	1,833	4	1,873
2001 Total	h	35	2	387	243	1	6	1,128	46	1,813	4	1,852
2002 Total	h	37	2	394	237	1	6	1,158	53	1,852	4	1,892
2003 Total	h	33	2	408	231	1	6	1,161	45	1,854	5	1,892
2004 Total	h	32	2	433	240	1	6	1,181	58	1,922	5	1,959
2005 Total	h	33	2	444	246	2	6	1,182	66	1,948	5	1,986
2006 Total	h	33	2	467	240	2	5	1,188	71	1,976	5	2,014
2007 Total	h	35	2	469	238	1	6	1,186	78	1,981	5	2,021
2008 Total	h	37	2	424	226	3	5	1,124	73	1,856	5	1,898
2009 Total	h	38	2	405	204	2	5	1,109	62	1,789	5	1,832
2010 Total	h	38	2	426	210	2	5	1,091	70	1,806	5	1,849
2011 Total	h	39	2	437	209	2	5	1,058	61	1,774	4	1,818
2012 Total	h	41	2	416	206	2	5	1,051	53	1,735	4	1,780
2013 Total	h	47	2	424	210	3	5	1,066	46	1,756	4	1,807
2014 Total	h	48	2	443	216	3	5	1,077	35	1,780	4	1,832
2015 Total	h	49	1	440	226	3	5	1,104	36	1,815	4	1,868

[a]Metric tons of carbon dioxide can be converted to metric tons of carbon equivalent by multiplying by 12/44.
[b]Natural gas, excluding supplemental gaseous fuels.
[c]Distillate fuel oil, excluding biodiesel.
[d]Liquefied petroleum gases.
[e]Finished motor gasoline, excluding fuel ethanol.
[f]Emissions from energy consumption (for electricity and a small amount of useful thermal output) in the electric power sector are allocated to the end-use sectors in proportion to each sector's share of total electricity retail sales.
[g]Excludes emissions from biomass energy consumption.
[h]Beginning in 1978, the small amounts of coal consumed for transportation are reported as industrial sector consumption.
Notes: Data are estimates for carbon dioxide emissions from energy consumption, including the nonfuel use of fossil fuels. Data exclude emissions from biomass energy consumption. Totals may not equal sum of components due to independent rounding. Geographic coverage is the 50 states and the District of Columbia.

SOURCE: Adapted from "Table 12.5 Carbon Dioxide Emissions from Energy Consumption: Transportation Sector (Million Metric Tons of Carbon Dioxide)," in *Monthly Energy Review: July 2016*, U.S. Energy Information Administration, July 2016, http://www.eia.gov/totalenergy/data/monthly/pdf/mer.pdf (accessed August 7, 2016)

FIGURE 9.7

Energy-related carbon dioxide emissions, 2000–15 and predicted through 2040

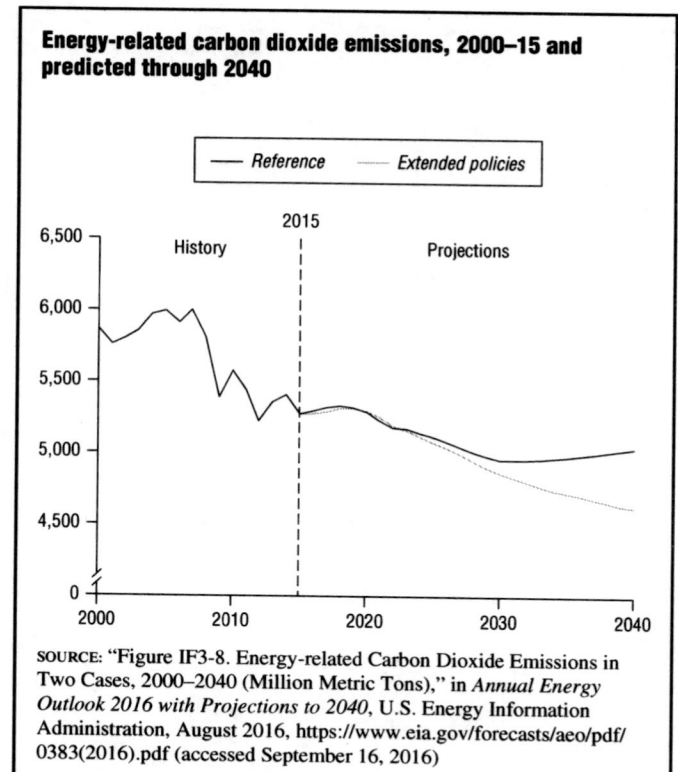

SOURCE: "Figure IF3-8. Energy-related Carbon Dioxide Emissions in Two Cases, 2000–2040 (Million Metric Tons)," in *Annual Energy Outlook 2016 with Projections to 2040*, U.S. Energy Information Administration, August 2016, https://www.eia.gov/forecasts/aeo/pdf/0383(2016).pdf (accessed September 16, 2016)

FIGURE 9.8

World energy-related carbon dioxide emissions by fuel type, 1990–2012 and predicted through 2040

[Billion metric tons]

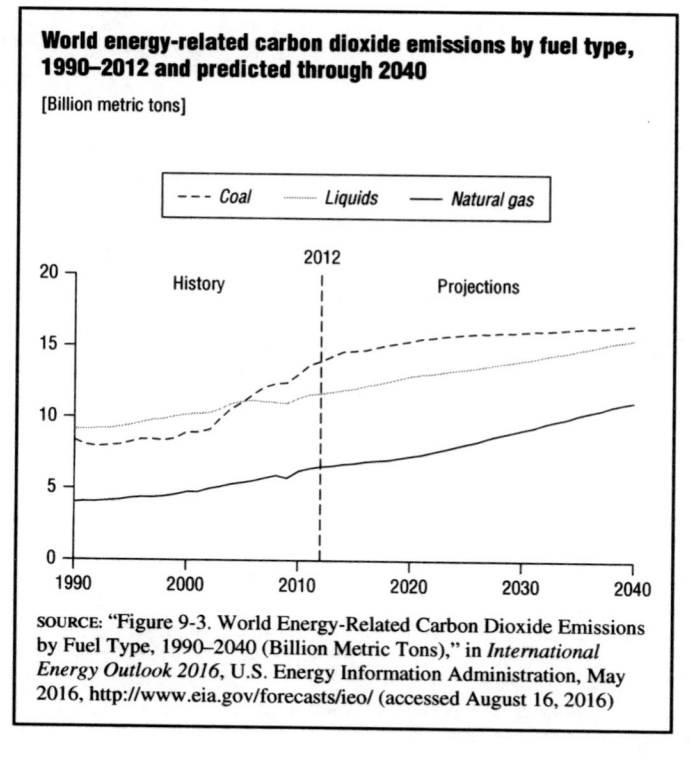

SOURCE: "Figure 9-3. World Energy-Related Carbon Dioxide Emissions by Fuel Type, 1990–2040 (Billion Metric Tons)," in *International Energy Outlook 2016*, U.S. Energy Information Administration, May 2016, http://www.eia.gov/forecasts/ieo/ (accessed August 16, 2016)

FIGURE 9.9

Coal consumption in China, India, and the United States, 1990–2012 and predicted through 2040

[Quadrillion Btu]

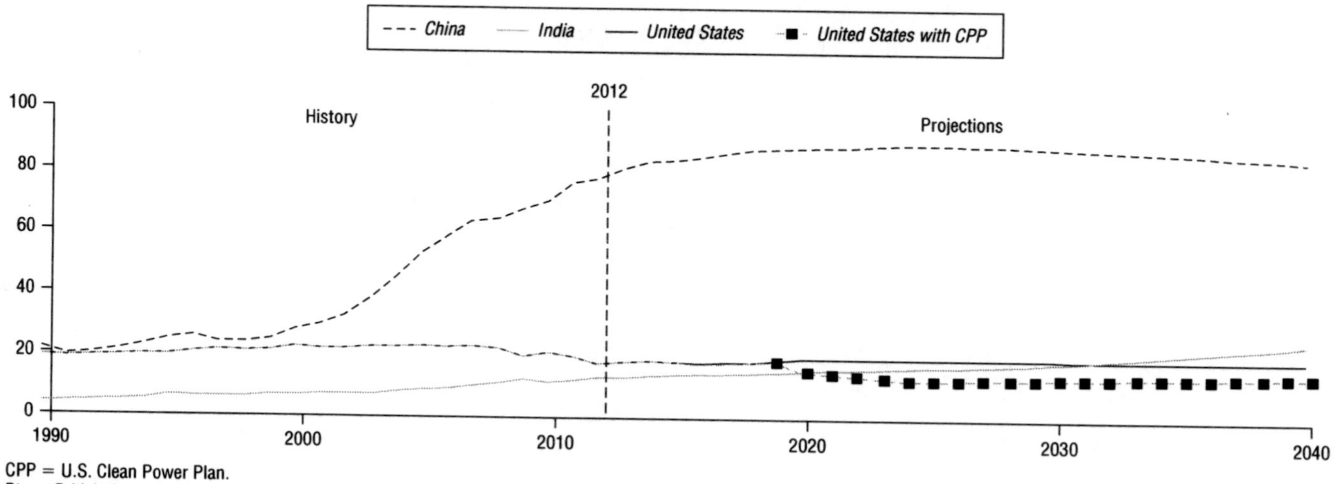

CPP = U.S. Clean Power Plan.
Btu = British thermal units.
Note: Dotted line for U.S. coal consumption shows projected effect of the U.S. Clean Power Plan.

SOURCE: "Figure ES-5. Coal Consumption in China, India, and the United States, 1990–2040 (Quadrillion Btu)," in *International Energy Outlook 2016*, U.S. Energy Information Administration, May 2016, http://www.eia.gov/forecasts/ieo/ (accessed August 16, 2016)

IMPORTANT NAMES
AND ADDRESSES

American Gas Association
400 N. Capitol St. NW, Ste. 450
Washington, DC 20001
(202) 824-7000
URL: http://www.aga.org/

American Petroleum Institute
1220 L St. NW
Washington, DC 20005-4070
(202) 682-8000
URL: http://www.api.org/

American Wind Energy Association
1501 M St. NW, Ste. 1000
Washington, DC 20005
(202) 383-2500
FAX: (202) 383-2505
URL: http://www.awea.org/

Bureau of Land Management
1849 C St. NW, Rm. 5665
Washington, DC 20240
(202) 208-3801
FAX: (202) 208-5242
URL: http://www.blm.gov/

Bureau of Ocean Energy Management
1849 C St. NW
Washington, DC 20240
(202) 208-6474
E-mail: BOEMPublicAffairs@boem.gov
URL: http://www.boem.gov/

Congressional Budget Office
Ford House Office Bldg., Fourth Floor
Second St. and D St. SW
Washington, DC 20515-6925
(202) 226-2602
URL: http://www.cbo.gov/

Congressional Research Service
Library of Congress
101 Independence Ave. SE
Washington, DC 20540
URL: http://www.loc.gov/crsinfo/

Edison Electric Institute
701 Pennsylvania Ave. NW
Washington, DC 20004-2696
(202) 508-5000
URL: http://www.eei.org/

Electric Power Research Institute
3420 Hillview Ave.
Palo Alto, CA 94304
(650) 855-2121
1-800-313-3774
E-mail: askepri@epri.com
URL: http://www.epri.com/

International Energy Agency
31-35 rue de la Fédération
Paris Cedex 15, France 75739
(011-33-1) 40 57 65 00
FAX: (011-33-1) 40 57 65 09
URL: http://www.iea.org/

National Highway Traffic Safety
Administration
1200 New Jersey Ave. SE, West Bldg.
Washington, DC 20590
1-888-327-4236
URL: http://www.nhtsa.gov/

National Mining Association
101 Constitution Ave. NW, Ste. 500 East
Washington, DC 20001
(202) 463-2600
FAX: (202) 463-2666
URL: http://www.nma.org/

Natural Gas Supply Association
1620 Eye St. NW, Ste. 700
Washington, DC 20006
(202) 326-9300
URL: http://www.ngsa.org/

Natural Resources Defense Council
40 W. 20th St., 11th Floor
New York, NY 10011
(212) 727-2700

E-mail: nrdcinfo@nrdc.org
URL: http://www.nrdc.org/

Nuclear Energy Institute
1201 F St. NW, Ste. 1100
Washington, DC 20004-1218
(202) 739-8000
FAX: (202) 785-4019
URL: http://www.nei.org/

Oak Ridge National Laboratory
PO Box 2008
Oak Ridge, TN 37831
(865) 576-7658
URL: http://ornl.gov/

Organization of the Petroleum
Exporting Countries
Helferstorferstrasse 17
Vienna, Austria A-1010
(011-43-1) 21112-3302
URL: http://www.opec.org/opec_web/en//

Solid Waste Association of North
America
1100 Wayne Ave., Ste. 650
Silver Spring, MD 20910
1-800-467-9262
FAX: (301) 589-7068
URL: http://www.swana.org/

U.S. Bureau of Reclamation
1849 C St. NW
Washington, DC 20240-0001
(202) 513-0501
FAX: (202) 513-0309
URL: http://www.usbr.gov/

U.S. Department of Energy
1000 Independence Ave. SW
Washington, DC 20585
(202) 586-5000
FAX: (202) 586-4403
E-mail: The.Secretary@hq.doe.gov
URL: http://www.energy.gov/

U.S. Energy Information Administration
1000 Independence Ave. SW
Washington, DC 20585
(202) 586-8800
E-mail: InfoCtr@eia.gov
URL: http://www.eia.gov/

U.S. Environmental Protection Agency
1200 Pennsylvania Ave. NW
Washington, DC 20460
(202) 272-0167
URL: http://www.epa.gov/

U.S. Geological Survey
John W. Powell Bldg.
12201 Sunrise Valley Dr.
Reston, VA 20192

(703) 648-4000
URL: http://www.usgs.gov/

**U.S. House of Representatives
Committee on Natural Resources**
1324 Longworth House Office Bldg.
Washington, DC 20515
(202) 225-2761
FAX: (202) 225-5929
URL: http://resourcescommittee.house.gov/

U.S. Nuclear Regulatory Commission
Washington, DC 20555-0001
(301) 415-7000
1-800-368-5642
URL: http://www.nrc.gov/

**U.S. Senate
Committee on Energy and Natural
Resources**
304 Dirksen Senate Bldg.
Washington, DC 20510
(202) 224-4971
FAX: (202) 224-6163
URL: http://energy.senate.gov/

World Energy Council
62-64 Cornhill
London, United Kingdom EC3V
3NH
(011-44-20) 7734 5996
FAX: (011-44-20) 7734 5926
URL: http://www.worldenergy
.org/

RESOURCES

The U.S. Department of Energy's U.S. Energy Information Administration is the major source of energy statistics in the United States. It publishes weekly, monthly, and yearly statistical collections on most types of energy, which are available in libraries and online at http://www.eia.doe.gov/. The *Annual Energy Outlook* projects future developments in the energy field. The website International Energy Statistics presents a statistical overview of the world energy situation, and the *International Energy Outlook* forecasts future industry developments. The Energy Information Administration also provides the *Domestic Uranium Production Report* and the *Monthly Energy Review*. The *U.S. Crude Oil, Natural Gas, and Natural Gas Liquids Proved Reserves* discusses reserves of coal, oil, and gas. The agency's websites Energy Explained, Energy in Brief, and Today in Energy contain a wealth of technical information about various energy sources.

The Department of Energy's Oak Ridge National Laboratory publishes the annual *Transportation Energy Data Book* and *Biomass Energy Data Book*. In addition, the Department of Energy makes available information on the development of alternative vehicles and fuels, renewable energy sources, and electric industry restructuring.

The U.S. Environmental Protection Agency maintains websites about hydraulic fracturing and global warming and publishes the annual *Inventory of U.S. Greenhouse Gas Emissions and Sinks*. The U.S. Geological Survey maintains extensive data regarding energy reserves. The U.S. Nuclear Regulatory Commission is also an important source of information and publishes the annual *Information Digest*.

INDEX

on exploration/development of oil/natural gas wells, 109

on foreign unrest, effects of on oil prices, 44

on Fukushima Daiichi nuclear accident, 85

on gasoline prices, 42–43

on history of coal use, 2

on hydroelectric plants, locations of, 95–96

on international energy reserves, 111

on international reserves of uranium, 114

on lease/plant fuel, 55–56

on market costs, 13

on natural gas, production forecast, 58

on natural gas imports, 54–55

on natural gas liquefaction, 53

on natural gas storage fields, 52–53

on natural gas wellhead, definition of, 56

on nuclear power plants in U.S., 80

on OECD petroleum consumption, 39

on offshore oil deposits, 26

on oil production forecast, 33

on OPEC imports, 44

on outlook for U.S. energy consumption, 135

on petroleum, definition of, 26

on petroleum product volume, 38

on proved reserves, 105–107

on renewable energy standards, 91

on renewables-generated electricity, 99–100

on residential use of natural gas, 56

on residential use of solar energy, 99

on technically recoverable resources, 107

on tight oil production, 32–33

on tight sand gas, 50

on transmission/distribution of electricity, 118

on uranium ore mines in U.S., 76–77

on uranium purchases, 78

on uranium reserves, 109–110

on U.S. refineries, 32

on volume of spent nuclear fuel, 87

on waste coal, 64

on world coal production/consumption, 71

on world electricity production/consumption, 127

on world energy production/consumption, outlook for, 22

on world renewable energy production/consumption/outlook, 101

U.S. Environmental Protection Agency (EPA)

coal power plant lawsuit, 129–130

environmental issues of electricity, 129–130

on fracking, 45–46

on "gas guzzler" tax, 16

on greenhouse gas emissions, 136–137

on lightbulbs phased out, 135

renewables-derived electricity, support for, 91

on uranium ore mines in U.S., 76

U.S. Exclusive Economic Zone, 27(f2.2)

U.S. Geological Survey (USGS)

Energy Resources Program, 105

on international reserves of uranium, 114

on oil/natural gas wastewater, 46

"U.S. HEU Disposition Program" (NNSA), 79

U.S. House of Representatives' Committee on Energy and Commerce, Subcommittee on Energy and Power, 15

U.S. Nuclear Regulatory Commission (NRC)

gas centrifuge process, 77–78

on low-level waste, 86–87

on nuclear generating units, global, 81–82

on nuclear generating units in U.S., 80–81

on nuclear power plant construction/operation, applications for, 81

uranium removal regulated by, 76

"U.S. Refineries, Crude Oil, and Refined Products Pipelines" (API), 29

"The U.S. Relies on Foreign Uranium, Enrichment Services to Fuel Its Nuclear Power Plants" (EIA), 78

"U.S. Ruling Loosens Four-Decade Ban on Oil Exports" (Berthelsen & Cook), 37

U.S. Supreme Court, 130

"Use of Natural Gas" (EIA), 56

USGS. See U.S. Geological Survey

V

Valero Energy Corporation, 90

Van Loon, Jeremy, 30–31

Vehicles

energy conservation efforts, 133

energy consumption by transportation sector, 132–133

fuel economy standards, 133–134

greenhouse gas emissions from, 137

motor vehicle fuel economy, by vehicle type, 133f

Vertical wells, 29f

Voltage, 118

W

War, 44

Warrick, Joby, 58

Waste, nuclear

issues concerning, 85–86

low-level waste, 86–87

spent nuclear fuel, 87

uranium mill tailings, 86

Waste, renewable, 91

Waste coal

description of, 64

increase of, 68

Wastewater, natural gas, 58

Water quality, 73

Watt, 117

Watt, James, 117

Wave energy, 103

Weather

electricity prices and, 122–123

oil prices, effect on, 43

Wellhead price, natural gas, 56

Wells

horizontal/vertical, comparison of, 29f

natural gas, drilling of, 49

Wells, Randy, 130

West Texas Intermediate (WTI), 42

West Virginia

coal production in, 66

coal reserves of, 109

proved reserves of natural gas, 107

Western region

coal deposits in, 62, 62f

coal production in, 64, 66, 68

Wet natural gas, 52

See also Natural gas

"What Is the Electric Power Grid and What Are Some Challenges It Faces?" (EIA), 118

"When Was the Last Refinery Built in the United States?" (EIA), 32

White House

"Advancing American Energy," 91

on Better Buildings Initiative, 135

on fuel economy standards, 134

Wind energy

horizontal-axis wind machine, 99f

outlook for, 100

production/consumption of, 97–98

Withdrawals

natural gas, 54t

natural gas, domestic, 53–54

World

carbon dioxide emissions, outlook for, 138–139

coal consumption in China, India, U.S., 143(f9.9)

coal production/consumption, 71–72

consumption of coal, by region/selected country, 72(t4.8)

electricity generation from renewable energy sources, by country classification, 103f

electricity generation from renewable/other energy sources, 102(f6.10)

energy conservation efforts, 135–136

energy consumption by country category, 24f

energy consumption by country/country category, 24t

CPSIA information can be obtained
at www.ICGtesting.com
Printed in the USA
FFOW05n2233100517